PRAISE FOR

Chaos Under Heaven

"Josh Rogin's superbly researched *Chaos Under Heaven* is the first book-
length dive into that newborn con t
of a thriller, Mr. Rogin traces Wa
threat . . . Mr. Rogin's research on t
is darkly fascinating."

l

T0115688

"A fascinating window into the dysfunction and shortsightedness that typified the Trump administration's approach to China . . . [*Chaos Under Heaven*] brings to light important details that will undoubtedly make their way into future histories of the bilateral relationship."

— *Washington Post*

"*Chaos Under Heaven* moves quickly, is well-written and draws the reader in."

— *Guardian*

"In *Chaos Under Heaven,* Josh Rogin tells a deeply reported, briskly written, and compelling story of how President Trump and his team struggled to deal with the significant economic and national security threats posed to the US by the Chinese government. This book is a must-read for anyone looking for insight into why this new cold war matters to every American."

—Jake Tapper, CNN anchor

"The ultimate insider's account of the making and mismaking of China policy by the Trump administration—a chilling twin portrait of the relentless advance of Xi Jinping and the venomous backbiting among Donald Trump and his advisers, who tried unsuccessfully to combat it. There are scoops on nearly every page. Read it and weep: *Chaos Under Heaven* reveals how China rose and America flubbed its response."

—David Ignatius, *Washington Post* columnist

"Josh Rogin is an outstanding journalist who breaks news all the time. And there's certainly lots of news in his extraordinary book. He takes us behind the scenes to get a real appreciation of this critically important relationship. *Chaos Under Heaven* is well written and incisive — and once you start reading, you won't want to put it down."

— Wolf Blitzer, CNN anchor

"Outstanding . . . That Mr. Rogin manages to capture the complexity and multi-faceted nature of the China challenge is a testament to his writing and reporting. This is a must-read book . . . *Chaos Under Heaven* is the best single volume on the totality of China's reach and influence, and our muddled policy over the last four years." — *Diplomatic Courier*

"*Chaos Under Heaven* is required reading for anyone who wants to know what happened between America and China during Trump's tumultuous four years in the White House. Josh Rogin's account is rich in detail and full of insight into the events and people that drove the United States as it began to change many of its longstanding policies in dealing with Beijing." — James Mann, *New York Times* best-selling author of *The China Fantasy* and *Rise of the Vulcans*

"Packing the account with insider details, Rogin makes a persuasive case that confronting China's rise is essential to world affairs. Readers will appreciate this in-depth look behind the headlines." — *Publishers Weekly*

CHAOS UNDER HEAVEN

America, China, and the Battle for the Twenty-First Century

JOSH ROGIN

MARINER BOOKS
Boston • New York

CHAOS UNDER HEAVEN. Copyright © 2021 by Josh Rogin. All rights reserved. Printed in the United States of America. No part of this book may be used or reproduced in any manner whatsoever without written permission except in the case of brief quotations embodied in critical articles and reviews. For information, address HarperCollins Publishers, 195 Broadway, New York, NY 10007.

HarperCollins books may be purchased for educational, business, or sales promotional use. For information, please email the Special Markets Department at SPsales@harpercollins.com.

First Mariner Books paperback published 2022
First Mariner Books hardcover published 2021

Designed by Chloe Foster

Library of Congress Cataloging-in-Publication Data has been applied for.
ISBN 978–0-358-69928-6

22 23 24 25 LSC 10 9 8 7 6 5 4 3 2 1

4500846784

To my parents, Michael and Sharon Rogin, for everything

There is great chaos under heaven . . . The situation is excellent.

— ATTRIBUTED TO MAO ZEDONG

Contents

Prologue

On Friday, December 9, 2016, a senior Chinese diplomat named Yang Jiechi took a seat at a table in the conference room on the fourteenth floor of 666 Fifth Avenue, a large skyscraper several blocks south of New York City's Central Park. Just over one month had passed since the election that had secured Donald Trump the American presidency, vaulting the real estate magnate and reality TV star into the role of leader of the free world. The president-elect's son-in-law, Jared Kushner, was also Trump's close adviser and clearly a power broker in the incoming administration; in fact, the flagship property of his family's real estate empire was 666 Fifth, the building in which Yang now sat. On the far wall, a large painting of Kushner's grandparents loomed over the men and women assembled beneath it, including the small band of Chinese dignitaries who had just arrived.

Yang, a former Chinese ambassador to Washington and a member of China's highest political body, the Politburo, was flanked by current Chinese ambassador Cui Tiankai and two other embassy officials. Yang himself had cut his teeth as the personal English translator for former Chinese president Deng Xiaoping in the 1980s. He knew English almost as well as he knew the history of the struggle between China and the West—and as soon as the meeting got started, he made clear that he would not be mincing words.

"The territorial integrity and sovereignty of the People's Republic of China is not to be questioned."

Staring back at Yang, on the other side of the table, was a motley crew of Trump campaign loyalists, family members, and staffers — among them Kushner, Steve Bannon, Michael Flynn, Peter Navarro, and K. T. McFarland, the meeting's official notetaker. Each would soon be a senior White House official. But none of them had believed, just one month prior, that they would be preparing a president-elect with zero real foreign policy experience to be the leader of the free world. And none of them were prepared to respond to these, the first words spoken by the leadership of China to the Trump transition team.

Yang had clearly come to New York on a mission. With a large binder sitting unopened in front of him, he held forth for an hour as he took the Trump team through a litany of Chinese government edicts, grievances, and demands. He educated the Americans on the long history of China and bemoaned China's two hundred years of modern humiliation at the hands of European and Western powers. He defended expansive Chinese territorial claims, including Beijing's assertion that 90 percent of the South China Sea belonged to China, based on what's called the "nine-dash line," the border line China wrote on its own map. He explained that China's behavior was motivated by the unhelpful actions of its aggressive neighbors (which was taken to mean Japan). And he called on the United States to join China in "win-win cooperation," a phrase Beijing's leaders use to dissuade any confrontation of its behavior.

Yang also laid out a list of demands. Beijing wanted the new administration to adopt its strategic framework for the twenty-first-century US-China relationship — what Yang called a "new model of great power relations." This was the same language often used by Chinese president Xi Jinping to say the United States should see — and treat — China as its equal. Yang also wanted Trump's public support for China's Belt and Road Initiative, a multitrillion-dollar worldwide infrastructure effort rife with political and diplomatic benefits for China. And the dignitary repeated well-worn Chinese government admonitions against US interference in whatever Beijing considered "core" issues. In essence, Yang was reminding the incoming administration that they should shut up about

Taiwan, Tibet, Hong Kong, and internal Chinese affairs — including issues of religious freedom and human rights within China's borders.

After an hour, Yang concluded his harangue. Both sides took a bathroom break. When they sat back down at the table, Yang pulled his materials toward him for the first time, lifted the first page, and began again:

"The territorial integrity and sovereignty of the People's Republic of China is not to be questioned."

He proceeded to repeat the entire diatribe for another hour. This was no longer a meeting; it was an elder lecturing a group of children.

At one point in the meeting, Bannon, Trump's final campaign chief and an avowed enemy of the Chinese Communist Party, turned to Kushner and said, "It's like foreign devils are so fucking stupid, you've got to tell them and then you've got to read it, and then you've got to tell the boss I told them and then I read it line for line. It's like we're morons." Bannon wanted Yang to know he wasn't buying it. In response to Yang's demands, he was defiant, telling Yang that Trump was a disrupter, that "everything is on the table," and that the Trump administration would not make any commitments before doing a full examination of US policy regarding China.

For his part, Flynn — a retired lieutenant general and former Defense Intelligence Agency director who had been Trump's chief campaign foreign policy adviser and would soon become Trump's first national security adviser — said almost nothing, other than to praise China's Belt and Road Initiative, which the other American officials considered odd and unhelpful. For months on the campaign trail, candidate Trump had railed against China's economic and trade policies, blaming China for stealing American jobs and outsmarting the US government on trade. By praising the Chinese project, the other US officials in the meeting felt, Flynn had laid bare his lack of actual China expertise.

Not everyone on the American side of the table was so clueless — or so restrained, even in comparison to Bannon. Navarro, a University of California at Irvine economics professor and five-time failed Democratic political candidate, had spent the campaign crafting the attacks on China that Trump used in his speeches. Now, he had a chance to tell the Chinese leadership what he thought to their face. Yet no sooner had he started to confront Yang on Chinese trade policy in heated tones, making accusations like, "You guys have been stealing our intellectual property for thirty years," than McFarland, who was poised to soon be deputy national security adviser under Flynn, placed her hand on Navarro's arm — a not subtle instruction to simmer down. Yang smirked. Navarro lost face. It would be the first of many times Trump's officials indicated to their Chinese counterparts that Navarro was not someone they needed to heed.

Despite the unproductive nature of their Friday meeting, the two sides decided to meet again the following day, but the same dynamic played out. Yang and Cui returned for another meeting at Kushner's office building Saturday. Kushner was absent because it was the Sabbath. There was more scolding of the American side by the Chinese officials. Yet Bannon and Navarro at least came away satisfied that the Chinese leadership would get the message that this administration was not interested in business as usual. They wanted Beijing to know that Trump's representatives had rejected its proposal to have the United States stand aside while China expanded its power and abused its leverage.

The Chinese delegation did indeed appear to have received that message. But it was only one of many conflicting signals that people close to Trump were sending — and which were coming from outside the new administration, as well as from within it.

What everyone could agree on was that the US-China relationship under Trump was clearly off to a rocky start. The meetings compounded the shock and confusion of the Chinese leadership, which had been banking on a Hillary Clinton win and a continuation of the Obama administration's soft-glove approach to China. Only one month earlier, exactly one week before the election, Yang had met with a team of high-ranking Obama administration officials. And from these outgoing American power brokers, Yang got a completely different message about the US approach to China.

There were several senior Obama administration and government officials in the room at the Palace Hotel on Tuesday, November 1, but the US contingent was led by National Security Adviser Susan Rice and Secretary of State John Kerry. The quiet confab was part of a series of personal high-level interactions the Obama team had with their Chinese counterparts over the course of the second term. For example, in 2014, Kerry had hosted Yang at his Boston home for two days, to build their personal ties. The Obama team was trying to establish relationships they thought would net positive changes in Chinese behavior. They were focused on areas of cooperation with China, not areas of contention. The outgoing Obama team was attempting to reassure Beijing's top leadership that the relationship was getting closer and Clinton would continue the trend.

One official who was in the November 1 meeting in New York said that Rice had tried to get Yang to help plan contingencies for a regime collapse scenario in North Korea. This official recalled that the attendees felt the meeting seemed to have gone very smoothly. "It was a table setting exercise for the new administration," this Obama administration official who attended told me. "We walked out of this meeting thinking this was one of the more constructive conversations we had with the Chinese side."

The Chinese government readout of the meeting claimed Rice, Kerry, and Yang were working to implement the "important consensus" that Chinese president Xi and Barack Obama had supposedly reached at their previous meeting in China. It also said Rice and Kerry agreed to "expand pragmatic cooperation and properly manage differences, so as to promote the sustained and stable development of China-US relations." The White House's readout of the meeting mimicked this language.

This meeting was not about confronting China on trade or human rights; quite the opposite. The Obama team wanted to coordinate with Beijing on everything from climate change to Iran to counterpiracy. In effect, without stating it publicly, they were giving in to Beijing's long-sought desire for a world governed by what Xi originally pitched directly to Obama at their 2013 Sunnylands summit as "the new model of relations between great powers"—a system in which the United States would no longer treat China as the junior partner in the relationship, would avoid criticizing China's internal actions, and would allow China greater influence over world affairs. Rice herself in 2013 pledged to "operationalize" that concept, and Obama said in 2014 when meeting Xi that he was "committed to continuing to strengthen and build a new model of relations."

Toward the end of his second term, Obama stopped referring publicly to Xi's "new model," but in effect he was still acceding to it, by directing his senior officials to explore a new US strategy to deal with China, one that would allow Beijing more influence in its near abroad and recognize a larger role for China in the region. Obama wanted his team to set new "lines of control" that would give in to some of China's desires for expansion and power. Ben Rhodes, Obama's deputy national security adviser and chief foreign policy speechwriter for eight years, said Obama wanted to figure out a way to have "the no bullshit conversation" with China's leaders about their real ambitions. For instance, Obama wanted to find a way to acknowledge the reality of China's increased presence in the South China Sea, without allowing Beijing to take over the entire area. Obama wanted to know "where do we have to draw our red lines and how do we communicate that to the Chinese," Rhodes said. Obama's view, he recalled, was, "Hey, they are going to play a bigger role in the world." The president wanted his team to "set up a capacity [with Beijing] to have a conversation about, 'What do you try to define as your sphere of influence?'"

To many foreign policy hands both inside and outside the Obama administration, allowing China to keep any part of the South China Sea that it had taken over through deception and international lawbreaking was naïve and even dangerous. Obama's willingness to set new red lines, these people felt, showed that he was prepared to retreat from the lines that America had previously established—thereby showing China that it could successfully obliterate any guardrails set up by the West to force China to follow the rules as it expands. But Rhodes, for one, felt that the approach was pragmatic, not an indication of American weakness or appeasement of Beijing's bad behavior. "You are suggesting that there's a degree of increasing Chinese influence that's going to happen. But you are trying to shape it," he said, describing the Obama administration's final approach.

At Obama's final meeting with Xi in September 2016 at the G20 summit in Hangzhou, Xi had referred again to the "new model of great country relations" that he had pitched Obama in 2013, purring that his vision had already "achieved substantial results." The Obama administration didn't have to say out loud that they were going along with Xi's program; Xi was saying it for them.

Perhaps the Obama team honestly believed this approach was the right way to go — their last effort to avoid a conflict that might result if the declining power and rising power clashed. Maybe they thought they were saving America from another Cold War. If they believed (as many at the time did, and still do) that the United States was destined to relinquish its role as a superpower, much less *the* superpower, then it would only seem pragmatic to organize a handoff of some global responsibilities to the rising power. And Obama was nothing if not a pragmatist.

But any reassurance that Yang gleaned from the Palace Hotel meeting was short-lived. One week later, Trump was elected; three weeks after that, Yang was back in New York, meeting with a team that had campaigned on the exact opposite message from the one he had gotten on his previous trip. The Obama team had told China that the United States would alter its behavior to accommodate theirs. Now the Trump team was telling China that *its* behavior had to change. For better or worse, America was rousing itself to confront the great power across the Pacific.

Awakenings

Virtually everyone I interviewed for this book had an awakening story; a moment in their personal or professional lives when they realized that the grand strategic competition between the United States and China was the most important foreign policy issue in the world and the most important project they would work on in their lifetime. Many also said this was an awakening to the aggressive and malign character, behavior, and strategy of China's leadership: the Chinese Communist Party (CCP), a hundred-year-old revolutionary organization that is determined to expand its influence and increase its power, and which has few limits to the methods it will use to advance its interests.

My own awakening was in the summer of 2003, in a tiny, windowless office at a law firm in Philadelphia's Rittenhouse Square. It is how I fell — unintentionally and unexpectedly — into journalism, and how I found myself on the path that led me to write this book. It's a journey you are now joining me on. And if you haven't yet had your awakening, this book aims to spark it.

Just twenty-four years old at the time, I had returned to Philadelphia after four years in Washington, DC, at the George Washington University, followed by a year teaching English at a conversation school in Yokohama, Japan. My new job was a paralegal position at Berger Montague, a firm that has made history using the American legal system to seek justice for human rights crimes committed abroad. I was assigned to a team working to sue the government of Sudan for genocide in what was then southern Sudan, and as I pored over the research on the case, I found a trove of State Department documents that revealed that China, in a bid to maintain a stable supply of oil from Sudan, had secretly helped to perpetuate the bloodshed. From providing a grant agreement worth $2.5 million for "any project" deemed worthy by Sudanese officials, to promising diplomatic support to remove international sanctions, to smuggling illicit arms to the government as it continued to target civilians, Beijing had helped to prop up Khartoum and enable its rampage — all out of a thirst for the oil that China needed to fuel its booming economy.

Confronted with the cold, calculated support of the CCP for the atrocities in Sudan, I was simultaneously impressed and horrified by the sophistication and ruthlessness of the scheme. China was outside the reach of the litigation, so I decided to send a copy of the files to an old college friend and China hand in Washington, Joshua Eisenman, who was then working at the New America Foundation, a relatively new, centrist-minded

DC think tank. Today, stories of China's corrupt practices in Africa have become ubiquitous, but in 2003, firm evidence of these examples was still scarce. Eisenman took one look at the documents I had sent him and said that we needed to publish this information. We coauthored an op-ed that was published on July 23, 2003, in the *Straits Times* of Singapore. Entitled "China Must Play by the Rules in Oil-Rich Sudan," the article revealed that Beijing was using bribery and corruption to secure energy resources and intentionally fueling crimes against humanity to do it. We argued the United States had a moral imperative and national security interest in opposing China's abuses in Africa.

I didn't think the article would get much attention. But within twenty-four hours, it had been shared around the world, appearing in energy trade publications and on websites covering Africa. The partners at Berger Montague were furious. They did not appreciate their twenty-four-year-old paralegal making international news on their case. Also, publicity was explicitly counter to their legal strategy.

I started to surf the internet for job openings, my law school applications sitting incomplete on my desk. I applied to the Japanese newspaper the *Asahi Shimbun* to be a news assistant in their DC bureau. I sent them the article from the *Straits Times.* At the interview, they said I had broken a big story. I got the job and moved back to Washington. Law school isn't going anywhere, I thought. This sounds like an adventure.

After two and a half years covering the Pentagon for *Asahi*, I got a job at a trade publication covering the IT industry called *Federal Computer Week.* The first article I wrote for the magazine was about Chinese cyber spying as detailed by the Pentagon in their annual report on China's military power; the first big scoop I broke was when the head of Naval Network Warfare Command admitted to me that Chinese government-sponsored hackers were attacking "everything and anything" inside the US military. I could see that the US government wasn't prepared for what insiders were watching unfold—a drive by a foreign power to use hybrid warfare to transfer huge amounts of knowledge in ways we couldn't stop and couldn't even really understand. I documented how the technology had outpaced US policy when it came to stopping China's cyberattacks and how the US government was so divided and bureaucratic that even senior leaders who recognized the threat could not properly address it. Eventually, I broke enough stories to be offered a more prestigious gig, working for *Congressional Quarterly,* then the premier trade publication covering the inner workings of Capitol Hill.

It was while reporting for *Congressional Quarterly* that, in a 2007 Congress, I found the beginnings of the effort to understand, call out, and then push back against a range of Chinese government actions. Other people in Washington had been experiencing awakenings of their own. There were different camps for different issues. There was a group of Christian lawmakers who were passionate about standing up to Beijing's human rights abuses. There was a group of defense hawks who were warning about China's nascent but growing capabilities. And there were the trade protectionists, who had tracked China's economic strategy since Congress granted Beijing most-favored-nation status in 2000 and China was admitted to the WTO the following year.

Soon after the Obama administration came in, I moved to *Foreign Policy* magazine, where I covered the State Department under Secretary Hillary Clinton. This was a period of great debate over how to deal with a China that had clearly become more problematic but had yet to abandon Deng Xiaoping's mantra, "Bide your time, hide your strength." The 2008 Olympics were Beijing's declaration of its status as a world leader and its claim for the respect that entails. But the accompanying crackdown on Tibetans protesting for basic rights simultaneously showed the world that the party was willing to do anything to crush dissent and maintain power. This was the same year Xi was anointed as the next president of the country and general secretary of the party.

I continued to track the China story as I migrated to the then-hybrid publication *Newsweek/Daily Beast,* and then to *Bloomberg View*—and finally, in June 2016, to the *Washington Post,* where I took up a position as a columnist for the paper's Global Opinions section, a post that I still hold as of this writing.

When I started out covering US-China relations in 2004, I and the other members of the twentysomething gang of Asia experts, congressional staffers, and government officials I became friends with were just starting out in our careers. By 2016, the young China hands of 2004 had become middle-aged China hands, now spread throughout the government, Congress, and even a few in the media. Over that time, we watched the generation of China hands and government leaders above us struggle mightily over the question of how to deal with a China that was steadily becoming more externally aggressive and internally repressive and using its rising power and influence in malign ways against us.

During all those years, an academic debate was also raging among the old-guard Asia hands who were in charge of managing the relationship. This debate is often summed up as "Who lost China?" Essentially, the United States had pursued a strategy of "open engagement," which meant that it actively promoted China's economic development and success while working to integrate China into as much of the international system as possible. The bet was that China was given this help on the promise that it would steadily reform economically and politically, a promise the West had no means to enforce once the help was accepted. Some of the older generation say that the only responsible course of action twenty years ago was to pursue open engagement with China in the hope China would become more like us, but China just decided to go a different way. Some will say that approach was always misguided. Some will say it's still the only responsible approach right now.

For the younger generation of Asia hands, the debate over "who lost China" didn't much matter, because we hadn't been around when the bet was made and we bore no allegiance to it one way or the other. The younger generation of Asia hands saw China for what it was, not for what the older generation said it was or wanted to believe it would become. They were not a monolith of opinion or analysis. But there was a lot less disagreement about the prognosis than about the solutions.

When the Trump administration came to power, the only thing that was ensured was that it would be disruptive. That was an opportunity for the young foreign policy hands, many of whom had been waiting their entire career for such a disruption to elevate the China issue to the top of the agenda. But still, the conventional wisdom was that China's rise was inevitable and there wasn't much we could or should do about it.

The most common way to dismiss the idea of confronting China in Washington is to point to the risk that such confrontation could lead to outright conflict. In 2015, Harvard's Graham Allison wrote in the *Atlantic* that the United States and China were headed into what he termed "the Thucydides Trap," a reference to the Greek historian's writings on the Peloponnesian War between Athens and Sparta. He later turned his article into a book. Allison's Thucydides Trap theory holds that, when the dominance of one power is threatened by another, the resulting tension often leads to bloodshed. But that theory doesn't fit the US-China relationship for a whole host of reasons. The simplest one is that shifting power dynamics are only one reason that nations historically have gone to war. Also, it's a variable that's impossible to measure, because the relative power of a nation isn't always clear, especially throughout the large sweep of history. This idea is also deeply rooted in a Westerncentric view of history. It also assumes that China's rise is inevitable, an assumption that ignores the severe economic and political challenges China faces as it grows. The Thucydides Trap concept is interesting, but we shouldn't base our strategy on it. One could just as easily use a comparison of domestic political systems as a basis for predictions. And of course, any serious student of history knows how other nationalist-socialist systems have fared.

Ultimately, the challenge that China poses is greater than can be contained in any single, simple vessel, whether "open engagement" or "containment" or "the Thucydides Trap." The fact of the matter is that the rise of China has been a complex, turbulent process with myriad repercussions and no single, simple solution. And while the root of much of the tension is the character and behavior of the CCP, the US response — especially under Trump — has been all over the map, making the problem more difficult to solve than it needed to be, or might have been otherwise.

Chaos Under Heaven

There are two basic narratives about Donald Trump and his handling of the US-China relationship during his presidency. The first—more popular among the media—is that this neophyte president bumbled his way through the most important bilateral relationship at a crucial juncture. According to this argument, Trump was flailing between tough but ineffective trade wars, a love affair with China's dictator-for-life, and a general disregard for traditional American values like democracy, freedom, and human rights. He made important decisions on a whim, based on the last person he talked to. He set his factions against each other in an Oval Office turned policy Coliseum and lorded over the battles, picking winners based on his instincts, which varied daily.

The second narrative—told mostly by those closest to the president—is that Trump actually has a firm view on China, an outlook that he brought into his presidency and that has stayed consistent throughout. Trump set his advisers against each other, this theory goes, because he wanted them to compete to serve him ideas that fit his vision, not because he didn't know what he wanted. The conflicting public statements by Trump's officials merely reflect their disagreements, in this view—not Trump's own internal confusion.

These two narratives are not mutually exclusive, and there are elements of truth in both—as well as myths and fabrications that future historians will need to separate from hard facts. It's true that Trump prioritized his trade deal above national security concerns and cared little about human rights. It's also true that he believed his friendship with Xi was constructive and close and that caused him to make concessions foolishly. And it's true that Trump was personally committed to confronting China on the issues that he did care about, such as trade, but that he constantly changed his mind about the tactics. The sheer chaos of the White House on all issues all the time made a steady, much less predictable, strategy impossible.

What's certain, however, is that the Chinese leadership misinterpreted and misunderstood Trump and his administration egregiously and constantly from the start. They can't be blamed; most of us were operating in the same fog. But the Chinese leadership over and over again came to the wrong conclusions both about Trump and about how his administration worked.

The chaos that defined the Trump administration came at a time when the US-China relationship was already entering a particularly unforgiving period. When the Trump administration unexpectedly came to power, US-China relations were at the center of three tectonic trends: the rise of nationalism and populism due to the unequal distribution of benefits from globalization; the rise of emerging and foundational technologies that have altered both daily life and the way governments, companies, and people interact; and the fraying of a world order that was built for an era when the United States was the only superpower and the spread of democracy everywhere seemed inevitable.

Over the course of Trump's presidency, awareness inside the US government and around the country steadily grew that China's rise and the Chinese government's strategy play into all three of those dynamics. Put simply, a China that is militarily expansionist, economically aggressive, internally repressive, and increasingly interfering in democratic societies poses enormous challenges for the United States along with all of our allies, friends, and partners. The effects are already being seen in our national security, our investments, our industries, our schools, our media, and even our elections.

Even in 2016, the FBI was flooded with cases of Chinese espionage they didn't have the resources or mandate to prioritize. US industries were watching Chinese firms steal their technology and then use it to vanquish them, including in their own country. Universities were contending with attempts by the Chinese government to curb their debates and silence their students. The Chinese propaganda machine was actively trying to shape American public discussion. Money was flowing into our politics in ways we couldn't track. Gradually, these problems became too big to ignore.

Different sectors of US society have awoken to these challenges at different times and in different ways. As the US government started to engage academia, the tech industry, and Wall Street on the national security implications of China's behavior, there was a lot of friction. Many were skeptical of Trump's claims and intentions. American institutions guard their independence fiercely and rightly, but these were challenges that required them to work with a Trump administration they didn't trust.

These challenges would have existed even if Donald Trump had not been elected president. To be sure, our reaction would have been different; if Hillary Clinton had won the presidency in 2016 instead of Donald Trump, her administration undoubtedly would have used different language, focused more on multilateral cooperation and alliances, perhaps figured out a way to have the United States join the Trans-Pacific Partnership. But it's unlikely she would have been able to continue the Obama approach to China. She would not have been able to avoid the conclusion that Washington had lost the bet it made twenty years ago, when it had granted China permanent normal trade relations in the hope that helping China expand economically would cause it to liberalize politically and that would lead to peaceful coexistence.

The frustration with China's long promise to liberalize inside the US government at the end of the Obama administration was reaching a boiling point. "As the Trump administration came in, everyone was beginning to realize that our grand forty-year experiment with Beijing was not working out as we'd planned, not because we didn't try, not because it wasn't well intentioned. It's just that the CCP has a different view," said former army officer Matthew Turpin, who served in Obama's Pentagon and on Trump's National Security Council staff. "They don't want political liberalization. They are going to fight us on that as much as possible."

The challenges of this historic moment were perhaps inevitable — but it is also unquestionable that the Trump team at times bungled its handling of the difficult situation they inherited, often due to the administration's dysfunction and the president's behavior. By mishandling important aspects of the new competition and mistreating allies, the administration committed damaging unforced errors. The outcome has been that this new era of naked competition with China is now seen by many as a spat between the United States and China, rather than an international response to China's actions as it rises. The Trump administration also got several things right, including the basic conclusion that the US government had to confront China's behavior not on a government-to-government level alone but in various parts of American society.

This sense that the world is becoming divided into two separate, competing systems that can't coexist is hardening into what many people — not without reason — have referred to as a second Cold War. The implications are just as troubling now as they were then, and the risks just as great. "When you look back on the details of how the first Cold War started, it's not as if the two sides in 1946 said 'OK, let's have a cold war,'" historian Michael Pillsbury, one of Trump's early China advisers, said at the Aspen Institute in January 2020. "It's a series of blunders."

Both the United States and China could be blamed for their share of blunders in the few years preceding Pillsbury's remarks, and China owned the lion's share. But the disorder of the Trump administration was baked into its DNA, and the China issue was not immune from the implications.

To think of the China story during the Trump administration as a binary fight between hawks and doves, panda sluggers and panda huggers, the blue team and the red team, or any other such construction is too simplistic. There were many camps that formed assorted alliances over time, based on overlapping interests. At different parts of the story, various camps gained and lost champions inside the administration. Also, individuals' views evolved over time; where many officials began on China is far from where they ended up.

There were the Superhawks, who wanted Trump to speed the downfall of the CCP. They were led by Bannon at first but included Navarro, Stephen Miller, and others. The Superhawks also believed in economic nationalism, the return of manufacturing from abroad, and the protection of domestic industries, even at the expense of free trade. Another, closely related group were the hardliners, mostly national security and law enforcement types who had been watching the China threat rise and were pushing for a stronger US response — but one that would stop short of pushing for regime change in Beijing. Matt Pottinger was this group's platoon commander and Marco Rubio was their spirit animal. John Bolton, Mike Pence, Mike Pompeo, and Robert O'Brien each fit into this camp and each led the charge at different times. They wanted to confront Beijing and reset the competition on better terms. But unlike the Superhawks, they didn't want to blow up the whole relationship for the fun of it.

On the other end of the spectrum, there was the Wall Street clique, led by investment banker and film producer Steven Mnuchin and Goldman Sachs executive Gary Cohn and later CNBC talking head Larry Kudlow. They came to the table with a coterie of billionaires that constantly injected itself into the middle of the US-China relationship. These pro-business players wanted to avoid confronting China on national security or trade, and to focus instead on opening up Chinese markets and integrating the two economies as much as possible. They shared overlapping interests with many of the bureaucrats, lifers in agencies all around town, who disliked the Trump team and worked inside the system to maintain the status quo.

There was also the Axis of Adults. This was the team of senior national security officials surrounding Trump — especially in the beginning of the administration — who came from long careers in the military or government and saw themselves as the grownups in a group of inexperienced and unqualified Trump campaign and political staffers. This included Defense Secretary James Mattis, Chief of Staff John Kelly, National Security Adviser H. R. McMaster, and others who viewed their role to be guardrails to keep the crazy president from driving the car off the road. Each of these officials would eventually annoy Trump or get fed up with his antics and leave the administration. On China, they tended to be hardliners on security matters but skeptical of the Superhawks' efforts to start a trade war.

Certain officials played unique roles and didn't fit into any one camp. Jared Kushner had a huge impact on the US-China relationship at the many points he was directly involved, because he was the closest to the president and because he maintained his own channels to the Chinese leadership. Wilbur Ross acted like a China hawk at times and a New York billionaire at others, because he was both. Pillsbury became a unique Trump whisperer on China but never joined the administration or committed to any one team.

This book tells the story of how this fractious team managed (or often mismanaged) the US-China relationship at a crucial juncture under the leadership of Donald Trump, a president so unpredictable that he could scarcely have been imagined by foreign policy makers on either side before 2016. Trump's own views on China and his own behavior set the tone as the relationship started rocky and spiraled downhill from there. But one level below him, his senior officials played their own games. And two levels below them, actors inside the system steered it toward the outcomes they desired.

This is their story. But it is also the story of how regular Americans in all walks of life over these four years gradually woke up to the fact that China's rise and the CCP's strategy are no longer faraway issues, but now pose direct and immediate challenges to their security, prosperity, freedom, and public health. This realization is not limited to Americans; people in countries across the world are undergoing it as well.

The Trump administration played the first round of this new game, for better or worse. But future administrations will have to pick up where it left off and hopefully come up with a strategy that the entire country and our allies can join. Many career national security officials are already well aware of the threat and have long been calling for a broader response. "You have a bunch of liberal democracies that realize by 2016 that Xi Jinping is taking China backwards and we probably better start protecting ourselves. That's the bigger story here," said Turpin. "We needed a new strategic approach." The Trump team mounted an imperfect and incomplete attempt to create that new approach. It will be up to their successors to continue, and improve, this vital endeavor.

Chaos Under Heaven

I

The Transition

There was no calm before the storm.

Trump's surprise electoral win on November 8, 2016, sent shockwaves through the global establishment. And it left everyone — in the United States and in China — to wonder what kind of a leader he would be, and whether his tough campaign rhetoric on China would become the basis for a new US foreign policy.

They would not have long to wait. The first indications about what a Trump presidency would look like in practice, not just in theory, came fast and furious during the ten weeks between his election and his inauguration on January 20, 2017. The signs were not reassuring to anyone in Beijing who might have held out hope that the incoming president would keep the relationship on an even keel. The transition showed a president who was already creating havoc and a team of advisers consumed over fighting for control of the policy and the attention of the boss. Relations between the two capitals were an early casualty of this tumult in Washington, DC.

When the Chinese diplomat Yang Jiechi berated his American counterparts in their meeting at Jared Kushner's office on December 9, he was not merely establishing the baseline of their relationship, or testing the Trump team for strengths and weaknesses. He was also conveying his government's intense displeasure at one of the incoming Trump administration's first official acts vis-à-vis China.

Everyone knew why the Chinese leadership was upset, but Yang made it clear anyway. Exactly one week prior, President-Elect Trump had taken a congratulatory phone call from Taiwanese president Tsai Ing-wen. This small act had broken four decades of precedent and sent shockwaves throughout Washington and Asia.

Beijing considered Taiwan a renegade province to eventually be subsumed back into China, one way or the other. But the majority of Taiwanese don't consider themselves Chinese; the island has never been governed by the Chinese Communist Party (CCP) and has a history and culture distinct from those of mainland China, characterized by its indigenous population, its period of Japanese colonial rule, and the waves of migration to Taiwan from mainland China. The CCP also thought of Taiwan as a "core issue," meaning that it was nonnegotiable and off-limits for other governments.

Every minor interaction between Washington and Taipei was grounds for a diplomatic protest. A contact at this level was an assault on all these understandings. Trump had brazenly provoked Beijing right out of the gate, but nobody knew why. If it was part of a plan, then the fight was on. But if it was some sort of accident or one-off gesture, that meant something completely different. Chinese leaders could not have known it was part of a plan, just not Trump's.

At the time, the mere fact that Trump had accepted a call from Taiwan's president—and that the White House put out a press release saying the president had taken a call from the "President of Taiwan"—was proof enough for most of the media that the incoming president was either a reckless China hawk or a neophyte who had clumsily failed his first foreign policy test out of sheer ignorance and naïveté. But the story of how, exactly, Trump came to take a call from Taiwan's president on Friday, December 2, remains in dispute, even among the people directly involved.

The story's outcome, on the other hand, is incontestable: Trump ended up conceding one huge issue in the US-China competition almost immediately, for nothing in return. This incident, in turn, became the foundation for Trump's personal relationship with Xi Jinping — a relationship that would have a massive influence on the course of history.

The Taiwan Call

In the first year of the Trump administration, the White House was a hall of mirrors. Like the Japanese movie *Rashomon*, every story was told from several perspectives, and even when all storytellers believed they were telling the truth, the stories often differed greatly. These competing narratives — not to mention the authorized leaks, the unauthorized leaks, the flat-out lies, and the fog of confusion — practically ensured that every story about the Trump administration during his first year in office got mangled as it was reported, and then mangled further as other versions emerged.

In the case of Trump's Taiwan call, the most often reported version of the story also is the one the least believed by people actually in the know. This version was largely accepted by the Washington establishment because it was plausible enough and because, in the chaos of the moment, there were too many other scandals drawing the media's attention to search for a better version after this basic explanation was printed.

This widely accepted version, as reported by the *New York Times* and others, credits the Taiwan call to former Kansas senator Bob Dole, whose lobbying law firm, Alston & Bird, gets paid $280,000 a year by the Taiwanese government. Dole "worked behind the scenes over the past six months to establish high-level contact between Taiwanese officials and President-elect Donald J. Trump's staff." The *Times* story even included an interview with Dole himself, speaking on behalf of the Taiwanese government. "They're very optimistic," Dole said.

But that's not the way it actually went down, according to the people who were directly involved. The real connection between the Trump team and Taiwan, they say, was made when Randy Schriver, a former Pentagon official who at the time led a small think tank called the Project 2049 Institute that was partially funded with Taiwanese government money, reached out to a friend of his who was a staffer on the State Department transition team. Schriver told the transition staffer that he had spoken with Taiwanese government officials about a call between Trump and Tsai. The staffer added the call to Trump's call sheet and sent the call sheet up to Trump Tower in New York.

Trump went through his calls that day until he got to the last one on the list: Taiwan. Because there was so much confusion during the transition, according to some White House insiders, nobody noticed in time to stop it.

But others involved still dispute that Trump was caught unaware. Steve Bannon, who at the time was set to become Trump's chief strategist, insists that the president-elect was briefed on the call ahead of time — and that Bannon warned Kushner, and they both warned Trump, that the Chinese government would protest. In Bannon's mind, however, provoking Beijing's ire was a good thing — and according to Bannon, Trump felt the same way. "If you take the phone call, it will explode around the region but you will have [the Chinese government] on the back foot," Bannon told Trump. "Well then, I'm definitely taking the phone call," Trump responded.

The phone call itself was only a few minutes long and contained not much of substance: Tsai congratulated Trump on his victory and Trump rattled off his usual platitudes and basked in the attention. But the fact of the call was explosive, and it didn't take long before the media was reporting it as a foolish blunder or, worse, a reckless provocation. Trump was surprised by the Washington media's response to the call, according to Bannon, although not by Beijing's — contrary to allegations from others on the transition team that Trump was blindsided by the Chinese government's swift condemnation.

Everyone involved could agree, at least, that Trump was livid. "However the phone call happened, the president reads about it in the *New York Times* as the biggest blunder in forty years, which he doesn't appreciate," a senior transition official said. "His wonderful staff had just told him to do the call and promised him positive results."

Trump's defensiveness was on display when he tweeted the next day that he hadn't initiated the call: "The President of Taiwan CALLED ME today to wish me congratulations on winning the Presidency. Thank you!"

This left Beijing in a pickle. Speaking with Taiwan's leader was an affront that the rulers in China could not ignore. At the same time, back in Beijing, they were receiving the opposite signal from the president — this one conveyed by the Chinese government's oldest and most trusted American friend.

Nobody in Charge

On the very same day of the Taiwan call, former secretary of state Henry Kissinger was in Beijing conveying a completely different message directly to Chinese president Xi Jinping. Trump, Kissinger said, wanted US-China relations to move forward in "a sustained and stable manner." With his president's personal approval, Kissinger had come to set a tone of cooperation and engagement with Beijing, and to reassure Xi that Trump's aggressive rhetoric during the campaign did not mean that he wanted to go to war — figuratively or literally — with China.

Kissinger has been among the most influential — and controversial — figures in US-China relations since he traveled there in 1971 to meet Premier Zhou Enlai, meetings that paved the way for normalization of the bilateral relationship in 1979 and established a relationship that would allow anti-Soviet cooperation during the Cold War. Since the establishment of his consulting firm, Kissinger Associates, in 1982, the former secretary of state has also been in business with China's "red capitalists." These party-backed businesspeople set up shop in Hong Kong in the 1980s and 1990s in part to generate capital for the Communist Party, but also to pilfer or purchase technology and intelligence from the rest of the world.

Kissinger's ties to the red capitalists date back to 1988, when Kissinger partnered with China International Trust and Investment Corporation, an investment company controlled by the Chinese government, to establish a boutique investment firm called China Ventures. Based in Delaware, it got off the ground with $75 million in backing, the bulk of which came from China. Kissinger served as chairman, CEO, and chief partner of the company, which described itself in its brochure as only investing in projects that "enjoy the unquestioned support of the People's Republic of China." Kissinger planned to publicize its establishment in June 1989, but the Tiananmen Square massacre put that on hold. Immediately after the massacre, Kissinger offered commentary on ABC and later criticized the US government's decision to impose sanctions on China. An ABC executive later said that, had he known of Kissinger's financial interests in China, he would never have invited him to comment on the massacre. In 2008, Kissinger played down Beijing's human rights record during the Olympic games and said to China's state media outlet, *Xinhua,* "Friends of China should not use the Olympics to pressure China now."

By the time of Kissinger's meeting with Xi on December 2, 2016, in short, the Chinese leadership saw the former secretary of state as a reliable friend and a trusted interlocutor. But that fact surely made their conundrum even more confounding.

Steeped as they were in the patterns and logic of diplomatic protocol and signaling, Chinese leaders must have struggled to believe that these two events—Trump's inflammatory Taiwan call and Kissinger's conciliatory Beijing meeting—could have occurred on the exact same day purely by coincidence. But how to explain the mixed messages? Were they supposed to listen to the personal message Trump sent through Kissinger or pay attention to the fact that Trump had just thrown down the gauntlet on Taiwan, a core national issue for Beijing? Who, they must have wondered, was in charge of Trump's China policy anyway?

The truth was, nobody was in charge of Trump's China policy. There was no China team. There was no written China strategy. The closest anyone ever came to articulating one was during the campaign, in candidate Trump's June 28, 2016, speech in Monessen, Pennsylvania, an address that was written by Peter Navarro and Stephen Miller, who at the time were writing Trump's foreign policy into his speeches. Miller would become

Trump's most trusted policy adviser and speechwriter. Navarro would be given a newly created job as head of the White House Office of Trade and Manufacturing Policy, which hadn't previously existed. It would take years for the ideas they infused into the campaign to make it into Trump's official policies — but even before the election, Miller and Navarro had succeeded in committing the new president to confronting China if he won office, and laid out the trade hawk's theory of the case against Beijing.

In his Monessen campaign speech, Trump blamed the administration of Bill Clinton — as well as the influence of Trump's 2016 electoral opponent, Hillary Clinton — for admitting China into the World Trade Organization, a move Trump called second only to NAFTA in the history of bad deals. "Then, as Secretary of State, Hillary Clinton stood by idly while China cheated on its currency, added another trillion dollars to our trade deficits, and stole hundreds of billions of dollars in our intellectual property," Trump said.

Trump went on to lay out a seven-point plan for restoring America's manufacturing base and righting the trade imbalance with China. Point 1 was a promise to withdraw the United States from the Trans-Pacific Partnership, the twelve-nation trade deal Obama spent years negotiating as a strategic play vis-à-vis China. For the Obama administration and many in Congress, TPP was not just about trade; it was the United States' attempt to counter China's economic rise in Asia and key to shoring up America's regional alliances. But in the campaign, both Trump and Clinton disavowed it due to its bitter unpopularity on the far sides of both parties. Trump made economic nationalism a cornerstone of his campaign and promised to kill it on day one.

Points 2 to 4 had to do with NAFTA and Europe. Points 5 and 6 promised to label China a currency manipulator and bring cases against China at the WTO, respectively. Point 7 was where Trump previewed the specific weapons he would later use to wage his trade war: "If China does not stop its illegal activities, including its theft of American trade secrets," he intoned, "I will use every lawful presidential power to remedy trade disputes, including the application of tariffs consistent with

Section 201 and 301 of the Trade Act of 1974 and Section 232 of the Trade Expansion Act of 1962."

Trump likely didn't know the specifics of these laws, but he was threatening to use unusual although not unprecedented tools to punish China through tariffs and other measures. George H. W. Bush had threatened China with a 301 investigation, which allows the US government to take drastic measures to protect the US economy, but backed off after Beijing signed a memorandum of understanding it didn't honor. Obama had used tariffs to protect the American steel and aluminum industries, but by invoking Section 232, Trump was threatening to use tariffs under a national security justification.

Bannon, Navarro, and Miller were previewing their ideas for the trade war they would spend the first year of Trump's presidency trying to implement. Their theory of the case was that the Chinese economy was vulnerable to pressure, if only real pressure could be brought to bear. There was evidence at the time to support this assumption. China's economy grew 6.7 percent in 2016, according to its own self-reporting, but even that was China's slowest growth year since 1990.

But at that point in the campaign, few noticed. The Hillary Clinton campaign didn't bother responding directly. Nobody thought Trump could actually win. If they had, they might have spent more time studying up on the man and his views — which, despite what many have claimed, had stayed relatively unchanged over several decades, and which centered on one grievance in particular: that America was being taken advantage of by China.

Trump on China

Donald Trump's views on China are unique and, in a way, remarkably consistent. They are not the views of Steve Bannon or Peter Navarro. They are not the views of Gary Cohn, the former Goldman Sachs executive who served as his chief economic adviser while the administration was first plotting its approach to China; or Steve Mnuchin, the former Goldman Sachs executive and movie producer who became Treasury secretary. They are not the views of Jared Kushner either. They are Trump's, and Trump's alone—and perhaps for this reason, they have never been fully understood.

Donald Trump has fashioned himself a foreign policy expert for most of his adult life. In the 1980s, he frequently appeared on television to offer his services to negotiate with the Soviet Union on behalf of the United States. "Why don't you negotiate the SALT talks for Reagan, Donald?" a man was quoted shouting at Trump in a 1990 profile by *Vanity Fair.* Even before he was focused on China, Trump thought he should be in charge of the government's dealmaking abroad.

Trump's views on China are scattered throughout the several books he wrote, cowrote, or paid a ghostwriter to write over the years. In his 2000 book, *The America We Deserve,* while he was rumored to be contemplating a presidential run, Trump wrote, "I believe the day of the chess player is over. American foreign policy has to be put in the hands of a dealmaker." The two greatest dealmaker presidents, in Trump's view, were FDR and Richard Nixon, whom Trump credited for opening up relations with China. But he also wrote an entire chapter entitled "How to Take on China," which Trump said was "our biggest long-term challenge." Trump argued that the United States had given China a pass on its bad economic behavior in the hope of gaining access to the Chinese markets. US businesspeople were too eager to believe Beijing's claims of reform, he thought. For his part, Trump saw investing in China as still too risky. "I'm not going to be opening a hotel there any time soon," he wrote, "but maybe someday it could happen."

Trump went on to complain about China's unfair trade practices, grousing that the foreign policy experts in the Clinton and Bush administrations had failed to stand up to Beijing, whose appetite for power had grown with the eating. Trump also predicted that the two countries would remain in a sustained state of confrontation as their values and interests diverged. And he noted that China was sliding quickly into patterns of brutal repression and human rights abuses.

Trump claimed that, unlike most of his business colleagues, he could not simply ignore these trends, because they showed the CCP's contempt for the American way of life. "[The Chinese government] fears freedom because it knows its survival depends on oppression," Trump wrote. "As such, it is a destabilizing force in the world, and should be viewed that way."

Trump's next book to talk in depth about China was published in 2011, when he was again threatening to run for president. Called *Time to Get Tough*, it claimed that Obama "bowed down to China and allowed them to steal our future" through such things as currency manipulation and technology theft. Trump wrote that Obama's defense budget cuts had put the country in danger as China built up its military. He called China's leaders "our enemy," and wrote, "Those who pretend China is our friend are either naïve, incompetent or both. The Chinese can be reined in easily—we are their biggest customer. All we need is a president willing to stand up, not bow down to China."

In 2015, during his presidential run, Trump put out another book, *Crippled America: How to Make America Great Again*. Here he noted his experience negotiating with the Chinese; specifically that he was the landlord to China's largest bank in Trump Tower. He complained extensively about China's unfair trade practices and shrugged off the idea that he shouldn't have his own products, such as shirts and ties, made in China. "I'm a realist. I'm a competitor," he said. Trump promised to use the power of the US economy to put pressure on Beijing to come to the negotiating table to make a deal. "When dealing with China we need to stand up to them and remind them that it's bad business to take advantage of your best customer. And then we should sit down and figure out how to make this a more equitable relationship," he said. "There are people who wish I wouldn't refer to China as our enemy. But that's exactly what they are."

Trump's professed concern for the human rights of the Chinese people did not carry over from his books to his presidency. But his long-held desire to reframe the US-China economic relationship by finally standing up to Beijing's trade and financial abuses became a major theme of his campaign, and would come to define his administration as well. His concerns clearly had resonated with American voters, who by this point were keenly aware that there was a problem with China — one that would require a very different set of solutions from those that had been attempted by the current occupant of the White House.

"Something Is Not Working"

Toward the end of the Obama administration, there was mounting evidence not only that the CCP under Xi Jinping was headed in the opposite direction of what their leaders were professing but also that Xi was determined to shape the international environment in his favor. The Chinese government was becoming more externally aggressive, more internally repressive, and more totalitarian in its politics and economics, fusing state and business in a coordinated strategy not to join the world order that the United States and its partners had built after World War II but rather to undermine that system and replace it with one suited to China's interests — and one that would protect the party's survival and success above all.

The Obama administration had been slow to realize that Xi's ascension to power at the end of 2012 marked a new era. Xi was a strongman nationalist who had a clear view that this was not a China that was rising, but a China risen. And his dream of an ascendant China — a vision that quickly became part of official Chinese rhetoric — was no secret. As CCP theorists crowed in late 2014, "Mao made the Chinese nation stand up, Deng made the people of China grow rich, Xi Jinping will make the people of China grow powerful." He had a hardline approach domestically and he had big ambitions on the world stage. In Xi's first major speech as general secretary, he pledged "to unite and lead people of the entire party and of all ethnic groups around the country while accepting the baton of history and continuing to work for realizing the great revival of the Chinese nation in order to let the Chinese nation stand more firmly and powerfully among all nations around the world and make a greater contribution to mankind."

Xi viewed China's interactions with the Western world as a battle of competing, incompatible ideologies. In 2013, the CCP issued an internal (later leaked) memo called Document 9, which reportedly was directly approved by Xi and reflected his views. It called on all Chinese officials to "see the ideological situation as a complicated, intense struggle." It warned that Western liberal values were just attempts to undermine the CCP and its system of "socialism with Chinese characteristics." Promoting democracy, human rights, civil society, neoliberal economics, and even journalism were all just Western excuses to attack the Communist Party. The memo called on all Chinese officials to "conscientiously strengthen management of the ideological battlefield." The official who leaked it, Gao Yu, was thrown in prison.

If one could dismiss Xi's words, it was harder to ignore his actions and his string of broken promises during Obama's tenure. Xi and Obama signed an agreement in 2015 that China would end cyber theft of intellectual property; that same year, Xi promised Obama in the Rose Garden that China did "not intend to" militarize its artificial islands in the South China Sea. But no sooner had the Chinese president made these promises than his government set about breaking them. The government-sponsored cyber theft lessened for a few months but then returned to its previous levels. In May 2015, Beijing unveiled its "Made in China 2025" plan, a commitment to revolutionize the Chinese manufacturing sector over ten years; this plan, which sought dominance of several high-technology industries of the future, including information technology, robotics, aerospace, and clean energy, was a direct challenge to the technological advantage that Western economies were depending on to fuel the next generation of economic growth. China steadily built out surfaces on reclaimed reefs and other features in disputed areas of the South China Sea, adding infrastructure, then radar, then all-out military defenses. Meanwhile, China was rapidly expanding its Belt and Road Initiative, debt-trapping developing countries on several continents. Xi's government was crushing domestic dissent, pressuring Taiwan, slowly suffocating Hong Kong's freedoms, and brutally repressing Tibetans, Uyghurs, and any other minority that resisted the official program of political loyalty and total state authority.

Over Obama's eight years in office, his China team battled internally over whether to continue an engagement-focused strategy based on encouraging the CCP to move toward economic and political opening, or shift to a strategy of competition based on a more realistic assessment of China under Xi. The internal dynamics were messy. The State Department under Hillary Clinton took a relatively centrist position on China while she was secretary. Her lead Asia official, Kurt Campbell, devised the "Pivot to Asia" policy, but the National Security Council, led by National Security Adviser Tom Donilon, forced him to change the name to "Rebalance to Asia" (although Campbell got the last word in his book, which was titled *The Pivot*). Meanwhile, her deputy, Jim Steinberg, came up with his own framework for US-China relations that he called "Strategic Reassurance." The problem was, Steinberg never bothered to include any other part of the government in coming up with his framework, so it never went anywhere.

Confronting China simply was not a priority for top-tier second-term Obama administration foreign policy officials such as National Security Adviser Susan Rice and Secretary of State John Kerry, who valued smooth relations as necessary for securing Obama's legacy. They didn't see China's aggression as an urgent problem that needed solving, and they needed Beijing for the things they cared about more, such as climate change and the Iran nuclear deal. Officials at the Pentagon, at the Justice Department, and in parts of the intelligence community, on the other hand, did become increasingly concerned about China's behavior as the Obama administration dragged on. "You had this whole team across the Obama administration who felt our approach to China is not working," one senior Obama administration official told me. "We are being shaped to our disadvantage. We are not doing the shaping."

In order for the Obama team to claim a successful China policy, it needed to portray the relationship as copacetic—a need that manifested itself as willful blindness to the changing reality. Toward the end of its tenure, indeed, the Obama White House went to great lengths to avoid disrupting relations with China. After Defense Secretary Ash Carter and Chief of Naval Operations Jim Richardson referred in speeches to "great power competition," Rice's National Security Council went so far as to directly instruct the Pentagon officials not to use the term "competition" when referring to the US-China relations and find a less inflammatory term.

Their deference was not rewarded with respect. On Obama's final presidential trip to China in September 2016 for the G20 summit in Hangzhou, the Chinese officials famously wouldn't allow the US advance team to bring over the stairs Obama uses to depart Air Force One. Obama embarrassingly popped out of a smaller exit under the wing. Chinese officials then manhandled the US press and prevented Rice from crossing their security line.

"At the time, many viewed the treatment as a metaphor for a rising power flexing its muscles with a young president from a superpower in decline," the *New York Times* reported.

A senior Obama administration official put it more bluntly: "When you are not respected enough for them to bring the stairs in, clearly something is not working."

The Backchannel

The Chinese government had taken for granted that Clinton would win, and that Beijing could continue flexing its muscles with little resistance from Washington. As a result, China had been utterly unprepared for Trump's surprise electoral victory. On November 9, it was forced to confront the unpleasant reality that it had no plan for dealing with an incoming administration whose China team Beijing didn't know, didn't understand—and certainly didn't want.

For Beijing, an American foreign policy run by hawks like Bannon and Navarro was the worst possible scenario. Chinese leaders had spent four decades grooming a generation of China hands to manage the relationship, investing in them with time and money and depending on them to steer the ship calmly. Bannon and Navarro had no skin in that game, and nothing to lose by burning those bridges.

In a search for answers after the election, and hoping to find another, less hawkish liaison with the new administration, Ambassador Cui reached out to Jared Kushner. Cui had met the president's son-in-law during the campaign, and had reason to suspect that Kushner would be easier to deal with than Donald Trump's other close advisers. After all, the ambassador and Kushner had been introduced, auspiciously, by a mutual acquaintance and longtime friend of China: former US secretary of state Henry Kissinger.

Kushner had reached out to Kissinger for help during the campaign. Privately, he also sought Kissinger's approval, which for Kushner represented the cachet that he would need in order to assume a major policymaking role for which he simply wasn't qualified. Kissinger, for his part, was pragmatic; he knew that Kushner was the quickest way to Trump's ear, and the best way to continue advancing the cause of improving US-China relations, to which he had devoted his life and on which he had staked his legacy. But Kissinger didn't pretend to be close to Kushner. When Kushner asked Kissinger to write his biography for *Time* magazine's 100 Most Influential People list in April 2017, Kissinger was decidedly lukewarm in his endorsement of the young man, "whom I first met about 18 months ago, when he introduced himself after a foreign policy lecture I had given. We have sporadically exchanged views since," Kissinger wrote. "As part of the Trump family, Jared is familiar with the intangibles of the President. As a graduate of Harvard and NYU, he has a broad education; as a businessman, a knowledge of administration. All this should help him make a success of his daunting role flying close to the sun."

In any event, the budding friendship between the real estate heir and the foreign-policy sage began to pay dividends immediately — at least, for Kissinger and his Chinese counterparts. Kissinger had gone to see Xi on December 2, the day of the Taiwan call, because he believed he spoke for the president; through Kushner, he had gotten Trump's blessing to make an overture to Beijing on behalf of the incoming administration. After all, Trump may have thought of China as an "enemy," but he still wanted a deal. It was Kissinger, too, who subsequently set up the meetings in Kushner's office with Yang after the Taiwan call, in an ultimately failed bid to undo the damage. But although the meetings were a bust, Kissinger had established the first functioning bilateral channel between Beijing and the incoming US administration — and that channel went straight through Trump's son-in-law.

Kushner was proving to be a good investment for Kissinger. Trump's son-in-law had wasted no time showing that, despite his meager title, he held the power at the White House. Just two days after the election, on November 10, 2016, Trump had traveled down to Washington with Kushner and foreign policy adviser Michael Flynn. While Trump sat with Obama in the Oval Office, Kushner took a very public walk around the property with Obama's chief of staff, Denis McDonough. "It was a really big deal because Jared was the one McDonough was dealing with, not Reince," a White House official said, referring to Reince Priebus, the chairman of the Republican National Committee, who was soon to be named White House chief of staff. "It was the first big sign Jared was in charge and Priebus was a pissant."

Kushner didn't want a job in the spotlight. He didn't want to be in the press. He just wanted to be in charge, playing a key role in almost every issue. For anyone who wanted to shape Trump's China policy, Kushner clearly was the most important official to know — and, like Kissinger, the Chinese leadership smartly invested in him by working primarily through him and ignoring the hawkish advisers they hoped to marginalize.

Reinforcements

The day after the December 2 Taiwan call, the transition staff in New York knew they had a problem. The president needed to be briefed about the US-China relationship, and fast. But there were no actual China experts on staff.

So the transition team called in reinforcements. Trump transition official K. T. McFarland, who had early on in her career been Kissinger's notetaker, called Michael Pillsbury, a historian and Mandarin speaker who had worked in policy and intelligence circles since the Nixon administration. We are forming a China team, she told him, and you're on it. Show up at Trump Tower at eight o'clock on Monday morning.

Flynn, meanwhile, called in Matthew Pottinger, a former journalist who had spent seven years in China reporting for the *Wall Street Journal* before quitting journalism and joining the Marines in 2005 at age thirty-two. He had worked under Flynn in Afghanistan, where the general was then a top intelligence official, and had coauthored with Flynn a consequential document: a 2010 think tank report on how to fix the intelligence effort in Afghanistan, a paper that brought Flynn out of military obscurity and into the attention of the Obama administration. Now, Flynn was filling his staff with his intel buddies, so he tapped Pottinger back as his top Asia guy. The morning after receiving his old commander's summons, Pottinger rode a Citi Bike uptown from his office at an investment consulting firm to Trump Tower to answer the call.

A semblance of a China team was taking shape. That was perhaps the only positive result of the Taiwan call. The negative was that Trump had started what was already poised to be a difficult relationship with China with a fight he didn't intend. It also ended up poisoning Trump on the issue of Taiwan, backfiring on the hawks who thought the call was a good idea. Bannon, Navarro, and the other campaign folks thought they could control the policy by cutting out the bureaucracy, and they assumed that Trump was on board with their plan to come out guns blazing. But they soon discovered they had no choice but to engage the other people who had real influence with the president-elect — his New York billionaire buddies.

Over the course of the transition, Trump's ragtag China team — Bannon, Navarro, Pillsbury, and Pottinger — set out to meet with the other stakeholders in Trump's orbit. Each of these players would try to claim a piece of the China policy and steer it to their interests as time progressed. Factions formed and battle lines were set, but there weren't just two teams, the China hawks and China doves. Opposing groups existed, to be sure—but even within them, there were disagreements all the time.

For example, during the transition, the team met with soon-to-be commerce secretary Wilbur Ross in his Fifty-Seventh Street apartment, which was packed with millions of dollars' worth of Chinese art and artifacts. Ross had been to China over eighty times, he bragged to the China crew, and had substantial business interests there.

Ross and Navarro had worked together to write memos about China for the campaign; in those memos, Ross had taken a hawkish line on trade, which led Navarro to believe they were on the same page. But when they met after the election, Navarro and Ross got into a spat about whether the Trump administration should welcome foreign direct investment from China. Ross's view was that Chinese investment was fine, so long as it did not affect US national security in any way. Navarro, on the other hand, believed—and had argued in several books—that essentially every dollar China sends to the United States should be rejected and every dollar that Americans invest in Chinese companies should be blocked. The hawks on Trump's China team had only just banded together, and already fault lines were beginning to show.

Unlike Ross, Navarro was not a close friend of the new president. He had first encountered Trump when he had read that Trump was a fan of Navarro's 2011 book *Death by China*. When it came time to make the movie, narrated by Martin Sheen, Trump provided a marketing blurb at Navarro's request. Navarro, an economics professor at the University of California at Irvine, had run unsuccessfully for local political office five times. The fact that he had done so as a Democrat didn't seem to bother Trump.

Class Warfare

In the few weeks between Trump's election and his inauguration, it quickly became clear that consensus on China would be elusive within his administration. Even the hawks couldn't agree with each other. But within Trump's foreign policy team, class proved to be as big of a dividing line as ideology, if not bigger — a phenomenon that resulted in an alliance between the New York bankers and the Washington policy wonks, whose opposition to the hawks on the China team sometimes seemed more about personalities than policy.

The officials from the Wall Street Goldman Sachs clique (Kushner, Mnuchin, Cohn, and Cohn's deputy, Dina Powell), upon arriving in Washington, naturally gravitated toward the DC Republicans one would find at fancy Georgetown spots like Café Milano (Priebus, Deputy Chief of Staff Rob Porter, Kellyanne Conway). "For Jared, Cohn and Mnuchin just made him more comfortable than a goofy California professor or a raspy voiced trade lawyer from Ashtabula, Ohio," one White House official said, referring to Navarro and Robert Lighthizer, whom Trump would appoint US trade representative. "Rob Porter didn't care about China. Reince Priebus didn't care about China. But they wanted to hang out with the cool kids."

Kushner was not a part of the "China team," but only because he was part of his own faction, the Trump family. That faction was the best one to be in. The Trump Organization was a family business and Kushner had grown up in his own. It soon became clear to the hawks that Kushner's instincts led him to agree more with the finance executives and billionaires he had known his whole life. Kushner was how these businesspeople, like the Chinese leaders, got to Trump outside any formal government process. The early China team saw Kushner as naïvely wading into geopolitics in ways that were sure to be unhelpful to their cause. Kushner saw his role as to help Trump get what he wanted — and if that was a deal with China, then so be it.

The official governmental China team also quickly realized it had to contend with another group of powerful figures who were determined to have their own influence over Trump's China policy: the president-elect's billionaire friends. Several of them had long-standing business interests in China and deep personal relationships with leading business and political figures in Beijing. The China team tried to co-opt these influencers as best they could; as they set about developing the beginnings of a real China strategy for Trump, the team sought out several of Trump's billionaire buddies for counsel. They also wanted to know what Trump's friends were likely to be saying in the late-night phone calls the staff knew were constantly occurring but couldn't track.

Along with Kushner, the team met with former Treasury secretary Hank Paulson, who while Treasury secretary under President Obama had led the Strategic and Economic Dialogue with China, a massive annual conference where hundreds of officials from both countries were forced to sit down and talk with each other for a couple of days. Paulson pitched the framework as a useful mechanism the Trump administration should continue. Mnuchin had worked under Paulson at Goldman and relied on him for advice on China. Kushner also gave Paulson an avenue to influence Trump.

Bannon told Kushner this was the kind of fake diplomacy that the CCP used to lull the stupid Americans into a false sense of security while they advanced their plan to spread misery and tyranny around the world. "My belief is pretty straightforward, that the CCP is exactly like Mussolini, Hitler and Tojo. These are gangsters, they are criminals. They think like criminals, they act like criminals and they need to be treated like criminals," Bannon explained later. "This is very much like the 1930s . . . They are at war with us. They are at war and we are not. It's pretty obvious." Bannon believed the only way to save our country and the free world is to bring down the CCP as quickly as possible. "CCP delende est," he loved to say, paraphrasing Cato the Elder, who ended every speech by declaring, "Carthage delende est," or "Carthage must be destroyed."

The team met with Hank Greenberg, the former CEO of AIG, whom Trump had known personally for decades. A businessman with decades of experience in China, Greenberg also happened to be a decorated World War II veteran. At this meeting, Navarro yelled at Greenberg for advancing the idea that the United States and China could be closer economic partners rather than rivals. "You're part of the problem," he yelled. Pillsbury stood up for Greenberg. "There's only one person in this room who landed in Normandy on D-Day and he deserves our respect," Pillsbury told Navarro.

The most active set of outsiders trying to get Trump's ear on China were his business buddies, several of whom depended on Beijing's good graces for billions of dollars in annual revenue. They included casino magnates Sheldon Adelson and Steve Wynn, Blackstone Group CEO Stephen Schwarzman, Blackrock CEO Lawrence Fink, and Barrick Gold CEO John Thornton. Adelson actually offered to set up his own team of China experts to assist Trump. That never came about, to the relief of Trump's actual China team. This was one less complication in their effort to manage the China policy, an effort that was getting more difficult by the day. Only later would it become clear just how much havoc the businesspeople could wreak.

Trump's Favorite General

During the November 10 visit between the outgoing and incoming presidents, Obama warned Trump about two things: North Korea and Michael Flynn. Obama had made Flynn director of the Defense Intelligence Agency in 2012, but had fired him two years later over Flynn's penchant for chasing conspiracy theories, including one that held that the Iranian government was behind the 2012 attack on the US consulate in Benghazi. Flynn's resentment of Obama and his outcast status among establishment Republicans had led him into the welcoming arms of the Trump campaign.

While Trump had met with Obama, Flynn had met with Rice and her deputy Ben Rhodes. You don't need secret sources to know how awkward that encounter was. Flynn — whom Trump named as incoming national security adviser a week after the election — had spent the campaign shouting "Lock Her Up" at the top of his lungs while working as an unregistered agent for the Turkish government and backchannelling with the Russian ambassador. What's more, Rice and Rhodes had been part of the team that fired Flynn from his job as Defense Intelligence Agency director in 2015.

Flynn held that grudge, and he would have been even more resentful had he known what had been happening behind the scenes in the White House. Obama officials had been tracking Flynn's interactions with Russian ambassador Sergei Kislyak during the transition, along with the FBI. The revelation that Flynn was caught on intelligence intercepts of Russian officials was the basis of the convoluted saga that spawned Trump's warped claim Obama had "wiretapped" him. Flynn's lies about these conversations—both to the FBI and to Vice President Pence—were the proximate cause of his firing twenty-four days after inauguration. In fact, Flynn was fired for a host of reasons, chief among them his sheer inability to manage the National Security Council staff or get along with any of the other White House factions. In Trump's world, the factions ganged up on whomever seemed weakest, for self-preservation and for sport.

Flynn's well-documented plan to mend relations with Russia was not just about Moscow. Like Bannon, Flynn wanted to engage Russia to fight what he saw as a common adversary—China. Rice would hint at it later, when she told the House Intelligence Committee behind closed doors during the Russiagate investigation that Flynn was not at all focused on Russia in their first meeting during the transition—in fact, he was focused on China. "Frankly, we spent a lot more time talking about China in part because General Flynn's focus was on China as our principal overarching adversary. He had many questions and concerns about China," Rice testified. "He downplayed his assessment of Russia as a threat to the United States. He called it overblown. He said they're a declining power, they're demographically challenged, they're not really much of a threat, and then reemphasized the importance of China."

Despite their differences and history, Flynn and Rice paraded themselves onstage two months later, on January 10, 2017, at the United States Institute of Peace for a time-honored Washington ritual known as the grip and grin. The institute, run by George W. Bush's national security adviser, Steven Hadley, held their quadrennial "Passing the Baton" conference, where the incoming and outgoing national security advisers pretend to like each other and preach about American exceptionalism, the international rules-based order, and other such catchphrases. The handshake between the incoming and outgoing national security advisers, according to Hadley, "symbolizes the transition of power from one admin to the next and the shared commitment to national security that transcends party lines."

Rice laid out her argument that the Obama administration's foreign policy had been a raging success on all fronts. To the extent that Rice referred to Asia in her remarks (which was not much), she praised the Obama administration's "rebalance," urged the new administration to support the Trans-Pacific Partnership—knowing Trump would likely scrap it but touting it as an accomplishment nonetheless—and said the Obama team had successfully managed a "complex but cooperative" relationship with China.

"General Flynn, I am rooting hard for you," she said, paraphrasing a note George H. W. Bush famously left for Bill Clinton.

The irony of this exchange is hard to overstate. The $100 million United States Institute of Peace building itself is a monument to the "blob," the foreign policy elite establishment Trump ran his campaign against. Across the street from the State Department, its very existence was meant to enshrine the professional foreign policy careerists' role as guardians of the type of bipartisan American muscular internationalism that Trump was promising to destroy. During the campaign, dozens of GOP foreign policy establishment figures signed public letters condemning Trump's candidacy. Those who didn't sign such letters were privately pressured not to join Trump's movement. That's why Trump had to rely on amateurs and unknown outsiders like George Papadopoulos, Carter Page, and J. D. Gordon to staff him on foreign policy during the campaign. They weren't Russian assets. They were fringe players in the GOP foreign policy scene who loved the idea of a huge payoff from a long-shot bet on a kooky candidate. Now, here in the grand hall of the United States Institute for Peace, former establishment outcast Flynn was being applauded by the likes of Hadley, Madeleine Albright, and all the rest. The establishment needed him now. They were welcoming him back in.

This was Flynn's proudest public moment: the comeback of comebacks. The crowd was happy to ignore the fact that his remarks contained no real substance and revealed nothing about how Trump would run US foreign policy. Flynn praised Rice's "grace" and "elegance" and rattled off the platitudes that had come to serve as the way Trump people spoke to DC establishment types to make their lack of strategic coherence digestible. He threw out catchphrases like "peace through strength," using alliances as a multiplier, "the unapologetic defense of liberty" as a "core element of American exceptionalism," and said not much else of substance.

In this, Flynn wasn't alone. McFarland, who had been named by this point as Flynn's incoming deputy, rambled on about everything and nothing at the same time in her panel at the event. She made up a statistic that 40 percent of Americans had long since checked out of the foreign policy discussion in our country. She said these were the Americans whom Trump was bringing back into our politics, by responding to their demands. Like Flynn, she rattled off promises to uphold American values, strengthen alliances, and preserve American leadership.

"So I would say, all of you, relax. It's going to be great. We are going to make America great again," she told the nervous crowd. "And welcome along for the ride."

2

All Aboard

Just shortly after noon on January 20, 2017, on the steps of the US Capitol building, Donald Trump delivered his first address as the newly inaugurated president of the United States. Five blocks away, a mix of diplomats, officials, and VIPs from various countries watched from a posh reception on the rooftop of the Canadian embassy. As Trump began speaking, these onlookers lowered their Bloody Mary cocktails and cups of poutine to listen. The guests were the diplomatic and foreign policy elite who had worried during the campaign about Trump's professed plans to abandon the international liberal order the United States had led since World War II. They were about to have their worst fears confirmed.

As millions of onlookers gaped, Trump scowled and barked about the end of "American carnage," lashing out at unnamed foreign countries that had allegedly stolen American jobs, sent immigrants over the United States' borders, and taken dollars away from its citizens. The new president promised to even the scales, and then some. "From this day forward, a new vision will govern our land," he bellowed. "From this moment on, it's going to be America First."

The only difference between this speech and those given during Trump's campaign rallies was that now Trump had the power to fulfill his pledge. Trump saw the American promises to champion values like democracy, human rights, and free markets as foolish in a world where every country had to fend for itself and might made right. This was the worst possible time for such a retrenchment, in the eyes of America's allies, who needed more US help to combat rising nationalism at home and expanding authoritarianism worldwide. For over a year, Washington insiders had been promising their foreign visitor friends in DC that there was no way Trump would win.

Every foreign government had been unprepared for Trump's election. Now, as he took the helm of the most powerful country on earth, his fellow heads of state — like many DC insiders — were panicking. They had no idea how to navigate the Trump team or which lobbyists and consultants to pay to help them do it.

Beijing's position was more precarious than the others. With slowing economic growth at home and ambitious investment plans abroad, an economic confrontation with the United States — which is what Trump was promising — was not in their carefully crafted plans. Like most observers, they had expected Hillary Clinton to win — and although the former secretary of state had not exactly shied away from criticizing China, with her in the Oval Office at least Beijing would have known what they were dealing with. Now, they needed to rebuild their network from scratch, and quickly. They had Jared Kushner, which was a start — but they had no way of knowing whether he would be enough to offset the hawks on Trump's team.

Clipped Wings

In the earliest days of the Trump administration, the hawks knew it would be a fight to control the China policy, but they felt up to the task. Steve Bannon, Peter Navarro, and Stephen Miller were all proven loyalists who had earned their Trump bona fides during the campaign and knew the president well. They believed the key to success was to make a more confrontational China policy happen right out of the gate. They knew that Kushner and Steven Mnuchin and Gary Cohn didn't agree with their views on China, but they didn't think they would be able to stop what they had in store. The hawks felt confident that Trump wouldn't immediately turn his back on a key promise from his campaign—and they had a plan to ensure that he didn't.

They could be forgiven for their assumptions. After all, Trump had run on a promise to disrupt the US trade relationship with China. The basic plan to make that happen—tariffs and all—had been laid out clearly in Trump's campaign speeches. Unlike Republican Party officials who hadn't been involved before the election but were scooping up all the staff jobs at the White House, the China hawks were prepared: they had a well-developed strategy to disrupt the way Washington and Beijing did business.

Trump went ahead and withdrew the United States from the almost complete negotiations for the Trans-Pacific Partnership on his fourth day as president. The Democrats were appalled he hadn't bothered to review it formally before withdrawing, at least. The free traders inside the White House knew the partnership was a lost cause, so they kept their powder dry for the fights they knew were coming down the line.

Reince Priebus may have ultimately landed the job of chief of staff, but Bannon was named chief strategist—a job he got to define. During the transition, he and Miller prepared a series of executive orders they planned to have Trump sign before the bureaucracy even realized what was going on. One of the first ones gave Bannon a seat on the principals committee of the National Security Council (NSC), the most senior level of national security decision-making. When the media learned that high-ranking military officials had been replaced on the NSC by the head of Breitbart News, there was a public outcry; Bannon would never actually attend an NSC principals meeting. H. R. McMaster formally removed him from the committee a few months later.

Bannon still had allies on the NSC staff, however, and meanwhile started his own policy shop that he called the Strategic Working Group, where he hoped to import his own national security staffers, including figures like Sebastian Gorka, an anti-Islam Hungarian American "expert" whose wife was working as a Trump appointee in the Homeland

Security Department. Bannon intended to bring in Michael Pillsbury as the China guy in the group while Pillsbury waited for a sweeter posting. But the group never materialized, denied the lifeblood of any bureaucracy—money.

Bannon had a separate plan with Navarro and others to set up a front line of China hawk ambassadors in Asia, not the donors and politicos who typically get these assignments. Pillsbury was to be appointed ambassador to Singapore (or be sent to Hong Kong or Taiwan, depending on who is telling the story). Admiral Harry Harris, who was finishing up a stint as the head of US Pacific Command, was to be sent to Australia. Council on Foreign Relations scholar Ashley Tellis would represent America in India.

Bannon felt that China had declared all-out economic war on the United States, and that previous presidents had been too stupid or scared to fight back. But he didn't see China as just a foreign policy issue. He also wanted China to be the rallying cry for his domestic political movement.

Bannon believed China was key to his grand scheme to link the American Far Right and Far Left in a nationalist, populist political realignment. His goal was nothing less than to overturn the neoconservative, neoliberal globalist order—the same sect that Trump had run against. Both Bannon and the new president shared a dream of destroying the power of the political elite in both parties, and Bannon thought he knew how to make that dream a reality. One flaw in his plan, of course, was that the Far Left and the Far Right arguably have much more antipathy for each other than they do common interests. But Bannon believed they could be united on the China issue.

It takes real nerve to lead a populist, anti-China movement when you started out as a Goldman Sachs executive—and when you have already made your money in China before turning against the system that made that possible. After he left Goldman, Bannon worked for six years with a Hong Kong startup called Internet Gaming Entertainment, which used cheap labor in China to mine virtual goods inside computer games to sell for real-world money.

But never mind all that. Bannon was going to get our jobs back from China. And he had a plan.

"The way to do this is to do a reverse Nixon, Russia has to be a potential ally," Bannon told me later. "Russia is a fucking sideshow, dude. This here is the deal . . . They [Russia] are only on their [China's] side because they have to be on their side. They hate these guys as much as I do."

Best-Laid Plans

Bannon's scheme did not go as planned. The FBI's Russia investigation took over the news, making any significant warming of relations with Vladimir Putin politically impossible. Putin and Xi Jinping, now both targets of the American establishment, only deepened their countries' ties and worked together to thwart the United States. The hawk's plans to do a "reverse Nixon" never got off the ground. And many of the key figures who played a role at the start of the Trump administration's relationship with China would not be around to see it develop. The endless scandals resulted in nonstop turnover, and one by one, several of the players closest to Trump during the campaign on the China issue found themselves sitting on the sidelines.

Flynn would be fired as national security adviser twenty-four days into the administration for lying to Vice President Mike Pence about his conversations during the transition with Russian ambassador Sergei Kislyak. McFarland had been Flynn's deputy before his firing, and she also had been involved in Flynn's dealings with Russian officials during the transition; after initially denying direct involvement, emails surfaced showing that she was in fact in the loop. She would step down from her White House role in April.

Trump subsequently nominated McFarland to be US ambassador to Singapore, but due to her links to the investigation into Flynn's contacts with Russian officials, she was unconfirmable and eventually withdrew. Bannon wanted Pillsbury to be nominated for the Singapore post, but Pillsbury's security clearance application was held up due to an unrelated matter — a wrinkle that ultimately prevented him from getting any official Trump administration job, despite the fact that he had Trump's trust and his ear.

Pillsbury had gotten caught up in the security clearance investigation of another NSC staffer: a well-known China hawk named Adam Lovinger who had been working at the Pentagon's Office of Net Assessment. That office had been run for decades by legendary strategist Andy Marshall, who had led the office well into his nineties, set on the mission of looking beyond the horizon at the strategic challenges facing the United States. He mentored a generation of China hands in the process, including Pillsbury and Lovinger. But Lovinger clashed with Marshall's replacement, James Baker, and was accused of mishandling classified information (a charge Lovinger denies). Pillsbury got dragged into the fray because he had worked with Lovinger on a project for the Office of Net Assessment. Pillsbury would not be able to get a clearance, Bannon was told firmly. He never stopped trying to fix his clearance problem. But others got the prime postings.

Trump did appoint an ambassador to Beijing, but not one that Bannon would have ever wanted. Iowa governor Terry Branstad's nomination had been announced before Trump even took office. A former friend of the Chinese president from Xi's time as a study-abroad student in Iowa, Branstad seemed a logical choice to the public, but he was not on board with the more confrontational policy that Trump's China team had been pushing. His easy confirmation in late spring 2017 placed him as a permanent but not overly important counterweight to the hardliners and the hawks — a thumb on the scale opposite Bannon's.

The leadership in Beijing should have been reassured by Trump's choice of ambassador, but they remained convinced that Bannon was in charge of the China policy — and they remained concerned that his views matched Trump's. If they had known just how limited Bannon's time in the West Wing would be, they might not have been so worried.

Picking on Peter

Unlike some of his comrades on Trump's early China team, Peter Navarro managed not to be sidelined — at least, not entirely. Instead, he settled in for a long struggle over policy and set about scheming with like-minded trade hawks to push forward the trade war against China that Trump had advertised during the campaign. He worked with Stephen Miller, US Trade Representative Robert Lighthizer, and others to convince the president — successfully — that national security tools should be used to implement broad and escalating tariffs to pressure China. But to reach that prize, he would have to walk over coals.

Navarro's call for confronting all of China's malign economic activity and decoupling the two large economies had fit neatly into Trump's campaign strategy, which was geared toward highlighting the economic grievances of rural Americans and blaming the current leaders in both Washington and Beijing. But once he joined the administration, the University of California at Irvine economist would be constantly attacked and ridiculed by Kushner and his free market–oriented Wall Street clique, which came to include Treasury Secretary Steven Mnuchin, National Economic Council director Gary Cohn, and others.

Almost immediately after inauguration, the other factions joined forces to marginalize Navarro. One news report said White House chief of staff Reince Priebus intended to assign Navarro to an office in the basement of the Commerce Department, rather than placing him in the Old Executive Office Building, which is on the White House compound grounds. Bannon claims he thwarted that plan. Navarro believes it was just a press leak meant to demean him. In any case, Navarro wasn't assigned an office on the White House campus and had to work out of his home for the first three weeks. After that, he was given the rank of deputy assistant to the president, a full notch below the rank of assistant to the president, which was granted to his West Wing counterparts such as Bannon, Priebus, Flynn, Cohn — even White House press secretary Sean Spicer.

There were other indignities. Whereas Cohn's spot at the head of the National Economic Council came with a robust staff and office space in the West Wing, Navarro was named the head of the National Trade Council, which had never existed before and had hardly any staff or money. He was eventually assigned an office at the Old Executive Office Building next to the White House. But he wasn't allowed to see the president for almost two months after Trump took office.

When Navarro finally was permitted to see Trump in the Oval Office in early March, he had a huge argument with Cohn in front of the president—what would be the first of many fights between the two men. It wasn't just about China. The US negotiations with Mexico over a new free trade agreement to replace NAFTA were already heating up, and German chancellor Angela Merkel was on her way to Washington to talk trade as well. Kushner, Cohn, and Mnuchin were taking control of all these relationships. Navarro was getting cut out of the loop, with the damaging leaks about his treatment adding insult to injury.

In Navarro's view, Cohn and his merry band of globalists were working to basically suppress the president's trade policy. In the view of Cohn, Kushner, and Mnuchin, they were the adults in the room, preventing Trump from following the crazy campaign crowd into economic and political calamity.

"The Trump trade agenda does indeed remain severely hobbled by political forces within the West Wing," Navarro wrote in a two-page memo to Trump and Priebus in late March, a document that was revealed in Bob Woodward's book *Fear.* Navarro specifically called out Priebus, Rob Porter, Mnuchin, and Cohn for preventing his trade proposals from reaching the president. Navarro said he, Bannon, Miller, and Wilbur Ross were fighting the good fight. (Ross's hawk credentials were a subject of dispute internally; both camps at times claimed or disowned him, depending on the moment and the issue.)

In that first battle between Navarro and Cohn in the Oval Office, in front of many top staffers, Trump sided with Navarro's call for the trade policy from the campaign. Clearly he hadn't given up on his core belief that China was robbing the United States blind on trade and that he was the president who would fix it. The rest of the officials knew, then, that Navarro could capture Trump's ear and attention any time. And that, in their minds, made him dangerous.

That meeting sheds valuable light on the way in which Trump set about making China policy after entering the White House. He never hired a China czar. He never empowered one person. He never let one side completely remove the other from the conversations. He didn't always side with the hawks because he was never really a hawk. But he didn't agree with the Goldman Sachs clique either. And he wanted both sides to know it.

The Cohn-Mnuchin-Kushner group was successful in those first few months in stopping the campaign hawks from doing a lot of what they wanted. For now, there were no tariffs. Kushner maintained a close relationship with the Chinese ambassador and used it to plan the upcoming Xi-Trump summit at Mar-a-Lago. Secretary of State Rex Tillerson, Defense Secretary James Mattis, and Vice President Mike Pence were deployed abroad to manage the alliances and conduct the top-level diplomacy with Beijing.

Trump chose his national security cabinet mostly on a series of whims. Tillerson was put forth for the secretary of state position by former secretary of state Condoleezza Rice and former defense secretary Bob Gates. The Exxon oil chief was a major client of the RiceHadley-Gates consulting firm. Tillerson was actually in Doha on the night of the election. The only country he had more experience with than Qatar was Russia. Trump offered him the job as the nation's top diplomat on their first meeting. He had no China experience and no government experience at all.

Retired general Mattis spent four decades in the Marines, mostly serving in the Middle East and retiring as the head of US Central Command. Mattis was a favorite of the DC crowd because of his warrior-monk reputation and his famous "Mattisms," the most famous of which was "Be polite. Be professional. But have a plan to kill everyone you meet." He had run afoul of the Obama White House by pushing for more aggressive tactics vis-à-vis Iran. That, plus the fact that some referred to him as "Mad-Dog" Mattis, was enough for Trump to put him in charge of the Pentagon.

Pence was head of the transition and can be credited with populating the top ranks of the Trump administration with foreign policy conservative hawks and neocons like UN ambassador Nikki Haley and Director of National Intelligence Dan Coats, a former Republican senator. Pence was an original neocon back to his congressional days. He supported the invasion of Iraq and still thinks it was the right call. He's fervently anticommunist. For that reason, he was a China hardliner well before that was the fashionable thing to be. But Pence's main goal was not to find himself in the crosshairs of the president. He would have to tread carefully when interjecting on behalf of the hardliners inside the administration. But he was on their team from the start.

As he became involved in so many other issues, Kushner began handing over responsibility for managing the China relationship to Tillerson, who had no real China experience to speak of. That became obvious when Tillerson traveled to Beijing in March to meet with Xi Jinping. Standing next to Foreign Minister Wang Yi at a press conference, Tillerson said the US-China relationship should be guided by "nonconflict, nonconfrontation, mutual respect and win-win cooperation."

Tillerson was not only parroting the talking points that Yang Jiechi had used to lecture the Trump officials in Kushner's office building during the transition. He was also contradicting all of Trump's campaign promises to confront China's malign trade and economic policies. Matt Pottinger sent Tillerson's chief of staff, Margaret Peterlin, a file of articles celebrating Tillerson's concessions in Chinese state-run propaganda media. Only then did Tillerson understand that he had fallen into one of Beijing's favorite traps: getting a US official to use their language and thereby endorse their vision. Obama had made the same mistake in 2013 when he repeated Xi's call for a "new model of great power relations." But

Trump's secretary of state was not endorsing it intentionally; he was just incompetent.

Bill's Paper

While most eyes were focused on the fights between the famous senior figures around Trump, one level down in the administration, a quiet effort to build the structure of a new China policy for the Trump administration was being hatched. As the big shots fought for control, the worker bees hunkered down trying to turn Trump's campaign rhetoric into an actual set of plans and get the bureaucracy on the same page.

Pottinger started day 1 as National Security Council senior director for Asia, inheriting most of his team at the Old Executive Office Building from the last administration. The first thing he did was brush off the very first memo he had written about China for the Trump campaign that past November and share it with his new team. This twelve-page memo became the starting point for the NSC to figure out what a new US strategy should look like. It ended up having more influence on the Trump administration's approach to China than almost any other single document.

The memo was saved on Pottinger's computer under the name "Bill's Paper." (There is no Bill; Pottinger used the name to throw off any person or entity who might be scouring his files surreptitiously.) It begins with the subtitle "A Balance of Power" and presents a set of concepts to explain the need for a new US approach toward China and how to get there.

The paper argues that the peace and prosperity that Asia has enjoyed since World War II, which was made possible by US hegemony, was being threatened by three shocks: the rise of the People's Republic of China, which is laboring to displace the United States in Asia and dissolve our alliances; the dramatic nuclear and missile technology advances by North Korea; and the rising sense among America's Asian allies that the

United States is withdrawing from its role as guarantor of their security and freedom.

While the United States was distracted by wars in the Middle East and the Great Recession at home, Pottinger noted, China had quintupled its economy and built a world-class military, all without compromising its authoritarian political system or state-controlled economy. "As a result, U.S. hegemony as we knew it no longer exists in East Asia," the memo argues. "What we have now vis-à-vis China is a dynamic and uneven balance of power (we have the military edge, they have the economic edge, and the political balance is roughly split). China's aspiration is manifestly not to settle for a balance of power with the United States. Beijing's intermediate-range goal is to achieve hegemony over its neighbors and the Western Pacific."

His claim about China's imperial ambitions was not a mere assumption, Pottinger wrote, but rather the inescapable conclusion that anyone would reach if they were watching the Chinese Communist Party's actions and listening to what it was saying—in its own language, to its own people. "The Party's goal of hemispheric supremacy isn't the whim of President Xi Jinping," he wrote. "It stems from Party aspirations going back decades; Xi is merely accelerating the timeline. But the United States has a big vote in whether China achieves this aspiration."

Unlike Bannon, Pottinger wasn't calling for the destruction of the CCP. He was calling for America to reinforce a balance of power with China in Asia that was slipping in the wrong direction. The idea was to fix the structural problems in the world order we built, which Beijing had been exploiting ever since we welcomed them into that order.

Pottinger didn't want to decouple the US and Chinese economies, like Bannon and Navarro. He argued for addressing China's abuses in trade, intellectual property theft, industrial theft, and the rest through tough negotiations. He warned that much would depend on how the United States treated allies. He called for finding a strategy that allowed both the United States and China to succeed, but not on Beijing's terms. "As such," he wrote, "this strategy, if executed, would constitute a viable and sustainable understanding with China that brings advantages to both sides. China can thrive whether or not our strategy succeeds. America will struggle if we fail."

The paper urged that when American policy makers think of China, they should "think Jupiter, not the Sun." Pottinger saw the countries in the region as the front lines of US competition with China and the places where the friction would be most prominent. Those countries were more influenceable and therefore needed more of our attention. "China shouldn't be the 'sun' around which our regional diplomacy revolves," Pottinger explained. "It should be considered but one of the planets — albeit a massive one — in a solar system of governments we continuously engage."

Pottinger also called for a robust program to counter Chinese influence and interference in various parts of American society. The United States, he wrote, must stop Chinese efforts to intimidate, censor, and punish the citizens, media, and corporations of democracies when Beijing objects to their viewpoints and activities. He said the expansion of China's propaganda outlets must be stopped and "reciprocity" — a concept that in the context of China meant demanding equal treatment from Beijing compared with how the United States treated China — should be enforced where possible. Why should the United States allow the CCP to send hundreds of "journalists" to Washington while restricting the number of US journalists in China and harassing them the entire time? Beijing had come to expect that an imbalanced relationship was their entitlement, and some balance needed to be restored.

Pottinger was arguing for a broad reset of US-China relations based on recognizing the basic principle that the United States was not going to be able to fundamentally change the nature of the Chinese system — nor should it try. The idea was to deal with the reality of China, to focus on stopping the worst of its behaviors and building resilience against the rest — all while protecting American values and interests.

China's malign actions, Pottinger argued, followed a simple pattern. Why, for instance, did China lie to the Obama administration by promising not to militarize the South China Sea? Because the United States didn't make it clear that such aggression would incur costs. And after Beijing did it, it was too late to impose costs. This pattern of China's is like "salami slicing," shaving sliver after sliver until they had eaten more than their portion, Pottinger warned. China's strategy is to nudge the strategic environment incrementally in its favor, sometimes acting so brazenly as to raise alarms in the region, but not quite aggressive enough as to provoke significant countermeasures by neighbors or the United States. After a backlash, China slows its activities until the world stops paying close attention again, then repeats the cycle, rearranging the continental order to its favor, one small earthquake at a time.

Pottinger argued that only by realizing this—and changing our behavior to stop the erosion of our relative power and influence in Asia—could US-China relations be set on a course that avoids confrontation without losing the strategic competition altogether. "China's former premier, Zhu Rongji, said in 2001 that U.S.-China relations will never be great, but they also needn't be awful . . . That goal, rather than a romantic one, would be wise for both sides to aspire to," he wrote.

"Bill's Paper" would later become the basis for two classified strategies on China, as well as the China section of the public-facing National Security Strategy, and feed into several initiatives and speeches made by senior Trump officials. Pottinger's efforts to make concrete policy based on these ideas blossomed over the years, but the seeds were planted on the administration's very first day.

When Doves Cry

Bannon, Pottinger, and Navarro were entrenching for a long fight. Meanwhile, the other member of Trump's original China team, Pillsbury, migrated to an outside advisory role and became a key backchannel connection between the two governments. Just days before the inauguration, he made his own trip to Beijing. There he met with various Chinese officials and experts who were frantically trying to assess what they were dealing with. Pillsbury would make five more trips to Beijing to help demystify the Trump administration for Chinese leaders. Slowly but surely, he also would become a trusted adviser on China to Trump and Vice President Pence.

Other hawks drifted in and out of favor with Trump—and their influence fluctuated correspondingly. Commerce Secretary Wilbur Ross was deeply involved in the China debate for the first year, as he partnered with Mnuchin to secure the deal that Trump had promised would correct a trade relationship that had fallen woefully out of balance. But Ross slowly and surely fell out of favor with the president, his friend for several decades. His tendency to freelance and his tendency to fall asleep in meetings eventually convinced Trump he was not up for the task. Nevertheless, his Commerce Department ended up taking tough actions against China many times, often when Mnuchin's Treasury Department refused to act.

The more pro-Beijing officials, for their part, also began to settle in for the war of attrition. Mnuchin, the former investment banker and movie producer, became the head of the Treasury Department and the lead official for dealing with Beijing on trade negotiations, along with Lighthizer. He also played a complex and covert game pushing back against the China hawks inside the system for years, defending the interests of his Wall Street associates and, some would say, the pro-China lobby in Washington. "I don't know why you guys keep saying China's a threat," Mnuchin said in an Oval Office meeting early on. "You live in your DC bubble. Nobody outside DC thinks China is a threat."

Did Trump see China as a threat? Economically, sure. But on national security, certainly not at first. He just wanted to make a deal. And in their own ways, both he and Mnuchin would find a willing accomplice in the president's son-in-law, Jared Kushner, who was emerging as one of the biggest advocates for China within the administration.

Kushner's role as a China adviser conflicted with his own personal business interests almost immediately. In early January, less than two weeks before the inauguration, it had been revealed that he had met with a senior Chinese business leader in New York only one week after the election, to discuss a deal that would have seen the Chinese conglomerate Anbang Insurance Group invest $400 million in the Kushners' tower at 666 Fifth Avenue.

The leak of Kushner's meeting with Wu Xiaohui, the chairman of Anbang, at the Waldorf Astoria hotel (which Anbang owns) on November 16 was so specific it had to have come from someone at the dinner. Even the $2,100 bottles of Château Lafite Rothschild got mentioned. The Kushner companies explained that the deal had been in the works for months before the election. Regardless, due to the clear conflict of interest after the election, the negotiations were scuttled.

Kushner did not suffer nearly as much as his would-be business partner, however. Chinese authorities would arrest Wu four months after the story broke; he subsequently was sentenced to eighteen years in prison for corruption. Whatever factional fighting there was in Trump world paled in comparison to what must have been going on inside the CCP system at the time. Perhaps Wu's outreach to Kushner was seen as a power play and therefore a threat to the leadership in Beijing, so he was purged. Perhaps he was punished for the fact that the scheme failed so publicly. It's impossible to know.

But what is certain is that, for a time, Kushner and his conciliatory views toward China seemed to have won out. After Trump's inauguration on January 20, 2017, Kushner was the official who had the direct line to Beijing, so he had the most influence. He was listening to Henry Kissinger, Mnuchin, Cohn, and the billionaires, all of whom steered him toward a friendly relationship managed at the very top of both governments. That was the way to get the deal Trump wanted, they assured him.

To that end, Kushner's main objective was to organize a summit between Trump and Xi at Mar-a-Lago. The summit, he felt, was crucial for the two leaders to forge a personal bond and set the bilateral relationship on a steady and stable course. If Kushner's father-in-law wanted a deal with China, this seemed like a necessary first step.

But Xi refused to even speak with Trump over the phone until the American president fixed the problem he had caused with his Taiwan call. "The Chinese began to punish the Trump administration for that phone call and would not actually have a summit anywhere until the president clarified his views," Pillsbury would recall several years later. "But the way he did that set the tone for the next three years."

After Dark

Xi wanted to come to Mar-a-Lago and cement his relationship with Trump. But he couldn't lose face. The Taiwan call had to be walked back. Otherwise, Xi would be seen as conceding on a core issue for China right off the bat.

Trump wanted the problem with Xi fixed as well. He had never intended to offend Xi with the call. Trump saw the two countries as two giant corporations and Xi as his opposing CEO. You need a good relationship with the other CEO to have productive negotiations, at least at the start. Trump also looked up to strongman rulers like Xi: he was jealous of Xi's power but at the same time sought Xi's validation. But most of all, for Trump, a close personal relationship with Xi was the prerequisite for getting what he wanted — a deal.

So Kushner, working with the Chinese ambassador, devised a plan to break the impasse. On the evening of Thursday, February 9, after most White House staff had gone home, Kushner called Bannon and Secretary of State Rex Tillerson to the president's residence. There, Trump took a phone call from Xi. And, as Kushner had arranged, his father-in-law promised Xi directly that he would accept no more phone calls from the leader of Taiwan.

In the official White House statement about the call, Pottinger secured a small but largely symbolic victory. The original draft had stated that Trump would commit to honoring "the one China policy." But Pottinger made sure the statement read, "President Trump agreed, at the request of President Xi, to honor *our* one China policy" (emphasis added). That edit maintained America's historical position of ambiguity as to whether the United States agrees with Beijing on its claims regarding what it considers a renegade province.

Regardless, the call showed that Trump had conceded Xi's main point: that the Taiwan call was wrong and would never happen again. "That removed the obstacle for the Mar-a-Lago summit," Pillsbury said. Kushner had delivered the meeting that Trump had sought, putting the president's son-in-law firmly in the driver's seat of US-China policy.

Not everyone was pleased about this outcome. Bannon, for instance, was livid. He saw the call as a naïve concession by Kushner and a misstep by Trump. "Why did we take the phone call from Xi? We had all the leverage. Xi was dying to go to Mar-a-Lago," Bannon told me later. "They got to Kushner. This is Kushner who drove that. Since that time, Trump doesn't want to hear about Taiwan."

After these two phone calls, Trump's attitude toward Taiwan would vacillate between indifference and disrespect, and would continue in that vein throughout his presidency. Because everybody in the administration was aware of the president's opinion, the Trump administration—despite being full of pro-Taiwan hawks at the bureaucratic level—avoided almost all public displays of sympathy or support for the island for the first three years. What minor increases in support the United States did muster were done largely without public fanfare and sometimes even without Trump's knowledge. For instance, despite the fact that Mattis chose Randy Schriver—a pro-Taiwan hardliner—to be the top Pentagon policy official for Asia, it took over two years to push through sales of new F-16 fighter jets to the island. The Pentagon didn't send any generals or admirals to visit Taipei for public events, which would have been a relatively benign move. For the first year, no senior Trump administration officials visited Taiwan at all.

When Trump officials did visit Taiwan and Beijing complained, Trump took China's side. In March 2018, a deputy assistant secretary of state named Alex Wong would visit Taipei, meet with senior Taiwanese officials, and give a speech praising Taiwan's democracy as an example for the entire region. Wong had been the foreign policy staffer for Senator Tom Cotton (R-AR) and had worked on Mitt Romney's 2012 presidential campaign before that. "The United States has been, is, and always will be Taiwan's closest friend and partner," he said during his trip to Taipei.

The Chinese government protested to the White House. When Trump was informed that Beijing was angry about the remarks of Wong in Taipei, he was furious.

"Who the fuck is Alex Wong?" he screamed, according to a person in the room. "And why didn't anybody tell me he was going to Taiwan? Get him out of there!"

Wong wasn't fired, but the rest of the administration got the message — one that, in the months and years to follow, would become clear to Taiwan's government, as well. In early 2019, when the American Institute in Taiwan was preparing a reception to celebrate the fortieth anniversary of the Taiwan Relations Act, there was an internal administration discussion about sending a cabinet-level official to attend. No senior cabinet member wanted to go, so Veterans Affairs Secretary David Shulkin was given the assignment. But a month before the ceremony, Trump fired Shulkin after it was revealed that he had been taking his wife on European shopping and sightseeing trips under the cover of official US government business. When Taiwanese president Tsai Ing-wen arrived at the reception, the highest-level US guests were an assistant secretary of state and former House Speaker Paul Ryan. There were no senior Trump officials in the room.

A Special Relationship

Trump's February 2017 phone call with Xi marked the beginning of a dynamic between the two leaders, one that would shape US-China engagement significantly over the next three years. Xi learned that if he really wanted Trump to do something, all he had to do was ask him for a personal favor. Xi called on these favors liberally, using them to keep Trump out of several issues China deemed sensitive and playing Trump against his own government.

The result was a chilling effect that was felt by even the most senior members of the new administration, and which lasted well beyond the first few months of Trump's presidency. "Trump once told me, I never want to hear from you about Taiwan, Hong Kong, or the Uyghurs," then national security adviser John Bolton, a vocal supporter of Taiwanese independence, would recall in 2019—adding, "I didn't even want to try him on Tibet."

The same year that Bolton made those remarks, one GOP senator would try to convince Trump to do everything possible to persuade China not to crack down on Hong Kong protesters. If Beijing ran roughshod over Hong Kong, the senator argued, China might feel emboldened to take over Taiwan next. That would be a black eye on Trump's record, he cautioned.

The senator admitted to me that he was exaggerating the possibility of a Chinese invasion of Taiwan in an attempt to get Trump on board with a stronger stance vis-à-vis Beijing. Based on my conversations with sources inside the administration, this was not unusual; everyone talking to Trump tried to play to his vanity, ego, and political sense, rather than making a case based on any national security interest. But the words that came back from the president's mouth were chilling.

"Taiwan is like two feet from China," Trump told the senator. "We are eight thousand miles away. If they invade, there isn't a fucking thing we can do about it."

If Trump had said those words publicly, he would have been abdicating forty years of American commitment to aid Taiwan in its defense, which is written into US law, and maintain the status quo that has kept the peace between Taiwan and China. The senator was speechless. *This is what Trump really believed. He just didn't give a shit.* Nobody could know—although by that point in his presidency, it's possible that nobody would have been surprised.

3

Mar-a-Lago and Beyond

At first, only a few officials in the new administration were focused on China. Then, suddenly, everybody was. Xi Jinping was coming to Mar-a-Lago.

The summit between the Chinese and American presidents, scheduled for April 7, 2017, clearly was going to be the biggest foreign policy test of Trump's still-young presidency. The media and the world were watching. How would this inexperienced and unpredictable US president match up with the seasoned leader of a dictatorship — one that threatened to topple America from its perch atop the world?

As far as Trump was concerned, there were two huge issues on the table: first, his need to make good on his promise to forever change the US-China trade relationship; and second, his need to confront the rising threat of North Korea's nuclear and missile programs. For many around the president, however, there was a single, simpler goal: to forge the beginning of a relationship between Trump and Xi that was as stable and constructive as possible.

Xi, as best we know, came to the summit hoping to stave off any move toward tariffs or trade punishments. He surely also wanted to convince Trump to ignore his hawkish advisers and resume the long-standing pattern of the US-China relationship, which until this point had been characterized by long dialogues that resulted in vague promises — thereby allowing China to avoid changing its behavior.

What emerged from the weekend was a clear victory for the Chinese delegation. They succeeded in delaying any punitive trade measures against China, and in reinforcing Trump's belief that he and Xi had a personal friendship. Beijing would use this belief to elicit favors from Trump throughout the next four years. The American president, for his part, got to claim he had successfully navigated a complex diplomatic interaction on the way to real progress, and the hawks on his delegation had been sidelined for the time being.

But although the hawks lost this battle, they didn't surrender in the larger war inside the administration. In fact, the Mar-a-Lago summit and its aftermath would set the stage for exactly what they had been gunning for, and what Xi most feared: a trade war between the world's two largest economies.

Japan's Play

Xi wasn't the first foreign leader to visit Trump's gaudy private club in Palm Beach. Japanese prime minister Shinzo Abe had dined there the month prior and played twenty-seven holes of golf with Trump. That visit produced the now infamous photos of Trump and Abe poring over secret intelligence about North Korea's missile launch at their dinner table, in full view of club members.

Not only was Abe the first in line at Mar-a-Lago; he also was the first foreign leader to visit Trump Tower after the election. In their congratulatory phone call, Trump had made a vague, offhand offer to the Japanese prime minister—something to the effect of, "Hey, if you are ever in town, come stop by." Abe seized the opportunity and showed up in New York City three days later. For the Japanese, the Abe-Trump relationship was everything. Japan's foreign policy was so dependent on the United States, Abe had no choice but to get as close to Trump as possible.

So high were the stakes for Japan—and such was Abe's anxiety about Trump's unpredictability—that the prime minister and his staff went to great lengths to ensure that these meetings went off without a hitch. One official in Abe's inner circle told me that a team in the prime minister's office took meticulous notes of every Trump-Abe interaction during their Mar-a-Lago visit, to create a database of words, topics, and mannerisms that elicited various reactions from Trump. The idea was to figure out what things people say that make Trump happy or upset or bored.

Abe's efforts paid off—for a time. Trump and Abe always got along well, and at first their rapport allowed Japan to navigate the relationship better than other allies, who were constantly the subject of Trump's Twitter rants and threats. Later on, however, when Japan's number one fear (a nuclear North Korea) was under discussion, Abe's ability to get along with Trump provided him no real advantage. Japan pleaded with Trump to take a hard line in the negotiations, not to release the pressure, and not to trust Kim Jong Un. He did the opposite.

Open Access

At the time of the Trump-Xi summit, Mar-a-Lago was a security nightmare. Members were prescreened by the Secret Service, but their guests weren't; they would get patted down at the entrance, but there were no background checks. Inside the club, anyone could get near the president or his conversations. Trump's table in the main dining room had a little velvet rope that separated it from the rest. When he was there, random people would constantly saunter up to the rope to chat him up or eavesdrop on whatever conversation he was in.

Trump's business friends abused their access all the time. For example, when Xi first walked into the club, Blackstone CEO Stephen Schwarzman was just lingering nearby, as if he was part of the official delegation. Trump himself had to nudge Schwarzman and tell him his presence at the historic occasion was inappropriate. "Xi Jinping was arriving and there's Schwarzman walking around the ballroom near the entrance," a senior White House official recalled. "That guy was in our receiving party. It was like, how the fuck did that guy get in here?"

Schwarzman was the rare billionaire cozying up to Trump on China who actually had known and been good friends with the president, his Palm Beach neighbor, for a very long time. He was also perhaps Wall Street's top dealmaker with large Chinese corporations, which meant that he was connected to China's political leadership as well. As CEO of the Blackstone Group, he made news in 2008 when he sold 9.9 percent of his company (under the limit for a security review) to a Chinese government-controlled firm called Wonderful Investments for $3 billion. When asked later how he did it, he said "the premier himself must approve" it.

Schwarzman had given over $100 million to a program to bring American students to study at Tsinghua University (Xi's alma mater) and liked to brag that people called him "an unofficial ambassador" to China. Schwarzman's business dealings in China gave him access to the very top. He had been close to Anbang Insurance Group chief Wu Xiaohui — the same executive whom Jared Kushner had met during the transition — before Wu was purged and jailed. (Blackstone sold $558 million worth of real estate to Anbang one month before the 2016 election.) Schwarzman also was close to HNA Group chairman Chen Feng; Blackstone did a ton of business with HNA, a mysterious but massive Chinese company with a murky ownership structure but clear political ties to the top of the Chinese Communist Party (CCP). For example, Blackstone sold HNA 25 percent of Hilton, also one month before the election, for $6.5 billion.

On top of all that, Schwarzman was good friends with Mnuchin. They had apartments together in the same New York building and would sometimes vacation together. They became close allies during the trade war, working together to persuade Trump to side with them against the hawks and working the Beijing side at the same time. Schwarzman describes his efforts to fight against trade tariffs on China and work toward a deal behind the scenes in his own book, *What It Takes: Lessons in the Pursuit of Excellence*. He claims he made several trips to China in 2018 to tell China's top officials that Trump "was not looking for a trade war."

But the North Korea issue was, in a sense, more urgent than the trade issue, and Trump needed Xi's help. That's what was on Tillerson's mind at Mar-a-Lago. He met Xi at the airport and told reporters that the Trump administration would work with China to "find ways to exercise influence on North Korea's actions to dismantle their nuclear weapons and their missile technology program." The secretary of state was focused on getting the thing Trump wanted perhaps as much as a trade deal, or maybe even more: a peace deal with North Korea. "China can be part of a new strategy to end North Korea's reckless behavior and ensure security, stability, and economic prosperity in Northeast Asia," Tillerson said.

Trump was holding to his tough rhetoric on trade before the summit started. "We have been treated unfairly and have made terrible trade deals with China for many, many years," he said before the summit started. "That's one of the things we are going to be talking about."

Some of Trump's advisers worried that their boss may have wanted a trade deal *too* badly. Matt Pottinger and Kenneth Juster, the senior director of international economic affairs at the National Security Council, prepared a memo for Trump ahead of the summit to warn him not to fall into the traps Xi was likely to set. Don't agree to grand bargains. Don't agree to strategic dialogues. Don't agree to get roped into a long personal entanglement with Xi, disguised as a friendship, that was aimed at neutering Trump's instinct to toughen the US stance vis-à-vis China.

If Trump read the memo, he hid it well. Because, among other things, the Mar-a-Lago summit marked the beginning of his long flirtation with Xi.

The Art of the Steal

On April 7, Donald and Melania Trump were all smiles as they descended the red carpet to greet the Chinese president and his wife when they exited their limousine at the Mar-a-Lago entrance. Trump nodded enthusiastically, but didn't bow, as he shook hands with Xi and Peng Liyuan, a famous Chinese contemporary folk singer, and thanked them for coming. As they posed for a photo at the top of the entrance's staircase, the reporters below stumbled over each other, fighting for the best shot. Trump pointed it out to Xi and made a crack that only Xi could hear. Xi nodded and smiled. He didn't have a strong command of English. Trump didn't seem to realize that.

Their first official meeting, which was supposed to last only thirty minutes, ended up stretching on for over two and half hours. Xi went through a litany of historical grievances, telling Trump about one hundred years of China's humiliation and his family's suffering during the civil war. Xi threw in a good deal of flattery for Trump, just for good measure. It worked.

"We've had a long discussion already. And so far, I have gotten nothing, absolutely nothing," Trump said at the dinner table that first night. "But we have developed a friendship. I can see that. And I think long term we are going to have a very, very great relationship."

Toward the end of that dinner, Trump leaned over and — while Xi was enjoying what Trump later called "the most beautiful piece of chocolate cake that you've ever seen"— the American president told Xi that the United States had fired fifty-nine missiles at Syria's Assad regime, something even the American public didn't yet know. China was not a party to the Syria conflict, but Trump's attack certainly ran counter to China's stance that authoritarian governments should be able to kill their own people, especially those who resist the regime. Was this meant to show Xi that Trump was willing to use force to solve problems and punish rogue regimes? Not really. Trump was just bragging, about the missile strikes and the cake.

Trump later told the *Wall Street Journal* he had told Xi he was willing to be more lenient on trade if Xi cooperated more on pressuring North Korea. "But you want to make a great deal? Solve the problem in North Korea," he said, describing his own logic. "That's worth having deficits. And that's worth having not as good a trade deal as I would normally be able to make."

That linkage was seen by the hawks as not only a betrayal of the campaign's promises, but a foolhardy one at that. By backing down on trade now, in exchange for promises of help on North Korea later, Trump was falling into an old trap. Xi was basically saying, "I will gladly pay you Tuesday for a hamburger today." By actually suggesting this linkage, Trump was enthusiastically walking into one of the traps his advisers had warned against. Trump was also signaling to Xi that he could use the North Korea issue to squeeze concessions out of Trump, which he did over and over again. Trump actually gave Xi incentive to never help solve the North Korea problem.

Trump may have walked away from their meeting with "nothing, absolutely nothing," but Xi won a lot of concessions at Mar-a-Lago. The threat of tariffs was tabled. The United States and China agreed to begin trade talks that would last the next one hundred days, with the goal of boosting US exports and thereby shrinking the trade deficit. Steven Mnuchin and Wilbur Ross would lead the negotiations. Trump also agreed not to name China a currency manipulator, breaking a campaign promise. And he entered into a "Comprehensive Economic Dialogue" with Beijing—a large and protracted set of meetings that would be the forum to discuss all the outstanding economic issues in the relationship. This was what the George W. Bush and Obama teams had done. Their meetings, which under Barack Obama had been called the "Strategic and Economic Dialogue," became what in Washington is called a self-licking ice cream cone: a system whose sole purpose is to perpetuate its own existence. This was also another thing Steve Bannon, Peter Navarro, and even Pottinger had warned against. The new Comprehensive Economic Dialogue was to be a mini version of the old Strategic and Economic Dialogue. Xi couldn't have asked for more.

Trump's family members, as usual, could not resist getting involved. Ivanka tweeted out a video of two of her children, Arabella and Joseph, regaling Xi and his wife with a Chinese folk song called "Jasmine Flower." How they had learned the Mandarin lyrics so well, most observers at the time could only guess.

Beijing had come bearing gifts as well: while Xi was at the resort, the Chinese government approved three provisional trademarks for Ivanka's company, allowing her to sell jewelry, hand bags, and spa services in China.

There's no evidence of a quid pro quo or even that Ivanka was granted the trademarks for any specific reason. Beijing wanted to co-opt her for the sake of it. By giving her a huge gift — and by her accepting it — the soft corruption of family-to-family favor trading, so common in China, was now under way in America as well, and with zero cost for Beijing. In the years ahead, China often would approve Ivanka's trademarks before big trade-related events between Trump and Beijing.

The family was happy, Gary Cohn and Mnuchin were happy, Trump was happy. Xi was elated. Only one group wasn't pleased. As far as the hawks and hardliners were concerned, the weekend hadn't gone well at all.

Bannon and his cohort did, however, see a silver lining in the clouds that hung over the summit. Trump had given the Wall Street guys a chance to try and make a quick deal with China that wasn't terrible. If Beijing reverted to pattern and failed to really negotiate anything substantive — as the hawks fully expected — then Mnuchin and Ross's plan would backfire and Trump might turn to a harder approach.

"We lost that fight but only temporarily and tactically," Pottinger later told me. "There was a one-hundred-day plan. But I knew that was going to be totally futile and of course the Chinese proved it was futile."

Where's My Peter?

At the end of the weekend, after Xi and his delegation had left the premises, Trump convened the whole US team for a "hot wash" debrief in the garden patio at the rear of Mar-a-Lago's main building. There, in front of the full team, Cohn gave a presentation about the trade talks between the US and Chinese sides, touting the progress that was made and the path forward.

A statement released later by the White House said that, in addition to the Comprehensive Economic Dialogue, there would be three other parallel high-level "dialogues," a Diplomatic and Security Dialogue, a

Law Enforcement and Cybersecurity Dialogue, and a Social and Cultural Issues Dialogue, whatever that meant. These dialogues would be the method, according to the White House, to address not only Chinese trade practices but their industrial, agricultural, technological, and cyber misbehaviors as well.

After Cohn finished his remarks, Trump looked around the room to find the one person he hadn't heard much from over the weekend. "Where's my Peter?" he asked, referring to Navarro. "You all have been very, very unfair to him."

Navarro, standing at the back of the room in his black sneakers, looked up. Trump whistled him over. He was on. He was going to get to speak to the whole team for the first time all weekend — and he was not about to waste the opportunity.

Navarro hadn't even been officially invited to the Mar-a-Lago summit; Bannon had pulled him onto the plane at the last minute. Navarro hadn't been allowed to sit at the table for any of the meetings between the US and Chinese delegations. At some of them, he could sit in the back with lower-level staff. But Kushner, Mnuchin, Cohn, and Ross had made sure that the Chinese visitors never had to stare at him directly across a table.

Now, Navarro went at Mnuchin and Cohn on full blast. He said that everything the Chinese side had put forth over the past two days was nothing but lies.

"You've got to be fucking kidding me, what are we, stupid?" he said. "Are we really going to do another SED [Strategic and Economic Dialogue] and just change the letters around to CED and pretend we're doing something different than the last few administrations?"

Trump just nodded and pointed to Navarro as if to say, "Listen to this guy." Trump was making it clear that he was going to give Mnuchin, Ross, and Cohn what they wanted, a chance to prove that they could convince Beijing to make a great trade deal that addressed Trump's core grievances without exerting any real pressure on China. But Trump wanted them to know there was a plan B, that it was Navarro's plan — and that, if they failed, he would turn to it.

"That's when people knew, don't fuck with Peter," one attendee told me. "Don't think you can remove him, because his worldview is closer to that of the president's [worldview] than that of any other person sitting around the table."

The writing was on the wall. If Navarro, Bannon, and Pottinger were right, the Chinese would simply fail to give any real concessions until or unless they were coerced into doing so. And if the hawks were right, they might have a shot at shaping Trump's China policy before too long. But for now, they had to take a back seat and let Mnuchin, Ross, and Cohn try to prove them wrong.

"They sold Trump so hard on this thing," Bannon said. "All we had to do is pull our knives out and just wait."

Rat Meat

As soon as the team got back to Washington, Mnuchin and Ross set their sights on getting a trade deal done before the expiration of the one-hundred-day timeline agreed to by Trump and Xi. If they could only give the president a trade deal that was politically defensible, they thought, the whole idea of tariffs and trade disruption would become irrelevant, the stock market would break records, and US-China relations could be saved.

They ran into trouble right from the start. In May, Ross announced that the two sides had struck a landmark agreement—China would be able to sell chicken inside the United States and US beef exporters would regain access to the Chinese market they had been shut out of since 2003. The deal also contained promises to open up Chinese markets to US financial services companies and US gas exporters. But while some beef exports did happen, they were not nearly on a scale that would have taken a chunk out of the multi-hundred-billion-dollar annual trade deficit. Chicken from China is not really in demand in America, in part due to a long history of Chinese food export scandals that included selling rat meat as lamb, passing off drainage ditch oil as cooking oil, and sending Americans baby formula contaminated with melamine, which causes kidney stones.

The idea of "reciprocity" in US-China relations is a big theme of the Trump administration's approach. It sounds easy: China buys US beef, America buys Chinese chicken. But in this example, as in many others, the concept of reciprocity falls short. Americans don't actually want the same goods and services from China that Chinese people want from the United States. Trading beef for chicken doesn't really make sense. Of course, trying to manipulate the trade deficit by setting arbitrary quotas while ignoring real market forces like supply and demand doesn't make sense either. But the commerce secretary thought Trump and the public would buy what he was selling. "This is more than has been done in the whole history of U.S.-China relations on trade," Ross told reporters on May 12. "Normally trade deals are denominated in multiple years, not tens of days."

Despite these boasts, the chicken-for-beef deal was not nearly enough to stave off Trump's appetite for the kinds of tariffs that would really get Beijing's attention. The most obvious targets for tariffs were aluminum and steel. Ross was no stranger to using steel tariffs against Beijing; in fact his companies had benefited from that exact tactic during the George W. Bush administration. But Ross's vast experience doing business in China cut both ways. In 2008, he entered into a joint venture with state-owned China Huaneng Group, led by a son of former Chinese premier Li Peng, better known as the "Butcher of Beijing" for his role in the Tiananmen Square massacre. China Investment Corporation, a state-owned sovereign wealth fund, contributed $500 million to Ross's investment in Diamond S Shipping, a company based in Connecticut.

Before he joined up with Trump, Ross often had warned against demonizing China, and he had openly disagreed with Trump on issues like Chinese currency manipulation. But after he started helping the campaign, he changed his tune to match Trump's song. Ross even coauthored a white paper for the campaign on trade with Navarro in September 2016 that argued for tariffs and other strong measures against China.

"Our view is that China's leaders will quickly understand they are facing strength on the trade issue in Trump rather than the kind of weakness on trade that has characterized the Obama-Clinton years," they wrote.

Ross's experience and long, personal friendship with Trump gave him confidence that he had authority to make his own deals with Chinese leaders. But he soon found out the hard way that, in this administration, even Trump's closest buddies could be the targets of his wrath.

The Humiliation of Wilbur Ross

In April, Trump had launched an investigation that would determine whether the United States could impose steel and aluminum tariffs on national security grounds, under Section 232 of the Trade Expansion Act. The last time a president invoked that law to impose tariffs was in 1986. The investigation made the tariff threat credible.

As the one hundred days were wrapping up, Ross and Mnuchin planned to unveil a deal with a high-level visiting Chinese government delegation that would have avoided imposing the steel tariffs in exchange for China agreeing to cut its steel exports. Ross had scheduled a news conference on the last day of the Chinese delegation's visit. There was a celebration dinner scheduled at his house the evening before. There was just one thing they forgot to do.

"The dinner was scheduled. They wanted to announce it the next day," Bannon said. "But they hadn't run it by Trump."

Just hours before the dinner, Ross was called into the White House to see Trump. Navarro, who had not been part of the bilateral negotiations, caught wind of the announcement and told Trump about it, making sure to point out its weaknesses.

Trump blew up at Ross when he arrived at the Oval Office in a meeting attended by several other senior staffers. Trump called Ross "weak" and "washed up" and said he "pitied Wilbur's wife," according to one official who was in the room. The deal was off, Trump declared.

The president was just as angry at Ross for not consulting him in advance as he was about the details of the arrangement. Trump wanted to make sure everyone knew that he, and only he, could agree to any deal. Just because he gave someone the authority to negotiate, that didn't mean he would accept whatever they came back with.

Trump's humiliation of Ross resounded across the administration. The dinner at the commerce secretary's house went forward, but the deal and the news conference were canceled. Ross never recovered in Trump's eyes, and the baton for leading the trade negotiations passed to Mnuchin and Robert Lighthizer, who had been confirmed in May as US trade representative. "Wilbur was about to sell us down the river," a White House official critical of Ross's gambit said. "But Trump made a call and it was over."

"We've Got to Get the Rapist"

In the months following the Mar-a-Lago summit, Trump's billionaires tested out his willingness to do personal favors for his new friend Xi, acting as a go-between in the effort to extradite one of the CCP's most vocal critics from the United States.

Xi and Trump had a lot of personal one-on-one interactions—a stream of communications that would blossom into over thirty letters and forty personal phone calls exchanged between the two leaders. Xi used these communications to incept Trump with pro-Beijing ideas, which Trump's team then had to contend with. But when Xi wanted to cut out the US government officials altogether, he would work through this network of private influencers, especially when he wanted something particularly shady. Trump's staff often had to scramble to figure out how to contain the damage from these gambits, when they even found out about them at all.

Such was the case on the morning of June 29 at the White House. By pure happenstance, Bannon was in the Oval Office. The president walked in around 10 a.m.; his next appointment was an intelligence briefing about an hour later, and in the interim, Bannon had a list of issues he wanted to raise with Trump. But before Bannon could begin, the president stopped him in his tracks.

"Hang on," Trump said. "We've got to get the rapist."

"Excuse me?" Bannon said.

"The rapist," Trump repeated. "We've got to get the rapist . . . the guy who's raping everybody. We've got to get him."

Seeing that Bannon was stupefied, Trump called out to Madeleine Westerhout, his trusted personal secretary, and demanded she bring in a letter Trump had received from his friend, casino magnate Steve Wynn, when the two had met the night before at the Republican National Committee fund-raiser at the Trump International Hotel in DC. This in and of itself was strange: many White House officials hadn't forgotten that Wynn had trash-talked Trump during the campaign, but the businessman had turned on a dime after the election and become one of Trump's buddies, a frequent visitor to Mar-a-Lago, and Republican National Committee finance chair. Trump, who often seemed to value personal loyalty above all else, didn't seem to hold it against him.

Westerhout came into the Oval Office and handed Trump a large envelope. "I want to get this guy out of the country, now," Trump insisted.

"Mr. President, what are you talking about, what is this letter?" Bannon asked.

"This letter that Wynn brought me from Xi," the president responded. "It's a personal favor from Xi."

Trump seemed to think Wynn was passing on a letter directly from the Chinese government. In fact, that's how the *Wall Street Journal* reported it later that year. As far as Trump was concerned, the president of China had sent a secret communication to the president of the United States through a casino owner with huge financial stakes in China. Wynn told Trump Xi wanted him to extradite a Chinese national named Guo Wengui. Also known as Miles Kwok, Guo was a Chinese billionaire who had close links to the Ministry of State Security, particularly senior vice minister Ma Jian, who recently had been purged and charged with accepting bribes from Guo, who fled to the United States shortly before the CCP completed its investigation into Ma. Two years later, Guo claimed to have switched sides and to now be working to expose the corruption of senior CCP officials — including China's vice president, Wang Qishan.

But it wasn't actually a letter from Xi. What Wynn had passed Trump was a research file on Guo, compiled by a team of billionaires and alleged criminals who were helping the Chinese government convince Trump to hand over Guo. The material laid out the allegations against Guo and showed Interpol had put out a "red notice" on the Chinese billionaire, seeking his arrest on corruption charges. Wynn was trying to help a foreign government manipulate the US justice system to have a critic of the regime handed over by the US president. Not only was this a brazen breach of US law and all norms of diplomatic interactions, but China also was passing the message through a casino owner its leaders knew they could leverage, who undoubtedly sold it hard to Trump before any US government officials or experts could possibly weigh in. In any normal environment, such a maneuver would never work. But Trump was a willing mark.

Trump didn't know who Guo was and didn't seem to care. He was willing to take it on Beijing's word — as conveyed by Wynn — that this "rapist" was a criminal who needed to be sent back to China to face punishment. (Guo denies these and all other charges brought against him by the Chinese authorities.)

Bannon, on the other hand, did know who Guo was. Not only was Guo an outspoken critic of the CCP, he was also in the process of being vetted by the FBI and CIA to determine whether he could be a source of crucial intelligence information on the Chinese government, the CCP, and its leadership.

"Hang on a sec," Bannon pleaded, as Reince Priebus happened to come into the Oval Office. Bannon went over to the desk of Communications Director Hope Hicks and picked up her phone to call Pottinger, whose office was in the Old Executive Office Building next to the White House.

"Get the fuck over here right now," Bannon told Pottinger.

Pottinger ran over to the West Wing. Bannon showed him the package of information that had come from Wynn. Pottinger said that Guo might have already sought asylum and simply extraditing him might not be a straightforward matter. And he pointed out that the United States did not have an extradition treaty with China. They urged Trump to let them handle it.

Eventually, Trump relented — but even as he did, he insisted that Guo eventually be delivered into the hands of the Xi government.

"We've got to get him outta here because he's raping everybody," Trump insisted.

Bannon called in a team of FBI and other intelligence officials to brief him on Guo. The intelligence community was still working to vet Guo and his information, but he was clearly someone with whom they wanted to continue to engage. Moreover, they feared the precedent of handing over a high-value antigovernment defector to Beijing absent any judicial process.

Bannon stuck Wynn's dossier on Guo in the safe in his office and never spoke of it again. He calculated that Trump would forget Beijing's request and move on.

Bannon calculated correctly. Eventually, Attorney General Jeff Sessions agreed to put Guo into the system that governs political asylum applications. "We've got to make sure this guy is protected by the courts, so even Trump can't send him home," Bannon told Sessions.

The incident laid bare to everyone in the White House that Xi Jinping was playing a different game from the one they had seen played by past Chinese leaders with past US administrations. The Chinese president was appealing to Trump directly and playing on Trump's belief in their close, personal relationship. By using American businesspeople including Wynn, moreover, Xi was attempting to cut out all the national security and political advisers around Trump who knew better than to give in to extravagant demands such as this one. It was just one of the perils of a presidency where private interests had as much sway as public servants, if not more.

The Steve Wynn Channel

Wynn denied that he ever gave Trump a "letter" about Guo Wengui but never denied talking to Trump about Guo on Xi's behalf. Indeed, Wynn's financial interests in pleasing Xi were huge and obvious. In 2017, Wynn Resorts owned four casinos: two in Las Vegas and two in Macau. However, his Macau casinos had been driving the company's revenue. In the last quarter of 2017, as Business Insider reported, "Wynn's corporate earnings jumped 30% entirely on the backs of the company's two Macau casinos, Wynn Palace and Wynn Macau, which saw revenue growth of 65.5% and 24.1%."

But his investments in the peninsula had long been rocky because Macau has been a key laundering point and destination for corrupt money in China. After assuming power in 2012, Xi ramped up anticorruption efforts in a bid to reassert the central government's control, limit capital flight, and lock up his political rivals. More than a million party members were caught up in the crackdown. High rollers got scared and Wynn's business tumbled. His Macau revenue dropped by as much as 35 percent a quarter. "Almost half the business of VIP is gone and may be shrinking," he told shareholders in 2015. "In my 45 years of experience, I've never seen anything like this before."

A year later, Steve Wynn was making nice with the Chinese government. In February 2016, instead of complaining about how CCP policy was making "planning and adjusting almost a mystical process," as he did in 2015, he praised its economic management as "unequaled in the history of civilization" in a call with shareholders. He also told them to "remember that the Communist Party is a meritocracy in China" and reminded them that "although one leader may be a bit more conservative than his predecessor or a bit more liberal, generally speaking they want a successful life for the citizens of China and for the people in Hong Kong and Macau."

Wynn Resorts' share price jumped. It would not be the only example of how his fortunes were tied to the whims of the CCP.

After Trump's victory in the November 2016 election, Wynn was named a finance vice-chair of the twenty-person Presidential Inaugural Committee. In January 2017, he was picked as finance chairman of the Republican National Committee. He stepped down the following year after a *Wall Street Journal* investigation revealed dozens of sexual misconduct allegations. Several former employees of his alleged that they were pressured to engage in sexual acts with Wynn. Wynn Resorts' share price dropped by 6.5 percent after the report. The Republican Party, however, continued to accept donations from Wynn. In 2019, it received at least $400,000 from him.

Over a year later, after Bannon left the White House, Guo returned the favor. The two formed a partnership to fight a common enemy: the current leadership in Beijing. Guo, who many administration officials believe is aligned with a rival CCP faction working against the faction led by Xi, started the $100 million Rule of Law Foundation to investigate Xi and his cohorts. Guo chose Bannon to run it. Later, Guo hired Bannon to help run his company GTV Media Group. His initial contract was $1 million.

The story of Guo Wengui is wrapped in mystery, and over the next three years, he would go on to become involved in several public and private scandals. He hired a private intelligence firm called Strategic Vision to spy on several Chinese nationals inside the United States for $9 million, according to the firm. Guo said they were connected to high-ranking CCP officials. He later sued Strategic Vision and the company responded by accusing Guo of being a CCP spy himself, a double agent hunting dissidents for Beijing. During the litigation over the Strategic Vision contract, journalist Bill Gertz admitted he had taken a $100,000 "loan" from an associate of Guo. The Washington Free Beacon fired Gertz, who had written extensively on Guo for that website and in his own book. Guo went on to sue the *Wall Street Journal*, CNN, another Chinese billionaire named Bruno Wu, Trump confidant Roger Stone, and former Trump campaign adviser Sam Nunberg. As of this writing, these lawsuits were in various stages of litigation and Guo was trying to sell his luxury apartment at the Sherry-Netherland hotel. His status as a member of Mar-a-Lago was unclear.

"Foreign Agents"

The line between advising and lobbying is vague and open to interpretation. US law states that if an American citizen is trying to influence government policy or public opinion on behalf of a foreign government or foreign government official, that citizen is working as a foreign agent and must disclose those activities by registering with the Justice Department under the Foreign Agents Registration Act (FARA). In recent decades, it has been sparsely enforced and violations were almost never prosecuted as felonies — until the Trump administration.

But while unregistered foreign agents were held to account more under Trump, it was a capricious form of justice. Trump's former campaign chairman, Paul Manafort, was tried and convicted of FARA violations, which contributed to his lengthy jail sentence, for his work on behalf of the pro-Russian former government of Ukraine. Obama's former White House counsel Greg Craig was working with Manafort on this very project, but he was acquitted at trial on similar charges. Michael Flynn was doing unregistered work for the government of Turkey during the campaign, laundering the money through a Turkish businessman, but was never charged. Most violators are allowed to register retroactively with little consequence.

When it came to China, the implementation of FARA was just as seemingly random and inconsistent. Bannon claims Wynn was the subject of a Justice Department investigation for possible violations of FARA, for lobbying on behalf of the Chinese government regarding the Guo case. The FBI doesn't comment on ongoing investigations. As of this writing, no charges were filed. But the Justice Department did indict another American who was working to extradite Guo, in August 2020. Nickie Lum Davis was charged with aiding and abetting the violation of FARA by working with Elliott Broidy, the former vice chairman of the Republican National Committee; rapper and member of the Fugees Pras Michel; and Jho Low, a Malaysian movie producer and financier who was indicted for his role in the pilfering of Malaysia's sovereign wealth fund, 1MDB, by the prime minister at the time, Najib Razak.

According to the indictment, Davis, Broidy, and Low met with senior CCP officials in Shenzhen in 2017 to strategize about how to get Guo extradited to China. Broidy acknowledges receiving over $8 million from Low but for years denied breaking the law. After Davis pleaded guilty and agreed to cooperate, the Justice Department raised the pressure on Broidy. In October 2020, the Justice Department released a thirty-one-page criminal information document tying Broidy to the lobbying scheme. As of this writing, he was expected to plead guilty. Meanwhile, federal prosecutors in New York were investigating Guo's finances related to GTV Media Group, the project Guo was working on with Bannon. New York federal prosecutors, in August 2020, indicted and arrested Bannon on accusations of fraud and embezzlement on an unrelated project to privately fund a sector of the border wall in Texas. There's no firm evidence of a connection between the two investigations, but it is at the very least a strange coincidence.

Navarro believed that the shuttle diplomacy conducted by John Thornton, Schwarzman, Wynn, Henry Kissinger, and others violated the spirit, if not the letter, of FARA because it was meant to influence not only the policy process but the media environment as well. Navarro kept a file tracking the stories about the trade war in financial and business news outlets, especially the *Wall Street Journal* and *Bloomberg News*. He was convinced he could demonstrate that these Americans came back from Beijing with specific messages and details from inside the trade negotiations that were leaked to trusted reporters. The goal was to shape the public discussion by leaking things that would benefit Beijing. Also,

Mnuchin and others would show Trump these articles, which supported whatever advice they were offering at the time.

"As part of a Chinese government influence operation, these globalist billionaires are putting a full-court press on the White House in advance of the G-20 in Argentina," Navarro said in a speech at the Center for Strategic and International Studies a year and a half after the Mar-a-Lago summit, right before Trump and Xi were set to meet in Buenos Aires. "The mission of these unregistered foreign agents — that's what they are; they're unregistered foreign agents — is to pressure this president into some kind of deal."

The John Thornton Channel

While many of Trump's billionaire friends played informal roles as message passers, one was more significant than the rest. Former Goldman Sachs copresident John Thornton became a behind-the-scenes player in the trade relationship, often shuttling back and forth between Beijing and Washington with delegations of other top US business leaders in tow.

Thornton had meticulously built one of the most reliable and high-level networks with the families that run the CCP, which operates more like a cartel with an aristocratic sheen than a socialist, much less communist, organization. His main claim to access and influence during the Trump years was due to his personal relationship with Chinese vice president Wang Qishan, whom Thornton had met in the 1990s when Wang was an official at the China Construction Bank and was Thornton's Goldman Sachs client. Wang had been instrumental in building ties between Chinese government entities and US financial institutions. In 2012, he joined the Politburo Standing Committee. In 2018, he became Vice President of the People's Republic of China.

Thornton was a proud proponent of smooth relations between Washington and Beijing based on economic integration and mutual investment. He was on the advisory board of China Investment Corporation, a sovereign wealth fund. He was chairman of the board of the Silk Road Financing Corporation, which is designed to fund the PRC's Belt and Road Initiative. The first Westerner to become a full professor at Tsinghua University (Xi Jinping's alma mater) since the founding of the PRC, he also had operated at the top levels of US-China business and political relations for decades. He had endowed the John L. Thornton China Center at the Brookings Institution and was good friends with its director, Chinese American scholar Cheng Li; Xi Jinping's nephew Xi Mingzheng had been an intern in that program while studying at Georgetown University. Thornton's chairmanship of Barrick Gold Enterprises was just the latest iteration of a career spent ingratiating himself into the halls of power in New York, Washington, and Beijing.

In turn, Thornton has often presented a rosy picture about the CCP's leaders and their intentions. In 2008, he wrote an essay in *Foreign Affairs* predicting (based on his conversations with senior Chinese leaders) that the CCP was moving toward democracy. In 2013 he predicted that party leadership would focus on strengthening the rule of law to respond to the grievances of regular citizens demanding more rights. If anything, the opposite has come to pass—but that doesn't seem to have shaken Thornton's faith in China's leaders.

Ironically, Thornton's entrée into the Trump administration was through Bannon, whose stated goal is to bring down the CCP. It would seem clear that Thornton represents everything Bannon is attacking: the co-opting of American elites by the CCP in exchange for corporate profits that leave American workers behind. But Bannon brought Thornton into Trump Tower and then the White House, where he ended up establishing an influential backchannel between Trump and the CCP's very top ranks. Bannon was trying to enlist Thornton into his scheme, but Thornton ended up helping the pro-engagement crowd that Bannon was fighting.

Bannon had worked for Thornton at Goldman Sachs in the 1980s. They didn't keep in close touch, but after Trump won, Bannon emailed Thornton and asked him to come to Trump Tower. "I need your help on China, because China is the whole thing," Bannon told Thornton. He replied, "Steve, I've been waiting for 30 years to hear someone in that chair make that comment." But when Bannon asked Thornton what role he might want in the administration, Thornton said he would be of greater value to Bannon — and Trump — if he stayed out and acted in private.

Thornton did, at least, meet with Bannon and Kushner several times before the inauguration. And in December, they brought him to meet with Trump in his Trump Tower office.

This late-2016 meeting arguably had real influence on how Trump approached Xi. "The president who recasts the US-China relationship, to the benefit of both countries and the world, that president is going to be seen to be great," Thornton told the then president-elect. "And by the way, Mr. President, if you don't do it, trust me, the next president is going to, because it's going to become obvious." Thornton told Trump that, over time, the United States and China should become "strategic partners." He said that Trump needed to have a strong personal relationship of trust with Xi. He told Trump that Xi, whom Thornton had known for twenty-five years, was a good guy whom Trump would get along with.

Fatefully, Thornton also had recommended that Trump invite Xi to Mar-a-Lago and just focus on their personal friendship at the summit. Trump turned to Bannon and said, "I like this idea, let's do this."

Thornton subsequently had gone to Beijing, where in January he met with Xi and Wang. He relayed this same message to the Chinese leaders, telling them that Trump wanted to develop a close, personal friendship with Xi and use that as the primary means of managing the US-China relationship toward the goal of a strategic partnership.

Thornton believed he had Trump's agreement to use this concept as a guide for how the relationship should be managed. Did he really? Yes and no. Trump often agreed to things in meetings but never followed through. Trump did invest time in building his "friendship" with Xi, and that had various implications down the line. But did Trump really buy into the Thornton's idea of a "strategic partnership"? Not really.

Thornton's interventions sometimes backfired. A few days before the Mar-a-Lago summit, Thornton had met with Trump at the White House and then flown to Beijing, where Chinese leaders had asked him to negotiate language for a joint statement that would symbolize the spirit of cooperation between the United States and China. Thornton passed their suggested language for the joint statement to Bannon and Kushner, to get Trump to sign off. But when the State Department and National Security Council officials who were supposed to be in charge of that process finally saw it, they stopped the Chinese wording from becoming the joint statement language. With expectations now too far apart to bridge, the entire effort to agree on a joint statement failed and none was issued. Beijing had tried to use Thornton to cut out the rest of the US government, but this time it didn't work.

Regardless, Thornton had opened a sanctioned secret channel directly between Trump and Kushner on the one hand and Xi and Wang on the other. After Bannon got fired in August 2017, Thornton and Kushner continued to consult closely. Kushner would sometimes take messages from US Trade Representative Robert Lighthizer and pass them to Chinese leaders through Thornton. The official channels included too many people to be leakproof. Both sides would call on Thornton to use that channel to relay messages or fix problems over the years. In September 2017, after Bannon left the White House, Thornton organized a meeting between him and Wang Qishan in Beijing. All three of them got along famously.

Time's Up

The months following the Mar-a-Lago summit saw many occasions for Trump's billionaire buddies to flex their muscles—but they didn't see much in the way of progress on the trade talks. By the time the one-hundred-day timeframe for negotiations expired in July, no meaningful resolutions had been made.

Ross and Mnuchin had failed. And Trump had become convinced that unless he first imposed real economic pain—not just the threat of pain—Beijing would never make real concessions.

The irony was, if Chinese leaders had just given Ross and Mnuchin something a little more concrete, Trump probably would have accepted it and declared victory. Beijing seems not to have understood that they'd had a chance to take the wind out of the hawks' sails. Otherwise, they never would have squandered the opportunity.

"China didn't give us anything during the one-hundred-day plan. They had made so many promises they didn't deliver on," a senior White House official said. "They're so arrogant, they didn't even bother."

4

The Road to War

By the end of the summer of 2017, the afterglow of the Mar-a-Lago summit had faded. There was no trade deal in the offing, which meant that the Trump team faced another fork in the road. Would they move forward with the legal and policy preparations that would be necessary to escalate the trade conflict and put real pressure on Beijing? Or would they once again delay real pressure in exchange for more negotiations and more promises?

A trade war was the very thing that Steven Mnuchin and Gary Cohn had been fighting to avoid — but preparing for a trade war didn't necessarily mean *launching* a trade war. Some officials who wanted to avoid outright confrontation hoped that the preparations themselves would convince Beijing to take Trump's demands more seriously. The hawks, meanwhile, were using their time to prepare for the day Trump realized he was again being strung along, by building the evidentiary case for the tariffs. It was a day they were betting would come sooner rather than later.

When the one hundred days of trade talks had failed, Trump convened his top team in the Oval Office and told them he wanted to move forward with a tougher approach. The president no longer believed there was a good reason to delay moving forward with the tariffs.

The most significant step the administration could take toward ratcheting up the pressure on Beijing — a move that would open up a range of options for tariffs and other punitive measures — was to initiate the investigation of China's economic aggression under Section 301 of the Trade Act. This was one of the legal weapons that Trump had first talked about in Monessen, Pennsylvania, during his June 2016 campaign speech there. Under the law, if a 301 investigation proved to the president's satisfaction that punitive action (such as tariffs) was needed to protect the US economy, he could act unilaterally — no Congress, no negotiation, no problem.

Because these remarks had come from Trump, the Washington intelligentsia had freaked out during the campaign, as if no previous US administration had gone down this road. But tariffs had been used on China before. For instance, Obama placed 450 percent antidumping counterduties on Chinese rolled steel in the summer of 2016. That's akin to a tariff. He also put 150 percent antidumping counterduties on Chinese aluminum in December 2016 — in essence, another tariff.

Cohn and Mnuchin, along with retired Marine four-star general John Kelly (who had by now replaced Reince Priebus as chief of staff) and others in Trump's inner circle, began a desperate effort to try to stop the tariffs from moving forward. Mnuchin and Cohn wanted to use the threat of tariffs as leverage to extract a deal from China. But the trade hawks warned that the threat on its own would only cause Beijing to concede just enough to avoid the tariffs. The first Bush administration used the threat of a 301 investigation to drive the Chinese to the negotiating table on the issue of intellectual property theft, which resulted in a memorandum of understanding that never got implemented by Beijing and was never enforced by Washington. That was 1991; in 2017, America was still dealing with the same problem.

If tariffs had any chance of working, the hawks believed, the United States had to impose costs on China first. They believed any negotiations were futile until the 301 investigation was completed and the tariffs were imposed. Then, the negotiations could be framed as a discussion about what China had to do to earn the right to have the costs lifted. The economic pain of the tariffs, felt by both sides but more so by China, would put Beijing under time pressure because China's economic pain would mount the longer it stalled. Without real pressure, on the other hand, time would always be on Beijing's side.

Hurry Up and Wait

Even the announcement of the 301 investigation on August 18 got caught up in internal factional infighting and the dysfunction caused by competing officials pushing competing priorities. Steve Bannon planned a big show, but Kelly canceled it because he feared antagonizing Beijing. Bannon had invited a bunch of CEOs whose companies had been victims of Chinese economic mischief to hold a news conference celebrating the investigation's commencement. The star of the show was to be Safra Catz, CEO of Oracle, whom Bannon had been pushing for several senior jobs, including director of national intelligence and national security adviser.

Catz and the other CEOs were already in town, but just hours before it was set to begin, Kelly called Bannon into his office for a meeting with James Mattis and Rex Tillerson. The two cabinet secretaries were objecting to announcing the 301 investigation because the UN Security Council was debating a resolution to condemn North Korea's latest round of ballistic missile launches and the United States needed Beijing's support.

Bannon was irate. Here, he said, was another example of backing down from confronting China's bad behavior in exchange for something Beijing should support anyway. Bannon argued that Trump should be afforded the right to make the decision, and he demanded to see the president. The room emptied except for Bannon and Kelly.

"This decision is above your pay grade," Bannon told Kelly. "I don't work for you. This is a mistake. He is going to sign this. This is going to happen. This train has left the station. We're all the way down the road on this."

Kelly told Bannon he would not be permitted to appeal the decision to Trump. Kelly was all about controlling the process. He saw no reason not to side with the secretaries of state and defense over the "chief strategist" who everybody knew would soon be out the door. Trump had soured on Bannon by this point, mostly because Bannon's feud with Jared Kushner had become public and Trump blamed Bannon for it.

"I'm going to make this call," Kelly said. The press conference was scuttled. The CEOs went home. Trump signed the 301 investigation two weeks later anyway, just without the fanfare. Kelly, Tillerson, and Mattis had slowed the path to the trade war, but not really by much.

Peter Navarro and Bannon knew what the conclusion of the 301 investigation was going to be, so they wanted it to be done as quickly as possible. But Robert Lighthizer was a professional — and a lawyer — and he insisted on doing it the right way. He wanted to go to the president and the American people with a full and thorough report that would make an airtight case for tariffs and other measures.

So Lighthizer began working with Matt Pottinger's team to declassify intelligence and collect information from all around the government to demonstrate the scope and scale of China's unfair trade practices. The investigation was set to take at least six months — which meant that no tariffs could be applied until the spring at the earliest.

"The Soul of Our Policy"

The arguments over trade inside the White House were about much more than just the narrow parameters of the actual negotiations. This was a fight over how the United States would approach the second-largest country in the world. The Wall Street clique was warning that a trade war could tank the markets, damage the economy, and sink Trump's chances for reelection. The hardliners were warning that Trump had one last chance to stop China's economic aggression or go down in history as having squandered it. The stakes could not have been higher.

The most contentious trade arguments during this time happened every Tuesday morning in the Roosevelt Room, the small West Wing conference room across the hall from the Oval Office. There, senior figures like Mnuchin, Wilbur Ross, Navarro, Bannon (until he was fired), and others would scream and yell insults at each other on a regular basis. It was personal, sure. But at the core of these battles was a deadly serious debate over the future of US trade policy and the future of the US-China relationship. "These were meetings about the soul of our policy," one regular participant said, "and efforts to make good on the promise that we weren't going to let China continue this kind of economic aggression against us."

China wasn't the only trade issue on the table. Trump was also trying to renegotiate NAFTA and threatening trade wars against various European and Asian allies. Each of these was highly controversial and divisive inside his team. But the China debates were the rowdiest, probably because the stakes were the highest. Other cabinet members also sometimes attended these meetings. This was the forum where Tillerson, Mattis, and H. R. McMaster, among others, first began to weigh in on the China trade war.

Tillerson never claimed to be a China expert. "China ain't got no oil," he liked to say. Mattis had spent his military career in the Middle East and Afghanistan, with no real Asia experience to speak of. Same for McMaster, an army general who was not directly involved in the trade negotiations but was often in the room. They were national security experts who saw China as a threat, for sure, but they came up in the system that prized free trade over protectionism and stable relations with Beijing over disruption.

For these three, the notion that China posed an increasing security challenge to the United States was clear. And they agreed China was wantonly hacking our data while scooping up chunks of the South China Sea. But they never came around to the idea that the way to confront this behavior was to invoke economic tools under national security justifications. The idea of protecting US industries like steel and aluminum by imposing tariffs using a law meant only for national security purposes was just a bridge too far for two lifetime military officials and the oil executive from Wichita Falls.

Of course, that's precisely what Trump had promised to do during the campaign. But officials like Tillerson, Mattis, and McMaster saw themselves as defenders of an order Trump didn't care about or, worse, was trying to unravel. Their default position was the Washington consensus. And the conventional wisdom at that time was that tariffs would tank the economy and the markets. Bannon and Navarro were the oddballs, the unpopular kids in the class. They were easy to dismiss, or at least they would have been except for the fact that Trump seemed to agree with them on this issue. Nevertheless, these meetings became a forum for condescending insults in both directions.

"Peter, you just don't understand how global trade supply chains work," Tillerson told Navarro one time, in his thick, southern drawl.

"Mr. Secretary, the way they work is to basically suck every job out of the country, so I think I understand that pretty well," Navarro shot back.

It's long been a standard line in the national security community in DC that "economic security is national security." But most Washington officials say that to mean we have to have a strong economy at home to support a robust foreign policy. For Navarro, Bannon, and Stephen Miller, economic security meant something different—keeping industries critical to national security on domestic soil and weening ourselves off of dependence on things produced in China—things that China could use as leverage against us if things got bad. China itself pursues this goal through its Made in China 2025 plan and its push for what it calls "indigenous innovation."

White House staff secretary Rob Porter was meant to referee the sessions and presented himself as an impartial observer. But the hawks always believed he was on the Mnuchin-Cohn side. Kelly and Porter had been trying to control the flow of information and documents to the president. That meant almost no access for people like Navarro and Bannon, who had no patience for bureaucratic process and were always on Porter's bad side. As Bob Woodward famously reported, Porter and Cohn once stole a document that would vitiate the US–South Korea free trade agreement off the Resolute Desk, hoping that Trump would forget about it — or at least that doing so would slow down the effort to get Trump to sign it.

Other officials told me that kind of thing happened all the time. One man's commitment to process is another man's manipulation of information. Kelly and Porter controlled the process, which meant that they also determined what information was appropriate for Trump to see.

Predicting Failure

The hardliners never believed China would change its industrial policies, no matter how much pressure or negotiation was brought to bear. But through tariffs and pressure, at least China would feel some costs for its behavior. And if the tariffs incentivized both American companies and others to shift away from China, that would ultimately redound to our benefit. "We had to assume they would remain as they are," David Feith, a hardliner who served in the Trump administration's State Department, said later. "They were going to be Leninist. They were going to be ideologically paranoid about us. They were going to be hostile to us. And we were going to have to work to make ourselves and our society resilient to their malign conduct and to help other countries do the same."

Of course, this was not the premise of the trade talks, at least not publicly. The stated goal of the talks was to convince or pressure China to essentially change its entire industrial strategy by changing its laws to accommodate Western ideas of regulatory standards, stopping its bad economic behavior on a range of fronts, and dropping its Made in China 2025 strategy, which was the basis for its innovation expansion and technological approach.

In public, that's what Trump, Lighthizer, Mnuchin, and even Navarro said was the goal. The hardliners couldn't stop that. Trump was dead set on getting a deal. But they could try to steer it in ways that would serve other China-related policy goals. The fact that the 301 investigation focused on technology was no coincidence. Focusing the conversation about China on its technological and industrial approach ended up setting the trade deal bar so high, Beijing could never cross it. Was that intentional? Some say yes. Either way, the problem set got defined in a certain way, and it was not just about soybeans.

Pottinger's Side Hustle

Pottinger, along with other members of the National Security Council staff, was heavily involved in the 301 investigation. But he also used the process to collect and declassify a range of documents he would use for his own parallel project: crafting a secret strategy for countering China.

Pottinger actually ended up drafting two classified, inward-facing strategy documents in the summer and fall of 2017, both of which he hoped would form the basis of government action going forward. One strategy was on countering Chinese economic aggression and included a lot of the work from the 301 investigation plus much more. The economic strategy also included calls for confronting broader issues in the US-China relationship that nobody at that time was talking about publicly. It talked about combatting China's efforts to steal knowledge from American schools and research institutions through students and researchers, Chinese predatory acquisitions, export controls, semiconductors, and telecom.

Pottinger also led a process to devise another classified strategy called the "Indo-Pacific strategic framework," which was more regionally focused. This was where Pottinger expanded on his idea to ramp up US engagement in what he thought of as the front-line states — those closest to China geographically and therefore the most affected by China's rise. This was where the first phase of the new grand strategic competition would play out, he reasoned, so it was where US attention and resources needed to be directed.

Both strategies took elements of Bill's Paper and built them into a more thorough, albeit secret, plan to reorient the US approach not just to China but to the rest of Asia as well. These documents were meant to provide direction and framing for national security and Asia-focused officials throughout the government and give them explicit permission to increase their attention to confronting Chinese malign activities of all kinds. They were also meant to harness the various parts of the government around the effort. And in this, they would prove to be more successful than Pottinger could have dared to imagine — but that would not be evident for years.

McMaster presented Pottinger's classified Chinese economic strategy to the president in October 2017 and Trump signed it. The Indo-Pacific strategy was blessed by the president in January 2018. The hardliners had succeeded in changing official US policy on China in the most significant way in a decade — on paper. Those inside the government who wanted to confront China now had explicit guidance to do it. Initiatives in various departments gained steam.

Many of these initiatives would spring into public view over the following three years at different times, often when the wind shifted in the trade negotiations. Inside the system, though, various agencies began working these issues, in more serious ways than before. If you were a China hardliner at any government agency looking for top-level cover to pursue that investigation you had always dreamed of but had been thwarted from doing, this was your moment to shine. The game was afoot. But it had to be done behind the scenes, while the trade negotiations took center stage.

When the trade talks were going poorly, Trump would lift the valve a bit and let some initiatives to confront Chinese bad behavior spill out into the open. When the trade talks were going well, and especially when they were on the verge of a breakthrough, Trump would shut down the anti-China measures and, in some cases, actually undermine them or roll them back. This was a dynamic Xi Jinping understood better than anyone, and he used that knowledge to set Trump against the China hawks on his team at crucial junctures.

Going Public

Pottinger's secret strategy documents formed the basis of several unclassified policy papers the Trump administration churned out in its first year, including an Indo-Pacific policy review and the China section of the National Security Strategy (NSS), on which Pottinger worked with Nadia Schadlow, an academic and historian who came in as deputy to Gen. H. R. McMaster when he replaced Michael Flynn as national security adviser.

The NSS named China and Russia as "revisionist powers" that wanted to shape a world antithetical to US values and interests. In so doing, the NSS announced a turn away from the focus on counterterrorism and the Middle East that had dominated US national security policy since 9/11. The administration was also declaring in no uncertain terms that China and Russia were American adversaries who were working in tandem to undermine US leadership and shape a world order more amenable to their authoritarian, illiberal model of government.

Several of the themes of Bill's Paper had made it into official US foreign policy. Pottinger had wanted to bring attention to China's influence operations, its predatory industrial policies, and its abuse of new technologies for repression and control. Now, he had the platform he had sought. "China seeks to displace the United States in the Indo-Pacific region, expand the reaches of its state-driven economic model, and reorder the region in its favor," the NSS states. "For decades, U.S. policy was rooted in the belief that support for China's rise and for its integration into the post-war international order would liberalize China. Contrary to our hopes, China expanded its power at the expense of the sovereignty of others."

This wasn't just an exercise in paper pushing. Pottinger and his team were also using the process of forming a written, official Trump administration Asia policy to outwardly socialize the ideas he was focusing on internally throughout various parts of the government.

As an extension of this effort, Pottinger brought in Australia's top expert on Chinese influence operations, John Garnaut, to meet with US officials and educate them on how Australia had been dealing with Chinese Communist Party (CCP) interference in their politics, their school system, their economy, and their media. Garnaut was one of a small group of Australian journalists and scholars who had spent years exposing corrupt and covert efforts by Chinese agents to infiltrate Australian society. The party used these methods and networks of "friends" to take over China during the country's civil war, with great success. Now it was applying what Chinese leaders since Mao have described as a "magic weapon" to guide its influence efforts around the world. Nowhere was this more apparent than Australia, where CCP proxies had become dangerously close to politicians and attempted to shift the country's policy on issues like the South China Sea.

Thanks in part to Garnaut's efforts, Australia had become aware of the CCP's comprehensive and well-funded United Front program — work that is still described by Chinese leaders in Maoist terms: to mobilize the party's friends to strike at the party's enemies. Garnaut became immersed in Chinese interference efforts and the United Front while working in the Australian government as a foreign policy adviser and speechwriter for Prime Minister Malcolm Turnbull. While journalists like Nick McKenzie and scholars like Clive Hamilton were waking up the public and building political pressure, Garnaut was working inside the Australian government to carry out a classified study on foreign interference that eventually led to counter–foreign interference legislation.

Now Pottinger wanted America to experience a wake-up call of its own. Over the course of 2017, he and Garnaut began sharing documents government to government — and using them to inform Trump's policies. "It was about introducing all US officials to the idea of the United Front and what is the United Front and what the hell is this stuff?" Pottinger said later about his collaboration with Garnaut. "It's stuff Americans haven't had to think about."

The United Front

The issue of foreign governments' influence operations inside the United States is difficult to talk about, because it's designed to be difficult to talk about. It exists in a gray middle ground somewhere between overt soft power, propaganda, and espionage. It entails activities that are public in a sense but that conceal a covert purpose. They are meant to influence the domestic political and elite conversation about foreign policy without coming out and stating as much. This is why they are malign. This is why they are dangerous.

The Russian effort to interfere in the 2016 American presidential election gave most Americans a general understanding and awareness of how Moscow's influence operations work — lots of state-run propaganda mixed with internet campaigns run by troll armies on Twitter and fake Facebook groups. Moscow's chief goal is to sow chaos into our political discussion and divide and inflame the democratic process in any way possible, to undermine the integrity of our system. In 2016, Russia could best achieve this by supporting Trump and attacking Hillary Clinton. But the truth is, Moscow played both sides at various times for sport and mischief.

The Chinese government's influence campaign inside the United States is a totally different animal. It's a long-term project based on developing relationships over time with elites and interest groups the CCP believes it can leverage. It's quiet, operating slowly and planting a thousand flowers that might bloom later. The scale is massive, involving huge networks of proxies funneling billions into the political systems in foreign countries around the world. And it's highly coordinated, led by a part of the party that dates back to Mao: the United Front Work Department.

The CCP's United Front Work Department leads and oversees the party's efforts to snuff out criticism and promote the party's interests both inside and outside China. Mao wrote in 1939, "Our eighteen years of experience show that the united front and armed struggle are the two basic weapons for defeating the enemy." And at the 2015 Central United

Front Work Meeting, Xi himself harked back to this metaphor when he said, "The United Front . . . is an important magic weapon for strengthening the party's ruling position . . . and an important magic weapon for realizing the China Dream of the Great Rejuvenation of the Chinese Nation."

The "magic weapon" that is the United Front Work Department is part of a broader program of Chinese international influence. Indeed, various parts of the party and Chinese government system engage in conduct that is defined as "united front work," which the Central Intelligence Agency defined in the 1950s as "a technique for controlling, mobilizing, and utilizing non-communist masses." For the party, it's not enough to quash dissent among its own population. Public opinion needed to be shaped for anyone who is not in the party, in every country, if possible.

The fact that united front work is conducted outside China shows that Chinese leaders are lying when they say they have a policy of noninterference in other countries' affairs. China has influence operations connected to the united front system in dozens of countries around the world. Those countries closer to China, like Australia, have been working on identifying and countering united front efforts for many years.

Australian researchers were ahead of their American colleagues in identifying how the United Front operated and why it was dangerous. "The united front system's reach beyond the borders of the People's Republic of China (PRC)—such as into foreign political parties, diaspora communities and multinational corporations—is an exportation of the CCP's political system," wrote Australian researcher Alex Joske in a report about united front work for the Australian Strategic Policy Institute. "This undermines social cohesion, exacerbates racial tension, influences politics, harms media integrity, facilitates espionage, and increases unsupervised technology transfer." United Front groups, Joske stated, are involved in scientific relationships and run Confucius Institutes on foreign campuses, and the United Front Work Department in particular plays a central role in coordinating the CCP's policy on Xinjiang—the northwestern Chinese province where the CCP was viciously repressing a variety of minority ethnic groups, to the horror of most of the international community. The efforts of these united front groups are directed at all non–party members, whether they be Chinese citizens, overseas Chinese, or you and me.

The CCP conducts united front work in American universities, in American media, on Wall Street, in Washington think tanks, and through a vast network of "civil society" groups that are propped up by Chinese government money while acting as if they were grassroots organizations. This is what FBI director Christopher Wray was talking about when he testified to the Senate Intelligence Committee in February 2018: "One of the things we're trying to do is view the China threat as not just a whole-of-government threat, but a whole-of-society threat on their end. And I think it's going to take a whole-of-society response by us."

"Building the Plane"

Through the process of drafting new US policy documents about the path forward vis-à-vis China, Pottinger pushed each part of the bureaucracy to challenge its long-held assumptions about China and the bilateral relationship. Each classified document began with a section that revisited old assumptions and, if needed, replaced them with new ones. Was the US goal still to entice China to adopt a political system that mimicked America's own? Pottinger believed it had become obvious that this was not where China was going, and that America's leadership had to acknowledge that fact and make decisions accordingly. "A lot of thinking had gotten stale and entrenched in many parts of the bureaucracy, not just the State Department," he said. "We were trying to pull people back from this narcissistic, solipsistic view that we have as Americans where we think everyone wants to be like us and we've got the power to make them into us."

Some journalists will tell you that, when it comes to the Trump administration, the official papers and strategy documents didn't mean anything. Trump didn't read them. The big decisions were made at the political level and the "strategies" were just busywork for the eggheads. But that misses the point. Two or three levels down, in agencies around Washington and around the country, there were fights over China policy going on every day that never reached the White House and never made the news. But in each of these nooks and crannies inside the national security system, there was a China hardliner who had lost battle after internal battle, probably throughout their career. By rewriting the official policy documents and getting Trump to sign them, Pottinger was empowering these officials and giving them ammo for their fights.

Pottinger was trying to connect the top-level politics with the mid-level policies. Like everybody else, he knew that the Trump administration would set the US-China relationship in a new direction. He just didn't know what direction that would be. Nobody did. As he put it to me later, "We were building the plane and flying it at the same time."

This plan's success, however, depended on one thing that Pottinger and those like him would never be able to convince Trump to commit to: a more aggressive foreign policy that required smart diplomacy, generous aid, and assiduous coalition building.

Trump wanted to fight allies and adversaries at the same time. His aversion to multilateralism ceded huge space to Beijing. Pottinger's warnings against this stance went largely unheeded by the person who mattered most.

Coming to Blows

The charged dynamic inside the White House during this time led to another monumental fight between Navarro and Cohn in front of Trump.

After one Tuesday trade meeting, the team went up to the Oval Office to debrief the president. Navarro brought with him a huge, colorful chart laying out everything that he believed needed to be done on China and trade worldwide. The chart laid out in pictures Navarro's plan for confronting what he called China's "Seven Deadly Structural Sins," including cyber hacking, intellectual property theft, forced technology transfer, government subsidies, dumping, fentanyl exports, and currency manipulation. Navarro knew Trump was always up for colorful charts. This one laid out the entire trade war — and Navarro's battle plan full of tariffs and moves toward decoupling and new industrial policies — in easy-to-understand illustrations.

Navarro never even mentioned the chart to the others before showing it to Trump, much less got it cleared through Porter's process. Cohn exploded, yelling at Navarro that he was giving bad advice to the president, that this was typical of him, and how dare he just spring it on everybody like that. "Cohn and Mnuchin never saw the chart," Bannon later recalled. "They were all pissed off it had never been approved. To be honest, they definitely had some justification."

Their anger didn't just lie in the breach of protocol. Trump loved the chart, and Navarro's suggestions for how to go about fighting the trade war.

"Let's do it," the president said. Even before the 301 investigation was complete, Trump was agreeing to move forward with the punishments — at least at that particular moment.

The officials went back down to the Roosevelt Room to fight some more. Navarro, like the old man in the bar who is always provoking everyone, told Cohn and Mnuchin that now that the president had been told the truth (or Navarro's version of it, anyway), there was no way to stop him from following the trade war plan. "You guys are shut down," he told them.

"For the first time, Peter in the Oval actually got twenty minutes to explain it to Trump," one of the participants in the meeting said. "It is essentially what happened over the next couple of years, to be sure, with fits and starts."

Another Trump administration insider would reflect on this time in more philosophical terms. "2017 sets the predicate for the economic war between the two countries," a senior White House official said. "But the biggest war was inside our own system."

Asia Is Calling but Nobody's Home

All around the government, the Trump administration failed to fill crucial Asia-related diplomatic and professional posts in its first year, leaving huge gaps in embassies and agencies that were meant to deal with the China challenge and manage the alliances around the region. There's no real explanation for this except gross negligence and broad dysfunction and a disdain for the bureaucracy writ large by some in the White House.

Ashley Tellis, the Council on Foreign Relations scholar whom Navarro and Bannon had wanted to become America's top emissary to India, was nixed for that post after the crack researchers inside the presidential personnel office found an instance where he had written critically of Trump. Bill Haggerty, the head of presidential appointments, essentially appointed himself as ambassador to Japan, a place he had worked as a lawyer in the 1980s. K. T. McFarland was actually nominated to be ambassador to Singapore twice, because her first nomination expired due to Senate inaction. She eventually got the hint and withdrew.

Even before Trump's election, the Chinese government had been so afraid of Admiral Harry Harris—another hawk whom Navarro and Bannon had penciled in for ambassador to Australia—becoming a senior US official dealing with China that it had mounted a multiyear smear campaign, even accusing him of being anti-China because of his Japanese "blood." (His mother was Japanese.) Beijing had good reason to be concerned about the idea of the former head of US Pacific Command being put in charge of the relationship between America and its close ally in that region. Harris came to fame in China circles during the Obama administration by coining the term "Great Wall of Sand" to describe China's building of artificial islands on reefs and other reclaimed features in the South China Sea. He had strong bipartisan support in Congress.

But Beijing must have been relieved by the bureaucratic malaise in Washington. Harris would not be officially nominated to be Australian ambassador for another full year, long after Bannon was gone. And then, after Mike Pompeo took over for Tillerson, he would jilt Canberra yet again. Pompeo had his sights set on North Korean nuclear diplomacy and needed to appoint an envoy to the still vacant post of ambassador to South Korea. So Pompeo withdrew Harris's nomination to be Australian envoy so he could send him to Seoul. The Australians were insulted, as well they should have been. They didn't have a permanent American ambassador until two years after Trump's election. This was one of the earliest instances of the Trump team mistreating the allies it needed to help it contest with Beijing.

The South Korean ambassador post had sat vacant for so long because the White House had, at the last minute, scuttled plans to nominate respected Korea hand and former National Security Council senior director for Asia Victor Cha after several months of vetting. The White House had even informed Seoul's Blue House of Cha's nomination and Seoul had signed off. But the nomination never came and was eventually abandoned without any real explanation. The news reports at the time concluded that Cha had been pushed aside because he opposed the idea of a "bloody nose" strike on North Korea. This "bloody nose" idea had been leaked as an example of an option under consideration at the White House—a limited strike to show Kim Jong Un who's boss. An insanely dangerous idea, it was never really under serious consideration, but Cha seems to have thought that was why he lost the gig. But he never actually got a real explanation. White House officials at the time told me his security investigation had surfaced concerns about his father-in-law's business relationships in South Korea. Nobody ever presented any evidence. Perhaps the notoriously finicky and paranoid White House personnel office staff saw his George W. Bush administration credentials and killed the nomination on principle. It's one of those Trump administration palace intrigue stories that even the actual players never figured out.

The State Department didn't have a confirmed assistant secretary for East Asian and Pacific affairs for over two years, in part because Tillerson had insisted on nominating career foreign service officer Susan Thornton. For Bannon, Thornton was the poster child for a China policy proven wrong and controlled by alleged apologists and fellow travelers determined to maintain the status quo.

Less than eight months into the Trump administration, Bannon had alienated the president whom he had worked so hard to elect. His self-aggrandizing in the press had annoyed Trump, and his public attacks on Jared Kushner had forced the president to choose between a staffer and his own son-in-law. One of Bannon's final acts before getting fired was to launch a public attack on Thornton.

Bannon called a reporter from the liberal *American Prospect* and ridiculed Trump's desire to enter diplomatic negotiations with Kim Jong Un. In that interview, Bannon also promised to make sure Thornton never got the job as the State Department's lead Asia official permanently. Bannon liked to call reporters and vent about the economic war with China. I had been on the receiving end of such calls as well. For Bannon, it was the last straw. He maintains he had already planned to resign.

After Bannon got fired in August 2017, Tillerson personally intervened on Thornton's behalf, and in December the White House nominated her for the job. Bannon continued his war on Thornton and lots of other bureaucrats from his perch atop the Breitbart News machine. But in the end, Thornton's bid was tanked by Senator Marco Rubio (R-FL). Working first behind the scenes, Rubio's staff slowed the nomination. When Tillerson was eventually fired in March 2018, Rubio announced he would formally oppose Thornton's nomination. Pompeo was not about to fight for her, and so she resigned and retired from the foreign service that summer.

Smearing McMaster

Meanwhile, the infighting between the factions never let up. Starting in the fall of 2017, pro-Trump forces had begun a smear campaign against Pottinger's boss, McMaster. According to the various articles with unnamed sources, McMaster was not sufficiently pro-Israel, not sufficiently pro-Trump, and some even accused him of having a drinking problem. His enemies spread a rumor he was having an affair with another senior

White House staffer. There was never any evidence of excessive drinking or the affair, and people who know them say there is no way it happened. But the rumors reached Trump — and Trump believed them.

"Have you heard who McMaster is fucking?" Trump once asked nobody in particular during a crowded staff meeting in the Oval Office. "He's gonna get us all in trouble if he can't keep his dick in his pants."

There's no way to know for sure where the smears were coming from, but McMaster knew who his enemies were. He had run afoul first of Bannon, by removing him from the National Security Council when taking over for Flynn. He also managed to eventually fire a Bannon ally, Ezra Cohen-Watnik, who was the senior director for intelligence on the National Security Council staff but had become entangled in the Russiagate investigation. Cohen-Watnik left the White House in August, just as the McMaster smears started coming out. He took a job at Oracle, working for its CEO, Safra Catz, a billionaire and major Republican donor who also had worked on the Trump transition.

In November, BuzzFeed reported that at a July dinner with Catz, McMaster had called Trump a "dope" and an "idiot" and had insulted Jared Kushner for good measure. But the dinner, which had been arranged by Kushner, was meant to be an opportunity for McMaster and Catz to get to know each other; it didn't make sense that McMaster would bash Kushner to Catz when he knew they were close friends. That dinner is also said to be the source of the rumor about McMaster and the other senior White House staffer (who attended the dinner), the gossip being that they had appeared too chummy when outside the White House grounds. Again, there's no factual basis for that allegation.

Catz denied every part of the reporting about the dinner. But the endless rumors and leaks eventually took their toll and helped to turn Trump against McMaster. He would resign in April 2018. He had been promised a fourth star and a prime posting in the army command, but the ice melted beneath him before that could be squared away. Cohen-Watnik would end up rejoining the Trump administration, eventually being appointed acting undersecretary of defense for intelligence in the final two months of the administration.

5

The Trumps Go to Asia

While the trade investigations were under way, and US national security officials were quietly putting together the plans and strategies for what might come out of them, President Trump was preparing for his next big in-person interaction with Xi Jinping after the Mar-a-Lago summit. This time, they would be meeting on Xi's turf.

Beijing was the key stop in Trump's first big, thirteen-day tour of Asia as president in November 2017. After short stops in Hawaii, Japan, and South Korea, Trump arrived in Beijing and Xi brought out all the pageantry Trump could have hoped for, and the two leaders had a largely friendly visit. Routine and unremarkable statements were issued on trade and North Korea, avowing that the two sides intended to work toward a resolution but without any specifics. Throughout, Trump focused on maintaining the positive atmosphere that he believed was key to maintaining his close friendship with Xi. "My feeling toward you is incredibly warm," Trump told his counterpart at his Beijing press conference on November 9, an event that included no questions from the press. "We have great chemistry. I think we'll do tremendous things, China and the U.S."

Before the trip, there had been a formal interagency process to determine what the goals would be, and how the president should approach his interactions with Xi. The process determined that the administration would take a firm stance and avoid making any concrete trade concessions or agreeing to any of Beijing's concepts of "great power relations" or "grand bargains." Trump followed these recommendations, to an extent, but he veered off message at various points as he always did. In their bilateral meeting, he surprised the Chinese side by pointing at each of his staffers and telling them to speak on the issues they were in charge of inside the US government.

H. R. McMaster delivered the talking points on the South China Sea. Robert Lighthizer delivered the points on trade and intellectual property theft. Rex Tillerson spoke on North Korea. And so on. After having failed to agree on a joint statement at Mar-a-Lago, the two sides decided to issue a joint statement that was fairly benign. It mentioned the trade issues in language that, for Trump, was relatively mild. Although the entire statement was negotiated, half of it was attributed to each leader. Trump's half of the statement didn't mention human rights or the unfolding story of Chinese repression of the Uyghurs in Xinjiang.

John Bolton, in his book, claims Matt Pottinger told him Trump endorsed the idea of the internment camps during this trip (which occurred before Bolton joined the administration). That's true—but Trump did not say that to the Chinese officials, only to his own staff. Still, it alarmed them to hear it.

Commerce Secretary Wilbur Ross brought with him a large delegation of American CEOs. The White House put out a list of $250 billion in "deals" that were supposedly signed during the trip for US businesses. A lot of them never panned out. For example, $83 billion of the total was attributed to an alleged deal to develop the state of West Virginia's shale industry between the state and Shenhua Group, a Chinese state-run mining conglomerate that was later absorbed into the China Energy Investment Corporation. The hastily arranged agreement didn't anticipate national security concerns regarding Chinese control of US energy resources, however, and has been held up by investigations and lawsuits ever since.

But absent any major public scandals, the Beijing stop was considered a success. Trump still had several days of travel to go, however, and many more meetings with other world leaders. And he was not enthused about it.

Diplomacy Fail

After Beijing, Trump moved on to the rest of his trip. He was set to attend the Asia-Pacific Economic Cooperation (APEC) summit in Da Nang, Vietnam, and make an official state visit to Hanoi. He was then to go to the Philippines, where he would meet President Rodrigo Duterte and then attend the US–Association of Southeast Asian Nations Summit and the East Asia Summit. The schedule was packed with bilateral meetings with the leaders of countries from all over the region.

American leaders had learned over the years that a huge part of successful diplomacy in Asia was doing the basic work of attending these events and showing that America was present and attentive to the region's issues. The annual APEC summit was where the CEOs of each country were supposed to convene to discuss the business of state. The East Asia Summit, also held annually, was more focused on regional diplomacy. Even in the Obama administration, just getting the president to Asia for one of these hallmark events was a major lift that occasionally didn't come off. The Obama administration joined the East Asia Summit in 2011 and Obama attended every year except 2013, due to the government shutdown.

At the APEC CEO Summit on November 12 in Da Nang, Trump gave what was billed as a major speech on economics, in which he declared the United States would never return to the Trans-Pacific Partnership. Since he had withdrawn the United States from TPP ten months prior, the other eleven countries had moved forward on it without the United States. The US move also strengthened China's pitch for its own regional trade deal, called the Regional Comprehensive Economic Partnership, which demanded less from countries in terms of labor standards and adherence to the rule of law. Beijing was rushing to fill the void Trump had left.

In his speech, Trump offered to make bilateral trade deals with any country "that will abide by the principles of fair and reciprocal trade," adding, "What we will no longer do is enter into large agreements that tie our hands, surrender our sovereignty, and make meaningful enforcement practically impossible. Instead, we will deal on a basis of mutual respect and mutual benefit. We will respect your independence and your sovereignty."

After Vietnam, Trump traveled to the Philippines. He arrived on November 12 and met with Duterte in Manila on November 13. In his remarks to the press, Trump praised the weather in the Philippines ("pretty good"), thanked Duterte for the music and dance show at dinner the previous night ("tremendous talent"), and laughed when the Filipino strongman called the journalists in the room "spies." To the journalists, it wasn't funny because Duterte had publicly condoned the killing of journalists and had been under fire for overseeing thousands of extrajudicial killings in his administration's heavy-handed "war on drugs."

The East Asia Summit was to be held the next day in the nearby city of Angeles. But Trump didn't want to go. Before he left Washington, I had received a tip that Trump would skip the event. Even before his tour had begun, Trump had been complaining about the length of the trip, and the White House didn't want to push the issue with him. I wrote a column on October 27 about Trump's plan to skip the event, and in the piece I quoted former US ambassador to Burma Derek Mitchell saying, "Multilateralism in Asia is often just about showing up, but even that appears to be hard for him."

The next day, the White House had announced that Trump had changed his mind; now he would attend the summit. I wrote another column about the reversal, giving Trump credit for doing the right thing. "The reversal tells us something very important: Trump is learning about and places a high priority on Asia," Southeast Asia expert Ernest Bower told me. "Credit to him and his national security team on this adjustment."

Bower spoke too soon. Trump and his entourage did travel to Angeles on November 14 to attend the East Asia Summit, which was his last stop before flying home to Washington. But the summit's main plenary session, with all the heads of state, was running about an hour late. "Fuck it, let's go," Trump told his aides. He boarded Air Force One and ordered the crew to take off, leaving Tillerson to sit in his chair.

Trump would skip all the remaining meetings of the East Asia Summit in his presidency. Apparently he had had enough of diplomatic conferences in Asia. But he never forgot the good times he had in Beijing.

A year later, Trump was still talking about how, while in Beijing, he praised Xi's decision to grant himself a never-ending term as president by calling him "King." "He said, 'But I am not king, I am president.' I said 'No, you're president for life, and therefore you're king,'" Trump recounted. "He said, huh. He liked that. I get along with him great."

"Meeting the Right Partners"

While the Trump delegation was in Beijing, Jared Kushner hosted a meeting that had nothing to do with US government business at the US embassy in the Chinese capital. This meeting, unlike the Trump-Xi conference unfolding nearby, was never announced; to this day, Kushner has never publicly commented on it. His silence is understandable, given the gross conflict of interest it represented—and the pattern of improprieties of which it was a part.

Hosted by Ambassador Terry Branstad, the "casual lunch" was filled with senior Chinese private equity executives; one, Hugo Shong, a prominent Chinese venture capitalist, confirmed his attendance afterward to CNBC. He did not mention that, at the time, Kushner was seeking out Chinese capital investments for a whole host of projects he was involved in, including in the Kushners' family real estate business. He didn't have to.

The Kushners, always on the hunt for investment dollars, should have known using the embassy to conduct this meeting was a glaring conflict of interest. Jared had failed to learn the lesson after his disastrous meeting during the transition with the leader of Anbang Insurance Group in New York. Nor had he been chastened by the fact that, in May 2017, the *Washington Post* had revealed that Kushner's sister Nicole Kushner Meyers had been in Beijing hawking New Jersey apartments by promising Chinese investors they could get special EB-5 visas to live in the United States. "Invest $500,000 and immigrate to the United States," her brochure read. The Securities and Exchange Commission later opened an investigation into the scheme.

The Kushners may have learned about that government money-for-visas program from the Trumps. In 2016, while Trump was running for office, he licensed his name to the Trump Bay Street project in Jersey City. His partners there reportedly raised $50 million from one hundred Chinese investors, or about $500,000 each, the minimum investment mandated by the EB-5 visa application process.

Ivanka's interests were clear; she had been working to bring her brand to China for many years. In 2012, Ivanka said the Trump Organization had a team based in Shanghai. "There's such interest in the brand being here," she said to the *Wall Street Journal*. "We're really ramping up our commitment to meeting the right partners and finding the right opportunities."

The Beijing meeting was not the beginning or end of the Kushners' efforts to monetize their privileged position in the Trump-China nexus. In June 2017, Ivanka had gotten some of her trademark applications in China approved for the third time since her father was elected. Her personal brand also depended heavily on Chinese labor. Of the 838 items listed on her merchandise website, 364 were made in China, according to PBS. That same month, she was also spotted dining with Alibaba chief Jack Ma at Fiola Mare, a high-end Italian restaurant on the Georgetown waterfront.

Ma was the single best Chinese businessman at getting access to the top levels of the Trump administration. He was involved in setting up meetings between US and Chinese businesspeople in partnership with Ross and Stephen Schwarzman, who would hold informal salons with top-tier Chinese businesspeople in a way that blurred the line between official and unofficial interactions. At the time of his dinner with Ivanka, Ma also was lobbying the administration to allow his investment company, Ant Financial, to acquire MoneyGram, the second-largest cash transfer outlet chain in the United States. The deal was later blocked by the board of the Committee on Foreign Investment in the United States, which consisted of nine national security agencies that vetted foreign acquisitions, due to concerns about a Chinese company having the data of millions of Americans and their spending habits.

But Ma wasn't the only well-connected figure who was helping Beijing's elite cozy up to the American president's family—or even necessarily the most successful. The guest list for Jared and Ivanka's secret meeting with Chinese investors in Beijing, for instance, had reportedly been arranged by none other than Wendi Deng Murdoch—the former wife of Rupert Murdoch, and a close friend of Jared and Ivanka's for many years. She was also a person of interest to the FBI—and had been for many years.

The Wendi Deng Murdoch Connection

Deng Murdoch was one of the most mysterious figures in the US-China relationship. Superhawks such as Steve Bannon believed she was an agent for the Chinese Communist Party (CCP). Her defenders said she was simply an amazingly successful immigrant whose relationships and influence were unmatched. One way or another, her connections to the Trump family were nearly unparalleled—and were cause, to some, for serious concern.

Deng Murdoch was born in Jinan, the capital city of the eastern province of Shandong, south of Beijing, in 1968. Her birth name, Deng Wenge, means "Cultural Revolution Deng," reflecting the fact that she was born at the movement's height. She was raised in the city of Xuzhou, in Jiangsu Province, which is just south of Shandong. She has said that her family was poor, but in fact her parents were engineers. In her youth, she moved to Guangdong to run a factory with the rest of the family.

In 1987, Deng Murdoch met a Los Angeles couple named Jake and Joyce Cherry. Jake was working in Guangzhou and Joyce became her English tutor. The following year, they returned to LA and sponsored her student visa so she could join them and live in their house while completing her degree. It soon emerged that she was having an affair with Jake Cherry. They later married after his relationship with Joyce ended, but then quickly divorced after she began studying at California State University—and began dating businessman David Wolf.

Her CSU economics professor Ken Chapman would later reflect that Deng Murdoch had lived a lavish lifestyle in California, with "more state-of-the-art computer equipment than anyone had ever seen before." He also said that she often served as an interpreter for visiting Chinese official trade delegations and bragged about contacts with top CCP officials. But even bigger things were in store for the young student.

After completing her undergraduate degree at CSU, she moved to Yale, earned an MBA in 1996, and got a job in Hong Kong working for Murdoch's Star TV, reportedly helping build the company's partnerships in China. She had responsibility over Phoenix, a Chinese-language channel owned by Star that is based in Hong Kong but well understood there to be friendly to Beijing and its propaganda goals.

She met Rupert Murdoch during a trip to Hong Kong to visit Star TV. They were soon married, but divorced in 2013 after fourteen years. She had reportedly been having affairs with multiple men, including Tony Blair and Google's Eric Schmidt. Murdoch has implied that the rumors Deng had an affair with Blair, at least, are true, and in 2014, *Vanity Fair* published the text of a diary entry allegedly written by Deng in which she confessed her love for Blair. It read, "Whatever why I'm so so missing Tony. Because he is so so charming and his clothes are so good. He has such good body and he has really really good legs Butt . . . And he is slim tall and good skin. Pierce blue eyes which I love. Love his eyes." Blair has denied the claims.

Deng Murdoch met Jared and Ivanka because they lived in the same building in New York City, and the two couples became fast friends.

In March 2013, a Chinese blog claimed that she had worked for the Propaganda Division of the People's Liberation Army General Political

Department's Liaison Department (reformed as the People's Liberation Army Political Work Department's Liaison Bureau in 2016). The article claimed that she had been recruited by the agency in 1986, and that the following year, she had met an American couple and begun an affair with the husband, migrating to America with their support. She "formally became a General Political Department spy" in 1996, the blog post claims, the year she returned to China—and the year before she met Rupert Murdoch.

The post was republished on dissident media sites, but its reliability is unclear; the author attributed their information on Deng simply to "an insider in Beijing." Still, this was one more brick in the wall of evidence against the Kushners' friend—and there would soon be others.

The Nanny

The mystery surrounding Deng Murdoch was enough for the FBI's Counterintelligence Division to brief Jared in early 2017 that she might be using her relationship with them to "further the interests of the Chinese government." The specific concern reported was a counterintelligence assessment that Deng had been lobbying for a high-profile project to build a $100 million Chinese garden at the National Arboretum in Washington. The project set off FBI alarms because it was set to be funded by the Chinese government and included a seventy-foot white tower that officials feared could be used for spying. The plans were shelved after the FBI's concerns were made public. Through a spokesperson, Deng denied to the *Wall Street Journal* that she knew anything about the concerns surrounding her relationships in China or about the garden project.

Jared and Ivanka issued a statement at the time saying they "have been friends with Rupert and Wendi Murdoch for a decade before coming to Washington and their relationship is neither political nor about China." There's no doubt they were close friends. Michael Wolff's book *Siege: Trump Under Fire* claims that Deng helped introduce Jared to Wu Xiaohui, the Anbang chairman who met him in New York during the transition before later getting purged. Deng and the Kushners vacationed together in Croatia in 2016. Ivanka was even a trustee for a time for a trust fund set aside for Rupert and Wendi's children.

When the Kushners started to have children, they hired Deng Murdoch's longtime nanny, a Chinese national who has only been referred to publicly as "Xixi." This nanny, in fact, was another cause of concern for counterintelligence officials looking at the relationship between Deng Murdoch and the Kushners.

The Kushner family rarely even acknowledges their Chinese nanny Xixi. Ivanka first revealed her existence in a 2012 interview with the *South China Morning Post,* where she said that her family had a nanny who was teaching Mandarin to her daughter, Arabella. Ivanka's 2017 book, *Women Who Work,* never mentioned Xixi or the family's other nanny, Lisa, until the acknowledgments section.

But Xixi's presence would make itself felt in other ways. During the Mar-a-Lago summit, Arabella and her brother, Joseph, had performed in Mandarin for Xi and his wife; later that year, when he had met with Xi in Beijing, Donald Trump had played a video of Arabella singing in Mandarin and dedicating her performance to "Grandpa Xi" and "Grandma Peng." But he made no mention of his granddaughter's teacher—her Chinese nanny. Ivanka also brought Arabella to the Chinese embassy in Washington to sing in Mandarin, videos of which went viral in China.

One senior White House official told me that the FBI assessment of security concerns related to the Kushners' relationship with Deng Murdoch included concerns about Xixi. Specifically, if Deng Murdoch was working on behalf of Chinese government interests, Xixi's proximity to the Kushners and long relationship with Deng Murdoch provided an additional risk factor. The FBI never mentioned their concerns about Xixi to Jared and Ivanka. They also didn't share any specific intelligence with them that would validate those concerns.

When the FBI's warning to Jared about Deng was first reported by the *Wall Street Journal,* the Chinese state propaganda outlet *Global Times* defended her on its official Weibo account, calling the idea that Deng had ulterior motives "American paranoia." Wolff tweeted in response that Rupert Murdoch had been telling anyone who would listen that he believed she was a Chinese spy—and had been throughout their marriage.

According to the senior official, Jared and Ivanka shrugged off the FBI's concerns about Deng Murdoch. They didn't want to hear that their close friend might be an agent for the Chinese government, and the FBI either didn't have or didn't want to produce any hard evidence of misconduct by Deng. As of this writing, there still is no firm evidence that Deng Murdoch is working for or with the Chinese government. She and the Kushners remain close friends. Xixi remains employed in their home. And the Wendi Deng Murdoch mystery remains unsolved.

Memories of Tibet

One place in Asia that Trump did not mention, much less visit, on his tour—which no American president had ever visited, in fact—was Tibet. The "autonomous region" had been occupied by China since the 1950s, and in spite of a robust advocacy movement—and widespread international sympathy—Tibet was regarded by Beijing as a core issue: an off-limits topic, much like Taiwan. On the ground, Beijing had spent decades crushing Tibetans' political, cultural, and religious freedoms; securitizing the region; importing Han Chinese; and placing all Tibetans in a state of perpetual surveillance and fear while jailing any who dared protest. The Dalai Lama, the spiritual leader of the Tibetan nation, had been living in exile in Dharamshala, India, since 1959. There, Tibetan leaders established a government-in-exile, claiming to represent the hundreds of thousands of Tibetans in the diaspora and the six million still living inside Tibet.

Every American president since George H. W. Bush had met with the Dalai Lama multiple times while in office, and at first there was no reason to think that Trump would be any different. The Dalai Lama had been circumspect in his comments about Trump during the campaign, and shortly after the election the religious leader had said that he hoped to visit with Trump once he was in office. Given Trump's general hostility toward China on the campaign trail and his widely reported call with the Taiwanese president during his early days in office, the Dalai Lama might even have been encouraged that, in Trump, he had found an American president who would once again stand up for Tibet.

As the Trump administration had come into power, the movement to bring Tibetans limited autonomy and basic human rights was at a crossroads, struggling to maintain visibility in a chaotic world full of stories of suffering, even as the Chinese authorities steadily tightened their grip on Tibetans, appropriated Tibet's resources, and worked to extinguish its culture. In Washington, the Tibet issue was simply getting drowned out — a dramatic change from a decade prior.

During the George W. Bush administration, Tibet had been a top-tier human rights issue. George W. Bush, Nancy Pelosi, and Mitch McConnell all had joined hands in 2007 to present the Dalai Lama with the Congressional Medal of Honor in the Capitol Rotunda. The Chinese government protested, of course, but nobody cared and nobody backed down.

But American support for Tibet had steadily ebbed. When Obama came into office, his top adviser, Valerie Jarrett, was dispatched to India to go see the Dalai Lama and gently break it to him that he would not be invited to the White House in the first year. When Obama finally did receive the Dalai Lama in 2010, he went out of his way to please Beijing at the Dalai Lama's expense. The meeting was held in the Map Room, rather than in the Oval Office. To avoid the photo of the Dalai Lama emerging from the main entrance, he was sent out the back, where reporters snapped photos of him walking past heaps of garbage bags.

Beijing had not rewarded Obama's deference; quite the opposite, in fact. Once the Chinese leadership concluded the United States was willing to downgrade Tibet and other human rights issues, the CCP abruptly cut off dialogue with representatives of the Dalai Lama, whom they had met with regularly throughout the Bush administration.

Tibet still enjoyed overwhelming bipartisan support and attention in Congress and around Washington — but the Trump administration proved to be a different story. Trump didn't pretend to see America's role as to promote human rights, much less democracy, abroad. After Trump's disastrous phone call with Taiwan's president during the transition, those in his administration who cared deeply about the Tibet issue — and there were many — dared not even suggest a meeting with the Dalai Lama. God only knew what Trump might say or do. After all, he had offered at various times to mediate the Israeli-Palestinian conflict and the India-Pakistan dispute; for all anyone knew, he might try to solve this one, too. If he treated Tibet as a bargaining chip, his ham-handed intervention could set the movement back decades.

The Trump administration didn't even bother to appoint a State Department special coordinator for Tibetan issues, even though it was mandated by the Tibetan Policy Act of 2003, until October 2020. Nikki Haley would tell me that she personally asked Trump for permission to visit the Dalai Lama during her June 2018 trip to India but he said no. "I won some and I lost some," she said, "this one I lost."

By the end of 2017, the Tibetan leadership worried that a meeting between Trump and the Dalai Lama was too risky, but they could not afford to wait out the Trump presidency. China's power was growing, its repression of Tibetans was increasing, the Dalai Lama was aging, and their nation's struggle for survival, dignity, and autonomy was steadily losing international visibility. They had to come up with a strategy to give new momentum to their struggle.

So it was that, before Trump even departed for his Asia tour, the Tibetan government-in-exile had decided to host their first ever international conference in October 2017, in the Himalayan mountain town of Dharamshala. I asked my boss, Fred Hiatt, if I could go. He just nodded his head and said, "I hope you find enlightenment."

The Dalai Lama, eighty-three at the time of the event, seemed in good health and was somehow always in good spirits. But he would not live forever. Upon his death, the Chinese government was expected to announce their own choice for Dalai Lama, so the leaders-in-exile had decided they might "discover" his successor, the fifteenth incarnation, somewhere in India — setting up two opposing Dalai Lamas. Beijing had set the precedent for this when it had kidnapped Tibet's second-highest reincarnated spiritual leader, the Panchen Lama, in 1995 at age six, replacing him with an imposter and foisting that imposter on Tibetans inside China.

The Dalai Lama addressed the conference, and when the time came for him to take questions, I asked him what he thought about Trump and whether the United States would continue its role as the leader of the free world. "In the very beginning, [Trump] mentioned 'America first,' and that sounded in my ear not very nice," he said with a laugh. "America, the leading nation of the free world also becoming selfish, nationalist. But then, of course the American people and both houses really have been very supportive. So I think there is a willingness to show their concern and I think that will continue."

The conference was led by Lobsang Sangay, the elected president of the Tibetan government-in-exile, also known as the Sikyong. Sangay, a Harvard-educated, English-speaking man in his late forties, was only the second person to occupy this position since the Dalai Lama decided to relinquish political leadership of the Tibetan community and separate it officially from his spiritual post as the fourteenth incarnation of their living deity. Having led both parts of the Tibetan movement in India since he had fled in 1959, the Dalai Lama was attempting to leave this world with a sustainable model of governance in place.

It was clear that the Dalai Lama's optimism was not shared by everyone. The conference's name, the 5-50 Forum, was a reference to the idea that the Tibetan movement would spend five more years pursuing an increasingly dim chance of a negotiated solution to their quarrel with Beijing, aiming to strike what the Dalai Lama called his "Middle Way approach," somewhere between Tibetan independence and China's total brutal dominance over Tibet. If that failed, the Tibetan movement would need to pivot and hunker down for fifty years of struggle.

The odds were looking better for fifty years than for five. During Trump's administration, the DC-based nongovernmental organization

Freedom House scored Tibet as the second least free country in the world, a close second to Syria and only marginally freer than North Korea. But the plight of those two countries got covered in the international media because their conflicts are bloody or dangerous. Until 1971, there was a small Tibetan militia group supported by the CIA. But when Henry Kissinger went to Beijing in 1972, that aid was cut off and the militia was slaughtered. By the time of the 5-50 Forum meeting in 2017, the Chinese authorities in Tibet were bulldozing Tibetan houses of worship, changing the human demographics of the province in their favor by importing millions of Han Chinese, and industrializing the Tibetan Plateau in a way that threatens the integrity of an ice reservoir that feeds ten major rivers that spring out to billions of people all over Asia.

Before ascending to power, in 2011, Xi Jinping promised to "smash any plot to destroy stability in Tibet and jeopardize national unity" there. And since his rise to power, Beijing had turned the entire region into an open-air prison, hiring tens of thousands of police forces both overt and secret and forcing neighbors to spy and inform on each other under promise of bribes or threat of imprisonment. Xi was so impressed with the performance of the CCP's top official in Tibet, Chen Quanguo, that in 2016 he moved Chen to be the top CCP official in Xinjiang, where he was tasked with creating a similarly Orwellian system of repression for ethnic minorities there, including the region's millions of Uyghurs—a Muslim minority group that speaks a Turkic dialect and that had been under Chinese rule more or less since Xinjiang came under Chinese control during the Qing dynasty of the eighteenth century. After taking over following World War II, the CCP discovered huge reservoirs of oil, natural gas, and rare minerals in Xinjiang and began an ever-increasing program of encroachment and repression in order to facilitate its exploitation of these resources. By late 2017, reports were already emerging out of Xinjiang of a new network of prisons that were taking in innocent Uyghur civilians by the thousands. There was evidence of mass incarceration of other Muslim and ethnic minorities in a systemized way that was devastating entire communities. The stories of torture and political indoctrination inside these new prisons were harrowing. But the world had as yet done nothing to react.

The Tibetan government-in-exile, formally called the Central Tibetan Administration, speaks for the six million Tibetans cut off from the world in Tibet, suffering greatly at the hands of the brutal and systematic repression of the Chinese authorities that rule every aspect of their existence. The movement has remained nonviolent at the insistence of the Dalai Lama, but after he's gone, Tibetans might rightfully conclude that their commitment to nonviolence has allowed the world to turn a blind eye to the extremely violent suppression their people inside Tibet are suffering with no end in sight. "The violence gets more coverage, more attention. Nonviolence gets less attention and less support," Sangay told me.

The building of Tibet's democracy-in-exile was in part an effort to convince the next generation of Tibetans that they had an alternative and options to continue after the Dalai Lama was gone. Their only hope was to hold out long enough for China's campaign of totalitarian control to fail, which they were convinced it eventually would.

"For the time, there's a sense of control. But you can't control people based on mistrust and fear forever. Eventually it will not work," Sangay said. "If you want to know China, you have to understand what is happening in Tibet."

Counterprogramming

Back in Washington a couple of months after the conference in Dharamshala, I met the Tibetan president-in-exile again. Lobsang Sangay was in town to testify at a hearing on Tibet at the House Foreign Affairs Committee. There was still enough bipartisan support of the Tibet movement on Capitol Hill to organize a hearing every once in a while. There was legislation moving that would push for more international access to Tibet by linking it to Chinese officials' access in the United States; it was another attempt to inject some reciprocity into the relationship. Sangay was in town to support its passage.

While we were catching up, Sangay told me that he had just come from Sweden, but his key meetings with Swedish officials were canceled at the last minute because a group of CCP officials had shown up the same day and pressured the Swedes to shun Sangay. That kind of thing was happening more and more, he said. CCP officials were following him everywhere he traveled, pressuring politicians in any country he visited not to meet him. Sometimes, they would arrange counterprogramming with propaganda events in the city he was in, to drown out his message.

I asked Sangay whether the CCP officials had followed him from Sweden to Washington and he said they had. He said that the CCP officials responsible for Tibet were in fact counterprogramming by holding a meeting in the US Capitol building that very day. That's how I learned about how the CCP was working Washington from the inside, seeking to co-opt American elite voices to change the US discussion of China and deflect any efforts to criticize Beijing.

These influence operations were everywhere, but nobody in the government seemed to be in charge of countering them. So the response began in an unofficial and quiet way.

6

The Bingo Club

The trade negotiations between the United States and China dominated headlines as Trump's first year in office gave way to his second. They also dominated the attention of the American president. But beneath the surface of the US government, tectonic shifts were taking place, of which a recalibration of US-China trade relations was only one part.

David Feith, who served in the Trump administration's State Department, came up with a useful analogy to describe this period. Think of the trade negotiations as the weather, he said, but the US government's strategy and the American people's awareness of the challenge presented by China as the climate. The media has to cover the weather; it often gets the most attention. But climate change is more significant over the long run. "The 'climate' was that China has done hostile and malign activity across all domains at an enormous magnitude and we were waking up to it starting in 2017," he said, "and turning the aircraft carrier that is the United States slowly but in important ways. The 'weather' was whether it was stormy or not that day in the trade negotiations."

Those fighting inside the government to move the China policy had to pay attention to the weather because it provided a political context for what they could or could not do. It also greatly affected Trump's attitude and, by extension, raised or lowered his tolerance for actions that might anger Beijing, settling a ceiling for a host of other China-related policies. Whenever Beijing wasn't playing nice on the trade negotiations, Trump lifted the ceiling and allowed the government to do more on whatever China issues were up. And then, when negotiations got tense or close to a deal, the ceiling was lowered again.

In the West Wing, the pro-trade, antitariff officials like Steven Mnuchin, Gary Cohn, Rob Porter, and the self-appointed adult supervisors like John Kelly, Rex Tillerson, James Mattis, and H. R. McMaster, won more battles in the first eight months of the administration than the China hawks. They had control of the process and better access to the president, and frankly, they were in positions that far outweighed their opponents' in terms of rank and authority.

But across the street, in the Old Executive Office Building—and in other government buildings around Washington—the China hawks were playing a longer game.

Peter Navarro and Steve Bannon, before his firing, had started holding their own separate China strategy sessions in a conference room near Navarro's office in the Old Executive Office Building. And they began networking, inviting in officials from around the government who were like-minded on China: people like Admiral Harry Harris and air force brigadier general Robert Spalding.

Spalding had come onto the National Security Council staff in April after serving only four months as the US defense attaché at the embassy in Beijing. The following year, he would be pushed out of the administration due to a mix of personality clashes and an industry lobbying campaign against his idea to have government help build a secure 5G telecom network. But in the first year, he was one of the Superhawks and an active member of the group.

Similar groups were forming in other parts of the national security bureaucracy as well. Two or three levels down from the politicians, there were officials in the State Department, Department of Defense, Justice Department, intelligence community, and elsewhere who had been banging their heads against the wall for years trying to push action on various China-related issues. They had been tracking the politics above them, knowing this was perhaps their chance to finally get their various departments and agencies to get tougher on China. But they knew there would be bureaucratic and institutional resistance at each and every stage.

The China officials two levels down, working at national security agencies, in congressional offices, and throughout the law enforcement and intelligence community, weren't focused on trade. They were focused on national security. More specifically, they were focused on the issue of China's audacious influence operations inside the United States. The problem was, there was no forum within the government where they could discuss it, much less deal with it. So these officials (unofficially) created one.

"This Is Our Time to Stand"

The secret group fighting China's influence operations campaign inside the United States met in a redbrick townhouse a few blocks from Capitol Hill. The group had no name and no membership list. The participants were not there in any official capacity. They convened around a common mission: to wake up the country to a new kind of threat — and devise a plan to fight back.

The host was Dimon Liu, known publicly for her longtime affiliation with the Voice of America, the US government-funded international broadcasting agency, but known privately as a leader in Washington's complicated Chinese dissident movement. Liu emigrated from China decades ago. The daughter of a prominent family on the losing side of the Chinese Revolution, she served as a rare and important connection between Washington and what was left of the prodemocracy movement outside mainland China. Liu loved her birth country but hated its current rulers. She, more than most, knew what they were capable of. As a child, she had suffered through the famine of the Great Leap Forward. She was determined to do anything she could to convince Americans to come to terms with the true character of the Chinese Communist Party, the sheer cruelty the party's security apparatus was capable of, and the dire threat China under CCP leadership posed to the United States.

The Tiananmen Square massacre in 1989 persuaded her to abandon her teaching and her architecture practice in Hong Kong and move to the United States. If the world was going to stand up to the CCP and for the Chinese people, then it would begin in Washington.

Her house held enough souvenirs of her old life in Hong Kong and travels through Asia to account for at least two lifetimes. By the time I arrived on a Thursday evening in mid-January 2018, the house was filled with the smell of the Guangdong- and Hakka-inspired Chinese dishes that Liu had prepared for the occasion. Around twenty people were already mingling and noshing. I recognized some of them — two White House officials, congressional staffers, a think tank expert, a tech industry insider, an FBI agent. Some introduced themselves as the night went on — often without saying exactly which agency they worked for during the day. And although it was Liu's house, the meeting belonged to Peter Mattis, a young man who held no official title and represented no government agency.

Mattis, by coincidence the nephew of Defense Secretary James Mattis, was the founder and the leader of this group. Tall, skinny, and bespectacled, in his late thirties, he had been a CIA counterintelligence analyst on China before leaving the agency to work in the private sector. Mattis may have left the CIA, but he never left the fight.

Mattis and I first met over a decade ago. We were both part of a twentysomethings' networking group called Young Professionals in Foreign Policy, the kind of thing you would go to on a Tuesday night in DC to trade business cards or seek out Washington connections of a romantic nature. Peter was never a source, but he became a friend. Fifteen years later, that friendship provided enough trust for him to invite me into his quiet meeting.

Later, I would dub the group the Bingo Club, a reference to a similar group of cops, spies, and experts who convened secretly in San Francisco in the late 1980s to confront the urgent espionage threat China posed at that time. But this new generation of the Bingo Club was designed to confront a new kind of challenge.

"First, thank you all for joining us for a conversation about Chinese Communist Party influence inside the United States and how to deal with it," Mattis said to start the meeting.

In his soft-spoken, matter-of-fact staccato, Mattis laid out the problem set. The CCP had been building political influence in the United States to create the opening for China's rise. Beijing's campaign, endorsed by the highest levels of the Chinese government, was complex, well organized, extremely well-funded, and growing each day.

The CCP was waging a type of political warfare, he explained, a mix of information operations, influence peddling, propaganda, and old-fashioned espionage with a high-technology twist. It was directed at all parts of American society: our educational institutions, our technology labs, our media, our industry, our stock markets, and of course, our politics. By operating in the gray zones between soft power and hard power, between covert and overt operations, China's leaders had been able to target for influence the sectors of American society whose strength underpins our national power and our national identity — the antibodies in our democracy that respond to threats. The CCP was not simply trying to compete with America's vision for the global world order. Beijing was trying to change our ideas from within, using American institutions to promote the CCP's interests. And our government had no idea what to do about that.

"It's a whole-of-society effort that Beijing is trying to mobilize," Mattis told the group. "This comes from the party. It's what the party does. And the question is how do we deal with this intrusive effort."

The primary goal of Beijing's campaign was to promote the interests of the CCP and protect the party from criticism, much less resistance, from the United States or any other country. The second goal of this campaign, which served the first, was to undermine American institutions and, in so doing, weaken American democracy.

Of course, the idea that China conducted influence operations inside the United States was not itself a secret. But Washington, along with most of the country, was slow to realize the sheer scope and scale of this new challenge. Sure, there were signs Washington was waking up. A bill introduction here, a think tank event there. It was akin to different members of a symphony orchestra arriving for a concert one by one. Many key instruments were still missing. There was no agreed-upon sheet music. And there was no conductor.

Mattis was doing what everybody in the Bingo Club knew needed to be done. He was doing what the US government should have been doing. He was bringing together the best minds to devise a plan to fight back. It was a conversation our leaders could not (yet) have in public.

"This is the right place to think, what are the policy problems that we are trying to solve," he said. "And then, thinking what do we need."

As each person in the room took turns telling tales of pernicious Chinese influence operations they had witnessed or heard stories about, the group began to realize how far behind the United States really was. These included the stories of Chinese students at American universities who were prevented from having a free and full experience by the interference of China's official missions or the monitoring of their fellow students. I heard of federal investigations into members of Congress suspected of taking donations linked to CCP front organizations. I heard about Chinese government security officers coming into the United States and kidnapping Chinese citizens off the street to take back to China, sometimes with the help of local police.

One of the first problems the group grappled with was how to talk about Chinese influence operations to others in government and around the country. How can anyone expect the American people to sign up to fight a threat they didn't even realize existed and don't necessarily understand? The Bingo Club's consensus answer was that American institutions and the American people needed to be educated about this threat, and fast—hence my invitation.

The CCP sought to frame the issue, whenever it was raised, as a form of McCarthyism or Cold War reductionism, with China playing the victim. The CCP sought to divide Americans by party or ethnicity, to divert attention from its actions. Somehow, the China issue had to be protected from the bitter bipartisanship that engulfed every other major debate in Washington. "This is an American issue. This is something that should unite us," one Bingo Club member put it. "This is not something that we should use as a political baton to beat the other side. It's that important."

Most of Washington had come around to the acknowledgment that the strategic competition between the United States and China would be the most important dynamic in foreign relations for the foreseeable future. But they hadn't yet been able to comprehend that this competition is being waged first of all inside our own country. "This is happening on our watch," another Bingo Club member said. "We can't leave this mess to our kids and our grandkids. This is our time to stand."

Over the next months and years, I witnessed this group of young, patriotic Americans work together to combat CCP influence operations in various ways. Sometimes I wrote columns about their successes for the *Washington Post.* Some of their stories are told here for the first time. Some of their successes can never be written about. Liu told me she started the group because she had given up on the older generation of China hands, who were too set in their ways. She set upon convincing the younger generation that the United States needed to change its China policy, before it's too late.

"I used my kitchen to slowly build a community by feeding them. Good food and good conversation was an old-fashioned salon approach, popular in the eighteenth century, and it is still going," she said. "You build it with one person at a time, until you have a community that can share knowledge. Peter was my first convert."

One day, not long after this meeting, I got a call from an Asia expert friend who previously worked in the military but now consulted for the private sector. He was holding his own secret meeting to bring together like-minded Washington folks to think through a separate problem emanating from China — the giant national champion technology firm Huawei. In less than a decade, this company had lied, cheated, and stolen its way to threatening domination over mobile networks around the world. This group wanted to strategize a way to stop it.

It dawned on me that my Bingo Club was quickly becoming only one of many. I heard of a group meeting quietly at Stanford University to examine Chinese influence operations, organized by the Asia Society. Another group was convened at the Council on Foreign Relations. Bingo Clubs were suddenly popping up everywhere.

Breaking into Mar-a-Lago

A lot of what the Bingo Club members did, both at the meetings and in between them, was to share information to try to piece together the CCP's network of shadowy front groups it uses for influence and intelligence operations of all kinds on our soil. Roughly a year after I attended my first Bingo Club meeting, for instance, a member of one of those groups was caught sneaking into Mar-a-Lago and was arrested with four cell phones, a laptop, a hard drive, nine USB drives, five SIM cards, and a device to detect hidden cameras. It didn't take the Bingo Club members long to piece together who she was and how she fit into the network of Chinese influence operations on US soil. Her handler was a Chinese businessman known as Dr. Charles, who founded and runs something called the United Nations Chinese Friendship Association. His real name is Li Weitian, and he is a key figure in Chinese united front efforts to get close to top Republicans.

In a statement posted on Business Wire in 2012, the United Nations Chinese Friendship Association said it was founded in 2011 and that Charles Lee (Dr. Charles's alias), the "Secretary General" of the group, immediately began holding meetings with dozens of high-level CCP officials, including You Lan, vice-director of the United Front Work Department. In addition to meeting with the likes of Trump and UN secretary general António Guterres, Dr. Charles was offering tours of the US military academy and opportunities to meet President Obama, Warren Buffett, and lots of others. The *Washington Post* reported that his organization has no connection to the UN and when reporters went to the location it listed on its website, there was no office there.

There are united front groups connected to the Chinese government all over the United States; some are involved in politics. The *Wall Street Journal* reported that the group Chinese Americans for Trump, which was founded by a Chinese citizen green card holder named David Tian Wang, was approached by Chinese consulate officials and enlisted to help them lobby the Trump administration. Wang then registered himself as the head of a new consulting firm and used it to give $150,000 to the Trump Victory Fund. He later bragged on Chinese-language television that he has used his access to the Trump team to argue against confronting the Chinese government's aggression in the South China Sea. He never registered under the Foreign Agents Registration Act as a lobbyist. This combination of influence peddling, fraud, and propaganda is a hallmark of united front work.

Dr. Charles wasn't even the only shady Chinese figure using a united front group to get into Mar-a-Lago. Florida businesswoman Cindy Yang became famous after New England Patriots owner Robert Kraft was busted soliciting sexual services in a massage parlor she had founded but since sold. After several years of allegedly building a prostitution empire in South Florida, she and her family became huge political donors, which put them in rooms with the Trump family (for example, at their Super Bowl party at Mar-a-Lago); Florida governor Ron DeSantis; Senator Rick Scott; Sarah Palin; the president's campaign manager, Brad Parscale; and many others. Yang's consulting company, GY US Investments, openly promised its clients access to President Trump and other top officials. *Mother Jones* reported that Yang herself was heavily involved in the Florida branch of the Council for the Promotion of the Peaceful Reunification of China and the Miami chapter of the American arm of the China Association for Science and Technology, both of which were known to be connected to the CCP and the united front. Who else would start a Florida group dedicated to forcing Taiwan to join the mainland? This is how united front networks have long operated on US soil.

"Any sustainable, long-term strategy for addressing China's challenge requires the integrity of U.S. political and policymaking processes,"

Mattis testified before the House Foreign Affairs Committee in May 2019. "This requires grappling with the challenges posed by the party's efforts to shape the United States by interfering in our politics and domestic affairs. The United States, its political and business elite, its thinkers, and its Chinese communities have long been targets for the Chinese Communist Party."

The Money Train

Both Mattis and Alex Joske, the Australian researcher who wrote some of the earliest work on the united front (and who served as a researcher for this book), identified one united front organization as the most influential nonparty body that works to coordinate with the party and advance its goals. This group is called the Chinese People's Political Consultative Conference (CPPCC).

The CPPCC includes both party members and influential non–party members inside and outside China. Its annual confab was attended by more than two thousand party-approved representatives from different sectors of Chinese society. It coordinated and oversaw hundreds of other united front organizations around the world. "Organisations that claim to speak for different interest groups — the China Association for Science and Technology and the All-China Federation of Returned Overseas Chinese, for example — are official components of the CPPCC," Joske wrote. "In practice, those organisations are controlled by the CCP."

The CPPCC had been chaired over the years by Mao Zedong, Zhou Enlai, Deng Xiaoping, and Li Xiannian. The current CPPCC chairman as of this writing is Wang Yang, the standing committee member responsible for the united front system. The vice-chairman of the CPPCC is a man by the name of Tung Chee-hwa.

Tung has an impressive résumé, and an impressive network in the United States and its allied nations. He served as the first chief executive of Hong Kong after the British handover in 1997. Tung is also a billionaire shipping magnate whose family has been doing business for decades with the family of Elaine Chao, Trump's transportation secretary and the wife of Senate Majority Leader Mitch McConnell.

Tung also leads one of the largest united front influence operations inside the United States under the cover of an organization he founded called the China-United States Exchange Foundation (CUSEF). The story of how CUSEF tried to fund the China program at a major university in 2017 is also the story of the first success of the Bingo Club in stopping a united front influence operation in its tracks.

A Showdown in Texas

When David Firestein, a former career foreign service officer, first laid out his plans to colleagues to build out the China center at the prestigious Lyndon B. Johnson School of Public Affairs at the University of Texas at Austin, he didn't tell all of them he planned to use a CCP-linked influence organization as his primary funding source and use that money to host affiliates of the Chinese intelligence services.

His friend and proposed donor, Tung Chee-hwa, was no stranger in Washington. Tung's CUSEF had given money or sponsored research at major Washington think tanks, including the Brookings Institution, the Carnegie Endowment for International Peace, the Center for Strategic and International Studies, the Center for American Progress, and the Atlantic Council. CUSEF funds the endowed professorship in the China Studies Department in Johns Hopkins University's School of Advanced International Studies and a research project called the Pacific Community Initiative. Obama's top Asia adviser, Jeffrey Bader, thanked CUSEF for its support in his book on Obama and China.

Firestein, who had worked with CUSEF at his previous job at the EastWest Institute, proposed to take over a million dollars from CUSEF for the LBJ School's new China center. This was a first for CUSEF. Usually, it funded specific research programs or projects. This would fund the center's operations as well, making CUSEF its primary financial backer, after the university itself, which put up an initial $2 million to get it off the ground. If successful, his plan would have established a CCP influence campaign within the walls of one of America's top public universities.

Several of the professors inside the LBJ School were shocked and concerned upon finding out (belatedly) that a CCP-linked billionaire would be funding their new China center. One junior assistant professor who specializes in Chinese politics and international relations, Joshua Eisenman, raised concerns about the plan during a faculty meeting in November 2017. It erupted into a feud that would become a pivotal first battle in the war to stop Chinese influence operations on American soil.

On a trip to DC in November, Eisenman saw his old friend Peter Mattis at a Bingo Club dinner and asked him for assistance in his effort to help the UT leadership understand CUSEF and its actual mission. Mattis passed Eisenman a memo he had written about CUSEF and a book chapter draft he had written on Chinese influence via the CPPCC. A few days later, Mattis also reached out to professional staffers at the offices of both Texas senators, John Cornyn and Ted Cruz, to inform them of the brewing controversy unfolding at UT Austin, and sent them the CUSEF memo as well.

Dr. Will Inboden, a senior professor and former congressional staffer and State Department official, also reached out to Cornyn's office and alerted UT president Gregory Fenves. Fenves initiated an investigation and Inboden arranged for Fenves to get a briefing from US counterintelligence officials about CUSEF and Chinese influence operations in general.

In early December 2017, soon after Eisenman questioned CUSEF funding for the LBJ School's China center at the faculty meeting, the faculty email list became a battleground over the nature of Chinese influence operations inside our country. I obtained a trove of these emails. Eisenman argued that there was wide and growing awareness of united front influence operations targeting US institutions of all kinds and pointed to Marco Rubio's statement at a hearing that, "We have a lot of discussion of Russian interference in our elections, but the Chinese efforts to influence our public policy and our basic freedoms are much more widespread than most people realize."

Firestein responded by defending CUSEF. He admitted that Tung was vice-chairman of the CPPCC, but said there's no evidence the CPPCC was connected to the united front. Eisenman replied all with a list of links to exactly this evidence, starting with the document posted in English on the official CPPCC website dated July 3, 2012, that states, "The CPPCC is a Chinese people's patriotic united front organization" and "is under the leadership of the Communist Party of China."

"The question is do we want our China center funded by the perception management and influence operations wing of the Chinese Communist Party?" Eisenman wrote.

That's when things went from bad to worse. Dean Angela Evans intervened to accuse Eisenman of making "unsubstantiated claims" (an accusation she declined to substantiate) using "an unprofessional and inflammatory tone." Professor Jeremi Suri came to Eisenman's defense and demanded Evans apologize to Eisenman for attacking him or resign her post as dean. Admiral Bobby Ray Inman, former director of the National Security Agency, concurred with Eisenman's assessment of CUSEF.

While Fenves's investigation was ongoing, Firestein held his first China center event at the LBJ School, cohosted by CUSEF and featuring a former Chinese vice foreign minister. A second event in New York included several People's Liberation Army generals, while a third at LBJ featured representatives from the China Institutes of Contemporary International Relations, a think tank that is affiliated with the Ministry of State Security, China's CIA. These events drew the attention of the local FBI office, whose agents attended them and interviewed attendees afterward.

"Every single event that the China center and Firestein would hold parroted the Chinese line," one UT tenured professor told me. "The worst was when he brought over people from [the China Institutes of Contemporary International Relations]. He didn't disclose at all who they really were. We had to warn our students, 'You need to be careful.'"

In mid-December, Cruz wrote a letter to Fenves demanding he reject Firestein's plan to fund the school's China center using Tung Chee-hwa's money. Cruz's office gave me the letter and I called Fenves and gave him a two-day deadline to respond or comment. Just before the deadline, Fenves's office told me he had decided that UT would not take the CUSEF money and Firestein's plan was squashed.

Evans accused Eisenman of orchestrating the campaign to kill the funding. Eisenman played a role, to be sure, but crediting him fully would ignore the important roles of Inboden, Inman, Mattis, Cornyn, and Cruz, not to mention Fenves, who performed the due diligence Evans never considered and Firestein fought bitterly against. In what many in the school saw as retaliation, Evans declined to provide any further research funding for Eisenman, multiple professors said. Emails show she also decided not to continue funding for his wife's post-doc at the University's history department. Evans denied retaliating and said Eisenman and his wife continued to receive funding support from the university. His wife ended up securing funds from an alternate source.

Eisenman left the school and was granted a tenured professorship at Notre Dame, where his wife is now an assistant dean. Back in Texas, Firestein was not finished. He simply took his plan to use CCP-linked funding to promote the interests of the CCP to a brand-new institution: the George H. W. Bush Foundation for US-China Relations, where he became its executive director a few months later. There he linked up with a like-minded spirit, Neil Bush, one of the CCP's best friends in a royal American family.

Things with Presidents' Names on Them

As the Bingo Club continued mapping out Chinese influence efforts in the United States, patterns emerged. One of them was that CCP-linked influence organizations like nothing more than linking up with a domestic institution whose name brings instant credibility and validation. In the United States, what could be better for that than the organizations named after former American presidents? That's why CUSEF funded the George H. W. Bush Foundation and the Carter Center, two nongovernmental organizations that have advanced Chinese interests in the United States under the most venerable of guises.

President George H. W. Bush was a former US ambassador to China. His leniency on Beijing after the Tiananmen Square massacre in 1989, resuming relations only six months later and sending his envoy to secretly smooth things out, doesn't look great in hindsight. But nobody argued that Bush 41 was outright pro-CCP, because during his presidency, there were signs that China might progress and reform into a country that respected the international system and its own people. Those signs were simply misleading—or hardliners in Beijing won out, whichever theory you prefer.

But his son Neil Bush was a totally different story. Since becoming the chairman of the Bush China Foundation, he has become a reliable mouthpiece for Beijing and worked directly with united front figures, including Tung Chee-hwa. In July 2019, he traveled to Hong Kong in the middle of the protests and gave a keynote speech at a conference hosted by Tung, where he said, "China is not an economic enemy or existential national security threat to the United States . . . The demonisation of China is being fuelled by a rising nationalism in the US that is manifested in anti-immigrant, anti-Chinese, pro-America-first rhetoric."

Neil Bush always was quite supportive of China when talking to the press and he, like Firestein, was often quoted in Chinese state propaganda outlets. He pushed for economic collaboration, argued against tariffs, and blamed bad relations on "propaganda and demagoguery in the U.S. political process," all the time representing the foundation named after his late father, the former president.

Neil Bush's financial and personal interests in China explain why he's so deferential to the CCP and so connected to its elite friends. He claims to have visited China over one hundred times since 1975. In 2003, he established an investment firm in China with Edward Lehman. Lehman-Bush provided cross-border and domestic transaction advice to leading multinational corporations, high-net-worth individuals, Chinese state-owned enterprises, Chinese entrepreneurial start-ups, and emerging Chinese multinational corporations. It had offices in Beijing, Shanghai, Ulaanbaatar, Guangzhou, Houston, and Hong Kong.

There are also troubling indications that China may hold coercive leverage over the younger Bush. In a 2003 deposition for his divorce, Neil Bush admitted having sex with several women in Thailand and Hong Kong who showed up at his door unannounced in hotels during business trips. This is what is commonly referred to as a "honey trap," where sex is used to compromise targets, who are usually being surveilled. "Mr. Bush, you have to admit it's a pretty remarkable thing for a man just to go to a hotel room door and open it and have a woman standing there and have sex with her," his wife's lawyer said. "It was very unusual," Bush replied.

The other former US president with a foundation that had become a mouthpiece for Beijing was Jimmy Carter. Carter presided over the formal normalization of US relations with China in 1979, finishing the process begun by Nixon and Henry Kissinger. His foundation, the Carter Center, had since become a key outpost for pro-China influence operations inside the United States. The Carter Center has partnered with the Charhar Institute, which had ties to China's Ministry of State Security. The center also had partnered since 2012 to run forums on US-China relations with a united front organization called the Chinese People's Association for Friendship with Foreign Countries (CPAFFC), a quasi-governmental organization that forms an important part of China's foreign affairs bureaucracy. The forums were sponsored by CUSEF.

CPAFFC is particularly active in building relationships with local governments. In a February 2020 speech before the National Governors Association, Mike Pompeo warned about it. "I was familiar with that organization from my time as the director of the Central Intelligence Agency," he said. In particular, Pompeo drew attention to the US-China Governors Forum, which is run by CPAFFC with the National Governors Association, and which Hillary Clinton established in 2011 by signing an agreement with the Chinese government.

These two Chinese influence operations sometimes align in striking ways. In June 2019, the Bush Foundation awarded its inaugural George H. W. Bush Award for Statesmanship in US-China Relations to Jimmy Carter. However, Carter was recovering from surgery at the time and the award was collected by his son. Chinese ambassador Cui Tiankai spoke at the event, warning, "Some are clamoring for a decoupling of the two countries and even a new cold war. These attempts are not only questioning the achievements we have made over the past four decades and challenging the very tangible outcomes of our cooperation, but also putting the future of our relations and the prospects for global stability and prosperity at great risk." One must wonder how Neil's brothers, former president George W. Bush and former governor Jeb Bush, feel about their brother allowing the CCP to use their father's foundation as a platform for its propaganda.

The Chao Family

For those in Washington trying to understand the way power and money flowed between Beijing and Washington, there was no bigger puzzle than the story of the family of Transportation Secretary Elaine Chao, who was married to Senate Majority Leader Mitch McConnell (R-KY). It was too high level and too sensitive even for Bingo Club members — with all their knowledge and access — to really investigate. But the subject came up at every single Bingo Club meeting I attended.

US government officials, when they sign up to serve their country, agree to disclose and then to rid themselves of any personal or financial conflicts of interest — not because they are planning to act corruptly, but because the existence of such conflicts carries the risk and perception of said corruption. But in the Trump administration, conflicts of interest were ubiquitous. Chao had clear conflicts of interest between her US government obligations and her family's business interests. Her actions throughout her tenure show a pattern of mixing those interests with little regard for these conflicts or even the appearance of impropriety.

In February 2019, Chao and I were seated two seats apart at the Metropolitan Club for a VIP dinner featuring Colombian president Iván Duque Márquez, hosted by Concordia, a nonprofit policy organization. At the end of the dinner, I politely introduced myself and offered her my card. She said she had read my coverage of China and asked whether I could stay to have a chat one-on-one.

After she shook the hands of half a dozen people who stopped by our table to pay their respects, we spoke for about ten minutes. She never said "off the record." She asked me, "Josh, if you were to give advice to the Chinese leadership on how to handle these trade talks, what would it be?" I thought to myself, what an interesting construction for the question. Chao was asking me how to help Beijing deal with Washington, not how the Trump administration (in which she was transportation secretary) should deal with China. I played along.

"I think I would tell them that this is their last chance to really make the changes Washington is demanding. If they don't do that now, this town is going to run out of patience and things are going to get worse," I said.

I was trying to give her advice that, if passed on, would honestly reflect the mood in Washington, but I doubted that Beijing would heed it, even if Chao did pass it along. She seemed to take it in and we talked for a few more minutes. She was perfectly nice.

When the *New York Times* published its explosive investigation into Chao's ties to her family's business and her family's ties to the very top level of the CCP, her sister Angela suggested the reporting was motivated by their ethnicity. But if you read through the report, it's clear why the Chao story is important. The Chao family is the only family to be considered American royalty and Chinese royalty at the same time. Their business interests and political activities are so intertwined, to say there's no conflict of interest is not credible.

Just looking at the facts that are not in dispute is jarring. The US transportation secretary held twenty-one meetings with Chinese state press and zero interviews with the US media in her first year. In over a dozen of them, she sat next to her father, James Chao, the founder of the family shipping company called Foremost Group, with the US government's and Transportation Department's flags as their interview background. She booked an official trip to China and asked the State Department to include her family members in official meetings and help them with travel. She canceled the trip when the emails were revealed.

Chao and her husband, McConnell, took somewhere between $5 million and $25 million from her father as a gift. The Chao family has donated over a million dollars to McConnell's senate campaigns. Elaine's sister Angela Chao, who now runs Foremost, sits on the board of the Bank of China. Foremost has accepted at least $300 million in loans from the China Export-Import Bank, according to the bank.

The Chao family story is a Chinese, Taiwanese, and American success story. James Chao, who grew up in Shanghai and went to school with former Chinese president Jiang Zemin, left mainland China with the Kuomintang after they lost the civil war to the Communists and settled in Taiwan. That's where Elaine was born in 1952. The family eventually immigrated to the United States and became American citizens. After the United States and China thawed relations in 1972, James got back in touch with his old friends, built a shipping business, and became a model of success in the Chinese diaspora.

"My family are patriotic Americans who have led purpose-driven lives and contributed much to this country. They embody the American dream, and my parents inspired all their daughters to give back to this country we love," Chao told the *Times*.

That's all well and good. But the long record of Chao helping her family business is too extensive to overlook. It calls into question why the Transportation Department under her watch proposed slashing budgets for American government mariner shipbuilding programs. Does it have anything to do with the fact that Angela and James Chao have served on the board of the holding company for China State Shipbuilding? Does it matter that Foremost ships don't fly the US flag, to avoid operating and labor costs, but the US transportation secretary is supposed to be promoting the US flagging system? That's why conflicts of interest are problematic. They present competing interests inside a person's head and in their wallets.

One of the families the Chaos have been close to for decades is none other than the family of Tung Chee-hwa. James Chao worked for Tung's father, Tung Chao-yung, who founded the China Maritime Shipping Line. Fifty years later, Tung still ran that company, now called Orient Overseas Container Line. The families and the companies remain close. And until new details come to light about their relationship, it will continue to vex the Bingo Club—and anyone else who believes American officials should unequivocally put the country's good over their family's wealth, let alone the interests of another nation.

7

Ploughshares into Swords

While the women and men of the Bingo Club worked behind the scenes to identify and counteract Chinese influence in the United States, their compatriots in government weren't always benignly neglecting these same issues. Sometimes, they were exacerbating them — spreading Chinese influence, or at least turning a blind eye, all while purporting to serve the American people. Indeed, as the White House wound down its investigation of Chinese economic aggression in late 2017 and early 2018, and national-security-minded officials in the Trump administration steeled themselves for the confrontation with China that they had long expected, they sometimes found that their adversaries weren't confined to the other side of the Pacific; sometimes, they were on the same side of the Potomac.

When the Chinese government wants a US politician to do its bidding, it typically invests in the relationship early on. The influence operations system of the Chinese Communist Party (CCP) is connected to organizations at the state and local levels all over the country. It's a numbers game. Some mayors will eventually become governors, or congresspeople or senators. Very rarely, the Chinese government finds a willing partner at the top of the food chain. This is what happened with Montana senator Steve Daines.

Daines, a freshman senator, came from the business world and had extensive experience in China. He had worked for Procter & Gamble, living for six years in Hong Kong and China. When he got to Congress, he naturally began using his China connections to advance the cause of opening up that market to Montana beef exports. He took a delegation to China in April 2017 and presented a plastic cooler stuffed with frozen steaks to Chinese premier Li Keqiang in Beijing.

The delegation also visited Tibet and Xinjiang. Tibet at this time was all but off-limits to foreigners. Upon returning, Daines said exactly nothing about his meetings with CCP officials in charge of both of those oppressed provinces — and he said little to nothing about the plight of the Tibetans.

It worked. In September 2017, Daines hosted the Chinese ambassador at a Montana ranch to talk beef exports. Montana ranchers were granted a $200 million beef contract from China.

But then came the phone call. The Chinese ambassador asked Daines to host a meeting with the CCP officials who oversee Tibet, who just happened to be in town on the day before the House Foreign Affairs Committee was set to hold a hearing on Tibet, featuring Lobsang Sangay, the Tibetan president-in-exile. Daines obliged.

Daines and Senator John Barrasso (R-WY) hosted the CCP delegation in Daines's office and posed for the assembled Chinese media cameras. No US press was invited or notified. The meeting was blasted out by Chinese propaganda outlets. The state-owned *China Daily* reported that Daines had praised Chinese officials in Tibet for doing "a good job in environmental protection and traditional cultural preservation."

Did Daines actually say that in the meeting? It didn't matter. Beijing had gotten their picture and their headlines. The Chinese media coverage of that meeting was meant to muddy any coverage of the real Tibet hearing over on the other side of the Capitol complex. The CCP had put their propaganda in a US senator's mouth. The damage was done.

The revelation that Daines had been co-opted by the CCP, exposed in a column I wrote on December 17 for the *Washington Post,* sent shock waves throughout Capitol Hill, but he faced no real consequences. When it was revealed earlier that year that an Australian senator, Sam Dastyari, parroted CCP propaganda while cozying up to a Chinese businessman and donor, the scandal was so big he had to resign. But when I broke the Daines story, his office just denied that anything was wrong with what he had done and Daines told his local newspaper that "Washington columnists" didn't understand what he was doing for Montana's ranchers.

Daines did other favors for Beijing. Over the summer of 2017, he worked behind the scenes to block progress of a bill put forward by Senator Ted Cruz that would rename the street outside the Chinese embassy in Washington after Nobel Peace Prize winner Liu Xiaobo, who died in government custody. The Chinese leadership told Rex Tillerson that preventing this bill from becoming law was one of their top three priorities.

Daines's trading of political favors to Beijing in exchange for economic rewards "confirms everything the Chinese believe about us and folks around the world, that anyone can be bought," former US ambassador to Burma Derek Mitchell told me. "We're only as strong as our weakest link, and that Daines would do this only encourages them to continue."

China's tactics didn't always work. Senator David Perdue was a former businessman, like Daines, with experience in China; like Daines, he sometimes did favors on demand for the Chinese embassy. When the Senate Foreign Relations Committee was planning a hearing to mark the anniversary of the Tiananmen Square massacre, the Chinese ambassador reached out to Perdue, who asked to use the committee room to host a meeting with CCP officials. It was another counterprogramming attempt, but this time the Chinese wanted the recognizable committee room to be the backdrop in the photos. To his credit, the chairman, Senator James Risch, said no way.

Friends in Low Places

The CCP doesn't just focus on the politicians; they cultivate relationships with congressional staffers of all levels. The main way this is done is by bringing staffers on lavish trips to China, something the China-United States Exchange Foundation is heavily involved in. The trips are run by a variety of organizations that are more or less connected to the government, with government or CCP-linked money all around. This is legal but a severe abuse of the spirit and intention of the Mutual Educational and Cultural Exchange Act (MECEA), a law that allows the State Department to approve trips for federal employees being sponsored by foreign governments.

When MECEA was passed in 1961, the idea was to foster goodwill, not open the door to a huge influence operation sponsored by an adversary government. In recent years, the number of MECEA China trips has outstripped by far the total for all other countries combined. Almost any level congressional staffer could apply, from staff assistant to press secretary. Many staffers traveled to China over and over again. It amounted to millions of dollars of free gifts. "There are chiefs of staff that go once or twice a year for several years," a senior GOP senate aide said. "The CCP has spent so much money taking people to China over the years. Then they call up all the friends and all of the people who have gone on those trips later and ask for favors."

There were a variety of favors that the Chinese government would call in from their former five-star travel guests. In yet another example of counterprogramming, the Chinese embassy once asked a congressional office chief of staff who had been on a free trip to help it host a photo exhibit in the halls of a congressional office building near a human rights hearing. Another congressional staffer — a Senate press secretary — who went on a MECEA trip to China told me that her handlers took her to a Uyghur village, where "reformed" Uyghurs who had been in the internment camps told her they loved Xi Jinping — as the CCP minders watched on.

"The point is to get visibility up from the staff assistants all the way to the chief of staff," the GOP official said. "It's just the sheer scope and scale of what they are doing. Everyone knows that it's a problem, and nobody wants to admit it."

Draining the Swamp

Capitol Hill is a land of many tribes. Inside the parties, and sometimes across them, members join forces for a variety of reasons. On China, there have always been passionate camps, but they have largely operated in their own lanes. You have the human rights champions, the defense hawks, the trade skeptics, the finance and business crowd. But as the China issue began to heat up, these camps all joined the fight. The first big battle was over whether to let national security or business decide where and when China could invest in the United States.

When Congress debated granting China permanent normal trade relations in 1999 and endorsing China's WTO accession in 2001, pro-business engagement folks lined up on one side and all the other amalgamated tribes opposed them on the other side. The business folks won out. But twenty years later, when it was time to reform the law that governs how Chinese investment and national security interact, the dynamic had changed.

Two decades of China's bad behavior — stealing intellectual property, spying, hacking, and attacking US industries — had made it harder and harder to defend the pro-business position. Xi was committed to a military-civil fusion strategy that obliterated the already thin line between Chinese firms and the People's Liberation Army. Under Chinese law, any Chinese company could be compelled to help the government and hand over its data at any time. Chinese acquisitions were entering new sectors so fast, nobody could keep track. And the technologies Chinese companies were scooping up here were sure to feed into the CCP's repression and military machine at home.

Not all Chinese investment was considered bad, of course — it's just that the rules were written for a long-ago era and new technologies posed new national security challenges that nobody could have anticipated, but that China was certain to exploit. The technology had outpaced the policy.

The body in charge of auditing Chinese investments to identify national security concerns — the Committee on Foreign Investment in the United States (CFIUS)—was operating on laws and rules designed for a past era. CFIUS had nine member agencies, including the State Department, the Defense Department, the Justice Department, and so on. These agencies often had competing interests and were focused on different parts of the issue. If it were to stand any chance of meeting the threat, CFIUS needed new marching orders, and it was going to be a fight over who would get to write them.

The drive to reform the CFIUS law in Congress began before Trump's election in 2016, when Senator John Cornyn (R-TX) tasked one of his senior intelligence staffers, Dave Hanke, to start a process to write a new law. Cornyn, a member of the intelligence committee and GOP Senate leadership at the time, had long been interested in China and had pushed for a more hawkish approach. He used his seniority to take a leadership role on CFIUS reform, and that led to tougher restrictions than otherwise would have resulted. Hanke began convening dozens of meetings and briefings with congressional offices, government officials, intelligence community representatives, business stakeholders, and anyone else he could think of. They soon realized that foreign acquisitions of American companies were only one part of the country's vulnerability to malign Chinese economic influence.

For one thing, the Chinese government forced American firms to form joint ventures with Chinese firms in order to secure access to the Chinese market. Those Chinese firms routinely stole the US companies' intellectual property and then used it against them, first inside China and then everywhere else. On top of that, there was a huge problem with the United States' export control regime, which wasn't set up to manage emerging technologies that couldn't have been conceived when the rules were written. The high-tech items the United States was exporting to China often were being used for military purposes; many of these products simply had never been restricted from export because they hadn't existed when the rules had been written.

The Treasury Department under Obama didn't want to come to the table. They believed that revisiting the CFIUS guidelines would end up expanding the committee's jurisdiction endlessly and giving the Treasury Department endless work to do. In the House and Senate, moreover, the financial services and banking committees viewed the very idea of CFIUS reform as an encroachment by the national security folks on the American business community and their interests. "We realized along the way that our opinions and conclusions were not shared by key committees and even key agencies," Hanke recalled. "The financial services guys were looking out for their interests. This is the beauty and also the weakness of capitalism."

After Trump was elected and Steven Mnuchin — a former investment banker who was as pro-business as they came — was sworn in at Treasury, things changed. CFIUS reform suddenly gained traction, with Mnuchin's support. For anyone who prized America's national security over its businesses' bottom lines, however, his involvement was an ominous sign.

Cornyn convened a meeting in his office and invited Mnuchin, Senate Banking Committee chairman Mike Crapo (R-ID), and then House Financial Services Committee chairman Jeb Hensarling (R-TX). He knew any reform would need the agreement of these three figures, and the strategy was to get them bought into the process early. These lawmakers weren't particularly involved in the China issue, and to the extent they were, it was from the economic and business perspective. They were in the position of key gatekeepers simply because the reform bill would have to go through their committees. But that meant the business lobby would have its say before any deal was done.

Mnuchin pledged to work with Cornyn to pass legislation that would overhaul the CFIUS guidelines — so long as Cornyn accepted his guiding principles. The new law needed to provide Treasury with flexibility it could exert through regulations, Mnuchin said, rather than micromanaging each issue. Treasury also would need more resources if it was to handle a lot more work. He did not reveal his true motivation for supporting the reform bill: subverting the drive for executive action to restrict Chinese investment. Cornyn and Mnuchin shook hands on the deal.

Crapo and Hensarling had no choice but to go along. The Republican committee chairmen believed that as the chairmen of the committees of jurisdiction, they should be in charge of writing the bill. But they were soon upset to discover Cornyn and Treasury had been exchanging drafts of the new bill for several months outside their visibility; Crapo and Hensarling also were annoyed that the intel committee staffers were negotiating a bill the financial services and banking committees would have to ultimately approve.

Their frustration would soon become more acute. When Cornyn introduced the new CFIUS legislation — called the Foreign Investment Risk Review Modernization Act (FIRRMA)— the bill already had the endorsements of Mnuchin, James Mattis, and Jeff Sessions.

At Mnuchin's insistence, FIRRMA never mentioned China by name. But at the first hearing on the bill in January 2018, which Crapo chaired, Cornyn made sure there was no doubt which country posed the threats the legislation meant to address. "The context for this legislation is important and relatively straight forward, and it's China," he testified. "It's not just that China poses a threat, though, it's that the kind of threat is unlike anything the U.S. has ever before faced — a powerful economy with coercive, state-driven industrial policies that distort and undermine the free market, married up with an aggressive military modernization and the intent to dominate its own region and potentially beyond."

It may seem surprising that Mnuchin, who resisted so many other national security actions against China, was so willing to work with Cornyn on a project that was meant to restrict investment from China based on national security concerns. But for Mnuchin, this was part of a bigger play. Because, at the same time the FIRRMA drama was unfolding, he and Robert Lighthizer were involved in a food fight over Lighthizer's 301 investigation, which finally had come out in March 2018.

The Lighthizer Report

By February 2018, Lighthizer had been ready to release the results of his 301 investigation into China's economic aggressions against the United States. The investigation was a crucial part of the Trump administration's efforts to impose pressure on Beijing by laying the groundwork for tariffs; the clear and present danger of a trade war, many inside the White House believed, would be enough to motivate Beijing to make meaningful concessions in order to alleviate the risk of tariffs. In that sense, the conclusion of the 301 investigation was one that everyone in the White House — whether pro- or antitariff — should have been able to get behind. But the rollout, like the announcement of the investigation back in August 2017, had gotten caught up in factional infighting.

On February 16, Wilbur Ross's Commerce Department announced the results of its own investigation to justify steel and aluminum tariffs, beating Lighthizer to the punch. Their tariffs, based on Section 232 of the Trade Expansion Act of 1962, were based on national security rather than economic concerns, which was rare and therefore controversial. And only 6 percent of those tariffs applied to China — the rest were against allies like Canada, Mexico, South Korea, and the European Union. "Had we timed it differently, it would have been better," one White House official later reflected. "Things just got confused with everybody just doing whatever they wanted."

Still, when Lighthizer's 301 investigation report finally came out in late March 2018, it was damning. Lighthizer reported that Chinese illicit practices, including intellectual property theft, forced technology transfer, and unfair subsidies, were robbing the US economy of at least $50 billion annually. He had given the hawks a lot to work with — not only with his diagnoses but also with his prescriptions.

Peter Navarro and Steve Bannon may have wanted Lighthizer's investigation to move faster, and Bannon surely still wished as much, given that he had been fired in the interim. But for Navarro and others in his camp, the results of the 301 investigation had proved to be well worth the wait. It called for drastic countermeasures: enhanced export controls, tariffs, and broad bans on Chinese investment in US companies.

Lighthizer's report gave powerful ammunition for those in Trump's orbit who were fighting for tariffs. His team proposed that the first tranche — 15 percent on $50 billion of Chinese exports to the United

States — should focus on industries that make up Xi's hallmark technology strategy, called Made in China 2025. The idea of those fighting for tariffs was to target the technologies of the future, thereby limiting the actual economic impact today. They thought that would be more palatable to Trump and cause less collateral damage to the US economy. "Technology is probably the most important part of our economy," Lighthizer said in announcing the report. "And we concluded that, in fact, China does have a policy of forced technology transfer; of requiring licensing at less than economic value; of state capitalism, wherein they go in and buy technology in the United States in non-economic ways; and then, finally, of cybertheft."

On April 3, the Office of the US Trade Representative released its list of 1,333 Chinese products that composed $50 billion worth of goods, adding detail to Trump's tariff threats, which were at that point still only threats. The next day, Beijing published its own list of 106 US products it was threatening to tariff, targeting the transportation and agriculture sectors hardest. An angry Trump responded the following day by announcing he was now considering tariffs on an additional $100 billion worth of Chinese goods and he warned China not to harm American farmers.

For the Goldman Sachs crowd inside the Trump team, it was now clear Trump was barreling toward the trade war they had been fighting against since day one. They reacted in different ways. As it became clear he was losing the internal fight over the tariffs, Gary Cohn resigned. Mnuchin was not done fighting and still believed he could find a way to stop the trade war before it started. As Trump and Xi traded threats, he prepared to go to Beijing to try to stave off the implementation of tariffs by negotiating a quick deal.

The hawks and the hardliners, meanwhile, were satisfied. They had gotten the president to embrace the idea of using pressure on China. What's more, they had shown that even when Trump played hardball, the Chinese leadership would still negotiate and the markets wouldn't collapse. "Remember, the initial Chinese position had been that they would never negotiate while the tariffs were in place," said former Trump National Security Council China official Matthew Turpin later. "Clearly, that didn't pan out. So the whole concept that if you take an action, the sky will fall, was disproven. We had to shift the Overton window of acceptable policy options."

The China Lobby

Lighthizer's report had made three broad recommendations: enhanced export controls, tariffs, and broad bans on Chinese investment in US companies. The tariffs, as well as the broad bans on Chinese investment, were anathema to a pro-business type such as Mnuchin. Sure, he had supported FIRRMA, which was aimed at halting Chinese investment that might jeopardize national security—but for him, shaping the new CFIUS guidelines was a way to outflank Lighthizer and convince the White House to avoid the harsher measures. "Mnuchin got behind FIRRMA so much because it gave him the opportunity to short-circuit the thing he didn't like," Hanke said later. "I'm not sure he was a true believer that Chinese investment was a big problem."

There were, of course, many others inside the Beltway who stood to lose out from new, stricter regulations on Chinese investment—and while they couldn't short-circuit parts of the FIRRMA legislation as easily as Mnuchin could, they weren't about to go down without a lobbying fight. Crapo and Hensarling were taking flak from several interest groups that stood opposed to the legislation, including the chamber of commerce, Wall Street lobbyists, and industry association groups. But Cornyn's staff chipped away at the opposition by working the industry groups from the inside, trying to gain key allies inside them to at least blunt their ability to criticize the bill.

This strategy required compromises that were uncomfortable for national security hawks involved in the process. The final language of the bill denied CFIUS the ability to create its own list of emerging and foundational technologies that would fall under its purview—in other words, to determine its own jurisdiction. This would provide Beijing with huge loopholes that it was sure to exploit.

There would be other compromises before the bill finally got enough support to become law. The thing that American companies hated most about FIRRMA was its restrictions on joint ventures—which, although they were often used as a pretense for Chinese companies to strip American firms of their intellectual property, also gained those firms access to the Chinese market and helped them make a great deal of money in the short term. In the process of getting the bill through committee and eventually attached to the National Defense Authorization Act, those restrictions were cut.

It was rare and significant that such a major reform bill got through the process at all, but nobody knew yet exactly how it would change the game. One thing, at least, seemed certain: without stronger rules to govern joint ventures between American and Chinese companies, Beijing's ability to transfer technology and knowledge through pressure would continue—as would the ability of certain Americans to profit from it. Because just as certain people in Congress see an advantage in aiding and abetting China, so too do certain American corporations. For instance, GE.

Nowhere were the problems posed by joint ventures in China during the era of military-civil fusion clearer than in the example of General Electric. GE has had a joint venture going back to 2011 with the Aviation Industry Corporation of China (AVIC), the state-owned aviation conglomerate, dealing with jet engines and avionics. Chinese commerce minister Chen Deming and then-US commerce secretary Gary Locke attended the public signing of the agreement in Chicago.

Every year, the Pentagon puts out an annual report on China's military power. Before the GE-AVIC joint venture, jet engines and avionics were both things this report identified for years as shortcomings in the technological advancement and ambitions of the People's Liberation Army. After the GE deal, avionics fell off the Pentagon's list as a Chinese shortcoming. GE essentially solved the People's Liberation Army's avionics problem.

AVIC is also a shareholder in another Chinese state-owned aviation conglomerate called Commercial Aircraft Corporation of China. The company's new C919 passenger jet is based on various technologies stolen from foreign companies, according to a report by the cybersecurity firm Crowdstrike. The technology was stolen by the same Chinese government hackers who stole the personal security information of twenty-two million Americans (including me) by hacking the Office of Personnel Management in 2015. What the Chinese government can't get us to give over, it takes.

"The Wheel Had Turned"

FIRRMA wasn't signed into law until August 2018, but the professionals at CFIUS didn't wait for it to be official before they started cracking down. Almost immediately after Trump got into office, the entire mood toward consideration of Chinese investment had changed. In January, CFIUS had blocked Jack Ma's Ant Financial from acquiring MoneyGram, the second-largest money transfer company in the country. In March, CFIUS had blocked the acquisition of US tech giant Qualcomm by Singapore-based Broadcom, a company with deep links to China.

In this, the actions of CFIUS are reflective of so much of the story about US-China relations in the Trump era—a story that involves different sectors of American society waking up to the reality of the competition at different speeds and on different calendars. When two of those sectors collided, the result was a struggle between them, often with Americans caught in the middle.

The rapid change in the way the US government treated Chinese investment caught a lot of Wall Street types, especially, by surprise—but none more than Trump's shortest-tenured senior White House official, Anthony Scaramucci. "The Mooch," as he is known, never set out to be a test case for the clash between the national security world and Wall

Street over China. But by the time he realized what he had gotten himself into, it was too late.

I was sitting in the CNN green room on the afternoon of April 28, 2018, waiting for my hit time, when Scaramucci walked in, talking very loudly on his cell phone. He was talking with a representative of HNA, the Chinese company that had agreed to buy his own "fund of funds" SkyBridge way back in January 2017 when the Mooch thought he was about to join the White House staff right off the bat.

There were a half dozen other people in the room, all chatting and waiting for their segments, but none of them were paying attention as Scaramucci told the person on the other end of the line that he knew HNA wanted out of the deal, which had been caught up in a seemingly endless national security review by the Committee on Foreign Investment in the United States. At first, Scaramucci suggested they try to work it out. But if HNA didn't meet his price for getting out of the deal, he said he would get President Trump to intervene.

"You have to pay a breakup fee if you want to end the transaction without mitigation," he said. If they didn't like that idea, he said, he would call "my friend the president," who has ultimate power over the CFIUS decisions. "Let the president decide," he said. "We'll contact the president and we'll ask him why they are abrogating his right to make a decision on the deal."

As I typed notes into my phone, I looked around and wondered whether anyone else in the room realized what Scaramucci was talking about. He was invoking Trump's name to pressure a Chinese company to pay him to get out of their deal to buy his company. Nobody seemed to notice.

There were several issues with the call. First of all, did Scaramucci still have a relationship with Trump sufficient to make that threat credible? Second, was this an indication Scaramucci was lobbying Trump on the deal? Lastly, why did HNA want out so badly that Mooch thought he had so much leverage to make them pay?

Two days later, HNA and SkyBridge announced they had agreed to scuttle the acquisition. The day after that, Scaramucci told CNBC the two companies would forge a joint venture in China.

When I interviewed Mooch two years later, he admitted to making the comments — but he assured me that it was just part of his impassioned negotiating style. He insists that he never spoke to Trump about the deal, and never intended to. He also said he never got a breakup fee. "I was emotionally charged about it, I had no problem letting them out, but we had money in the deal," he told me. "We were going to do a joint venture with them, so we never asked for damages. Then the joint venture never materialized."

He also told me the story of how his wild, albeit brief, political career got tangled up with the rising tensions between Washington and Beijing. "By accident, I ensnared myself in the drama of the United States versus China," he said. Scaramucci learned the hard way that Wall Street's open door to selling US companies to China — especially when they dealt with technology — was closing fast.

After Trump was elected, Scaramucci was all set to join the administration as the director of the White House Office of Public Liaison, a job that meant managing the White House's relationships with any number of outside civil society organizations. Trump was the third presidential candidate Scaramucci had supported in 2016, but after his first two picks, Scott Walker and Jeb Bush, were eliminated, "the Mooch" became a reliable TV surrogate for the Trump campaign and his earlier comments calling Trump a "hack politician" were forgotten.

In order to serve in the Trump administration, Scaramucci needed to divest his personal assets and decided to sell his investment firm SkyBridge Capital, which was basically a hedge fund that invested in other hedge funds and allowed individuals to buy in, for a fee. He hired Gregory Fleming, a former head of Morgan Stanley's retail brokerage business, to organize the SkyBridge sale. They reached out to about fifty potential investors, of which about fifteen were foreign, but none of them Chinese.

It was another firm, RON Transatlantic, which already owned 10 percent of SkyBridge, that introduced the massive Chinese conglomerate HNA to SkyBridge. RON Transatlantic was best known for having President Obama's former body man Reggie Love as part of its management team. RON Transatlantic introduced Scaramucci to HNA executive Guang Yang, a Chinese-born American citizen who had raised money for Jeb Bush's 2016 presidential campaign. HNA came in with what Scaramucci says was the second-highest bid. Scaramucci took it because HNA promised to keep SkyBridge's people employed.

The exact amount of the transaction was not made public, but Scaramucci said it was around a couple hundred million dollars. For HNA, which had scooped up some $50 billion of US assets the year prior, this was not a big money deal. Scaramucci thought the deal would get signed off by the CFIUS board because CFIUS hadn't stood in the way of HNA acquiring US financial technology firm Ingram Micro for $6 billion in 2016.

Until then, financial technology wasn't something the CFIUS investigators were focused on and HNA was not in their sights. "Remember at that time, they were very well regarded," Scaramucci said. "So this is pre-Trump administration, when CFIUS was being more fair to Chinese companies. We thought that because HNA was buying other asset managers, that was an okay thing to do."

Scaramucci broke the news of the deal himself — before it was actually completed — during his trip to Davos for the World Economic Forum, where he gave a speech about free trade and warning against protectionism. "The United States and the new administration does not want to have a trade war," he told the Davos crowd. The *Wall Street Journal* declared that Scaramucci, in Trump's absence, was "the new administration's ambassador to the global elite." He spoke after Xi Jinping, who defended the concept of globalization that Trump had campaigned against.

The first sign of trouble was on January 31, when the *New York Times* ran a front-page story alleging top officials were concerned about Scaramucci's White House appointment due to his "tangled interests" with a

Chinese company. Scaramucci is convinced that Reince Priebus or Bannon planted the story to sour Trump on bringing him to the White House. It worked. The job disappeared. But the deal was still moving forward.

Scaramucci's lawyers at Wachtell Lipton predicted that CFIUS would sign off on HNA's acquisition of SkyBridge in about three months' time, similar to the time it took to sign off on HNA's acquisition of Ingram Micro. But HNA was simultaneously being investigated by CFIUS over several much larger US acquisitions it had in the pipeline. Government regulators had asked for more information about HNA's murky ownership structure and its ties to the Chinese government. New Jersey software company Ness Technologies alleged in a lawsuit that the regulators found discrepancies in HNA's explanations. In July 2017, Bank of America backed out of negotiations on a separate deal.

This was about the time Trump forgot about his previous concerns about Scaramucci and hired him to be White House communications director. He lasted only eleven days, fired after the *New Yorker* published his four-letter insults about Bannon and others — comments that Scaramucci had wrongly assumed were off the record. He was out of politics and out of Trump's favor again, but the deal was still in limbo. Scaramucci still was willing to see it through.

The CFIUS investigations into HNA's various US acquisitions — including the SkyBridge deal — dragged on and on, until eventually the CFIUS board came back with a mixed verdict. The deal for Scaramucci's firm could go through only if the two companies completely separated their data and information technology systems. CFIUS didn't want US investors' information in Chinese hands.

But that made the whole point of the acquisition moot, Scaramucci said. Meanwhile, the tide had turned at HNA and orders from Beijing were to change course to reduce debt. "It never happened because they got forced to de-lever by the government," he said. "The wheel had turned, it turned quickly, and this deal was toast."

Scaramucci returned to SkyBridge and joined the anti-Trump resistance. He said he has no regrets, and that he simply did not realize that the risks of doing deals with Chinese companies had gone way up, both because of the mood in Washington and because of the behavior of those companies and the government they report to.

"I've made a lot of mistakes in my life," he said, "but none bigger than working for the Trump administration."

In that opening skirmish, the national security folks won out against the Wall Street crowd and their Chinese partners. That was new. For so many years, these deals had gone through without much scrutiny. Now, almost any firm connected to sensitive technology or the data of American citizens could be considered national security sensitive and worthy of government protection. This was the beginning of what became the greater US-China tech war.

8

The Battle for the Future

In the spring and summer of 2018, the trade war between the United States and China was starting to heat up. But within that war, there were the opening salvos of another: a tech war was in the offing between the world's two largest economies.

China's largest tech companies, such as Alibaba, Tencent, HNA, Huawei, ZTE, China Mobile, and others, had grown in just a few years from second-tier players to national champions that were expanding worldwide and threatening to dominate key sectors like telecom and high-end manufacturing. Beijing's Made in China 2025 strategy had accelerated what was already a huge national investment in science and technological innovation that China combined with their diplomatic and military expansions into a project it called "military-civil fusion," which blurred the line between the state and private industry.

US national security agencies had two fundamental problems with this development. These firms were benefiting from the ongoing theft of US intellectual property, huge government subsidies, and other unfair trade practices, meaning the competition was fundamentally unfair for American and European firms. Also, the US intelligence community believed these firms either were working directly with Chinese military and intelligence agencies or were at the very least susceptible to being forced to do so at any time. Chinese tech embedded in the national infrastructure of the United States or any allied country was a security vulnerability that had to be avoided at all costs.

Top-level US officials like Steven Mnuchin, Robert Lighthizer, and Larry Kudlow were focused on making it through the opening curves of what they expected to be a long roller coaster of negotiations with their Chinese counterparts, led by Vice Premier Liu He. They knew that a crackdown on China's tech industry would only complicate their job and make a deal harder. But inside the national security agencies, officials were figuring out how to wage the tech war at the same time the trade war was playing out.

Shooting the Messenger

Trump, for his part, conflated the two wars—the trade war and the tech war—all the time, mixing national security considerations and economic concessions and regular old favor trading in a way that made his officials crazy but made Xi Jinping very happy. The first glaring example of this was on May 13, 2018, when he tweeted that he was going to give a reprieve to Chinese telecom giant ZTE, which the Commerce Department had just announced penalties against as punishment for ZTE violating US sanctions on North Korea and Iran. Trump said he had ordered the Commerce Department to find a way to get ZTE "back into business, fast. Too many jobs in China lost."

Trump had agreed to help ZTE during a phone call with Xi as a favor, according to John Bolton's book, without getting anything in return. Mnuchin encouraged the move. Bolton, Lighthizer, and Peter Navarro tried to talk Trump out of it, but he wasn't having it. After Trump's tweet, White House spokeswoman Lindsay Walters tried to claim the president hadn't just overruled his commerce secretary Wilbur Ross, saying in a statement that Trump wanted Ross to "exercise his independent judgment" to resolve the ZTE case "based on its facts."

The commerce secretary's judgment was good enough to know that he had to redraw the clear line between the economically driven trade war and the national-security-driven tech war—a line that his boss had just tried to erase, and not for the last time. Ross told the National Press Club on May 14 that the issue of punishing ZTE for violations was "separate from trade," but he admitted he was looking at "alternative remedies." But Trump just tweeted again, completely contradicting him. "ZTE, the large Chinese phone company, buys a big percentage of individual parts from U.S. companies. This is also reflective of the larger trade deal we are negotiating with China and my personal relationship with President Xi."

Trump had now confirmed the linkage twice. National security and law enforcement issues were bargaining chips in his larger quest to make a deal on trade. This was Xi's dream come true. For Beijing, every time there was a national security or law enforcement action against their illegal or corrupt behavior, Xi would try to throw it into the trade negotiations. It often worked.

I know for sure that Beijing asked Trump to pardon ZTE as part of the trade negotiations because I obtained a secret document from inside the talks that spelled it out in black and white. The document was a list of China's demands that was handed over to American officials during the US delegation visit to Beijing the week prior. Bullet point 5 said, "Having noted China's great concern about the case of ZTE, the U.S. will listen attentively to ZTE's plea, consider the progress and efforts ZTE has made in compliance management and announce adjustment to the export ban."

The column I published on May 15 for the *Washington Post* got a lot of attention. I was booked on CNN's *New Day* the next morning at six o'clock to talk about it with Chris Cuomo and Derek Scissors, resident scholar at the American Enterprise Institute, who told me Trump "just got blackmailed" by Xi. Trump saw the segment and tweeted that my reporting was fake news. "The Washington Post and CNN have typically written false stories about our trade negotiations with China . . . We have not seen China's demands yet," the president tweeted.

Trump didn't realize that it was just one story, me writing for the *Washington Post* and me talking about it on CNN. But more importantly, I had the document of demands. I knew for a fact that US officials had seen it. The president of the United States was calling me a liar. Later that day, Ross confirmed that the list of demands did exist and he had seen it.

That same week, several stories started leaking to the press about the US delegation's trip to Beijing, all of them disparaging Navarro. In Beijing, before the key meeting with Liu, Mnuchin decided last minute to change the format to a one-on-one, meaning Lighthizer and Navarro couldn't come in. Navarro was furious and the two had a shouting match within earshot of the Chinese officials.

White House officials began whispering in reporters' ears that Navarro had acted strangely on the trip, only his second ever in his life to China. He insisted on keeping his luggage with him at all times. He wanted to sleep inside the embassy because he feared hotel surveillance. He rudely refused to eat the food served to him in official functions. That sort of stuff. White House officials opposed to Navarro even started looking for reasons to file workplace complaints about him. They initiated a process to interview anyone who worked for him to try to find cause to push him out. The investigation ultimately never went anywhere.

Game On

Despite all that drama, Mnuchin wasn't able to quickly strike a small deal that would be sufficient enough to convince Trump to hold off on tariffs. The trade war was going forward, whether he liked it or not.

On May 20, after meeting with his Chinese counterparts, Mnuchin announced that the trade war was "on hold," because the two sides had made substantial progress, vitiating the need for actually going through with the tariff threats. Nine days later, the White House released a statement totally contradicting Mnuchin and promising the first tariffs would be announced on June 15. That day, the Office of the US Trade Representative updated their list of Chinese tariff targets and Beijing did the same. On July 6, the first $34 billion of US tariffs went into effect and China retaliated in kind. Beijing targeted industries in states that make up Trump's base. He didn't like that at all, and so he ordered the Office of the US Trade Representative to come up with a list of $200 billion worth of potential tariffs on Chinese goods. The trade war was on, and it was escalating quickly.

On July 6, the first $50 billion of tariffs went into effect, and it escalated from there. Before that month was over, Trump was publicly threatening to tariff all $500 billion of imports from China. He also pledged billions to bail out US farmers hit hard by the Chinese retaliatory measures. Throughout August and September, relations soured as threats of tariffs and new rounds of tariffs came about every couple of weeks.

These looked like terribly stormy weather conditions for US relations with China, and most of the public focused on these twists and turns. But these conditions were also the result of the changing climate. The national security hardliners were ready to capitalize on that shifting climate in a major way. They had a plan and a champion to carry it out — Vice President Mike Pence.

The Hardliners Strike Back

The national security officials in the Trump administration were largely cut out of the trade negotiations, by design. But that didn't mean they were sitting still on China. By the summer of 2018, Mike Pompeo had replaced Rex Tillerson as secretary of state. John Bolton had consolidated control at the National Security Council (NSC). And in June, as the White House's announcement of impending tariffs on Chinese goods was still resounding around the globe, James Mattis became the first defense secretary under Trump to visit Beijing.

On his way to China, Mattis made a big show of stopping in Hawaii to formally announce that the United States was changing the name of US Pacific Command to US Indo-Pacific Command. He also attended the Shangri-La Dialogue and announced that the United States had a new Indo-Pacific strategy. This was one of the first visible demonstrations of the classified and unclassified Indo-Pacific strategic framework documents Matt Pottinger had helped spearhead in 2017. Now, there was a defense-specific strategy to go with it and Mattis was rolling it out to the region.

Mattis had never been to China, having spent his four-decade career in the Marines mostly in the Middle East. He didn't understand the Chinese system. For example, Mattis was very impressed with his meeting with Chinese defense minister Wei Fenghe, but he didn't get that the defense minister in the Chinese system is a relatively weak official. That's not his direct counterpart because the systems are different. His staff had to convince him to meet with air force general Xu Qiliang, who, as the senior military member of the Chinese Communist Party (CCP) Central Military Commission, holds a lot more actual power than the defense minister.

Xu drained the clock, taking up the whole meeting lecturing Mattis on the one hundred years of Chinese humiliation, and didn't offer much happy talk about win-win cooperation. Mattis didn't like that meeting as much, but the staff felt like he at least had a more honest picture of who was really leading China and what they were saying, not the barbarian handlers they put forward.

When he met with Xi Jinping, Mattis told him that he wanted to have a relationship starting from a position of clarity and objective truth, so that the United States and China could operate in a competitive environment without stumbling into a conflict neither side wanted. "We can do what the Europeans stupidly did twice in the twentieth century and destroy ourselves," he told Xi, "or we can sit down and talk about confidence-building measures, keeping operations safe, and the like."

Mattis, unlike most Trump officials, had a real reputation as a military leader in foreign capitals that brought with it respect — and he used that to drive home his point. "Hey, if you want to fight, great. I know how to do it. I'm pretty good at it," Mattis said to Xi. "But we shouldn't be so stupid and we shouldn't underestimate the huge costs for both of us."

Mattis wasn't the only Trump official trying to convince China's leaders that the new frame of the relationship would be competition, whether they liked it or not. Pottinger made multiple trips to Beijing in 2017 and early 2018 to brief Chinese officials on what these new policy documents meant and what Beijing should expect from the Trump administration — namely, a harder line.

Of course, the Chinese leaders at this point trusted the people in Trump's inner circle with whom they by now enjoyed fairly established relationships, more than they did the boyish-looking staffer Matt Pottinger. But in a September event at the Chinese embassy, Pottinger got his message through by giving a speech partially in Chinese. He argued that Confucius himself would have wanted the United States and China to speak honestly about the competition they were in. "We in the Trump administration have updated our China policy, to bring the concept of competition to the forefront," he said, pointing back to the National Security Strategy he helped write. "To us, this was really an example of what Confucius called the 'Rectification of names.'"

Pottinger quoted Confucius from *The Analects,* first in Chinese and then translated to English: "If names cannot be correct, then language cannot be in accordance with the truth of things. And if language cannot be in accordance with the truth of things, then affairs cannot be carried on to success."

The United States and China were obviously in competition with each other, he said, and there was no benefit to avoiding saying that out loud. By presenting the Trump administration's policy as one of honesty and realism, he sought to dispel the Chinese ambassador's notion that Washington was somehow the aggressor. "For us, competition is not a four-letter word," he said.

Pottinger was trying to call out the change in climate in US-China relations, but he was not senior enough to really break through. That's why he and other like-minded officials pushed for a major speech on China to be delivered by the most senior official the hardliners counted as one of their own, Vice President Pence.

Pence on China

Pence had kept up a steady role on foreign policy, traveling to the Munich Security Conference in 2017 and touring Asia in early 2018. I traveled with him to the opening ceremony of the Winter Olympics in Pyeongchang, where he sat feet away from Kim Jong Un's sister but never made eye contact. We traveled to the border and peered over into North

Korea. Pence was a true neocon from way back in his congressional days. I once asked him, just to see what he would say, if he thought the CCP was a "fascist" organization. He replied, "No, they're Communists." He saw the CCP similarly to how he once viewed the Soviet Union.

When Pence delivered his China speech on October 4, 2018, at the Hudson Institute, a conservative think tank, he instantly became the champion of the new tough-on-China strategy. Pence had always been a hardliner on China, but he hadn't taken such a public stance until this point, perhaps not wanting to get in the middle of the fight over the president's trade negotiations. Knowing Pence's speech would be controversial, Pottinger worked on it quietly with Pence's speechwriter Stephen Ford. They didn't show any other agencies (especially the Treasury Department) until the night before. Mnuchin tried to delay the speech at the last minute, but he was too late. Pence shared the speech with President Trump the night before delivery and Trump made some edits and then blessed it.

"I come before you today because the American people deserve to know that, as we speak, Beijing is employing a whole-of-government approach, using political, economic, and military tools, as well as propaganda, to advance its influence and benefit its interests in the United States," Pence said. "China is also applying this power in more proactive ways than ever before, to exert influence and interfere in the domestic policy and politics of this country."

Pence had just made two huge accusations. First, he was calling out Beijing's united front influence operations, which was a first for a US official of this ranking. Then, immediately after, he was accusing China of interfering in politics against Trump. Pence pointed to how China targeted its retaliatory tariffs against pro-Trump counties and planted anti-Trump ads disguised as news articles in newspapers in Iowa.

Pence name-checked Michael Pillsbury, who was sitting in the front row. For those like Pottinger, this was the public explanation of the work they had been doing since the election and a senior-level endorsement of the strategy documents they were pushing down through the bureaucracy amid significant resistance. The *New York Times* immediately ran an article characterizing Pence's speech as clear proof that the Trump administration was "declaring" a "new Cold War." I got a call from a senior administration official who insisted that this was exactly the wrong way to look at it. The speech was meant to acknowledge the reality and put Beijing on notice, not start a conflict from scratch.

"It's saying to the American people that we need to wake up to this. And the Chinese need to wake up to the fact that if they continue to pursue this policy—which is unacceptable—there will be consequences," the official said.

Pence on the Road

When the time came for the next round of major Asian diplomatic confabs, it was clear Trump had no intention of going. He hated those things, and besides, Pence was more than happy to stand in. I joined Pence for his trip in November 2018 to South Korea, Japan, Singapore, Australia, and Papua New Guinea. In Singapore he led the US delegation to the East Asia Summit, and in Papua New Guinea he sat in for Trump at the Asia-Pacific Economic Cooperation (APEC) CEO Summit, the most important gathering of leaders from the Asia-Pacific region each year. The fact that the vice president even gave a major speech on China policy was significant. Now he was on a ten-day tour of Asia to explain to our allies what it meant. There was a brief window for the administration to convince people it had its act together on China.

One got the distinct sense, traveling with Pence, that he was happy to get out of DC for a bit. We all were. Democrats had just taken back the House in dramatic fashion in the midterm election, but they had lost ground in the Senate. That meant the next two years would be characterized by the paralysis of divided government and an endless drumbeat of new congressional investigations that were sure to turn up an endless string of scandals.

When we got to Tokyo, our first stop, Japanese prime minister Shinzo Abe gave Pence the full red carpet treatment as they posed for the cameras and doled out boilerplate statements about the alliance and North Korea. The vice president was in his element.

As we flew from Tokyo to Singapore for stop number two, I went up to the little cabin at the front of Air Force 2 to talk with Pence. I sat on the futon that folded out into the bed he slept on. Karen Pence sat at the desk nearby, very polite but clearly (and justifiably) annoyed a reporter had invaded their personal space.

The first thing Abe had said to Pence, the vice president told me, was to bring up Pence's speech on China that he delivered at the Hudson Institute. Abe told Pence it was important that the United States be clear on its stance toward China because countries like Japan, which supported a tougher stance, could only do so if Washington first took the lead.

The credibility of this new approach was also important because it was announced just before Trump and Xi were set to meet in Buenos Aires on the sideline of the G20. Trump was threatening to impose another $250 billion worth of tariffs on Chinese goods if Beijing didn't play ball. For Trump, that meant buying more US farm goods. For Pence and others, it meant actually addressing the structural issues in the economic relationship, including intellectual property theft, subsidies, and the like.

This was one of those instances where the trade war and the strategic awakening—the shift of the US government and society to a more competitive stance vis-à-vis China—intersected. If Trump were savvy, he could have pointed to his government's tougher China policy as evidence that Xi had better take him seriously on trade. Trump did the opposite. He folded on the new tariffs when Xi asked him for another favor, thereby undermining the overall strategy and getting nothing real in return.

But while Pence was traveling around Asia just before the Buenos Aires summit, he was telling everyone that Trump's new China strategy meant that the days of falling for Beijing's pattern of staving off action by making promises about promises were over.

"They've basically been running that game for at least twenty-five or thirty years in the modern era. And administrations say it's going to change but nobody really pushes it, nobody takes any action to demand the change. Eventually the subject changes and they keep going," Pence told me. "I think China, going into Argentina, is starting to realize this is different."

Shortest Asia Trip Ever

Bolton and Pence had a quiet but close alliance on foreign policy matters during Bolton's tenure as national security adviser, a relationship neither side saw any benefit in advertising. Bolton was not actually a neocon like Pence. Ideologically, he was more of a conservative hawk, like Pompeo. (The difference between neocon and conservative hawk — often overlooked even in DC — had to do with how much one felt the values of democracy, freedom, and human rights should factor into America's foreign policy and its use of hard power. That distinction most often surfaced when policy makers were talking about bad governments that the United States worked with, such as Egypt and Saudi Arabia. Neocons wanted them to change; conservative hawks wanted them to stay close allies.) Pence and Bolton shared staff and worked together on foreign policy, but they stayed quiet about their cooperation. They were both establishment Republicans viewed skeptically by the Make America Great Again crowd and the officials inside the White House who viewed the old GOP as the enemy.

On China, Pence and Bolton were two peas in a pod. While neocons and conservative hawks may disagree on how hard to push our values on our allies, they come together in agreeing we should push our values on our adversaries. Both Pence and Bolton had a long record of speaking out about China. In a speech at the Daniel Morgan Graduate School in DC, given just before he became national security adviser, Bolton called for Washington to lead the whole region to push back against Chinese aggression across the board. "Without effective American resistance, the countries of ASEAN [the Association of Southeast Asian Nations], the Southeast Asian countries, obviously don't have the strength to deal with

China individually, and I don't think we've provided adequate leadership," he said. "For two decades now, we have not had an effective China strategy . . . We've got to do what we can, or we will simply be outmaneuvered time and time again."

Bolton was committed to traveling to Asia as much as possible to try to manage alliance relationships Trump was damaging, so he planned to join Pence in Singapore (the second leg of our Asia trip) for the ASEAN summit and the East Asia Summit — the national security adviser was so excited that he flew directly to Singapore from the ceremony celebrating the seventy-fifth anniversary of D-Day in Normandy, France. Bolton intended to then travel on with Pence to the APEC CEO Summit in Papua New Guinea, with a short stopover in Australia. But he ended up attending zero of those events.

On Bolton's first night in Singapore, there was a crisis back in Washington involving his deputy, Mira Ricardel. A longtime GOP foreign policy hawk, Ricardel had kept out of politics during the campaign and had held several Trump administration positions over the years. Famously sharp-elbowed, she was Bolton's enforcer and, as such, battled with several administration factions during her short months as the NSC's number two official.

But Ricardel's mountain of bad will was built beginning in the transition, when she was the head of the White House personnel office for the Defense Department. There, she immediately clashed with Mattis. Mattis was putting forth not only career Foreign Service officers like Ambassador Anne Patterson for senior Pentagon jobs but outright Democrats like Michèle Flournoy, who was assumed to be a top contender for the defense secretary job if Hillary Clinton had won.

Ricardel wanted to be the Pentagon's number three official, undersecretary of defense for policy. Mattis blocked her, but not before she had blocked several of his picks and soured much of the White House on Mattis. Ricardel eventually got a posting at the Commerce Department as a consolation prize. But she returned to the White House in April 2018 as Bolton's right-hand woman, with a mandate to get the Pentagon under control.

But before she would do that, Ricardel ran afoul of the powerful Trump family faction, when she told Melania Trump's staff that if they wanted NSC officials to help the First Lady on her four-country tour of Africa, they would have to be allotted seats on Melania's plane. It seemed reasonable to Ricardel that her people shouldn't have to follow the First Lady's entourage from African country to country on commercial flights. But Melania's staff wouldn't budge. It became a test of wills, and in the Trump White House, the president's family wins those battles almost always. Melania's staff appealed to John Kelly, who ordered Ricardel to comply, which she did.

But even though they had prevailed, Melania's staff couldn't let it go. They waited until it was 3 a.m. in Singapore (so Bolton was asleep) and released a statement from the Office of the First Lady bashing Ricardel as undeserving of working in the White House. The East Wing was openly attacking the West Wing in a bizarrely public way. Privately, Melania's staff was also leaking that Ricardel was an angry, lying, leaking woman.

A few hours later in Singapore, Bolton and his traveling staff got on a plane back to Washington to deal with the Ricardel mess. The national security adviser missed all the meetings with our Southeast Asian allies because of the factional infighting back in DC. Ricardel resigned shortly thereafter.

Tantrum Diplomacy

Pence moved on to Papua New Guinea without Bolton, but with Deputy Secretary of State John Sullivan, Pottinger, and his own national security adviser, retired general Keith Kellogg, a perfectly nice but inconsequential official who had been a policy adviser on the campaign and had hung around ever since. This was the main event of the trip. Xi Jinping had arrived a week earlier for an official state visit. China had a plan to dominate the event or, if not, at least make sure they spoiled any chance the United States would gain any benefit from it.

The signs of China's influence on the small third-world island were everywhere. In advance of the conference, China had ceremoniously opened a huge highway through the middle of Port Moresby they had built for no money down (debt trap to come later). The road led up to the sparkling new and quite stunning parliament building, also built and paid for by Chinese firms working on government orders. The new Supreme Court building, another gift (with strings) from China to Papua New Guinea, was visible but still under construction.

In honor of Xi's state visit, the Chinese delegation had lined the new highway with Chinese flags. As the other national delegations poured in, the Papua New Guinea government asked the Chinese delegation to take the flags down. They refused. Pressed further, they finally took down the Chinese flags — but then replaced them with solid red flags that looked like the Chinese flags from any distance. But that was only the beginning of their weird and aggressive bullying over those few days.

When Xi hosted the leaders of the eight Pacific Islands that don't have diplomatic relationships with Taiwan for dinner at his hotel, all the international journalists who showed up to cover it were thrown out. When it came time for the awkward group photo where all the leaders stand together on rafters wearing brightly colored island shirts, Xi made the other leaders wait for him by delaying his arrival, a power move.

Inside the meetings, the Chinese delegation complained loudly that the United States was "scheming" against China and dragging these other Asian countries into it to their detriment. Pottinger was in charge of negotiating a joint statement that was supposed to represent the consensus of the twenty-one countries. The Chinese delegation objected to language about combatting unfair trade practices, a vague enough line that said, "We agree to fight protectionism including all unfair trade practices."

Chinese officials tried to go see Papua New Guinea's foreign minister in his office, to persuade him to intervene on their behalf. The foreign minister refused to see them, so the Chinese officials literally busted into the foreign minister's office and he had to call the local police to force them out. Back at the conference hall, Chinese officials were entering uninvited into meetings of the smaller countries, to demand they toe Beijing's line.

"This is becoming a bit of a routine in China's official relations: tantrum diplomacy," a senior US official involved in the negotiations told me at the time. "Them walking around like they own the place and trying to get what they want through bullying."

Xi and Pence were set to give the last two speeches in the public-facing side of the event. The speeches were being held on a cruise ship docked off the coast of Port Moresby, for security reasons. The international media was following it from a tent on shore. But when Pence started speaking, the internet in the international media center suddenly shut off, meaning the journalists couldn't cover the speech in real time. When Pence was finished, the internet mysteriously started working again.

Pence's staff was getting increasingly frustrated by the Chinese delegation's childish behavior, but they had a more pressing concern. Just hours before Pence was about to speak, Trump had made some comments on China in the Oval Office, totally oblivious to what Pence was up to on the other side of the world. Pottinger and Ford were furiously trying to work those comments into Pence's speech until the last minutes.

Here's how it came out:

> As President Trump said just a few hours ago in the Oval Office, we have "great respect for President Xi . . . [and] great respect for China." But, in the president's words, "China has taken advantage of the United States for many, many years." And those days are over.
>
> As the president has added, China has "tremendous barriers"; they have "tremendous tariffs"; and, as we all know, their country engages in quotas, forced technology transfer, intellectual property theft, industrial subsidies on an unprecedented scale. Such actions have actually contributed to a $375 billion good trades deficit with the United States last year alone. But as the president said today, "that's all changed now."

Pence was mashing together the official policy and the ongoing diplomatic negotiations in Port Moresby with Trump's utterances, in real time. It kind of made sense, but it kind of didn't. Trump was sending mixed signals and Pence was pretending they all fit together perfectly. Nobody could blame the audience for being confused.

When Pence finished speaking, there was scattered light applause. Pence was stunned. Why wouldn't the crowd be receptive to this tough-on-China, "America is here to stay" messaging? He found out later the Chinese delegation had maneuvered to scoop up all the tickets for the live audience and packed it with Chinese businesspeople. Their attention to detail in their mischief had to be admired.

On the final day, Pottinger worked with his Chinese counterparts to try to get consensus on the APEC joint statement. The Chinese delegation refused to budge. The vote was 20 to 1, with every country except China supporting the statement. But without consensus, the statement failed. As the leaders voted, the Chinese delegation watching through glass in an adjacent room broke out in cheerful applause. For China, America's failure was its roaring success.

The Buenos Aires Disaster

All of the hard work Pence, Bolton, and Pottinger had put into devising and then announcing America's new and tougher strategic approach to China was completely undermined only days later, when Trump traveled to Buenos Aires for the G20 summit and his next big meeting with Xi. This was also when national security officials and the trade team clashed, when Canadian officials, on behalf of the US Justice Department, arrested the CFO of Chinese telecom giant Huawei, Meng Wanzhou, the daughter of the founder and CEO, Ren Zhengfei.

Bolton admits in his book that he was alerted by Justice Department officials that Meng might be arrested the day before, but he decided not to tell Trump about it because it struck him as "straightforward" and he didn't want to bother the president until he had "all the facts." The news broke as Trump was sitting down to dinner with Xi. Afterward, Trump was angry he hadn't been told. Press Secretary Sarah Sanders called over to the Justice Department to ask them whether they had purposely withheld this information. The Justice Department said they had informed the NSC. Trump later complained that we had arrested "the Ivanka Trump of China."

Meng's arrest was based on an indictment for Huawei busting US sanctions on Iran. The evidence was strong, but that wasn't the point. Arresting a senior Chinese executive at this level on criminal charges for actions taken by the corporation was unprecedented. Using law enforcement tools at this senior level was an escalation that clearly had diplomatic and political implications. It would have been inconceivable in any normal administration for such a move to be made without the most senior White House officials involved or at least aware, particularly during a summit where the United States and Chinese presidents were set to meet.

Larry Kudlow was telling the truth when he told Fox News the next day that Trump didn't know about the arrest until after the dinner. The Justice Department move was covered in the press as "threatening a resolution to the U.S.-China trade war." In fact, it was the opening salvo of the US-China tech war. Were those two things linked? Of course. Was linking them deliberate? Well, that depends on who was doing the linking and at what point.

Xi Blames Canada

Xi tried to link easing pressure on Huawei to the trade negotiations at several points. From Xi's perspective, the linkage made sense. He took two Canadians hostage, arresting them on trumped-up charges, as leverage over Justin Trudeau while Meng litigated in Canadian courts to prevent being extradited to the United States. It backfired. Trudeau could never make such a trade because the politics in Canada wouldn't allow what was basically an abandonment of rule-of-law principles for political expediency.

But for Trump that was totally something he might do. Therefore, it was something the people inside his own government had to worry about. Their worries were not unfounded. My *Washington Post* colleague Ellen Nakashima heard from her sources that Mnuchin's chief of staff, Eli Miller, had initiated a quiet effort to negotiate a trade whereby Meng's charges would be dropped or reduced in exchange for Huawei accepting some other type of corporate punishment. Miller met with Chinese officials outside the government process, with Mnuchin's tacit approval. The deal never got done.

Bolton wrote that Mnuchin "fretted constantly" about the Justice Department's criminal prosecutions of Chinese officials and corporate entities and that Trump implied Huawei could be a bargaining chip in the trade negotiations "on several occasions." He said Trump saw it as a telecom company, the Justice Department saw it as a criminal organization, and Bolton saw it as an arm of the Chinese intelligence apparatus.

All of them were correct; Huawei was and is all of those things. Over the next year, Trump would repeatedly offer to include Huawei in the trade talks. Again, he was mixing national security and economic dealmaking to Beijing's advantage. The result was a policy that lurched back and forth, with the United States punishing Chinese tech companies only to have the president give them a reprieve, leaving much of the world confused.

Lighthizer in the Lead

After Buenos Aires, Lighthizer took over the lead role in trade negotiations from Mnuchin at Trump's direction. Navarro was largely cut out of the process. Lighthizer and Liu He conducted shuttle diplomacy for five months, ironing out the details of a lengthy agreement that would include Chinese commitments to buy US agricultural goods, open market access to US financial firms, and change a series of Chinese laws to show a commitment to end unfair trade practices like intellectual property theft and forced technology transfer.

But in early May 2019, Liu He returned a draft with a huge chunk of the agreement (all the proposed legal changes) crossed out. On May 6, Lighthizer said the Chinese were not ready to make structural changes yet, and so there would be no deal, for now. Inside the administration, this was known as "the Big Renege."

Although the talks would go on, the hardliners had another break in the weather to push forward something that had been sitting idle for months, an escalation of the fight against Huawei. With no trade deal imminent, Trump went along. On May 15, he signed an executive order effectively banning the US government from doing business with companies that are beholden to foreign adversary governments — that is, Huawei. He also signed off on Wilbur Ross placing Huawei on a Commerce Department list of banned entities. But even as he acknowledged the threat, he kept saying it could be negotiated away.

"Huawei is something that's very dangerous. You look at what they've done from a security standpoint, from a military standpoint, it's very dangerous," Trump said in the Oval Office on May 23. "So it's possible that Huawei even would be included in some kind of a trade deal. If we made a deal, I could imagine Huawei being possibly included in some form of, or in some part of, a trade deal."

The restrictions on Huawei had implications for both Chinese and American firms that supplied Huawei with everything from semiconductors to chips to software. It also had huge implications for countries that were already lousy with Huawei equipment and planning to buy more to build their 5G infrastructure. The Trump administration was making decisions that affected them, without consulting them, and then telling them afterward to go along.

And none of Trump's officials working on this problem could promise that Trump would stay the course. During a call on June 18, Xi brought up the Huawei restrictions and told Trump they should be removed as part of the trade deal. They discussed it again over dinner on June 28 at the G20 Summit in Osaka. The next day, Trump seemed to completely reverse his stance.

"US companies can sell their equipment to Huawei," he said at a press conference, adding that this means "equipment where there's no great national security problem."

Huawei tweeted out, "U-turn?" Pottinger was apoplectic. The whole thing was a mess. But the national security team had another big problem. For months, they had been pushing for measures to respond to China's persecution of the Uyghurs. For them, an important part of standing up to China was calling out their human rights violations and standing up for American values.

During the Trump-Xi dinner in Osaka, the subject of China's "re-education camps" for Uyghur Muslims and other ethnic minorities in Xinjiang Province had come up. Evidence was piling up about mass detention, forced indoctrination, and other human rights violations against the over one million innocent people in these camps. Confronting Xi about these brutal abuses would not only be the moral thing to do; it also would ensure that Xi understood the West would not be able to ignore mass atrocities on such a large scale.

But Trump didn't care about the plight of the Uyghurs. Bolton wrote, "According to our interpreter, Trump said that Xi should go ahead with building the camps, which he thought was exactly the right thing to do."

9

New World Order

In October 2014, Xi Jinping had traveled to Xinjiang, where he made a series of historic speeches. In full view of the United States and the rest of the international community, he had laid out his new plan to counter what he called the rise of "ethnic separatism and terrorist violence" in this far northwestern province of China. His declaration had grim implications for the majority of the residents of Xinjiang—and for Uyghurs living around the world and their families. The policies that Beijing went on to enact in Xinjiang would serve as a preview of the repressive system that the Chinese Communist Party (CCP) would surely enact if it could extend its control even further beyond its pre–World War II borders. It was the harbinger of a new world order—with Chinese characteristics.

In Xinjiang, which came into the possession of the CCP in 1949 after Mao Zedong's People's Liberation Army defeated Chiang Kai-shek's Nationalist army with extensive support from the Soviet Union, twenty-five million ethnic minority citizens live at the time of this writing under various levels of Chinese government control and repression. The largest minority group among them, the Uyghurs, numbers about eleven million. They practice Islam and speak a Turkic dialect. Their unique language, culture, art, and traditions give them a distinctive national identity, which in turn earns them the resentment and suspicion of the Chinese authorities.

Similar to what it had done in Tibet, Beijing was seeking to develop the resource-rich and strategically important region of Xinjiang by importing Han Chinese by the trainloads and slowly but surely clamping down on the locals' rights to practice their religion, speak freely, or have any control over what was happening in their homeland. But unlike with Tibet, not all Uyghurs confined themselves to nonviolence, and some trained in Afghanistan and Syria, coming back to Xinjiang to stage attacks.

On the second day of Xi's trip there, two Uyghurs blew themselves up at a train station, injuring eighty people. But Xi's speeches, as revealed later by the *New York Times*, show that he had already been planning—well before his trip—a brutal crackdown using mass surveillance, mass internment, political indoctrination, and forced labor. And he didn't care what the world thought about it. "We must be as harsh as them," Xi said in one of his speeches, "and show absolutely no mercy."

In 2016, Xi appointed the CCP's top man in Tibet, Chen Quanguo, to be the new party chief in Xinjiang. Chen quickly issued orders to "round up everyone who should be rounded up," purging any local officials who didn't obey. He began constructing a network of what he called "vocational skills, education training and transformation centers." But based on what could be seen from satellite imagery and on-the-ground reporting, they were identical to prisons. The region's already omnipresent networks of AI-powered cameras and other surveillance tools were tasked with identifying entire classes of people to jail, based on the most random and previously innocent behaviors, such as refusing to eat pork or having a beard.

Years later, the International Consortium of Investigative Journalists would release a series of internal documents it called "the China Cables," which revealed how Chinese authorities used technology to justify interning people they suspected of future crimes. They also persecuted Uyghurs living abroad, tracking them and trying to get them deported back to China for jailing. Anyone with exposure to the West was a prime target. Entire communities of academics, artists, students, and authors were disappeared. Leaked manuals detail instructions for the prisons to prevent escapes, indoctrinate inmates, and, above all, keep the entire system a secret from the outside world.

Secrecy was China's goal, at least. But by the second half of 2018, the circumstantial evidence was so strong, the world could no longer ignore the camps and China could no longer deny their existence. The confrontation that resulted would expose the naked truth of China's bid for international power — and the implications for ordinary people the world over, in China or beyond.

"You Shouldn't Talk About the Uyghurs"

After UN ambassador Nikki Haley mentioned the plight of the Uyghurs publicly at the UN for the first time in the summer of 2018, the Chinese permanent representative Ma Zhaoxu asked to see her. He came to Haley's residence the very next day for a meeting she was hosting for the representatives from all the permanent security council members, but asked to stay after to talk with Haley one-on-one. Once he had her alone, he handed her a thick dossier of information. Here's how the conversation went, according to Haley:

MA: You shouldn't talk about the Uyghurs. You don't understand. You need to understand why we do this.

HALEY: Help me understand why you were putting them into this situation and forcing them to think differently.

MA: But you don't know who these people are.

HALEY: Who are they?

MA: They're criminals.

HALEY: What crimes have they committed?

MA: They do bad things. They rob, they steal.

HALEY: Are you saying they've been arrested?

MA: Yes.

HALEY: So, they have all committed acts of crime?

MA: Well, some have, and some we know will.

Haley described the meeting as "bizarre." The Chinese leadership had seen the outrage in the international community about the reporting on the internment camps, and this is what they had instructed their UN representative to tell people. Ma went on about how they were teaching the Uyghurs a trade, for their own good, so they can steer clear of a life of crime.

"It was a very telling conversation," Haley told me. "He wasn't honest, but this is how they were selling it."

Despite Xi's best efforts, over the course of 2018 the awareness and alarm steadily rose about the Chinese government's ever-tightening control over its own citizens and its brutal mass internment of over one million Uyghur and other ethnic minorities. Large proportions of the adults in towns and cities across Xinjiang Province were being swept into prison camps that were popping up all over the place.

The Uyghurs in Xinjiang already lived in an open-air prison, monitored 24/7 by the most invasive and pervasive technological and human surveillance system ever deployed on a civilian population. The Chinese government had already sent one million or so Han Chinese to Xinjiang to live with Uyghur families in their homes without their consent, so they could spy on them and report back. The CCP called the program Pair Up and Become Family. One day, a new Han Chinese "relative" would just show up at a Uyghur household and start taking notes. The government was also attempting to snuff out the Uyghurs' religion by leveling hundreds of mosques and making the practice of Islam on a daily basis grounds for being thrown into a camp. Using the guise of fighting terrorism, the CCP waged war on all non-Han Chinese in the province.

The Chinese government was trying to sinicize the region and dilute, if not extinguish, the religion, identity, and culture of over eleven million people. The Uyghurs saw this as ethnic cleansing; the Tibetans prefer the term "cultural genocide." The stories of torture in the camps, forced sterilization, political indoctrination, and family separation are too numerous to recount, but they make a strong case for the charge of crimes against humanity. So many children were effectively orphaned after their parents were sent to the camps that the authorities began shipping them to orphanages in other parts of China by the thousands. Some parents got their kids back when they got out; many didn't. Thousands of innocently imprisoned civilians, meanwhile, were "released" only to be sent to work at factories in other provinces, without being offered any choice. That's called mass forced labor—just one crime against humanity on the long list of offenses for which China will someday have to answer.

Trump may not have objected to China's human rights depredations, but in Congress there was a unique bipartisan coalition coming together to call for sanctions. Steven Mnuchin fought against them tooth and nail. Whenever the subject of sanctioning Chinese officials or entities came up, the Treasury Department would have an objection. Sometimes, Mnuchin used delay tactics, like withholding documents from the White House that were necessary for sanctions to go forward. Sometimes he would call for a meeting of the principals committee, which caused a delay and gave him a chance to weigh in personally against a sanctions measure. Sometimes, Mnuchin would have his allies on Capitol Hill throw a wrench in a sanctions bill on his behalf. He had a full box of tools for protecting Beijing from sanctions, and he used them liberally.

Orwell on the East Side

The Chinese government was so sensitive about even discussing the situation in Xinjiang, it worked in March 2018 to bar the head of the World Uyghur Congress, Dolkun Isa, a German citizen, from even speaking at the annual UN Permanent Forum on Indigenous Issues at UN headquarters in Manhattan. The Chinese UN office had Isa flagged as a terrorist by the UN security office to keep him from entering the building.

It took two days for Kelley Currie, a top US UN official, to convince the UN security apparatus that Isa was not a terrorist but in fact a dissident and human rights activist. Isa was allowed to speak on the final day. But that was not the end of it for Beijing. The Chinese delegation then tried to revoke the consultative status of the German nongovernmental organization that sponsored Isa, the Society for Threatened Peoples, essentially trying to throw them out of the UN as well.

In a heated exchange, Currie called out the Muslim-majority countries like Pakistan that had defended the Chinese position, just out of blind loyalty, and she called on the Chinese representative to produce evidence of his charges.

"This is a very sad and disappointing day to see this committee and particularly members of this committee who espouse to uphold the tenets of Islam indulging in the Chinese delegation's islamophobia today, in which they conflate the efforts of an individual to advance the religious and human rights of a persecuted minority in China with terrorism," she said.

The Chinese delegate scolded Currie for "using very bad words" and said, "I can't understand why she was so emotional." The Chinese government has always paid attention to and protected the rights of all the ethnic minorities, including the Uyghur people, he said. Beijing, he said with a straight face, respects their religious freedom and their freedom of speech. "A long time ago we have abolished the reeducation through labor system," he said. "The Uyghurs and other ethnic minorities in Xinjiang have seen the best protection of their human rights in history."

China didn't just want the world to ignore its atrocities in Xinjiang; Beijing actually tried to change the international human rights rules to avoid accountability and justify their actions. In March 2018, China introduced a resolution at the Human Rights Council called "Promoting the International Human Rights Cause Through Win-Win Cooperation." It would encourage "dialogue" and "cooperation" to resolve human rights complaints, rather than punishment.

Currie traveled to Geneva to oppose it. She referred to Xi Jinping's "win-win" mantra and accused Chinese diplomats of using the resolution "to glorify their head of state by inserting his thoughts into the international human rights lexicon."

The resolution passed overwhelmingly. Only the United States voted no. Australia, Japan, Britain, and Switzerland abstained.

These moves by Beijing should not be dismissed as mere politics or propaganda. For a long time, China had economic power but not "discourse power"—the ability to shape the ideas that underpin the international order. But as its material power has grown, its self-confidence and leverage have increased. And now China's leaders are putting into action their plan to reshape international norms to protect the party and China's interests, said Nadège Rolland of the National Bureau of Asian Research.

"An authoritarian illiberal power is not going to want the world to be liberal and free. It wants an order that mirrors its own nature," she told me. "So what China wants for itself it wants for the rest of the world."

Beijing pretended they wanted to play along with our conception of the international order as much as they could, but this is over now, she said. China wants to shape that order and that system in a way that not only gives them a better say. It's about changing the concepts and principles that undermine the current order because they threaten the CCP's survival.

Of course, Trump himself made these kinds of efforts much easier for China by expressing open disdain for multilateral organizations and the order they enforce, abdicating America's historical leadership on this issue beyond anything Nikki Haley or Kelley Currie could make up for, no matter how hard they tried.

"America should be the embodiment and leader of the free world. It has to be," Rolland said. "If you don't believe in those values and don't lead in that direction, there's a whole powerful side of your strategy that is missing."

China's United Nations

Haley told me the biggest shock for her as UN ambassador was how China had not only taken over so many parts of the UN but also enlisted the parts they didn't run to do China's bidding. For example, few people realize that China has signed twenty-six memorandums of understanding with UN organizations for cooperation related to their massive Belt and Road Initiative (BRI).

China has effectively enlisted the United Nations to help organize and fund their own economic expansion, a $2 trillion infrastructure project known for trapping countries in predatory debt schemes, flooding elites in developing countries with bribes, wreaking havoc on the environment, and spreading Chinese influence.

One reason that Beijing has worked so hard to control areas populated by ethnic minorities and repress the freedom of people there is that these regions of China are critical to BRI and China's economic expansion into central Asia. The crackdowns in Xinjiang are partially in service of Beijing's need to develop that land for a major BRI project that runs through the region to Pakistan.

The US policy is to discourage other countries from participating in BRI, but US officials didn't even notice when twenty-six UN agencies signed up with China to be involved in the project. When they figured it out, much of it was already too far along to reverse. But to at least do something, the US delegation started insisting that language supporting BRI be removed from new UN documents, statements, and memorandums. "This was their strategic map for military installations, for utilities, for all of those things and that's why they were so incredibly aggressive about BRI," said Haley. "The more they could get other countries to sign on, the more they could get multilateral organizations to buy in, they all became advertising arms for BRI."

It didn't help that Chinese officials had successfully taken over four of the fifteen official UN organizations. In each case, there followed some mischief or shadiness. After a Chinese official took over the International Civil Aviation Organization (ICAO), the organization stopped inviting Taiwan to its annual assembly. ICAO hid for months a major hack of its servers that originated from China. The ICAO leadership then retaliated against the whistleblower who exposed the cover-up.

Since China assumed leadership of the International Telecommunication Union in 2015, the organization has drastically increased cooperation with Beijing, among other things by defending Chinese telecom giant Huawei. The United Nations Department of Economic and Social Affairs, also led by a Chinese official, is pushing BRI and is building a "big data research institute" inside China in partnership with Beijing. In 2018, Chinese official Meng Hongwei, then the head of Interpol, was secretly sent back to China, where he was prosecuted for corruption and given a thirteen-year prison sentence.

Secretary General António Guterres was among the most deferential to Beijing, Haley said, endorsing the BRI project and generally backing down when Beijing exerted pressure, even on small items. When Haley tried to change the rule barring Taiwanese citizens from being able to enter the UN headquarters with a Taiwanese ID, she raised the issue with the secretary general personally. But Ma, the Chinese ambassador, went to see Guterres about it and threatened him. "As we started to fix it, the Chinese blew such a gasket," Haley said. "[Guterres] was so shaken by the meeting afterwards. They had come down on him so hard that if this happened, there would be hell to pay."

The secretary general backed down. As of this writing, you still can't visit the UN headquarters with a Taiwanese ID.

A Cluster of Lanterns

Perhaps the most egregious story of China making a power grab at an international organization centers not on the United Nations but rather on the World Bank. There, Beijing has received the help of the bank's American, Obama-appointed president, Jim Kim, to advance the CCP's interests and expand its program of economic aggression—all at an institution that is nominally one of the bastions of global capitalism.

When the Chinese government hosted a major international conference for the Belt and Road Initiative in Beijing in May 2017, World Bank president Jim Kim didn't just attend the event; he went out of his way to praise Xi Jinping and endorse BRI on behalf of the World Bank.

"Asian countries are just like a cluster of bright lanterns. Only when we link them together, can we light up the night sky in our continent," he said at the opening session, quoting Xi. "As someone who was born in Korea, I'm inspired by the Belt and Road Initiative . . . And the World Bank Group very proudly supports the government of China's ambitious, unprecedented effort to light up that night sky."

Kim and the heads of several other multilateral development finance institutions signed agreements to participate in BRI at the forum. It would only be the beginning of Kim's involvement in the project.

In November 2018, Kim traveled to Beijing again, to attend the International Forum on China's Reform and Opening Up and Poverty Reduction at the Diaoyutai State Guest House. In his speech, Kim praised the CCP's development policies, its lifting up of hundreds of millions of its citizens out of poverty, and its "reform and opening up." "With the 19th party congress of October 2017, China has positioned itself as an example to emulate," Kim said. He quoted Xi's speech, in which Xi said China's model "offers a new option for other countries and nations who want to speed up their development while preserving their independence; and it offers Chinese wisdom and a Chinese approach to solving the problems facing mankind." "Other countries," Kim said, "are looking to China as a source of knowledge and experience, and the World Bank Group will continue to support China's growing international role."

This trip was the crowning achievement of Kim's multiyear effort to help the Chinese government gain a huge amount of influence and control at the World Bank and to get the World Bank to help Beijing expand its economic strategy. But it was only his latest, greatest triumph.

In January 2016, Kim had given the number two position at the World Bank to a Chinese official named Yang Shaolin, a former Chinese finance ministry official who had served as China's representative at the bank for several years, reportedly in response to a personal request by Xi. Yang's title was managing director and chief administrative officer, a new position that didn't exist before, and with a broad mandate that gave him general control over the budget of the World Bank. The human resources staff and the information technology department also reported up to him.

While Kim was president, other top bank officials from China included Wei Wang, the head of "human resources business partnerships," and a man named Jin-yong Cai, who had been the CEO of the International Finance Corporation (IFC) and was known for helping Chinese state-owned enterprises get business in developing countries.

When Cai took over the IFC in 2013, European journalist Elliot Wilson wrote, "Cai knows China inside and out. He has strong contacts at key regulators and ministries, and within the all-powerful grouping of state-owned enterprises, and his logical career progression, post-IFC, will surely be as a member of China's political elite."

Cai stepped down from the IFC in 2015 along with Kim's CFO, Bertrand Badré, amid a scandal over their involvement in an unusually structured $1 billion Chinese loan to the World Bank's development fund. Cai landed at a private equity firm called TPG Capital, but he remained close with Kim and spent lots of time with him at the World Bank. TPG wanted to raise billions of dollars from Chinese investment. He didn't last long before leaving the firm.

Two months after his speech in Beijing, Jim Kim abruptly quit his job as president of the World Bank with barely an explanation. He took a job within days with a firm called Global Infrastructure Partners, which was a private equity fund heavily involved in projects related to BRI. Four months later, Global Infrastructure Partners hired Kim's friend Cai to work with him there.

Kim's philosophy, that it was the World Bank's job to help China succeed economically, could arguably have fit into the Obama administration's basic approach, which was to engage with China economically as much as possible. But by 2018, this was counter to US policy. More importantly, the information coming out of Xinjiang showed the truth of how China's development policies were being implemented—with no regard for the rights of the people in the way of the projects or the environment they lived in.

And although Kim, as World Bank president, had to consider the interests of lots of different stakeholders, including China, on his watch China was the bank's number one recipient of aid as well as the country whose companies received more World Bank contract money than any other nation.

Kim went out of his way to steer World Bank money into China and help China reap benefits from its exploits in the rest of the developing world. Why he did it, we can only speculate. But the fact that he is profiting from the Belt and Road Initiative he helped to push provides one explanation.

Vera's Story

China's efforts to co-opt the United Nations and other international organizations to help its development plans were part and parcel of its drive to hide Chinese atrocities in Xinjiang. Foreign governments were threatened with losing lucrative deals if they dared speak up. Most Arab- and Muslim-majority countries looked the other way. But the issue gained traction in the United States because Beijing's persecution of Uyghurs and other minorities affects Americans as well.

Hundreds of American citizens and permanent residents have family members in the camps. All twenty-six Uyghur reporters for Radio Free Asia, a US government media outlet that has been reporting on the situation, have family members who have been arrested or disappeared.

Sometimes the survivors come back to the United States and tell their stories. One of those survivors told her story to me. Her name is Vera Zhou.

On October 17, 2017, Zhou, a sophomore at the University of Washington in Seattle, was visiting her father in Xinjiang. She was scheduled to return to Seattle, where she lived with her mother, on the 25th. On the 23rd, she logged in to her school's VPN to file her homework. At eleven o'clock that night, the police called her and asked her to come to the local police station right away. She arrived at midnight. The local officials wouldn't say anything except that police from the nearby city of Urumchi were on the way. Three hours later, officials in plain clothes arrived and told her they needed to bring her back to Urumchi immediately.

"I asked them what this was about. They didn't tell me anything. They just told me to get into their van. After I got in the van, they handcuffed me. No explanation. That's when I started to cry."

When they arrived at the Urumchi police station, the officials asked her some basic questions about her visit to China and whether she had used a VPN. She said she had, to submit her homework. They took her fingerprints, took her photo, and took a blood sample. At about eight in the morning, the police took her to the hospital for a more thorough checkup, handcuffing her for the ride. About four hours later, the lead official announced the verdict.

"He told me I had to go study at the relocation camp," she said. Zhou received no other explanation. The authorities refused to answer any questions. She was allowed to call her father, but he didn't pick up. They confiscated her passport and her US green card (she is a US permanent resident) and all of her other possessions. Two hours later, she was delivered to the camp, a three-floor prison building about thirty minutes outside the city center. Vera didn't know anything about the camps before her arrest. She didn't know the hell she was about to endure.

Vera was led to a small room with six bunkbeds and told to change into a prison uniform. There were two cameras in the room and a speaker, so the twelve women packed in there knew they were being watched twenty-four hours a day. Her father eventually was allowed to come to visit the camp for a fifteen-minute heavily supervised visit. He was too afraid of retaliation to say anything. That was the only time she saw him during her five-month imprisonment.

The women were only allowed to leave the room for "class," where they would be taught simple Chinese and forced to sing patriotic CCP songs. They were never allowed to go outside. They got their meals by passing a plastic bowl out of the cell door to be filled with slop. Vera only left the building once, when she had to go to the hospital. She had recently had major surgery. Aside from that one checkup, though, she was not allowed the medical care that her surgery required.

One of the women in Vera's room was still breastfeeding her baby when she was arrested, but they were separated. Some women had entire families imprisoned in the camp. One of Vera's cellmates was a reporter for the Chinese state media but was a Uyghur. She was arrested because another Uyghur man the authorities deemed an extremist had been on her flight, completely unbeknownst to her. Once, by chance, that woman saw a group of men from the floor below pass by in the hallway and she recognized her father among them. That was how the woman discovered her father was also in the camp.

The women had to talk carefully. Prisoners were rewarded for snitching on each other, creating fear even among the cellmates. Vera wasn't allowed to talk about her life in the West. None of the minority women were allowed to speak their native languages. The guards had a point system, where prisoners could earn the right to see or even have dinner with their families.

"You can earn points by doing good on the tests or you have to tell the director something that happened in the room, like spying on others," she said. "That's the really scary part. We were afraid of each other."

But Vera's nightmare was just beginning.

She was eventually released five months later with no explanation, although she was told to stay inside her father's apartment and told cameras on the street would recognize her face if she disobeyed. She still didn't have her US passport or her green card, so she couldn't leave China.

Back in Seattle, her mother, Mary Caiyun Ma, was furiously trying to get her daughter help. She called the University of Washington, but they said there was nothing they could do to help. Adding insult to injury, the university kept billing Vera tuition and then trying to collect the unpaid debt. Her federal loans lapsed. Her unpaid rent destroyed her credit.

Finally, Ma got in touch with Pastor Bob Fu, a nongovernmental organization leader with good connections in DC. Fu got her meetings with the State Department, the National Security Council, and members of

Congress. The State Department officials reached out to the Office of the President at the University of Washington, with Vera's mom and Bob Fu in the room. The response from the university official was chilling.

"They said bluntly we can't do anything for her, we have a $3 million deal negotiated with China," said Fu.

The State Department pressed the Chinese government to let Zhou leave China and return to the United States. On September 15, 2019, the authorities gave her back her passport. They told her not to speak out about the camps and threatened her father's safety if she disobeyed. She returned to Seattle with no school, no apartment, and no job. She spoke out, despite the threats, because she wants people to know the truth.

"What they did to a lot of people, this should be published," she told me. "We have a right to know what they are doing to those Uyghurs and Kazakhs and other innocent people."

Despite Trump's comment to Xi endorsing the Uyghur internment camps, the US government did gradually work to raise awareness of these atrocities and pressure the rest of the international community to respond. In September 2019, the State Department hosted an event featuring camp survivors on the sideline of the UN General Assembly in New York. Later, the State and Treasury Departments would sanction Chinese officials involved in the repression and companies profiting from the forced labor.

But like many other parts of the Trump administration's China strategy, the effectiveness was undermined by the overall unpredictability and incoherence that characterized the Trump administration's foreign policy. There were too many signals coming from too many different parts of the administration for anyone else to understand what they were trying to do. The State Department would try to correct this by laying out the overall argument for a Trump administration China approach in 2019. But that wouldn't go so well either.

10

Cold War Redux

Over the cold early months of 1946, a diplomat typed away in the bowels of the American embassy in Moscow. He sent an eight-thousand-word document over the wires to the State Department in Washington, where its conclusions caused a stir. George F. Kennan's "Long Telegram" was the first official document to warn that the Soviet Union, America's erstwhile World War II ally, whose armies had been indispensable to defeating Hitler, now posed a direct and dire threat to US national security. Buried deep within the Soviet DNA, Kennan warned, was the belief that its security could only be ensured by a "patient but deadly struggle for total destruction of rival power." He penned a public version that appeared in *Foreign Affairs* the following year under an anonymous byline "X" and entitled "The Sources of Soviet Conduct."

These two documents were Kennan's attempts to focus his government and the American public on what he believed was the key challenge of his time. The documents also became the basis for a decades-long policy of containment, the notion that America's goal should be to slow down and limit the Soviet expansion at all costs. The containment policy is credited with America's victory over the Soviet Union in the Cold War. "Letter X," as Kennan's anonymous essay in *Foreign Affairs* came to be known, argued that the Soviet threat required "a long-term, patient but firm and vigilant containment of Russian expansive tendencies."

"Soviet pressure against the free institutions of the Western world is something that can be contained by the adroit and vigilant application of counterforce at a series of constantly shifting geographical and political points, corresponding to the shifts and maneuvers of Soviet policy, but which cannot be charmed or talked out of existence," he wrote.

Kennan became the State Department's first-ever director of the Office of Policy Planning, known as the department's internal think tank, and there he helped Secretary of State George Marshall devise his plan to support Europe's revival after the war. But Marshall's successor, Dean Acheson, had his own ideas about how to counter Soviet expansion, and he brought on his own policy planning director, Paul Nitze, to help him implement them. Kennan had defined the problem, but Nitze and those like him got to devise the solution.

The document Nitze and his cohorts produced in 1950, called NSC 68, took Kennan's containment theory in a distinctly militarized direction. NSC 68 was a top-secret document that painted the challenge of the Soviet Union's rise in stark terms. "The issues that face us are momentous," the document stated, "involving the fulfillment or destruction not only of this Republic but of civilization itself." It called for a tripling of the US defense budget and a military buildup to prevent the Soviet Union from achieving "world domination." The document called for the United States to rally the free world to increase its military and economic strength, as well as its nuclear arsenal.

Kennan, out of government when NSC 68 was written, rejected Nitze's call for mass conventional and nuclear arms buildups. He believed the Soviet threat could be contained chiefly through political and economic means. When John Foster Dulles became secretary of state, Kennan warned him that US policy was becoming overconsumed by "emotional, moralistic attitudes," which, "unless corrected, can easily carry us toward real conflict with the Russians." For example, Kennan supported the US participation in defending South Korea from North Korean invasion in 1950, but not the plan to forcibly unite all of Korea under an anti-Soviet regime.

The fact that Kennan opposed much of the Cold War policy he is often credited with inspiring is lost on most Americans. Even in Washington, his name is casually invoked several times a month at various think tank panel events as the man who devised the Cold War plan that defeated the Soviet Union. And while it's true, of course, that the United States won the Cold War, there's actually no agreement on why the Soviet Union collapsed.

Was it really because the United States had fought or funded third-party proxy wars while building up a military arsenal that the Soviet state bankrupted itself trying to match? Was it the clever diplomacy embodied by the Helsinki Accords and several series of arms control agreements that drew Soviets into so many binding commitments they just couldn't pursue their own aggression? Or was it that the people of the Soviet Union sought a better life and a better government and placed enough internal pressure on their leaders until the system cracked?

Never mind all that. On most days in Washington, the discussion boils down to a simplistic remembrance of history: Kennan crafted the Cold War containment strategy and we won the Cold War. That leads to another common refrain: we need another Kennan and another Long Telegram for the new struggle with China.

On one particular day in Washington, April 24, 2019, the Trump administration's answer to Kennan managed not only to bungle the history of Kennan but also to create a worldwide and completely unnecessary scandal in the process. This is the story of the State Department's failed initial attempt to devise, much less articulate, an overall argument for dealing with China.

Clash of Civilizations

When Mike Pompeo became secretary of state, he was determined to leave his mark as a China hardliner. He knew Trump prioritized the trade deal above all, but he wanted to make China a focus of his tenure, and so he staffed up for that purpose. He filled the post of assistant secretary of state for East Asian and Pacific affairs with a brigadier general from Indo-Pacific Command named David Stilwell, a proud hardliner. He hired as a senior adviser Mary Kissel, a *Wall Street Journal* columnist who had lived and reported from Hong Kong. Pompeo held what he called "Saturday Sessions" on China outside the State Department and invited outside experts like Michael Pillsbury to come and talk through various China-related issues.

But Pompeo made one big mistake when he chose Kiron Skinner to be his new policy planning director (the same job Kennan had) and gave her the project of devising an overarching strategic argument for how to deal with China.

On paper, Skinner was perfectly qualified. Like Kennan, she had a PhD from Harvard in political science. At age twenty-three, she had met then Stanford junior faculty member Condoleezza Rice and enlisted her to serve on her dissertation review committee, the beginning of a long mentorship. Skinner had done research for the memoir of another secretary of state, George Shultz. She was a tenured professor at Carnegie Mellon with a list of publications to her credit and strong ties to the national security community in Washington.

Skinner had a political identity too. She served on the foreign policy staff of the presidential campaigns of George W. Bush, Rand Paul, Newt Gingrich, and eventually Donald Trump. The Trump campaign was like the film *The Dirty Dozen,* where the rejects of the GOP foreign policy establishment were assembled and sent on a mission of certain suicide. Not many of them survived to actually serve in the administration. Skinner lasted only a few days on the transition team before she clashed with other early Trump administration officials and vanished from the scene.

Rex Tillerson chose Brian Hook, a conventional GOP establishment type, to be his policy planning director. Hook's focus was Iran. When Pompeo replaced Tillerson, he wanted new blood. Skinner seemed like a logical choice. What Pompeo didn't know was that she was a management disaster and a public relations liability. But that became clear when Skinner took the stage on April 24, 2019, for a public event hosted by the New America Foundation, run by another Harvard alumnus and former State Department director of policy planning, Anne-Marie Slaughter.

The State Department's policy planning shop "is the place where the containment doctrine was born," Slaughter began. "Everybody who holds this role serves in the shadow of George Kennan and containment and the Marshall plan."

She asked Skinner, what exactly is the Trump doctrine? This was a popular question to ask Trump officials in public, because there was no real answer and each official who answered it usually just inserted their own worldview mashed up with whatever Trump had said recently. Skinner simply said it was "evolving" and that her job was to develop it.

"Part of my job is to provide the intellectual architecture for the Trump doctrine," she said. "If it doesn't happen at policy planning, the only foreign policy think tank in the government, it doesn't happen."

She laid out what she saw as the pillars of a Trump doctrine: a preference for national sovereignty above international organizations and international law, a laser focus on the American interest, a push for reciprocity from our adversaries and more burden sharing from our friends.

"He provides the hunches and instincts and it's my job with Secretary Pompeo to turn those hunches and instincts into a hypothesis," she said, adding that there was a "Pompeo corollary" to the Trump doctrine, which she was also in charge of developing, details to come later.

Nobody in the crowd likely believed that Skinner was in charge of Trump's foreign policy. But that kind of vague pablum was common enough in these think tank panels even before Trump. The problems started when the topic turned to China. Skinner said the White House economic crew had gotten hold of the China issue early on in the administration and that the State Department needed to reassert its role. Then she revealed that Pompeo's shop was working on their own paper that would trace the sources of Chinese Communist Party (CCP) conduct and how America should respond.

"State is in the lead in that attempt to get something like a Letter X for China, that Kennan wrote," she said. "You can't have a policy without an argument underneath it. What hasn't happened in this century is to advance the argument, and that is what we are working on at State. And if it will happen, it will happen at the State Department."

It's true Pompeo had initiated an effort to produce an internal document to guide US-China policy. Skinner called it "Letter X," incorrectly referring to the *Foreign Affairs* article Kennan wrote and misremembering which Kennan document she was attempting to re-create, the Long Telegram. But the bigger problem was what she said next.

"This is a fight with a really different civilization and a different ideology and the United States really hasn't had that before," she said. "It's also striking that it's the first time we will have a great power competitor who is not Caucasian."

Slaughter, hearing the word "civilization," immediately responded by invoking the only foreign policy trope more common at think tank events than invoking Kennan. "It's like Huntington's 'Clash of Civilizations,'" she said, referring to yet another Harvard PhD holder, Samuel Huntington, whose famous work dividing the world into a set of civilizational entities was the first item on my International Affairs 101 syllabus as a freshman at the George Washington University.

Slaughter could have just pointed out that what Skinner said was totally inaccurate (see Japan). Instead, she decided to point out that the United States is not all Caucasian (which is true, but not the point). Skinner replied that the foreign policy elite establishment is actually very heavily Caucasian (which is also true, but also not the point). The event ended without either realizing the controversy they had just unleashed.

Losing the Battle of Ideas

The condemnation and ridicule of Skinner after the event came swiftly and from all sides. For some, it was proof that the Trump foreign policy doctrine was racist. For others, it was proof that the Trump team was provoking the "clash" in the "Clash of Civilizations." For others, it was just evidence that Skinner was out of her depth.

Skinner was put into what I call the "senior official witness protection program," never to be allowed to speak in public again. Four months later, she was fired amid allegations of management abuse and chaos in her shop. Her staff had reported that she was prone to yelling, making homophobic remarks, alleging her staffers were sleeping with each other, and retaliating against anyone who complained.

If Skinner's Long Telegram project was primarily meant to offer an opening salvo in the US-China war of ideas, the scandal ensured that Beijing won this skirmish. The Chinese media had a field day with it and the Chinese government never let it go.

"The Director of Policy Planning Kiron Skinner seems to be quite blunt about her deeply-rooted racism," read a commentary in China's *Global Times,* accusing her of disrespecting her own African American community's victimization at the hands of Caucasians. "What she believes is groundless, as harmony remains a major feature of Chinese civilization."

This accusation of racism is a feature of CCP criticism of any person or policy in the United States that dares call out China for its aggression or calls for an approach that is more hawkish than the current one. It's particularly astonishing coming from the regime that is imprisoning over one million ethnic Uyghurs and other Muslim minorities, repressing millions of Tibetans, and systematically discriminating against all non-Han Chinese inside China.

But Beijing didn't let it go. At the largest international conference of Asian defense ministers in early June, called the Shangri-La Dialogue (named after the hotel that hosts it), China's state councillor and minister of national defense, Wei Fenghe, brought up Skinner's remarks in his official speech: "History witnessed the enslavement of Africans, the expulsion of Native American Indians, the colonization in Asia, Africa and Latin America, and the killing of Jewish people. These are scars and tragedies in the history of human civilization which do not go away. Unfortunately, some people recently picked up the decadent idea of the clash of civilizations. As racist and narrow-minded as it is, this is not right. How can we tolerate such a regress of history?"

Wei's speech was a clear signal the Chinese were feeling confident in their position and their argument that Beijing was pursuing "win-win" outcomes, peaceful development, and all the rest. The Chinese delegation's confidence was bolstered by the tone struck by countries like Singapore, whose prime minister, Lee Hsien Loong, gave a speech warning against "zero-sum outcomes" and also criticized Skinner's remarks about civilization and ideology.

If the Trump administration were organized, this event would have been a great opportunity for US government officials in attendance to correct the record, fix the misperception, and push back on the Chinese gaslighting about which side was being aggressive and which side was racist in its policies. But unfortunately, the US delegation was led by an acting secretary of defense named Patrick Shanahan, a tragic figure even in the context of an administration full of them.

The Rise and Fall of Pat Shanahan

Patrick Shanahan, a former Boeing executive, was thrust into the role of acting defense secretary after James Mattis resigned in protest in response to Trump's sudden decision to withdraw from Syria in December 2018. Speaking on his very first day as acting head of the Defense Department in January, Shanahan said his focus would be "China, China, China."

Five months later, standing at the podium in Singapore representing the United States at the Shangri-La Dialogue, Shanahan had been nominated to be the defense secretary on a permanent basis, but he was not yet confirmed. This was his chance to show the assembled officials and lawmakers in the audience he fit the role. But in a disappointing performance, he delivered basic talking points on the need for both cooperation and competition with China. He didn't bother to push back on the Chinese defense minister's racism accusations or talk about how Skinner's reference to a clash of civilizations was a misunderstanding.

Minutes after Shanahan's speech, the Pentagon released its first-ever *Indo-Pacific Strategy Report*, a sixty-four-page document that declared Asia was the Defense Department's "priority theatre" and reaffirmed the National Defense Strategy's declaration that China was a "revisionist power."

Was this the Long Telegram for China, Pentagon edition? Not at all. For one thing, it only dealt with the military part of the equation. Neither Shanahan nor the report ever got to the larger issue at hand—namely, what were China's intentions and what does that require us as a country to do? Hoping to force Shanahan to address that point, I asked him in the open plenary session how his promise to elevate the China issue was any different from the same exact promise made by every US defense secretary who had stood behind that same podium.

He responded that the Trump administration had fully resourced its pivot to Asia, unlike past administrations, which wasn't true. He said the United States was finally talking openly about China's bad behavior, as if that was something new. And he praised the Trump administration's engagement with regional allies and partners, which is actually one of the worst parts of the Trump administration's China policy. "Those are the three areas," he told me, "where I think fundamentally, if you were to measure the difference, people would look at those and say, 'This is a departure from what has been done in the past.'"

That was the last major event Shanahan ever spoke at while employed by the US government. He never got confirmed as defense secretary. Later that month, it was revealed that he had failed to disclose that he had been accused of spousal abuse as part of a tragic series of family events years prior that had resulted in the arrest of his then wife, her subsequent violent assault at the hands of their oldest son, and Shanahan's alleged efforts to hide that son from law enforcement after the attack. When the news broke, Shanahan withdrew from consideration.

Shanahan thought that in the Trump administration, personal scandals were forgivable, and he also wanted to protect his family from the publicity. But he wasn't really an insider on the Trump team whom the president was willing to stand behind. And when the scandal broke, the White House cut bait. Shanahan resigned in disgrace. He never got to implement his "China, China, China" plan, if he did indeed have one.

Cold War by Another Name

Throughout the Trump administration, officials who were pushing for a pivot to Asia repeatedly came to realize that for a variety of reasons, the money just wasn't there to make credible the claim that America was shifting its focus to the region. Similar to what had happened under Obama, cabinet members made speeches, strategy documents were released, but then the actual support for doing the things promised got delayed or diverted or just never materialized.

While in Singapore, I met with the head of Indo-Pacific Command, Admiral Philip Davidson, who had replaced Harry Harris after he had become the ambassador to South Korea. Davidson came from Fleet Command, a position that wasn't focused solely on Asia and wasn't in the public eye. It was the first interview he had done since assuming command a year prior. There was simply no upside in the Trump administration for generals and admirals to risk speaking to the press.

I asked him the same question I had asked Shanahan in open session: How is this Asia pivot different from all the others? Like Shanahan, he pointed to the new consensus that had allegedly come together in the US government. But privately, Davidson knew that the US government was talking a big game but not doing all that was needed to actually win it.

Davidson wrote a letter in April 2019, later leaked, calling on Congress to provide "immediate and necessary resources" to fill gaps in Indo-Pacific Command's budget: military construction, Aegis missile defense, the defense of Guam, and much more. He called it his "Regain the Advantage" plan, which was understood to be referring to China. The implicit suggestion was that our military advantage in the Pacific had dangerously eroded.

About a year later, a senior aide to Davidson called me in Washington and asked me for my analysis on why—even at that point—the administration and Congress had failed to give Indo-Pacific Command the money it needed to make their new Indo-Pacific strategy work. I told him if the leadership of Indo-Pacific Command was asking me why they weren't getting support from Washington, the problem was worse than I thought. I checked it out anyway. There were no good answers. Bureaucratic intransigence, competing priorities, budget delays in Congress, lack of strong leadership atop the Defense Department to advocate these interests, and overall Washington dysfunction. New administration, same claims of a pivot to Asia that were never realized.

I asked Davidson whether the United States and China were entering or perhaps had already entered a new cold war.

"I'm not calling this a cold war. But the idea of competition and how long it took in the actual Cold War, that may be what it's all about," he said. "We've been in the beginning stages for many years now, but we weren't in the competition. Now we are in the competition."

His answer was telling. It didn't matter if we call it a Cold War with big capital letters, in his view. It's the closest analogy we have in our collective modern historical memory. It's not the same as the Cold War for the obvious reason that China in 2020 is not the same as Russia in 1950. If anything, the China challenge is orders of magnitude more difficult because of China's massive economic power and our economies' deep interconnectedness. But if you believed, as Davidson did, that China's ambitions were in fact worldwide — that the CCP was trying to reshape the global order to fit its interests and that this posed an unacceptable threat to the security, prosperity, and health of free and open societies — then the comparison to the Cold War was useful, insofar as it helped one grasp the scope and scale and stakes of the challenge.

When I asked Pence the same question during a flight on Air Force 2 from Tokyo to Singapore in 2018, he told me it was up to China to avoid a new cold war. His point was that Beijing, not Washington, was changing its behavior in a way that was fueling the deep tensions between the two sides. In Bangkok in late 2019, Defense Secretary Mark Esper gave me a similar answer: "We're not the ones looking for a Cold War. All we are asking is for China to follow the rules, live by the international norms, live up to your commitments and obligations," he told me. "If

China wants to do it, China can do it. But China is either choosing not to or ignoring it."

For the CCP, the term "cold war" is a cudgel to swing at any American who dares criticize its actions — half gaslighting, half threat. It's part of their information operation against us: Why would you crazy Americans want to start a cold war when all China wants is win-win cooperation? The term is so loaded and abused it is basically no longer useful. CIA deputy director for East Asia Michael Collins probably put it best during a panel at the 2018 Aspen Security Forum: "What they're waging against us is fundamentally a cold war. A cold war not like we saw during the Cold War, but a cold war by definition," he said. "The Chinese do not want conflict. They do not want war. They do not want conflagration. But at the end of the day, they want every country around the world, when it's deciding its interests, its decisions on policy issues, to first and foremost side with China, not the United States, because the Chinese are increasingly defining a conflict with the United States and what we stand behind as a systems conflict."

At the Bloomberg New Economy Forum in Beijing in November 2019, Henry Kissinger gave a speech in which he said the United States and China were in the "foothills of a cold war" that could be avoided by first completing the trade negotiations and then having a bilateral political discussion to minimize tension and points of friction around the world. His speech followed (and agreed with) that of Chinese vice president Wang Qishan, who said, "We should abandon the zero-sum thinking and cold war mentality."

No matter how much Pompeo, Pence, Esper, Davidson, Collins, and the rest of the national security officials believed that the new Cold War with China was on, whatever you wanted to call it, there was one person who just didn't see it that way — the president of the United States.

"There are many voices inside the administration," Pillsbury said at the Aspen Institute in January 2020. "I don't think the president wants a cold war with China at all."

Pompeo's China Play

Pompeo's Long Telegram for China never got completed. After Skinner was fired, the work of it was delegated to Miles Yu, a historian on loan from the Naval War College and an affirmed China hawk. Although he never completed the project, his work found its way into a series of speeches Pompeo made over the course of 2019 and 2020 on China that focused on exposing Chinese malign influence in various sectors of American society. Yu crafted these with the help of Stilwell, Kissel, and David Feith.

In October 2019, Pompeo gave a speech called "The China Challenge" at a Hudson Institute gala (with Kissinger in the audience) in which he said, "It is no longer realistic to ignore the fundamental differences between our two systems and the impact, the impact that those two systems have . . . on American national security." In January 2020, he spoke in Silicon Valley, warning tech executives that their partnerships with Chinese government-associated companies were being abused by the CCP under their "military-civilian fusion" project.

"So even if the Chinese Communist Party gives assurances about your technology being confined to peaceful uses, you should know there is enormous risk, risk to America's national security as well," he told them.

In February, Pompeo spoke at a meeting of the National Governors Association, to warn them that the CCP's outreach to local and state officials across the United States was part of the work of the United Front Work Department. He referenced a report by a Chinese think tank that rated each of the fifty governors as "friendly," "hardline," or "ambiguous."

"Governors can ignore orders from the White House . . . and State-level officials enjoy a certain degree of diplomatic independence," the report stated. That think tank itself is reportedly associated with the United Front Work Department.

Pompeo had decided early on that he wanted to be on the leading edge of the administration's China approach in the most hawkish manner practically available to him. But he had to deal with the reality that

Trump didn't agree with that approach and didn't want to provoke Beijing unnecessarily during the ongoing trade negotiations.

Pompeo had a list of thirty or so China-related moves he wanted to make, ranging from Huawei sanctions, to sanctions on officials responsible for abusing the Uyghurs, to clamping down on the Chinese media and intelligence presence inside the United States. He gave each move a rating from 1 to 10, 1 being the most benign and 10 being the most aggressive. Uyghur sanctions, for example, were a 7. In the environment inside the administration in the middle of 2019, that was too high a number, so those sanctions sat on the shelf for months and months.

Pompeo knew Trump didn't want to hear about Taiwan or Hong Kong, which was already heading into what would become a full year of prodemocratic street demonstrations. He was pushing where he could, without hitting the ceiling of what Trump would allow—and without really knowing where that ceiling was at any given time.

As his public profile on the China issue grew, the Chinese government and its media made him into their favorite target, calling him an arrogant, hysterical, reckless troublemaker hell-bent on steering the relationship into a new cold war. But domestically, Pompeo was actually ahead of the political curve. Everybody knew he was building a case for running for president in 2024. His prospective competitors like Nikki Haley had to rush to make sure they did not get outflanked on the China issue, as more and more Americans (especially Republicans but not only Republicans) came around to Pompeo's view.

As a top White House official told me, "The most interesting thing about Pompeo is that he made a political calculation almost before anyone else that taking a tougher stance on China was going to be the smart political move."

The Real Letter X?

Still missing from the conversation of US strategy toward China was an explanation of how the Trump administration—or at least the China thinkers inside it—thought about why Beijing was rising in this way. To understand where the CCP was going required understanding the sources of CCP conduct. Trump officials often talked about the symptoms, but rarely the cause. Pottinger, who had written the original memo (Bill's Paper) tackling this question during the transition, wanted to put out a public version, but he wasn't in a position to do it. So he turned to an old friend, now a congressman representing Wisconsin, Mike Gallagher, to do it for him.

Gallagher, a military vet and rising GOP star with a PhD of his own, first met Pottinger in 2007 in Baghdad, when the two Marine intelligence officers' deployments overlapped. Gallagher was a young Arab linguist; Pottinger was a not-so-young Mandarin linguist who was well known in the small Marine intelligence community because of his unique story as a former journalist who needed an age waiver to join the Marines in his thirties.

The two became friends, and later they would both work as reservists in the Defense Intelligence Agency under its then director, Michael Flynn. Years later, Gallagher was hired as the Middle East professional staff member for the Senate Foreign Relations Committee under then-chairman Bob Corker of Tennessee. He left that job in 2015 to become the national security adviser to a presidential candidate from his home state, Governor Scott Walker. He turned to Pottinger for help on all things China. Pottinger sent him a 2015 version of Bill's Paper.

"That document, more than anything else I had read, really forced me to change my focus as a young foreign policy hand and change my perception of Asia," Gallagher told me. "That document really is the closest thing we've had to a Long Telegram that I've come across, despite numerous attempts by various people to write one . . . That was when I realized that Matt was smarter than everybody else."

Walker dropped out early, but Gallagher parlayed his new Wisconsin political connections into an unlikely run for Congress in Wisconsin's Eighth District, where Republican Reid Ribble was retiring. He won. In November 2016, Pottinger sent Gallagher an updated version of the memo.

As Pottinger moved into the administration and Gallagher moved into Congress, the two kept in close touch, meeting once a month for breakfast to strategize about China. In mid-2019, as the State Department's Long Telegram effort floundered, Pottinger and Gallagher decided to put out one of their own, with Gallagher's name on the byline. "With his help and over the course of many conversations, I just started to write something that would serve as a framework for thinking about this," Gallagher said. "George Kennan was from Wisconsin, so I figured why not."

His article, written with input from his foreign policy adviser Charles Morrison, appeared in the *American Interest* in May and was entitled "The Sources of CCP Conduct." It began by quoting Kennan's Long Telegram, which stated that the Soviet intention was to break "the international authority of [the American] state" and that countering this effort was the "greatest task our diplomacy has ever faced and probably [the] greatest it will ever have to face."

Gallagher identified the sources of CCP conduct as rooted in China's long history of viewing itself as the center of "all under Heaven," a central node around which other nations revolve. He pointed to China's historic focus on strong centralized leadership as a means of avoiding foreign domination or internal rebellion, which had toppled so many regimes in Beijing over time. He traced the CCP's long record of using underground influence operations at home and abroad as a means to overcome military asymmetry and shape the environments of its adversaries.

Kennan wrote that the Soviet strategy involved a "cautious, persistent pressure toward the disruption and weakening of all rival influence and rival power." The CCP's efforts can be understood the same way, according to Gallagher. Therefore, the United States should learn from the Cold War experience to counter Beijing's strategy now. Don't let smaller countries fall prey to China's influence and pressure campaigns. Work with allies and promote our more attractive set of values, as we did against the Soviet Union.

Don't fall into the trap of trying to "out China China," he wrote, pointing to Kennan's warning that "the greatest danger that can befall us in coping with this problem of Soviet communism, is that we shall allow ourselves to become like those with whom we are coping."

There were mistakes from the Cold War that Gallagher believed must not be repeated. For instance, Joseph McCarthy, whose virulent anti-communism led to a witch hunt that cost the careers of many patriotic Americans, was also a former Marine Corps intelligence officer who represented Wisconsin. But McCarthy's legacy had to be a warning, not a guide. "McCarthyism is an example of ideological warfare done the wrong way," Gallagher told me. "The primary way we avoid descending into cartoon hawkishness or McCarthyism is to repeatedly reinforce we don't have a problem with China or the Chinese people, but with the Chinese Communist Party."

Gallagher's version of "Letter X" went largely unnoticed. He had pitched it to *Foreign Affairs* magazine, which had run the original "Letter X," but they rejected it. Three months later, *Foreign Affairs* published a different article entitled "The Sources of Chinese Conduct," by Norwegian historian Odd Arne Westad.

For Pottinger and Gallagher, the issue wasn't whether the United States and China are in the "foothills" of a new cold war. They wanted to push Washington to make the grand strategic competition with China — whatever you want to call it — the most important thing on the minds of the greatest number of people. They knew it was an uphill climb.

"Within the foreign policy community, many are loitering in the foothills," Gallagher said. "But some of us have begun to climb the hill, because we realize that the CCP has been climbing the fucking hill for at least a decade now. And we better get moving, otherwise we are going to lose."

Kennan Is Dead

The truth is, in today's chaotic information environment, no one document or one proposal could have the impact or unique insight that Kennan's had in the early days of the Cold War. Everyone wanted to be Kennan but nobody could repeat what he had done. Nevertheless, various actors competed to put forth what they believed was the best theory of the case.

In early 2020, the Trump administration issued what was to be their most comprehensive document that spelled out their China strategy. The report, called the *United States Strategic Approach to the People's Republic of China*, laid out the administration's China policy in more clarity and detail than ever before.

"To respond to Beijing's challenge, the Administration has adopted a competitive approach to the PRC, based on a clear-eyed assessment of the CCP's intentions and actions, a reappraisal of the United States' many strategic advantages and shortfalls, and a tolerance of greater bilateral friction," it states.

Pottinger, the document's lead author, told me this was the closest thing the Trump administration would be able to issue to NSC 68, the Truman-era document that sought to provide the actual programmatic plan to respond to Kennan's Long Telegram and his Letter X. It spelled out how the administration was taking the analysis from its earlier documents and applying them in the real world. Historians will be quick to point out that this was not a perfect analogy. Unlike NSC 68, the strategy didn't get into the operational details of how the United States was supposed to implement all of its policies. There was scant discussion of resources, much less the trade-offs that would be necessary to carry it out. Those details did exist, but only in classified form, a set of still-secret plans Pottinger revised and updated constantly.

But it was significant in that all the relevant agencies had signed off. No longer were the Treasury Department and the National Economic Council disputing the basic theory of the case, that the Chinese government was mounting a comprehensive assault on America's position of world primacy and the United States had no choice but to respond to it in a massive, comprehensive way. "This is now the prevailing view," Pottinger told me when it was issued. "It is quite literally a consensus and it wasn't necessarily a consensus before."

For some reason, the night the Trump administration's update on NSC 68 was issued, Pillsbury went on Lou Dobbs's Fox Business show and bashed the document. He said it was "puzzling" that the document didn't have any quotes from Trump and that the president hadn't signed it. (Trump had approved it.)

"It appears to have been written by a committee that has a lot of consensus points that frankly even Obama or Vice President Biden would sign up for. It does not present a strategy," he said. "I'm not one of the authors, I'm sorry to say. It wouldn't read this way if I had been involved."

Dobbs called it "utter nonsense . . . written by insensate individuals who seem to have no intellect or experience." K. T. McFarland appeared on the same Dobbs broadcast and went even further to bash Pottinger's strategy document. "Throw it in the trash. That doesn't reflect President Trump's thinking," she said. "I talk to the people in the White House National Security Council on China . . . and that's not how they are thinking. They are much more hawkish than this wimpy little document."

McFarland was 100 percent wrong. This was exactly how the National Security Council was thinking about China. She could have just picked up the phone and asked them, but she didn't bother. She was just rambling on TV, saying what Dobbs had prompted her to say. But why would Pillsbury bash Pottinger's strategy document on Fox? Sure, it wasn't as hawkish as Dobbs wanted, but nobody could honestly argue it was something Obama would have put out. There's only one reason that makes sense. Pillsbury was trying to communicate directly with Trump, who never missed an episode.

By signaling to Trump that this document was not sufficiently taking his views into account, he was trying to sour Trump on it. Why? Well, Pillsbury at this very time was still battling to get his security clearance and get himself a formal position in the administration. Pillsbury's gambit got Trump's attention. "Get him his fucking clearance already!" Trump told his staffers on a call after the segment.

Even among the hardliners, they all distrusted each other and maneuvered behind each other's backs. Trump never did give a comprehensive speech laying out his actual thinking and strategy on China. He never explained to the American people or the world his theory of the case. The new cold war was on, but without a clear direction or a clear explanation from the man who mattered most. Kennan must have been rolling in his grave.

The fact that the Trump administration was having so much trouble articulating its China strategy was particularly unfortunate at this moment because Beijing was taking advantage of the confusion to export a new strain of its authoritarian system to the rest of the world. China was waging an ideological battle of its own, both inside its borders and increasingly inside ours. This made American leadership on the world stage more vital than ever — at the exact moment that it was weaker than at any time in living memory.

11

The Big Chill

The Chinese Communist Party (CCP) has gone to enormous lengths to control information inside China and control the behavior of Chinese citizens by tracking their every action and severely punishing any stray word or indication of disloyalty to the party's agenda. By merging technology and authoritarianism, Beijing created a system of "social credit" to create a fear incentive to deter misbehavior. Inside China, sooner rather than later, every single person will be assigned a social credit score, where every word online and every public action feeds a person's algorithmically calculated political loyalty rating. A bad social credit score can result in punishments that make employment, travel, basic comfort, and success nearly impossible.

It's too easy to call everything the CCP does Orwellian, but in this case, the shoe fits. What the CCP is doing is attempting to control people through the abuse of technology, and it is totalitarian by design. Its defenders will say, doesn't the West also have "credit"? When you apply for a mortgage, don't they look into your behavior? But in China your credit score is not related to following the law, or having sound finances or even loyalty to the country. It's about loyalty to the party. It's political. The apt comparison would be if an American were denied a mortgage unless they pledged total loyalty and devotion to the country's sitting president.

Most Americans might not care if the CCP deployed its "social credit" system only against its own people. But increasingly, Beijing is using it against foreigners as well. In 2018, the CCP began enforcing its social credit system and doling out punishments to US companies and US citizens on US soil. The most famous example was in 2019 when China punished the NBA for one manager's tweet. But Beijing had already been threatening and punishing US companies for more than a year by then.

"China's 'social credit system' . . . — the use of big-data collection and analysis to monitor, shape and rate behaviour via economic and social processes — doesn't stop at China's borders," Samantha Hoffman wrote for the Australian Strategic Policy Institute in 2018. "Social credit regulations are already being used to force businesses to change their language to accommodate the political demands of the Chinese Communist Party (CCP) . . . It's part of a complex system of control — being augmented with technology — that's embedded in the People's Republic of China's (PRC's) strategy of social management and economic development."

The concepts of "social management" and "social governance" date back to the Leninist roots of CCP governance and have featured prominently in the Chinese system at various times over the decades. But under Xi Jinping, the effort to push the social credit system on other countries, to shape ideas and compel political loyalty from foreign businesses and foreign citizens, was put on steroids. That would place American businesses and even entire industries in the middle of the growing US-China feud, as Beijing began to use economic coercion to force international companies to advance its political goals. The Trump administration struggled at first to convince US companies that they should do the right thing for their country, even if it hurt their bottom line. But over time, the Chinese government hurt its own cause, by pushing its attempts to control foreign companies to extreme levels.

"China Is Out of Control"

In May 2018, the Chinese government tried to force international airlines to literally erase the name Taiwan from all of their websites and other online materials and declare the island was part of the People's Republic of China. The letter from China's Civil Aviation Administration demanded every airline remove any reference to Taiwan, Hong Kong, and Macau that "mistakenly describes them as countries or anything otherwise inconsistent with Chinese law." All the international airlines were to change all their maps to show Taiwan as part of China, in the same color even.

The White House issued a statement calling the Chinese demands on international airlines "Orwellian nonsense." (Again, if the shoe fits.) The Trump administration was standing up for American companies and calling on them to stand up for American values. "The United States strongly objects to China's attempts to compel private firms to use specific language of a political nature in their publicly available content," the White House statement said. "We call on China to stop threatening and coercing American carriers and citizens."

A White House official put it to me more simply: "China is out of control."

The airlines didn't know what to do. One senior airline executive told me the airlines would probably still cave to Beijing's demands: "This is lose-lose for us. We aren't a political organization, we answer to our shareholders. We don't want to get caught in the middle of your US-China cold war." I asked the executive, what about the bad press the airline would get if it was seen to be kowtowing to China? "This is an airline, all we get is bad press. Nothing new there."

After the initial statement, the National Security Council handed off the issue to the State Department, whose officials at that juncture weren't as enthusiastic about standing up to the CCP's Orwellian behavior. They convened the three major US airlines and the related industry associations and tried to come up with a strategy to push back. They decided to meet Beijing halfway. If you look at the United Airlines website today, you will see a listing for Taipei that identifies it neither as part of Taiwan nor as part of China. The CCP initially protested the half measure but ended up accepting half a loaf. They had made their point. They had forced a group of huge international corporations to literally erase Taiwan from the map.

A senior State Department official told me they had engaged the Chinese government on the issue but the Chinese side totally refused to participate in the conversation.

"We tried to demarche them and they basically said no," the official said. "They basically put their fingers in their ears."

Loyalty or Else

The airlines weren't alone. Other major corporations were being leaned on by Beijing to toe their political line or face economic punishment. Marriott Hotels and Mercedes-Benz both folded to Chinese government pressure and removed online content related to Tibet. Marriott even fired an American worker for "liking" a tweet by a pro-Tibet group. That employee, Roy Jones, didn't even remember "liking" the tweet while working the overnight shift at the Omaha, Nebraska, branch of the Marriott technical support operation. After the Chinese authorities shut down Marriott's website in China and started a "criminal investigation," the company fired Jones from his fourteen-dollar-an-hour job, and then the president of their Asia division apologized profusely in the Chinese press. (Their PR team refused to even give me a comment.)

In the summer of 2019, as the Hong Kong situation heated up, Beijing went after (among others) Versace, Coach, Asics, and Givenchy for listing Hong Kong separately from China on their websites or on their products, for which they all profusely apologized. China threatened to boycott Apple for not listing Hong Kong, Taiwan, and Macau as part of China in their mobile operating system.

No perceived slight was overlooked. No amount of groveling was ever enough. And Beijing's bullying increased. The US government did not have a plan to convince US companies to side with America and not China—or to protect them if they wanted to defy Beijing. The vulnerability of the companies to financial pressure created an asymmetric advantage for Beijing. Somehow, the US side was going to have to figure out how to raise the costs for this kind of behavior, or the CCP would grow emboldened to escalate its demands on how US companies and their employees behaved.

As the CCP forced company after company to capitulate, its appetite grew with the eating. But in October 2019, that all changed when the Chinese government bit off more than it could chew by going nuclear on the NBA over a tweet.

"Stand with Hong Kong"

Just like Marriott's Roy Jones, Houston Rockets general manager Daryl Morey had no idea the crisis he would create by tweeting something that offended the delicate and paranoid sensibilities of the CCP. He couldn't have predicted that his tweet while in Tokyo on October 4 of an image that said, "Fight for Freedom, Stand with Hong Kong," would cause the biggest and costliest scandal in the history of modern sports.

But Morey did know what he was tweeting. He is not your average sports executive, having been a trained researcher and technology expert who worked for years in Washington's national security community before joining the NBA. He worked as a technology project lead at the MITRE Corporation, a federally funded research center, and contributed to projects at the National Security Agency, the CIA, and the Pentagon. The statistics-based technology strategy that he often published on was part and parcel of his work for Stats, Inc., the company that used the model featured in the Michael Lewis book *Moneyball.*

Even though he deleted the tweet, within hours, the Chinese Basketball Association, sportswear brand Li-Ning, SPD Bank, state broadcaster CCTV's sports, and tech giant Tencent all announced they would suspend business with the Rockets. Only with Chinese government direction could all these various organizations act in concert so quickly. Morey was hounded with death threats and lots of other bile on Twitter as China's "50-cent Army," the thousands of online trolls the government directs, blasted him for supporting "violent separatists," attacking China's dignity, violating its sovereignty, and offending all 1.4 billion Chinese people.

NBA commissioner Adam Silver, at first, followed the same playbook every other corporate executive had pursued until that point — apologize profusely, discipline the employee, take your lumps, and promise it will never happen again. The league pressured Morey to issue an outright apology. He refused, issuing a carefully worded statement: "I did not intend my tweet to cause any offense to Rockets fans and friends of mine in China. I was merely voicing one thought, based on one interpretation, of one complicated event."

The NBA actually issued two different statements in two languages. In English, the NBA statement said, "We recognize that the views expressed by Houston Rockets General Manager Daryl Morey have deeply offended many of our friends and fans in China, which is regrettable." In the Chinese-language version, the NBA statement said, "We are extremely disappointed in the inappropriate remarks made by Houston Rockets General Manager Daryl Morey."

Rockets owner Tilman Fertitta claimed on Twitter his team is "not a political organization." But the NBA supports players' and staffers' rights to speak out politically on non-China issues. The NBA supported Boston Celtics star Enes Kanter's right to speak out about the abuses of Turkish president Recep Tayyip Erdogan, who has jailed Kanter's family on false accusations of terrorism and even tried to put him on Interpol's fugitive list.

"NBA stands with me for freedom and democracy. It's made all the difference," Kanter tweeted on October 6 as the controversy got even hotter.

Silver, perhaps understandably, turned to the one man in his world who knew the CCP the best, Brooklyn Nets owner Joseph Tsai. But Tsai is not just any Taiwanese-born naturalized Canadian billionaire. He is a cofounder of Alibaba and its second-largest independent stockholder after Jack Ma. His ties to Beijing run very deep, and his politics are completely in support of the CCP's aims.

On Facebook, Tsai posted a message that had all the markings of a Chinese government statement. He purported to speak for "hundreds of millions" of Chinese citizens who were supposedly offended by Morey's tweet. Never mind that Twitter is banned in China and Chinese citizens aren't allowed to publicly disagree with their government regarding Hong Kong. Tsai also parroted a CCP line by calling Hong Kong protesters a "separatist movement" and said Hong Kong was a "third rail" issue Americans are no longer allowed to comment on in public.

By the time Silver realized that this was not the right PR strategy and delivered a belated, half-hearted statement of support for Morey's free speech rights, it was too late. Everybody from Mike Pompeo to Ted Cruz to Beto O'Rourke had weighed in to criticize the NBA for choosing its financial bottom line ahead of an American's basic rights. To this day, the NBA is held up by China hawks as an example of a US company that betrayed American values in pursuit of the Chinese dollar. And the league still lost hundreds of millions of dollars in revenue because they didn't sufficiently prostrate themselves in Beijing's eyes.

Lawmakers criticized the NBA for not doing the right thing but largely ignored the fact that the league and the teams were victims of the Chinese government's tactics. The companies had no idea how to handle political pressure from the CCP, and by the time the scandal had begun, it was too late. The risk had gone up for the NBA because the CCP had become more aggressive. But the league didn't have any plans to deal with that risk. And the US government only got involved to admonish the NBA, without offering them any real protection or support.

The Chinese government might have thought twice about punishing the NBA if the costs for doing so had been higher. For example, some government officials proposed organizing a full-on NBA ban on playing in China until the retaliation against the Rockets was lifted. The thinking was to put pressure on Chinese authorities to explain to their own people why LeBron James is not coming to China anymore. But absent real government cooperation and more support, the US companies were too weak to stand up to Beijing on their own.

On October 7, the Commerce Department announced it was adding twenty-eight Chinese organizations to its list of banned entities due to their connection to the abuse of ethnic minorities inside China. This action banned US exports to the public security bureaus in Xinjiang and companies related to them. This Commerce Department move fell short of what a lot of officials were pushing, which were full State and Treasury Department sanctions on top CCP officials and a broader range of companies — sanctions that had been sitting on the shelf for many months.

The timing of these sanctions, released in the middle of the NBA scandal, was a coincidence. But it showed that the United States was not completely impotent when it came to standing up for human rights in China. "I consider this to be our response to the NBA bullshit," one official told me.

"Google Uyghurs"

On October 30, 2019, fifteen young Uyghur activists stood outside the Capital One Arena in Chinatown before the Washington Wizards home opener against the Houston Rockets, chanting for all they were worth. "Google Uyghurs! Free the Uyghurs! Free Hong Kong! Educate LeBron!"

They were mocking Los Angeles Lakers star LeBron James for defending the Chinese government's severe punishment of the NBA after Morey tweeted out support for Hong Kong protesters. James said Morey was "either misinformed or not really educated on the situation."

The activists were mostly American citizens, all American residents — and each and every one of them had a family member in the camps back in Xinjiang; many had more than one. They had just enough people to spell out the words "Google Uyghur" one by one on their T-shirts, a simple plea to their fellow Americans to educate themselves on the plight of eleven million ethnic minorities in China suffering under brutal repression, with over one million of those imprisoned for no reason other than that the CCP seeks to crush their spirit and erase their culture from the face of the earth.

One thing I learned in my visit to Dharamshala to meet the Tibetan exile community is that national identity is a very difficult thing to wipe out, no matter how much technological surveillance and control, forced indoctrination, and cruel physical punishment is applied. Through it all, even after losing their homeland, not only have the Tibetans managed to preserve their language, religion, and culture, they have preserved their movement and passed it on to a second generation to continue their struggle for dignity. That's the same spirit I saw on the faces of the twenty-something Uyghur activists who invited me to the Wizards game to learn about their struggle and hear their cries for attention and help.

One of the activists, Bahram Sintash from Chantilly, Virginia, has lost contact with his entire family. His father, Qurban Mamut, was a leading Uyghur academic and journalist who had been arrested and then disappeared with zero information or explanation. Mamut once was editor in chief of the CCP-controlled Uyghur journal *Xinjiang Civilization.* Almost all Uyghur intellectuals, academics, and other civic leaders were rounded up in the early stages of the atrocity.

Sintash's mother and sister live in the open prison that is Xinjiang. They can leave their house but not without being under constant surveillance. Because of his activism, Sintash hasn't been able to talk with his mother or sister for over two years. He wanted regular NBA fans who had heard about China's treatment of the Rockets in retaliation for their manager's one tweet about Hong Kong to know what else the CCP was capable of.

"I'm feeling in pain every day because my father is in a camp. So other American people should know there are these people called Uyghurs and we need their support," he told me.

Also in the group was Ferkat Jawdat, from Fairfax, Virginia. Three days after he met with Secretary of State Mike Pompeo and protested his mother's internment, his aunt and uncle back in Xinjiang were also sent to the camps. They were later sentenced to seven- and eight-year prison terms, without any trial whatsoever. The authorities released his mother from the camp under pressure from the State Department, but CCP officials contacted him over WeChat and warned him she would be arrested again if he didn't shut up.

But Jawdat didn't shut up. He told me the movement can't allow the CCP to use their family members as political leverage. Quietly waiting for the world to do something was not working. Millions of people were suffering greatly, including lots of Americans with family members in the camps. Speaking out as much as possible was their only hope.

"It's not really about my mom anymore; it's about the entire nation," said Jawdat. "We ask the US government to stand up to protect American citizens like myself by pressuring the Chinese government to release our family members and the rest of our people."

Inside the arena, the security guards stood close by as the activists stood silently, lined up with their shirts imploring the other fans to "Google Uyghur." The arena security demanded they put down their signs because the NBA had a policy of not allowing political signs. But how could asking people to Google something be political? they argued. It's a call for education, that's all.

After the game, the group resumed chanting outside the arena on F Street as fans poured out. Coming from the other direction, a Chinese man in a knock-off Nike track suit starting shouting at them in Mandarin. He was calling them traitors and terrorists and telling them to stop smearing China with false accusations. This is not completely uncommon at China-related protests. Some Chinese and Chinese Americans support the government, to be sure. But then the man leaned in to Jawdat specifically, looked him in the eye, and said in Chinese, "Your mom is dead."

This was not a random counterprotester. This man knew who Jawdat was and threatened him with specific information. He ran away before anyone could find out exactly who he was.

For the Uyghur activists, China's punishment of the NBA was a good thing. It brought the reality of the CCP and its repression of Uyghurs, Hong Kongers, and everyone else into the mind of the entire country. These young activists were not demoralized. They were encouraged. They were determined. They were trying to use that brief moment of awareness to elevate their cause and maybe even save their family members' lives.

Hong Kong Goes Under the Bus

Of course, the Uyghur activists, the Hong Kong protesters, the Christian community members, the political dissidents, and all the other groups protesting China's worsening human rights practices knew they had a president who refused to give them even rhetorical support. Trump never missed an opportunity to miss an opportunity when it came to standing up for human rights, especially in China.

Trump's first reaction to the nationwide student protests in Hong Kong against a new extradition bill, Beijing's latest effort to violate its 1997 commitment not to suffocate Hong Kong's freedoms and autonomy for at least fifty years, was to say, "I don't want to get involved . . . We have human rights problems too," according to Bolton's recollection. Bolton also claimed Trump told Xi in a June 18 phone call that he had ordered all his officials to shut up about Hong Kong.

All you have to do is look at what happened next to know Bolton's tale checks out. On July 8, Trump literally parroted Beijing's line by calling the protests "riots" and promised to stay out of it. He noted that the Chinese government was said to be preparing for an all-out assault on the protesters but said it was none of his business. "That's between Hong Kong and that's between China, because Hong Kong is a part of China," said the president. "They'll have to deal with that themselves. They don't need advice."

That same day, the news broke that the Trump administration had barred the US consul in Hong Kong, career diplomat Kurt Tong, from giving a tough speech about the Chinese government's actions in Hong Kong as his final message before departing the post. The State Department's official statements were watered down to the point of uselessness, not condemning the growing crackdown, but calling on Hong Kong authorities "to ensure proper consultation" and "take into account the significant concerns" of the Hong Kong people.

Pompeo, clearly champing at the bit but not wanting to contradict the boss, walked up to the line of Trump's patience but still had to talk in gentle tones. On July 29, as the preparations for a crackdown mounted and tensions rose, Pompeo said Chinese authorities should "do the right thing" and maintain Hong Kong's autonomy. The next day, on his way to Southeast Asia for a diplomatic conference, he said, "These are the people of Hong Kong asking their government to listen to them. So it's always appropriate for every government to listen to their people."

By early August, it looked like Beijing was prepping for a Tiananmen Square–style massacre in Hong Kong, massing thousands of police and military troops just across the border. Chinese propaganda outlets were spreading videos of People's Liberation Army troops using machine guns against protesters, with the social media tagline, "A blunt warning for #HongKong secessionists and their foreign backers?"

By October, as the streets and universities in Hong Kong burned, the mood in Congress over China had turned very sour. More and more Republican senators were publicly breaking with Trump on Hong Kong. For example, Trump marked the seventieth anniversary of CCP rule by tweeting, "Congratulations to President Xi and the Chinese people on the 70th Anniversary of the People's Republic of China!" Senator Josh Hawley's statement read, "Seventy years ago, the Chinese Communist Party seized power from the Chinese people. Since then, its ruthless rule has resulted in the deaths of millions of its own citizens."

Multiple officials noted at the time the absence of the American billionaire "friends of China," who were supposed to have close relationships and influence inside the top tiers of the Chinese system. None of them spoke out in public (or, as far as we know, in private either) to explain to Chinese leaders that violently crushing a student movement for basic rights on international television was a bad look.

These folks were too busy lobbying the administration and Congress against taking action that would harm their business interests and Beijing's business interests—and their efforts paid off. I learned in early November that Trump and Mitch McConnell had been intentionally thwarting the progress of the Hong Kong Human Rights and Democracy bill, which the Senate Foreign Relations Committee had approved unanimously two months prior.

When I wrote a story for the *Washington Post* on November 7 entitled "Trump and McConnell Are Failing the People of Hong Kong," Chuck Schumer took the article to McConnell's office and laid it on his desk in front of him. For McConnell, this was particularly embarrassing because he had helped pass the law in 1992 that originally established US support for Hong Kong's autonomy and in August he had penned a now hypocritical-looking op-ed in the *Wall Street Journal* endorsing the bill, entitled "We Stand with Hong Kong."

A week later, Senators James Risch and Marco Rubio started the process to pass the bill by unanimous consent. No senator objected, and the bill finally passed the Senate. In the House, the vote was 417–1, with only Rep. Thomas Massie voting no. Trump reluctantly signed it and attached a signing statement reserving his right not to enforce any part he didn't agree with. In an appearance on *Fox and Friends* before he signed it, Trump said he had considered issuing a veto.

"We have to stand with Hong Kong, but I'm also standing with President Xi," he said. "He's a friend of mine."

US-China relations were spiraling downward throughout the first half of 2019, as the factions on each side of the relationship working to forge a new consensus seemed to be failing and the hardliners on each side seemed ascendant. China's actions internally and externally showed a new boldness, and the Trump team was struggling to respond without clear guidance from the commander in chief.

Trump had wanted to take a tougher approach toward China, but he hadn't wanted the relationship to actually unravel. He still wanted to make a deal. And his leverage was slipping away. The closer Trump got to his election, the more he needed that deal to run on — and Beijing knew it.

12

Waking Up

In the third year of Donald Trump's presidency, as US-China relations continued to sour amid the ongoing trade war, the escalating tech war, and the growing furor around Beijing's ever less subtle efforts to influence Americans' conversations about China, a new set of clashes emerged. As was so often the case, these were internecine skirmishes on the US side — but the clamor they created would help to raise awareness about China's interference and attract support for a more muscular response by Washington to Beijing's aggression. Slowly but surely, America was waking up to the China threat, even if some of its people and institutions — and leaders — would have preferred to remain asleep.

The domestic implications of Chinese Communist Party (CCP) power meant that the US-China competition was no longer just the State Department's turf. National security and law enforcement agencies were becoming a bigger part of the China relationship and setting China policy more than ever before. More and more parts of the machinery of the US federal government were reorienting to confront China.

Specifically, more and more officials were beginning to comprehend not only the degree to which China was having a chilling effect on American freedoms but also what the Chinese government was doing on US campuses, how they were interacting with Silicon Valley, and how they were involved in our stock exchanges and capital markets. US policy toward China was changing fast, and the academic universe, the tech sector, and

Wall Street found themselves caught up in a chain of events that affected them but that they were struggling to understand, much less navigate.

The US national security community was now reaching into these other areas of society that had not previously been keen on taking orders from the US government in ways it had never done before, enlisting them in the China competition whether they liked it or not. In China, the government and the schools, tech firms, and investment companies worked in very close tandem — with the party in charge of all of the above. In the United States, the system had never worked that way; US institutions and companies were proud of their independence, and although they were having their own difficulties regarding China, the vast majority would not consider calling for the US government to come in and help them. So unsurprisingly, when the national security community in Washington began forcing these institutions to grapple with confronting China's malign behavior on US campuses, on the US internet, and in US markets, each of these sectors resisted the call for more coordination with the government on the China challenge.

This intransigence was baked into the distinction between America's private and public sectors, each of which had its own relationships in China. In this sense, US firms and universities were like autonomous foreign policy actors, each with its own domestic lobbying efforts. Beijing used these relationships to resist the growing calls for scrutiny of the CCP's activities on American soil. But because these calls were now coming from a widening swath of the federal government, they were becoming harder and harder for private institutions to ignore.

The stakes could not have been higher — because America's universities, its scientific research community, Silicon Valley, and Wall Street all are crucial to the US response to China's rise. Universities influence public opinion and knowledge but also spearhead innovation. Silicon Valley is the kitchen for all the technologies of the future. Wall Street holds the world's greatest source of money by far — and gives access to over one hundred million US investors. Beijing has realized their importance for many years and invested in each of them strategically and heavily. The United States was just beginning to realize the scale and scope of the problem—and the immense challenge that China's abuse of US institutions poses for Americans' security, prosperity, freedom, and public health.

"Political Tools"

The CCP views the American values of academic freedom and free expression (and other freedoms) as not only antithetical to its model but also as direct challenges to its governance—a threat, in fact, to what the party defines as China's existential and ideological struggle with the West. Document 9, the 2013 memo approved by Xi Jinping and later revealed to the world, emphasizes the importance of controlling the public discussion and deems civil society, the free press, and the promotion of individual rights to be "political tools" used by "Western anti-Chinese forces." As part of the CCP's effort to "consciously strengthen management of the ideological battlefield," the party has developed extensive programs to promote its political views in American academic institutions, blunt any criticism of CCP policies on campus, and stifle the free speech of Chinese students studying in the United States.

China has been seeking influence on American campuses for decades, in a variety of ways. The most controversial ones are through Confucius Institutes, Chinese student organizations, and direct funding and donations. Each of these avenues of influence provides the CCP with relationships on campuses that have both positive and negative implications.

The Chinese government sponsors language programs, education exchanges, and research, much of which is constructive or benign. Independently or through these programs, hundreds of thousands of Chinese students study at American universities, bringing value to these schools and taking a better understanding of the United States back to China. The vast majority of these students have no connection to the Chinese state and are simply trying to get an education and better their lives. They are the victims both of their own government's abuses and of

Americans' discrimination and racism, which are exacerbated by some of Trump's statements and policies.

At the same time, grave concerns about China's influence on US campuses are warranted. This poses a tragic dilemma—albeit one whose urgency isn't diminished by its intractability.

Over the course of 2018 and 2019, parts of the national security community, law enforcement agencies, the intelligence community, and Congress began forcing a difficult conversation in academia about how to manage increasingly malign Chinese interference on US campuses. This caused a clash with the universities and others who were invested in their projects with the Chinese government. The first major battle was over Chinese government-sponsored language schools embedded in US colleges, called Confucius Institutes.

Confucius on Campus

The most visible signs of China's influence operations on American campuses are Confucius Institutes, Chinese government-sponsored and government-run language and cultural teaching outposts that are embedded inside foreign universities. The CCP has built over five hundred Confucius Institutes and over two thousand Confucius Classrooms in over 154 countries since the program was established in 2004. The Confucius Institute system reports to a part of the CCP's educational ministry, called the Hanban, which in 2020 was renamed the Ministry of Education's Centre for Language Education and Cooperation. Universities typically sign contracts that—in exchange for funding—allow the Chinese government to choose the instructors and the curriculum. The program was founded by a former head of the United Front Work Department.

FBI director Christopher Wray launched the opening salvo against Confucius Institutes when he testified in February 2018 that they are among the entities used by the Chinese government as "nontraditional collectors [of intelligence], especially in the academic setting," in large and small cities all across the United States. He said the FBI was "watching warily" and investigating in "certain instances." Wray accused the US academic sector of naïveté for hosting these CCP outposts — and accused the CCP of "exploiting the very open research and development environment that we have, which we all revere."

At their peak, Confucius Institutes existed on more than one hundred North American college campuses. *Around sixty still exist at the time of this writing.* Not all Confucius Institutes are the same. After Wray made his comments, I signed up to join the Confucius Institute at the George Washington University, my alma mater. I registered for Chinese Language 101. There was nothing nefarious going on in that classroom, just some college students learning Chinese.

But at some other schools, there were real concerns. FBI agents had alerted the University of West Florida that they suspected its Confucius Institute staff were conducting espionage and they had opened an investigation. The university closed the institute, quietly. When I called the president of the university, she told me it was closed due to a lack of interest and denied the FBI had spoken to her. She had other interests to protect. The university has been collaborating with China to bring students and teachers back and forth since 1987.

One of the first clashes between the national security community and academia regarding Confucius Institutes occurred quite by accident, but it had a cascading effect around the country. In an April 2018 panel at the National Press Club, former Arizona congressman Matt Salmon, now Arizona State University's vice president for government affairs, bragged (incorrectly) that the Pentagon was funding ASU's Confucius Institute. He claimed that the Pentagon did not see the institute as a national security concern, and in fact used the Confucius Institutes to recruit Chinese speakers into the US government. Salmon also said those who are concerned about the institutes were engaged in "McCarthyism," adding that "if it does pose a security threat, then the Department of Defense has made a big mistake by funding our program."

Pentagon officials, upon hearing about this, were incensed. They determined that ASU had mixed together the resources and programs of their Confucius Institute program and their Pentagon-funded Flagship Chinese-language programs, which was not what the Pentagon had intended or wanted. The Pentagon worked with Congress to pass new legislation that required any university that had a Confucius Institute and a Pentagon language program to separate the two and then get a waiver from the Defense Department if they wanted to keep both on the same campus. But even though about a dozen schools applied for the waivers, zero were grated. ASU and about a dozen other schools closed their Confucius Institutes as a result.

Following the ASU revelations, members of Congress began to put pressure on universities in their districts to jettison their Confucius Institutes. In April 2019, GOP representative Jim Banks called the president of the University of Indiana and told him in no uncertain terms that if he didn't shut down his Confucius Institute, Banks would personally make sure the school never got one more dime of Pentagon money. The university closed the institute later that day, midsemester.

The institutes mean big money, especially for smaller schools. In addition to paying millions for the actual programs, hosting a Confucius Institute gets any university into a special club that opens doors to all types of opportunities. According to a report by the National Association of Scholars, "In addition to providing funding and free textbooks and teachers, Confucius Institutes help attract full-tuition-paying Chinese students, fund scholarships for American students to study abroad, and are the conduit by which college presidents and administrators enjoy trips to and state dinners in China."

The report raises three chief concerns regarding Confucius Institutes: their restrictions on intellectual freedom, their lack of transparency, and their improper entanglements with the Chinese government, which end up implicating not just teachers and administrators but also students. Not only are the Chinese teachers at Confucius Institutes forced to adhere to Chinese law on so-called sensitive topics, such as Tibet and Taiwan, but Americans who are hired to work at the institutes also get pressure to self-censor. Their contracts and the institute's hiring policies are rarely public. And the relationships between the institutes and their American host universities often end up mixing China's state interests with academic ones.

By inviting Confucius Institutes onto their campuses, in short, American academic administrators have allowed a generation of US university students to be taught as their primary source of information on China the regime's official version of its history, ideology, and policies. This is a travesty, but it is one that is slowly being made right. Over the past six years, at least twenty-nine of more than one hundred US universities that had Confucius Institutes have closed them. This seems only fitting, given the counsel of Confucius himself in *The Analects:* "Not to act when justice commands, that is cowardice."

Surveillance by Students

Confucius Institutes are not the only way in which the CCP makes its presence felt on American university campuses. Chinese Students and Scholars Associations (CSSAs) are student organizations on campus that are in many cases supported by the Chinese government, sometimes publicly. Individual CSSAs are often financially sponsored and monitored by Chinese embassy and consular officials, who have used these student organizations to support Chinese senior officials' visits to US universities, facilitate trips to China, and mobilize support on campus for Chinese government objectives.

The expansion and establishment of CSSAs seems to have been a response to the Tiananmen Square massacre. After 1989, the Chinese government started putting a lot more effort into patriotic education and making sure Chinese students abroad wouldn't cause problems if they came back. But since Xi came to power, the CCP's efforts to surveil and control overseas Chinese have increased vastly. The party wants Chinese students, according to a 2016 directive, to "build a multidimensional contact network linking home and abroad — the motherland, embassies and consulates, overseas student groups, and the broad number of students abroad—so that they fully feel that the motherland cares." CSSAs are just one way Xi does this.

The CSSAs are collectively overseen by the CCP's United Front Work Department (which gives them a more direct connection to that organization than the Confucius Institutes); the associations' actual management is carried out by the education ministry. The CSSAs enable the CCP to monitor Chinese students by creating an environment where they are incentivized to report on each other. As with Confucius Institutes, much of their activity is benign; the average CSSA member is not seeking to interfere in academic freedom on campus. But the leaders of these organizations often work directly with the CCP to surveil their fellow students. "The effect of that surveillance is less that certain people are caught and punished and more that virtually all Chinese students know they could be reported and, therefore, watch what they say in public fora," Perry Link, a professor and China expert, told the *New York Times* about the CSSAs.

CSSAs also work with the Chinese government to blunt criticism of the CCP by anyone else on the campuses where they operate. The power of the CSSAs made headlines in 2017 when the University of California, San Diego, announced that His Holiness the Dalai Lama would be the 2017 commencement speaker. The university was blindsided by nasty remarks on Facebook and other social media sites: "Imagine how Americans would feel if someone invited Bin Laden," said one post. The outrage primarily poured from UCSD's CSSA, whose leaders admitted they had spoken with the Chinese consulate in LA about the controversy. The commencement took place as planned. But the Chinese government retaliated by banning students and scholars with funding from the Chinese government's China Scholarship Council from attending UCSD.

Other examples of repressive behaviors by CSSAs abound. When University of Maryland student Yang Shuping gave a speech in 2017 praising the "fresh air of free speech" in the United States and expressing her gratitude to the university for showing her that her "voice mattered," her CSSA denounced her. The Yale CSSA threatened Hong Kong student democracy activist Nathan Law when he began his studies at Yale last fall. They (along with other CSSAs) have also heckled some of his speeches both on campus and off.

One Thousand and One Talents

Across the country, American universities have been receiving billions of dollars of unreported foreign donations. This is being repeated at all levels down to the individuals carrying out research. By law, US universities have always been required to publicly report any foreign gifts or contracts above $250,000 in one calendar year, but that law was rarely observed and never enforced from its enactment in 1965 until last year, due to pressure from federal law enforcement agencies. When the Department of Education started looking into it in July 2019, in a few months it uncovered more than $6 billion worth of unreported foreign donations to major US educational institutions. The department opened specific investigations into Harvard and Yale.

A 2019 report by the Senate Permanent Select Committee on Intelligence found that over 70 percent of US colleges taking money from China's defense ministry failed to properly report it. The Hanban had given over $113 million to one hundred US universities since 2012, more than seven times what those schools had publicly disclosed.

In June 2018, Senator Marco Rubio and Congressman Jim Banks wrote to Education Secretary Betsy DeVos to demand she look into the fifty or so Huawei research centers located on American campuses. At the very least, they said, these universities should have to disclose the details of these arrangements, particularly when the federal government is involved in the research as well.

The Justice Department, in late 2018, began a huge program called the China Initiative, which brought together US attorneys from around the country to pool information and resources to get a handle on the vulnerability of American schools, research centers, and businesses to Chinese espionage and theft by "nontraditional collectors" of intelligence — that is, researchers. Part of their mission was to go around and educate academic institutions about threats to academic freedom posed by their hosting of these Chinese organizations.

The FBI and National Institutes of Health also began warning universities and research centers about CCP talent-recruitment plans, another major pipeline for research and technology theft. The CCP has established more than two hundred of these plans that pay leading scientists and entrepreneurs around the world to bring their expertise and technology to China. In many cases, the scientists are allowed to serve in place — covertly taking salaries from both China and America. As the FBI warned in 2015, these efforts allow the CCP "to acquire advanced technology without research costs." In other words, Beijing uses these programs to reap the benefits of the billions of dollars the US government pumps into research and development. After looking into these efforts, the FBI soon uncovered dozens of cases of American researchers who had been recruited and paid by the Chinese government but didn't tell anyone. If those researchers omitted that information from a federal grant application, they had committed a crime.

In April 2019, after a visit from the FBI, the MD Anderson Cancer Center in Houston fired three top scientists for not complying with center policies on disclosing their participation in the Thousand Talents Plan, the largest of over two hundred Chinese government programs to recruit Western scientists to work in China and to bring with them the secrets of their research. The scientists were never charged with any crime. Because they were ethnically Chinese, the incident raised concerns about racial profiling. But when the Moffitt Cancer Center in Tampa fired its CEO and five other researchers a few months later for hiding their Thousand Talent Plan affiliations, all but one were Caucasian.

By the end of 2019, the Education Department, Energy Department, and National Science Foundation had all banned their employees and grantees from participating in foreign talent-recruitment programs. The FBI program reached full speed. In December 2019, the FBI would arrest Chinese researcher Zheng Zaosong after he was caught with twenty-one vials of biological samples stolen from Boston University, hidden in a sock in his luggage; he subsequently would be charged with smuggling and making false statements. In January 2020, the chair of Harvard's chemistry department would be arrested and charged with hiding his own paid participation in Thousand Talents.

How can scientific research, which is collaborative and open by nature, be such a valuable thing that the CCP is working so hard to steal it? Because some of the research in which China is interested is not publicly available; it is proprietary or being developed for government or military use. The interest in protecting those things is clear. Some of it is stolen for commercialization, giving Chinese companies a huge and unfair competitive advantage. More broadly, even if Americans believe in an open knowledge economy for the sake of elevating humankind, the CCP might not see it that way. China is exploiting the fact that Western scientists want to advance human knowledge, whereas China wants to dominate strategic and emerging technologies, wean itself off Western technology and research, and use those advantages to repress its people, influence the rest of the world, strengthen its economy, and arm its military.

The danger is even clearer in those cases where China has used these collaborations to help commit mass atrocities. As the reality of China's expanding use of technology for the purpose of repression became clear, especially with regard to the Uyghurs, US universities were forced to examine whether they were making themselves complicit in these crimes against humanity. A top geneticist at Yale claimed ignorance when it was revealed in February 2019 that his collaboration with Chinese scientists was helping police in Xinjiang build a DNA database for Uyghurs without their consent. MIT had announced what was meant to be a five-year collaboration with Chinese artificial intelligence firm iFlytek in June 2018, but would cut ties in 2020 after reports accused the Chinese firm of selling technology to the government that is used to oppress Uyghurs. At the time of this writing, the University of Illinois at Urbana-Champaign is collaborating with the Chinese facial recognition firm CloudWalk, which is working to automate the detection and tracking of Uyghurs and

Tibetans based on phenotypes — technology that can be used to track people with certain DNA types based on their physical appearance.

In mid-2020, the FBI began a sweep to find researchers in US academic institutions who had hidden their histories or affiliations with the Chinese military. This investigation would uncover disturbing examples of researchers affiliated with the People's Liberation Army (PLA) who are working on sensitive topics including artificial intelligence, machine learning, supercomputers, and underwater robotics — all areas where the Chinese military is seeking a technological advantage over the United States. (When the State Department shut down China's Houston consulate in July of that year, it was in part because it had been central to helping these researchers hide their true identities and evade US justice.)

The only way for Xi's "China Dream" to come true is for America's own values to wane. College campuses are but one of the many battlegrounds. Safeguarding free speech at universities is critical to the health of any democracy. Yet the US academic sector has struggled with defending two competing values — academic freedom and openness — at the same time. The national security and law enforcement communities struggle with two competing priorities as well: protecting the nation's security while avoiding turning into the very repressive system they were opposing, by targeting people based on ethnicity or national origin. It had proved to be a vexing challenge — one made all the more difficult by the fact that it is far from the only one on these defenders' plates.

Chips on Their Shoulders

When the Trump administration came into power, there were two big things happening in Silicon Valley. One was the global feeding frenzy to get ahead on artificial intelligence, which was beginning to take off. The other was a competition for engineers that was heating up because major US firms like Facebook, Amazon, and Google were growing faster than the schools could turn out graduates. China provided a way to success for American firms on both these fronts — much to the consternation of those in Washington who were trying to warn the tech industry of Beijing's efforts to infiltrate their companies and exfiltrate their data.

The Chinese government was seriously investing in the technologies of the future, and Chinese universities were supplying skilled technicians to companies around the world. Inside US high-tech firms, there were national-security-minded people who were deeply wary and skeptical about China, but from a business perspective, cooperation made sense. The Chinese market of over seven hundred million internet users was too valuable to ignore.

The risks for US tech firms working with or in China were apparent for years before the Trump administration came into power, but were largely ignored. Google took a principled stand in 2010 and pulled out of China after their servers were compromised by hackers. But while they hadn't completely reversed themselves, by 2017 Google was building an AI center of excellence in partnership with Chinese tech giant Tencent in Beijing. Secretly, a team at Google was also working on a censorship-friendly web browser called Dragonfly, but that project was put on ice after employees blew the whistle.

Like academia, the tech sector also had a hard time working with the US government to push back against Chinese depredations. The legacy of the Snowden revelations had poisoned Silicon Valley's relationship with the national security community in a fundamental way. The firms felt that the National Security Agency had undermined the trust they needed to do business in every other country, and also resented the fact that they had been enlisted to serve national security priorities without their knowledge. Trust needed to be rebuilt, but for many years those conversations simply weren't happening.

At the end of the Obama administration, a group of Pentagon officials had sought to change that by attempting to reset the relationship with Silicon Valley. Matthew Turpin had been in charge of the plan. He asked the White House to send over one of the tech geniuses that he knew had recently joined the administration on a temporary basis as part of its Presidential Innovation Fellows program, to do a research report on

Chinese investment in Silicon Valley. The White House sent over Mike Brown, the former CEO of Symantec. Brown brought in his friends Dan Rosen, an expert on the Chinese economy and founding partner of Rhodium Group, and Pavneet Singh, a trade policy expert and former National Security Council (NSC) official. They set up shop in San Francisco.

They wrote up an internal report on China's technology strategy, which explained in detail how US tech firms didn't have to go to China to have their crown jewels stolen; it was already happening here at home. They didn't release the report, but they didn't classify it either. Soon it leaked to the *New York Times*, which first wrote about the Pentagon's "new White Paper" in March 2017. The full report was made public in January 2018. It stated China was participating in about 16 percent of all new Silicon Valley venture deals, with little to no national security vetting. "China is investing in the critical future technologies that will be foundational for future innovations both for commercial and military applications: artificial intelligence, robotics, autonomous vehicles, augmented and virtual reality, financial technology and gene editing," it stated. "The U.S. government does not have a holistic view of how fast this technology transfer is occurring, the level of Chinese investment in U.S. technology, or what technologies we should be protecting."

Brown stayed on to lead the Defense Innovation Unit Experimental, a new Pentagon office meant to help the military keep up with emerging technologies, and Turpin moved over to the NSC. Their work fed into the effort to reform the Committee on Foreign Investment in the United States, but also established a baseline for looking seriously into China's behavior in our own technology industry. As the tech war heated up more and more over the course of 2018 and 2019, however, every big US firm reacted differently.

Mnuchin Bails Out Google

When the battles among the tech giants of Silicon Valley became entangled in the Washington battles over China, the result was often confusion and chaos. At the National Conservatism Conference in July 2019, Trump-friendly billionaire Peter Thiel launched a public attack on Google, accusing the company of "treasonous" activity for working with the "Chinese military" but refusing to work with the US military (on a project called Maven, which used AI for intelligence sorting). He alleged that Google was thoroughly infiltrated by the PLA, but didn't provide any specific evidence.

That same month, on July 16, Trump said in a cabinet meeting that his administration would "take a look" at Google's work in China and suggested that his attorney general might investigate. Eight days later, Steven Mnuchin announced that he had done so instead of the attorney general and that he had discovered that everything was just fine. "The president and I did diligence on this issue, we're not aware of any areas where Google is working with the Chinese government in any way that raises concerns," Mnuchin said.

Obviously, there's no way that Mnuchin could have seriously examined the issue in eight days. Two weeks after that, Trump tweeted that Google CEO Sundar Pichai had visited him in the Oval Office and worked "very hard to explain how much he liked me, what a great job the Administration is doing, that Google was not involved with China's military."

Case closed. But in their haste, the Trump team appeared to have missed some crucial details. Although Google wasn't working directly with the PLA, Chinese military scientists have worked with Google employees on research papers on multiple occasions. And their cooperation with Chinese tech firms on artificial intelligence, according to the testimony of Joint Chiefs chairman General Joseph Dunford, is "a direct benefit to the Chinese military."

Facebook Flips

The US social media giants had less exposure to the shifting tides of the US-China relationship at first, because Beijing didn't allow them to operate in the Chinese market and created local domestic copies, such as

WeChat, to serve Chinese social media users while still being controllable by the CCP. But over the course of the Trump administration, Chinese internet companies began penetrating the US market and threatening American firms on their own turf for the first time. That forced US tech firms to rethink the nature of the China challenge.

The clearest example of the shift was at Facebook. CEO Mark Zuckerberg made a conscious decision in late 2019 to reorient Facebook's approach to China 180 degrees. After many years of trying everything he could think of to convince the Chinese government to allow Facebook to operate in China, including asking Xi personally to give his first child a Chinese name (Xi declined), Zuckerberg changed his mind and pledged in an October 2019 trip to Washington that Facebook was no longer seeking access to the Chinese market. Instead, he was now calling on the US government to help US tech firms fight back against China's tech strategy and pledging that Facebook would fight for American values. "China is building its own Internet focused on very different values, and is now exporting their vision of the Internet to other countries," he said on October 17 at Georgetown University. "Until recently, the Internet in almost every country outside China has been defined by American platforms with strong free expression values. There's no guarantee these values will win out."

The motivations for Zuckerberg's 180 were clear. He was racing to establish his Libra electronic payment system ahead of a competing system being developed by Alibaba and needed help from Congress and the administration to work out the regulatory structure. Lawmakers were concerned that Zuckerberg's international electronic payment system would undermine legal oversight of international transactions and weaken the dollar's role as the dominant world currency. But as Zuckerberg pointed out, if China won the race, Beijing would not afford the US government any of the cooperation and concessions Facebook was prepared to offer.

Facebook was also losing eyeballs by the millions to TikTok, which was owned by the Chinese firm ByteDance, giving Zuckerberg another huge incentive to back US lawmakers' efforts to rein in China's ever-increasing technological expansion. TikTok was the first Chinese social media company that caught fire inside the United States. Yet despite its popularity—and despite ByteDance's protestations to the contrary—reports kept coming out that TikTok's content managers were censoring anti-CPP messages in users' videos. There also was evidence that some of the US user data was being routed through China—which, if true, revealed that the company couldn't be trusted and exposed the personal information of millions of young Americans to Chinese government exploitation.

ByteDance insisted that it was immune from pressure from the Chinese government, should Beijing ever demand the company hand over user data—but that didn't match what Chinese national security laws stated. Lawmakers in both parties demanded action, and eventually President Trump declared that ByteDance would have to sell TikTok or shut it down. A series of chaotic negotiations commenced, led by Mnuchin, with the goal of forcing ByteDance to spin off TikTok's international operation and cede its control to a US company. Trump bizarrely demanded a kickback he called "key money," for brokering the deal. Beijing was incensed and withheld permission for ByteDance to go along. The company sued the Trump administration in US courts.

Although the national security officials had pushed the ban of TikTok and its larger tech cousin WeChat, the dealmaking was handed over to Mnuchin, who tried to turn it into a windfall for Wall Street and the US tech firms close to Trump, like Safra Catz's Oracle. This was the kind of ad hoc flailing that made the Trump administration's policy look capricious and self-serving. Mnuchin was also handing Beijing a talking point and a grievance; now it was the United States who was trying to force Chinese companies to hand over their technology for access to the US market. As of this writing, the company's fate is still in limbo.

Another Bite of Apple

Large tech companies that were already dependent on the Chinese market or dependent on Chinese factory labor reacted to the rising tensions in US-China relations by assuming a stance much more favorable to Beijing. Apple is the prime example of a US firm that was still determined to stay in the good graces of the CCP, even if that meant making ethical compromises. As the Chinese government tightened control on foreign firms inside China, increasingly using a corporate social credit system to reward or punish them, Apple tried its best to accommodate Beijing.

In July 2018, using the excuse it was "just following the local law," Apple agreed to move its data for Chinese users to cloud servers inside China, giving up any power to deny those users' data to Chinese authorities. During the Hong Kong protests in 2019, Apple bent over backward granting Beijing's demands, including by hiding the Taiwanese flag emoji, removing the news outlet Quartz from the Chinese version of its app store for covering the protests, and removing HKmap.live, an app that protesters were using to organize and avoid police.

With $44 billion in revenue annually coming from the Chinese market, not to mention all its factories there, Apple's stance makes sense. But it didn't protect them from Beijing's ire. In May 2020, China's *Global Times* would report that the Chinese government was considering punishments and restrictions on Apple to retaliate against Trump for clamping down on Huawei. Apple wasn't the CCP's friend — it was just another corporate hostage.

Sheep of Wall Street

While every other US industry was making the determination that the risks of doing business with China were going up, the leading financial firms on Wall Street were racing faster than ever to not only bring Chinese firms into US financial and capital markets but also invest and direct the money of tens of millions of unwitting Americans into huge Chinese companies at an astonishing rate. Their strategy was based on the assumption that nobody would stop them from sending hundreds of billions of US dollars into the Chinese system. But as the national security community in Washington expanded their activities in this arena, another major clash was in the offing.

For years, the main method through which Chinese companies raised money in US markets was to get themselves listed on the NASDAQ and New York Stock Exchanges, but since Chinese companies didn't follow the accounting and transparency rules mandated for listing by US law, they found workarounds. For example, Chinese firms would buy out dormant companies that were already listed on the exchanges—a process called a reverse merger, which allowed the Chinese firms to get listed on US stock exchanges without going through the regular process of disclosure and scrutiny. If the companies made money, the US investors were happy. But if they failed, the US investors had no recourse. In its 2017 report, the U.S.-China Economic and Security Review Commission observed that "these listings could pose significant risks for unsuspecting U.S. investors who buy into U.S.-listed Chinese companies."

Through a combination of lax oversight and rampant abuse, the problems associated with Chinese firms listing on US exchanges mounted. The commission found that through fraud schemes alone, Chinese issuers have stolen billions from US investors with no fear of punishment inside or outside China. The Public Company Accounting Oversight Board (PCAOB), which was created under the Sarbanes-Oxley Act of 2002, lists foreign companies that deny it the ability to inspect their audits, including more than two hundred firms based in China or Hong Kong. After a string of reverse mergers that went bad, hurting US investors, Chinese companies largely began focusing on getting listed directly on US exchanges and conducting initial public offerings (IPOs) to raise US cash. But there was still the problem of them not following US laws on disclosure and accountability.

In 2013, the PCAOB entered into a memorandum of understanding with its Chinese government counterpart that was meant to ensure Chinese companies would adhere to high standards of transparency and disclosure. But Beijing invoked its own national security laws to prevent Chinese firms from actually complying. The CCP didn't want the cash flowing between the party and its state-controlled companies to be revealed. If those relationships were laid bare, the nature of the party's control over these companies, their use for strategic purposes, and the corruption endemic in those relationships would be exposed.

Huge Chinese firms like Alibaba took the effort to the next level by launching massive IPOs on American exchanges with the help of Wall Street consultants. Even for these companies and transactions this big (Alibaba raised $25 billion in its 2014 IPO on the New York Stock Exchange), their financial disclosures and filings could not be independently verified. US investors simply could not perform due diligence on Chinese companies in which they were invested.

When the Trump administration came to power, the chairman of the PCAOB, James Doty, was in the middle of trying to negotiate a new arrangement with Beijing. But Doty was removed in 2018 by Securities and Exchange Commission chairman Jay Clayton, who was chosen by Mnuchin. Clayton was also a legal adviser to Alibaba. As he had so many times before, Trump's pro-business Treasury secretary had effectively short-circuited America's response to China's economic aggression.

The massive fraud and corruption these practices allowed eventually became well known enough that a cottage industry of short sellers cropped up. By simply performing basic research on these companies, firms like Muddy Waters Research were able to expose fraud after fraud. They were featured in a 2018 documentary called *The China Hustle,* which chronicled the efforts of Wall Street whistleblowers to call attention to the huge scope and scale of the problem. But as so often happened, when China's economic aggression was exposed, it simply changed its tactics.

The Big Con

After US stock market listings for Chinese firms began to attract too much scrutiny, Chinese firms found a way to raise billions from American investors without going anywhere near American markets. Beijing began to push major Wall Street index providers to include hundreds of Chinese companies in their offerings. These index providers were offshoots of major banks or financial firms whose business was to compile lists of companies based on extensive research that other investors could use to guide their investment decisions, either by licensing through the index providers or just by tracking the lists on their own. The index providers wielded huge influence in the global markets because their decisions caused a cascading effect on other investors — and also because they could include in their listings companies on any exchange, not just the American ones, meaning they were rainmakers for companies all over the world that wanted investment from Americans.

Once Beijing realized that it could obtain US investments much more easily by listing Chinese companies on less scrupulous markets and then having the index providers bless these companies by adding them to their lists, it pushed that strategy with all its might — and the index providers played along. For example, the world's largest index provider, MSCI, has been steadily increasing its holdings of Chinese assets, reportedly "after it came under heavy pressure by the Chinese government." MSCI quickly began adding Chinese firms to its international index listings, particularly emerging market indexes, which had the effect of steering billions of US dollars toward those Chinese firms.

Large investment vehicles like exchange-traded funds and mutual funds often track indexes like MSCI. This means that, whenever the index added Chinese firms, these large funds followed suit and took them on as well. Large institutional investors like pension funds and university endowments stocked up on these exchange-traded funds and mutual funds, often investing in them passively, which resulted in them taking on the risk of bad-actor Chinese firms. Investing in Chinese companies that were sanctioned by the US government, aiding the Chinese military, or contributing to human rights abuses would normally be seen as very risky. But when the index providers endorsed these firms, US investors' dollars flowed to them.

One implication of this new, surreptitious flow of US investment toward Chinese companies was that it made the Trump administration's trade negotiation strategy less effective than it might have been otherwise. MSCI quadrupled its mainland Chinese holdings in 2019, which sent about $80 billion of US cash into the struggling Chinese economy right as the Trump administration was trying to apply pressure on Beijing to make a trade deal. These Chinese firms never had to list on the US exchanges but were able to raise cash from the US capital markets through this backdoor method.

But there were even greater and more insidious implications as well. US investment funds worth nearly $14 trillion follow the MSCI indexes or use them as yardsticks for their investment decisions. That means asset managers all over the country are compelled to increase their holdings of Chinese stocks and bonds when MSCI does it. Millions of Americans, without doing anything, are all of a sudden betting on Chinese companies with their pension funds, mutual funds, and exchange-traded funds.

All the big index providers were doing it. The Bloomberg Barclays Global Aggregate Bond Index in 2019 began a twenty-month plan to support 364 Chinese firms by directing an estimated $150 billion into their bond offerings, including 159 companies controlled directly by the Chinese government. Pension and retirement funds all over the country that track these indexes passively were putting millions of Americans' financial futures in the hands of these Chinese companies.

What's worse, the companies the indexes were shoveling money into included companies that build weapons and ships for the PLA, companies that stood accused of cyber hacking, firms that are complicit in mass atrocities, and firms that are already sanctioned by the US government. The Wall Street firms weren't just betting our money on China; they also were helping Beijing fund China's expansion, which undermined the entire US government strategy to compete with Beijing and to maintain America's technological and economic primacy.

American investment firms were not disclosing this material risk to their investors, much less telling them what the impact of their investments was. At the same time, they were making it very difficult for the

US government to undo the damage. Once millions of Americans were invested in bad-actor Chinese firms, there would be a huge constituency inside the United States pushing against any punishment of those firms.

"While we thought we understood the scope and activities of the active 'China lobby' in the United States," Roger Robinson, the former chairman of the U.S.-China Economic and Security Review Commission, told me, "little did we know that China was in the process of recruiting well over 100 million American retail investors with a vested financial interest in opposing sanctions against Beijing for fear it could hurt their portfolios." Robinson wasn't in government anymore, but nevertheless, he decided to do something about it. And he was not alone.

The Opening Salvo

When Robinson talked about economic warfare, he knew whereof he spoke. The son of a senior FBI counterintelligence official, he had started his career as a Wall Street banker, but he made his name as a cold warrior. As a thirty-two-year-old head of international economic affairs at the National Security Council under President Ronald Reagan in 1982, Robinson was among the first to identify the vulnerability of the hard currency cash flow of the Soviet Union and then come up with a plan to exploit that vulnerability. Many would argue that the secret economic and financial strategy waged against the Kremlin centering on constraining its hard currency cash flow and access to Western credit was ultimately responsible for the collapse of the Soviet empire.

Before working in the Reagan administration, Robinson had been the vice president heading the Soviet and Eastern European division of Chase Manhattan Bank. He served for two and a half years as a personal assistant to then–Chase chairman David Rockefeller. On April 1, 1981, he had coauthored an article in the *New York Times* entitled "Europe's Big Gamble on Soviet Gas," warning about the perils of Western Europe's dependency on Soviet gas and warning that the Siberian pipeline would double the USSR's annual revenues. Ronald Reagan used this argument as a basis for his intervention on the issue, which became known as the Siberian pipeline dispute. He brought in Robinson to work the issue.

During the Trump administration, Robinson — by now a private citizen with a small research and risk management consulting firm — had been working behind the scenes to wage a new war against the Chinese corporate bad-actor companies trying to attract the money of average Americans and those on Wall Street helping them for fees. (The Trump administration looked into this issue in 2017, when Robert Spalding, the short-tenured NSC official, commissioned a quiet study on China's presence in US capital markets. Among its findings was that China had a much more expansive footprint inside the US capital markets than anyone understood, replete with bad actors. By the time the study was complete, Spalding had left the administration, and for still unclear reasons, the report never saw the light of day.)

Separately, over the course of 2017 and 2018, Robinson also was conducting an intensive research effort into the national security and human rights implications of China's expanding corporate presence in the US capital markets. In the fall of 2018, he began quietly and informally briefing officials, lawmakers, and journalists around Washington, hoping to instill in them the same outrage that he felt about the uses to which American dollars were being put in China. Robinson was at the nexus of two worlds, the national security community and Wall Street — and he was determined to connect them.

To help with these briefings, Robinson produced a presentation laying out the issue. It showed that if MSCI instituted its plans, millions of Americans would be passively investing in bad-actor Chinese companies, including China Shipbuilding Industry Corporation (which supplied the PLA Navy), the Aviation Industry Corporation of China (which supplied the Chinese air force and manufactured advanced weapons such as air-to-air missiles), China Unicom (which had been accused of cyber hacking and spying), and Hikvision (which produced the AI cameras that tracked Uyghurs in Xinjiang before they were arrested and sent to camps).

Seeking to build pressure on Wall Street, he reached out to the office of the lawmaker he thought most amenable to his plan, Marco Rubio, and began working with Rubio's senior foreign policy adviser Robert Zarate. He also sought out those industry groups that were meant to protect US investors. He began working with Christopher Iacovella, who headed up the American Securities Association, an industry organization meant to defend investors' interests. Iacovella, like Robinson, was keenly aware of the danger posed by China's unfettered access to US capital markets, and wanted to shake the rest of his countrymen awake. "The real issue was the Chinese companies that weren't listed in our markets but money was flowing to them anyway, through the indexes," Iacovella told me later. "We decided we really needed to start to get the word out because this was a huge problem."

In June 2019, the battle between Washington and Wall Street over Chinese companies listed by US index providers became public when Rubio sent a letter to MSCI asking them to explain how these Chinese companies in their listings were structured internally and how connected they were to the Chinese government. Of course, there was no way for MSCI to answer, because nobody knew the answers to those questions. That was the point Rubio was trying to make. "In reality, what MSCI is doing is allowing the Chinese Communist Party controlled market, and its state-owned national champion companies, to access a critical source of capital and clothe itself in a façade of legitimacy," the letter stated. This US financial firm, like so many others, was investing Americans' savings, adding up to hundreds of billions of dollars, without an ounce of awareness or concern for where the money was going and how that might affect the country.

The index providers, backed by Mnuchin, simply ignored Rubio and others who raised concerns. So Robinson decided to try a new approach. If pointing out what the index providers were doing in a general sense wasn't moving the needle, he thought, perhaps more lawmakers and officials would get involved if they realized that one of the funds that was set to increase its holding of problematic Chinese companies was the pension fund that managed the retirement savings of five million federal employees, including US military service members.

This was Robinson's next target. Called the Thrift Savings Plan, it was governed by the Federal Retirement Thrift Investment Board, which was planning to switch the plan's investment options. In the new proposed scheme, the only international option available to five million US federal employees to invest would be one that tracked a specific MSCI index that contained a number of problematic Chinese companies.

At first, Robinson's new approach seemed to be working. More lawmakers joined the fight. More letters were written. More articles were published. But the Federal Retirement Thrift Investment Board refused to budge.

Rubio tried to advance legislation to force the board to change its mind, but Mike Crapo, chairman of the Senate Banking Committee, thwarted that plan at Mnuchin's request. Mnuchin went to the president and told him if he intervened to stop the board, he would be disrupting the markets at the worst time and undermining the credibility of the biggest market index in the world. For the time being, Trump — who always had a hard time distinguishing the markets' performance from his approval ratings — declined to intervene.

California Dreaming

Undeterred, Robinson turned his attention to another retirement fund: the California Public Employees' Retirement System (CalPERS). Robinson had so far failed in his attempt to get the administrators of the Thrift Savings Plan to share his outrage about the index providers who were quietly channeling money to bad-actor Chinese firms. But if anything, CalPERS was an even bigger contributor to the problem. The California state pension system had the distinction of being the largest in the country — and its new chief investment officer, Ben Meng, also had a clear and troubling connection to the CCP.

Meng had taken the job of CalPERS CIO after returning from Beijing, where he had spent three years helping to manage the investments of China's gargantuan State Administration of Foreign Exchange (SAFE), which has assets under management of more than $3 trillion US dollars. China's foreign exchange reserves are a crucial part of the CCP's financial security. In recent years, Beijing has clamped down on capital outflow, showing just how seriously they take the issue of obtaining and holding foreign money, especially US dollars.

At CalPERS, Meng guided investment decisions that increased the pension system's already substantial exposure to Chinese companies, including major state-owned enterprises. During his first year, CalPERS tripled the number of Chinese companies it was investing in, including twenty-one connected to the PLA or sanctioned human rights abusers, according to research compiled by Robinson's firm. CalPERS said it was just passively tracking the MSCI and FTSE Russell indexes, but its own disclosures showed that it was actually following a homegrown investment strategy that used the indexes as a guide but didn't track them 100 percent.

Robinson's efforts to draw attention to the CalPERS problem appeared to bear fruit when Representative Jim Banks (R-IN) wrote a letter to California governor Gavin Newsom in February 2020, alleging that Meng was recruited to work in China through the Thousand Talents program. The allegation was true, but Banks was accused of racism for targeting Meng, who is a Chinese-born naturalized US citizen. Trump's Wall Street cabal reacted angrily as well — mounting a public campaign to stave off any efforts to force CalPERS to change course. But these friends of Meng didn't disclose their own conflicts of interests or how driving US investor dollars into Chinese companies benefited their bottom lines as well.

One prominent Trump adviser who spoke out in Meng's defense was Stephen Schwarzman. Not only did his private equity group, Blackstone, invest money on behalf of CalPERS, but Meng also was part of the Schwarzman Scholars program at Tsinghua University. "This type of attack on an accomplished American citizen is unwarranted," Schwarzman told *Bloomberg News*. "Ben is a talented investor who has done a tremendous job for the pensioners."

Robinson also used his deep connections and reputation to put his research in front of as many senior government officials as possible. He reached out to the NSC staff and shared his firm's research on CalPERS. On March 13, national security adviser Robert O'Brien joined the battle, telling a crowd at the Heritage Foundation that the CalPERS investments in firms helping China's military were extremely concerning. "I don't see why we should be underwriting the Chinese defense industry," he said.

Backed by the Treasury Department and the big banks, not one American index or pension fund has voluntarily divested one Chinese stock or bond in the face of congressional and administration pressure as of the time of this writing. But on May 20, 2020, Trump directed O'Brien and Larry Kudlow to issue a letter expressing the president's opposition to the Thrift Savings Plan board's proposal to increase its holding of Chinese stocks and bonds. The board relented. It was the first time China's effort to secure American investor capital was rebuffed on national security grounds.

Meng resigned from his position as CIO at CalPERS in August 2020, just days after he was publicly accused of failing to properly disclose his own personal investments in Chinese companies at the same time he was steering California pension funds into China. CalPERS claimed Meng did nothing wrong and that his sudden resignation had nothing to do with his personal scandal or the controversy over the fund's Chinese investments.

"The Greatest Financial Scandal in World History"

The Wall Street argument is that if Chinese companies can't raise money in the United States, they will just do it somewhere else—and that US financial firms have a fiduciary obligation to get the best return for their investors. But Robinson points out that the US capital markets are still the largest and most respected in the world by far; simply put, there is nowhere else for Chinese corporations to go for money—at least, no other financial wells that have anywhere near the depth, volume, and liquidity of the US markets. China's domestic currency, the renminbi, isn't tradeable outside its border. In order for China to expand economically and press its interests by spreading money around the world, it first needs to collect said money from outside China.

What's more, US financial firms' fiduciary responsibilities are not the extent of their duty as American corporations. Indeed, Wall Street's chief obligation, Robinson argues, is to protect American investors from fraud and from becoming complicit in China's military expansion and internal repression, which can represent asymmetric material risk to these American investors.

Wall Street's contention, that its investment in Chinese companies is separate from and unrelated to Washington's drive to compete with China and confront Beijing's malign behavior, was never true. Nor is it a defensible position, now that Chinese companies have become the most prominent implementers of Beijing's strategy. How can the Commerce Department sanction Hikvision while US financial firms are sending American dollars to it at the same time? How can Wall Street steer the pensions of American soldiers into Chinese companies that are building the weapons pointed back at them? As the Chinese government has speeded up its fusion of military and civilian activities, it has forced the US system to respond—whether all parts of that system want to or not.

Wall Street's behavior was not just undermining the short-term US goal of pressuring the Chinese government into a deal that would correct the trade imbalance and secure Beijing's promise to end its unfair trade practices. Robinson said the larger point is that China is going around the world buying elites, countries, even continents with a seemingly endless supply of money that they are getting from US citizens. Americans are contributing mightily to the funding of the Chinese government's strategy to surpass the United States. If the United States wants to thwart that plan, it must force Chinese companies to comply with US laws or be denied access to US investors. In doing so, the United States can preserve its primacy, protect its citizens, preserve the integrity of its markets, and thwart Beijing's malign activities all at once, Robinson said.

"We have used little, if any, of the leverage associated with our utter dominance of the global financial domain," Robinson said, "even though it involves China's single greatest weakness and one of America's greatest strengths — access to money. How have we done nothing about this over the past twenty years? This may well be the greatest financial scandal in world history."

13

Endgame

As 2019 wound down, Trump's trade team was still traveling back and forth to Beijing, trying to get a deal in place so that Trump could enter his election year with a foreign policy accomplishment that he could run on. Beijing had called his bluff. They had reneged on their pledges from earlier in the year, and Steven Mnuchin and Robert Lighthizer were still at the table. The time advantage had flipped back to Beijing. The Chinese economy was not breaking. Xi Jinping was president for life. But Trump had an election coming up.

Meanwhile, the effort by several national security agencies across the government to push back on China was humming along as fast as ever, if not faster. The Justice Department was scooping up more and more Chinese spies and prosecuting more and more cases against Chinese businesspeople and researchers thieving inside the United States. The Commerce Department kept sanctioning more companies complicit in the Xinjiang atrocities. The State Department put in new rules for Chinese diplomats, requiring them to report if they were going to meet with federal, state, or local officials of any kind while they were posted inside the United States. This was advertised as an example of "reciprocity," in response to China's severe restrictions on American diplomats there. But it was nice for State to know who the Chinese were meeting with, as well.

Vice President Pence gave another big China speech in October, which had previously been delayed because of the trade talks. But while the vice president was talking tough against China, US and Chinese economic officials were meeting to work out a deal. This dissonance did not go unnoticed by the general public. Was this an example of two camps inside the administration pursuing two different China policies? Or was there a logic to it? The argument some officials made at this time was that the US government was learning to walk and chew gum — to pursue some engagement and negotiations with Beijing while getting tough at the same time. But the notion that the Trump administration had a coherent approach to China, or on anything related to foreign policy, was hard to defend when Trump got directly involved. His swings back and forth — sometimes within the same day — ensured that nobody ever really knew what his China policy was at a given moment.

The last few months of the trade talks were full of threats and brinksmanship that ultimately ended in capitulation. In early August, when Mnuchin returned from his latest trip to Beijing, Trump was getting antsy. No longer trusting Mnuchin's advice, he denied the Treasury secretary's request to delay the next round of tariffs and announced that the United States would impose 10 percent tariffs on another $300 billion of Chinese imports, including consumer goods like toys, shoes, and clothes. These represented a new class of products coming from China that had been largely left untouched, because tariffs on consumer goods were likely to raise prices for US consumers, also known as voters. But Trump threatened it anyway. "When my people came home, they said we're talking. We have another meeting in early September," said Trump. "I said, 'That's fine.' But in the meantime, until such time as there's a deal, we'll be taxing them."

It was a major escalation, and China responded in kind — but with an underhanded reprisal that would allow it to hit back not once, but twice. In the short term, Beijing reacted to the new tariffs by allowing the tightly controlled yuan to slip to an eleven-year low, a move that could only result from a deliberate decision by Beijing. The move made Chinese exports cheaper and US exports more expensive, offsetting the effect of Trump's tariffs. It also spooked the markets and led to the Dow Jones dropping 3 percent in one day. Late in the day on August 5,

Mnuchin's Treasury Department, under White House orders, formally named China a "currency manipulator," the designation Mnuchin had talked Trump out of in 2017.

Two weeks later, the administration announced it would split those tariffs into two tranches, delaying tariffs on toys and consumer electronics (about $160 billion worth of imports) until December 15. The idea was to give a break to Americans who were buying and selling holiday presents. It was also an implicit admission that Trump was fibbing when he said the tariffs only cost China and didn't have costs for the United States.

Trump's billionaire friends were trying hard to steer him toward making a deal, any deal, and quick. Sheldon Adelson met with Trump at the White House on August 20 and told him in no uncertain terms he was risking not only the health of the US economy but also his reelection prospects with the new tariffs.

On August 23, Beijing released its plan to formally retaliate against Trump's early August tariffs, in addition to the currency moves, which included upping its tariffs on $75 billion of US goods. The Chinese counterattack hit automobiles hardest, with a tariff of 42 percent. Xi, knowing that many of Trump's voters were also in the manufacturing sector, was going straight for the jugular.

Trump reacted angrily and promised on Twitter a re-retaliation by raising his tariffs on the first $250 billion of Chinese goods from 25 to 30 percent and raising the tariffs on the new $300 billion worth of Chinese goods from 10 to 15 percent. The president also went on a Twitter rant in which he declared, "Our great American companies are hereby ordered to immediately start looking for an alternative to China, including bringing . . . your companies HOME."

The president had just announced a new policy of decoupling the two largest economies in the world as a threat — and seemingly on a whim.

After firing off the tweet, Trump boarded Air Force One for the meeting of the leaders of the Group of 7 (G7) countries in Biarritz, France, where I had arrived the day before. If the previous few days were any indication, it was going to be a wild weekend.

The France Fiasco

Trump had treated the ritual of the G7 summit — and the G7 itself — with a mix of disregard and disdain. He often referred to this gang of the seven leading Western democracies — Canada, France, Germany, Italy, the United Kingdom, Japan, and the United States — as "an outdated group of countries" that no longer reflected the reality of world power. He never stopped trying to bring Russia back in, after it was expelled following its invasion of Ukraine. Trump's behavior at all international summits was generally awful, but the G7 really brought out the worst in him.

At the 2018 G7 summit in Charlevoix, Canada, Trump bickered with his world leader counterparts over the joint statement and then infamously withdrew the United States from that joint statement on the plane ride leaving Canada, because he didn't like how Canadian prime minister Justin Trudeau had talked about him on television. Trump didn't even want to go to the 2019 summit, hosted by French president Emmanuel Macron. "Trump was wildly unenthusiastic about attending yet another G-7 after the fun at Charlevoix in 2018, and several times told me and others he would arrive late and leave early," John Bolton wrote in his book. "Trump was so uninterested in the G-7 it was hard for [Larry] Kudlow and me to schedule a briefing for him."

By the time Trump arrived in France on August 24, the media was all over his sudden call for US companies to start leaving China. But Trump didn't mind the outrage; rather, he minded that some news outlets said he didn't have the authority to order such a drastic maneuver. After Air Force One touched down, Trump tweeted that the "Fake News Reporters" were wrong to say he couldn't order US companies to leave China, citing the Emergency Economic Powers Act of 1977.

The main story at the G7 Biarritz summit was that Macron was quietly trying to arrange a meeting between Trump and Iranian foreign minister Javad Zarif, who was flying in secretly at Macron's invitation. Bolton and others worked successfully to thwart that idea and never forgave Macron for trying to pull it off without telling them. But that alone wasn't going to satiate the hundreds of reporters from around the world who had traveled to Biarritz for the event. And Trump insisted on doing a press conference before each bilateral meeting he had with the other heads of state. He was asked several times about the China controversy he had just ignited. And each time he answered, he made the predicament worse.

On the morning of the 25th, Trump was asked whether he was having second thoughts about his threats to raise tariffs on China just a few days earlier. The markets were reacting badly to his bombastic tweets and threats. "Yeah, sure, why not?" he said. "Might as well. Might as well. I have second thoughts about everything."

The press immediately reported that Trump had reversed himself. The markets jumped at the news — but then dropped again when White House press secretary Stephanie Grisham said those comments were "misinterpreted" and Trump actually meant that he had had second thoughts "because he regrets not raising the tariffs higher."

Kudlow and Mnuchin were sent to the hotel where the American press was headquartered on a public relations clean-up mission. Kudlow said Trump had trouble hearing the question. But Trump was clearly trying to back down and calm the markets. At his next open press event, he said, "Actually, we're getting along very well with China right now. We're talking."

A few hours later in Beijing, Liu He, the lead Chinese trade negotiator, just happened to be giving a speech at the Smart China Expo in Chongqing and indirectly referred to Trump's bombastic tweets. Liu said that China "resolutely opposes escalation of the U.S. trade war" and prefers "calm negotiations." This was clearly meant as a criticism of Trump's statements. But Trump misinterpreted it as a concession, focusing on the word "calm."

Trump praised Liu's comments at his next Biarritz press conference. "Very big things are happening with China," Trump said, sitting next to Egyptian president Abdel Fattah el-Sisi. "You probably read the breaking news a little while ago that they want to make a deal — they just came out — and they want calm. And that's a great thing, frankly. And one of the reasons that he's a great leader — President Xi — and one of the reasons that China is a great country is they understand how life works."

Trump became fixated on the comments by Liu, which he had misunderstood and was now repeatedly misrepresenting. Trump said during a news conference with Macron, "I think they want to make a deal very badly. I think that was elevated last night. The vice chairman of China came out, he said he wants to see a deal made." He also said the Chinese had called to relay the message, but Trump just didn't realize Liu was making a public speech and there had been no direct outreach.

The president had created at least three different competing news cycles in three days and manufactured a controversy only to back away from it, sending the markets up and down — for no reason. Trump's brinksmanship had escalated into total confusion, but the end result was that the president was still looking for a deal. So he sent his negotiating team back to work.

"Phase One"

In October, Liu He came to Washington and met with Trump in the Oval Office. After the meeting, Trump announced that a "Phase One" deal was all but struck. He didn't reveal the details of the near-complete deal, but he broadly claimed the terms would represent real progress on reducing China's theft of intellectual property and forced transfer of US technology, while also noting that "the banks and all of the financial services companies will be very, very happy with what we've been able to get."

In fact, the Phase One agreement would take months longer to play out, and even then Trump officials would caution that it was only a down payment on fixing the imbalances in the US-China economic and trade relationship. By calling it the "Phase One" deal, Lighthizer and Mnuchin were conceding that it was incomplete and promising to start negotiations on a "Phase Two" as soon as possible. Nobody thought that would really happen, unless or until Trump was reelected. The actual terms of the new trade agreement remained a closely held secret for weeks.

The uncertainty about the deal continued because the text remained missing in action, under the explanation that the translation was taking a long time. There was some planning to release it at the next G20 summit in Chile in November, when Trump and Xi could meet and maybe even have a signing ceremony. But that summit was canceled due to violent unrest on the Chilean streets. Meanwhile, every time Trump spoke publicly about the deal, he said something different about whether it was actually complete, confusing everyone.

In early December, on a trip to London, Trump was asked again about why the announcement of the Phase One deal seemed to be held up. This time, Trump indicated it might not happen at all. He played it off by saying he had "no deadline" for the trade talks and "in some ways I think it's better to wait until after the election with China." He continued to casually threaten to decouple the world's largest economies using his self-proclaimed economic powers. Sitting next to Justin Trudeau in London, Trump commented, "I don't want them to lose their supply chains, but if it happens, it happens." He also claimed he didn't watch the stock market, which was tanking due to his comments.

There was a firm reason the deal was not yet done. The sticking point for those two months was over whether China would receive substantial tariff relief up front. The US side wanted to freeze tariffs in place and delay any tariff relief until Phase Two of the deal could be finished, whereas the Chinese side insisted on substantial tariff rollbacks as part of Phase One. In early December, the US side largely conceded this point, removing the final obstacle.

On December 13, Lighthizer announced that the two negotiating teams had struck a deal. Jared Kushner had weighed in heavily in favor of the deal with Trump and Trump had accepted it. In the final weeks, Kushner reinvigorated his personal channel with Ambassador Cui Tiankai and they talked constantly. The announcement, which came two days before the next tariff deadline, promised that China had agreed to make broad structural reforms to its economy and purchase enormous amounts of US products.

Lighthizer later explained his personal belief that the success of the Phase One trade deal would be determined by whether "reformers" inside the Chinese system, like Liu He, won the internal struggle over the direction of China's economic development. Lighthizer was convinced that if these reformers could be empowered, China might actually fulfill its promises to become more market-oriented and obey the rules of the international economic and trade system. "Whether there will be a Phase 2 depends on whether China complies with the terms of Phase 1 and whether it is willing to fundamentally change its model of state-run capitalism," he wrote later in *Foreign Affairs.* "Regardless, the policy in place today protects American jobs, blunts China's unfair advantages, and minimizes the pain to U.S. exporters and consumers."

Most of the tariffs remained in place under the Phase One deal. There would still be 25 percent tariffs on the first $250 billion worth of Chinese goods and 7.5 percent tariffs on the $120 billion worth of goods that were added in September (down from 15 percent). For the economic warriors like Peter Navarro, there could have been worse outcomes. The tariffs were being institutionalized. These tariffs, over time, would have the collateral effect of pushing the decoupling Navarro envisioned, simply by making the costs of doing business in China higher for US firms. Moreover, businesses could now make decisions to reduce their presence in China because the unpredictability was reduced and the tariffs would be here to stay. Even politically, if Trump lost, a new president would find it hard to just let all those tariffs go. They now represented long-term leverage that would give Beijing incentive to keep negotiating, and maybe even to live up to some of its commitments.

The criticism of the Phase One deal, however, was broad and swift. Democrats maintained that Trump had upended the world economy for scant gains. Superhawks criticized Trump for agreeing to promises of structural reforms that—again—would be nearly impossible to enforce down the line. The enforcement mechanism boiled down to Lighthizer, or his successor, being in charge of determining whether China was living up to its commitments. If the United States thought Beijing was in violation, it reserved the right to reimpose the sanctions. But of course, that would mean starting the trade war all over again.

Trump, having decided that an imperfect deal was better than no deal at all, leaned all the way into it. He invited Liu He and his team for a signing ceremony in January. Two days before the ceremony, Treasury announced it would no longer designate China as a currency manipulator. The trade war was over. Both sides claimed victory but neither really won.

Celebration Time

The January 15 signing ceremony for the Phase One deal in the East Room of the White House was a quintessentially Trumpian event. Ever a showman, the American president had invited a coterie of billionaires, lawmakers, senior officials, family members, and friends to be part of the day's big event. By collecting powerful people to celebrate his accomplishment and presenting it as a group effort, he was giving them respect and validation while collecting both from them at the same time.

For about an hour, Trump called out the attendees at the event and thanked them for supporting him and for helping him secure the deal, whether they helped or not. In the front row sat Henry Kissinger, Stephen Schwarzman, Nelson Peltz, Adelson, Hank Greenberg, Michael Pillsbury, and others. Navarro was seated a few rows back. The Chinese delegation, led by Liu He, was featured prominently and given the full red-carpet treatment. Xi did not attend, but Trump thanked him and called him "a very, very good friend of mine." He then praised Liu He as "a good friend of mine." Then, one by one, Trump pointed to and set up applause lines for several other officials, including Pence, Mnuchin, Lighthizer, Kushner, Kudlow, and (for some reason) Ivanka.

Trump touted the Dow Jones's record-setting numbers that day and sarcastically referred to the fact that the billionaires were more interested in their bottom line than the US-China relationship: "The market is up substantially today," he said. "We have all these business leaders. I'm sure they don't care." Trump started ad-libbing, at one point teasing Ambassador Terry Branstad for being obsequious to the Chinese leadership. Trump told a story about how Branstad had asked Trump to tamp down his criticism of China before the election. "He just said, 'Don't say bad about China,'" Trump recalled. "So I had to rip up about half of my speech, right? And I said, 'Why?' And he said, 'Well, we do a lot of business.'"

Trump teased the China hawks as well. He pointed to Navarro as the example of the opposite of Branstad. "Right, Peter? He's a little different. We have all types. We have all types." He then praised Wilbur Ross, Sonny Perdue, Elaine Chao, Kevin McCarthy, Sheldon and Miriam Adelson, Lou Dobbs, Kissinger, and Pillsbury.

When he got to Schwarzman, Trump joked about the fact that the deal is chock full of goodies for Wall Street firms. "A friend of mine, Steve Schwarzman, is here. Steve, I know you have no interest in this deal at all," Trump joked. Schwarzman, Peltz, and Pillsbury actually conducted the postceremony press conference with reporters.

All the backslapping and happy banter was premature, to say the least. Trump and Xi had come together under a flag of truce, but they hadn't agreed to much of substance—and if Trump didn't make it through that fall's election, they never would. The signing ceremony, however, had never really been about celebrating a real achievement. Rather, it was about putting on a good show for the American people.

Trump tipped his hand when, after finishing his comedy routine, he returned to his prepared remarks, which presented the deal as a campaign promise fulfilled. "In June of 2016, in the great state of Pennsylvania, I promised that I would use every lawful presidential power to protect Americans from unfair trade and unfair trade practices," Trump said. "Unlike those who came before me, I kept my promise."

But Trump wasn't content to simply claim he had fixed the US-China economic relationship. He then went on to claim, quite absurdly, that he had solved several other huge problems in the US-China relationship. He claimed that China was helping the United States with North Korea (although Beijing was in fact loosening sanctions and pressure on the rogue regime). He said Xi had made great progress on stopping fentanyl from coming into the United States, despite the fact that there was zero evidence of that.

Not everyone was in such a celebratory mood. The fear among the hardliners was that after the signing, Trump would refuse to allow any more tough-on-China actions, in order to protect his new baby. They were mortified as they watched him present the Phase One trade deal — which they considered only moderately consequential — as a broader détente in the US-China relationship. For them, it was simply a limited agreement for a short-term truce on one front of the wider war with China.

Their boss, clearly, did not see it this way. "This is something that — far beyond even this deal — it's going to lead to an even stronger world peace," Trump said. "We now have a big investment in each other and in getting along with each other." He added that it was important for the whole world to keep "these two giant and powerful nations together in harmony." This kind of language reminded the hardliners of the "new model of great power relations" Xi had originally pitched to Obama. Trump seemed to be nodding to it.

That was January 15, 2020. The Chinese officials flew home satisfied that they had cemented a new path forward for US-China relations. Throughout their entire visit, they never once mentioned the issue that would soon dominate not only the relationship but the attention of the entire world — a mysterious flu was already spreading throughout China.

"They just got on the plane and never said a word," a White House official said. "Almost the next day, information about the virus started pouring in."

14

The Coronavirus

The first National Security Council (NSC) meeting on the strange new flu spreading around China had been held on the 14th of January, just one day before the White House ceremony to sign the Phase One trade deal. The meeting was held at the Policy Coordination Committee level, meaning the issue was not deemed important enough yet for cabinet officials, so each department was represented by lower-level officials. NSC senior director for weapons of mass destruction and biodefense Anthony Ruggiero chaired the meeting. Matt Pottinger was traveling abroad. "At that point, we didn't know how bad it was," Pottinger later recalled. They wouldn't have long to wait.

There in the room were representatives from all the related agencies, including the Centers for Disease Control and Prevention (CDC). The objective of this meeting was simply to try to get the lay of the land — and get answers to some basic questions. *What do we know about this thing? Do we have eyes on the ground? Where is the best information coming from? What are the Chinese saying about it?* But all that came back were shrugs. The health officials said that information was scarce. The US government had been trying to get permission to send CDC personnel to Wuhan for over a week without success. The World Health Organization (WHO) had been issuing statements about virus outbreak, but they hadn't been allowed to visit Wuhan yet either, so they didn't have any firsthand information.

Throughout all the festivities the next day at the White House surrounding the Phase One trade deal signing ceremony, the Chinese delegation acted as if there was no health crisis in their country that was in the process of spreading around the world; during their visit, the Chinese representatives didn't say a word about the virus. Nothing. It was never brought up — by either side.

It didn't even occur to the US officials who were hosting the Chinese delegation to ask about the coronavirus. The Chinese officials left after a two-day visit marked by the trade deal signing and press conference, giving no warning about what they must have known at the time: that the emerging pandemic was much worse than publicly known — more contagious, more present in asymptomatic cases, and more out of control than they wanted to admit.

Over the next ten days, Pottinger's email inbox was flooded with messages from credible sources telling him the outbreak in China was far worse than the Chinese government was telling. He began to scour Chinese social media, picking up firsthand accounts of the outbreak in Wuhan as they appeared and then were quickly deleted by Chinese censors. Ai Fen, a senior doctor at Wuhan Central Hospital, posted about the virus on WeChat. Wuhan doctor Li Wenliang also shared information. Both were admonished by the Chinese authorities for releasing information not previously approved by the government. The cover-up was already under way. Any Chinese health officials who publicly warned that the virus was more dangerous than the authorities would admit were forced to apologize or arrested.

On the evening of January 24, Pottinger went to Dimon Liu's house for a Chinese New Year's dinner celebration. It wasn't a formal Bingo Club event, but it was the same crowd. (I was out of town that weekend and missed it.) The Chinese dissidents at the party pleaded with Pottinger to investigate further, insisting that the crisis in Wuhan was far worse than advertised.

Pottinger came home from the party rattled and immediately started reaching out to doctors inside China who had been his sources when he covered the SARS outbreak in 2003 as a reporter for the *Wall Street Journal.* That public health crisis had marked the global debut of — and the first known pandemic risk from — coronaviruses, a type of pathogen that until then had been little studied and only poorly understood.

The deputy national security adviser was shocked, but not surprised, to think that history could now be repeating itself. The 2003 outbreak of what became known as severe acute respiratory syndrome coronavirus (SARS-CoV) had originated in China's Guangdong Province, where it was thought to have spread from bats to a type of tree-dwelling mammal called a palm civet, and from there to humans. The outbreak had ultimately been contained, but not before infecting over eight thousand people in over two dozen countries and causing 774 deaths. The Chinese government had actively undermined the containment efforts by failing to alert the WHO in a timely manner, suppressing information about the outbreak and allowing it to spread around the world without proper warnings.

Pottinger's response was not informed solely by his personal experience with SARS. It just so happened that he had two other close contacts who could provide him with information and insights on the subject of the new outbreak. Yen Pottinger, Matt's wife, is a trained virologist and former CDC official. Paul Pottinger, Matt's brother, is a professor of infectious diseases at the University of Washington School of Medicine in Seattle.

Between his ability to read Chinese social media in Chinese, his sources inside China, and his family expertise with infectious diseases — not to mention the US intelligence trickling in — Pottinger found himself at the nexus of more streams of information about the coronavirus than anyone else in the US government. He saw the pandemic coming before anyone else. But he had a problem: most people in the Trump administration didn't wanted to believe what was unfolding — or at least didn't want to speak up.

"Holy . . ."

On Monday, January 27, with Robert O'Brien's blessing, Pottinger called a cabinet meeting and chaired it, with the number one or two officials from all the relevant agencies in attendance: Health and Human Services Department secretary Alex Azar, CDC director Robert Redfield, Deputy Secretary of State Stephen Biegun, and National Institute of Allergy and Infectious Diseases director Anthony Fauci were all there. Pottinger told them all about his experience covering the SARS epidemic in China in 2003, the cover-up, the lack of real information coming out of China, and how we were seeing those exact patterns again.

"Look, you all need to convince me why we shouldn't shut down travel from China," Pottinger told the group. "Our default position should be to shut it down."

Not one of the other officials agreed. They thought Pottinger was out of his mind. The next morning, Pottinger had a conversation with a very high-level doctor in China, one who had spoken with health officials in several provinces, including Wuhan. This was a trusted source who was in a position to know the ground truth.

"Is this going to be as bad as SARS in 2003?" he asked the doctor, whose name must remain secret for his own protection.

"Forget SARS in 2003," the doctor replied, "this is 1918." He was referring to the deadliest pandemic of the twentieth century: an influenza outbreak that killed roughly fifty million people worldwide.

The doctor told Pottinger half the cases were asymptomatic and the government must have known all about it. He added that there was evidence of sustained human-to-human transmission in several provinces. SARS didn't have asymptomatic spread. O'Brien and Pottinger briefed Trump in the Oval Office the next day, Tuesday, January 28.

"This is the single greatest national security crisis of your presidency and it's now unfolding," O'Brien told the president.

"It's going to be 1918," Pottinger told Trump.

"Holy fuck," the president replied.

O'Brien and Pottinger recommended that Trump immediately ban travelers who were coming to the United States from China, or who had recently been to China. Every single other Trump official opposed the move, even the health experts like Fauci, for two more days. Only on Thursday, January 30, the day the first US case of human-to-human transmission was confirmed, did the health experts switch sides and decide to support the travel ban. But White House chief of staff Mick Mulvaney and Steven Mnuchin held firm, warning Trump that it would tank the markets and hurt the airline industry.

Trump sided with O'Brien and Pottinger. He announced the ban on Friday, January 31.

"It wasn't a consensus view, by any stretch of the imagination," Pottinger told me later. "Trump went with his instinct and shut it down."

All Hell

When Trump announced the ban on travel from China, it seemed drastic. It *was* drastic. This was an election year, and the success of the economy was the core of Trump's argument for a second term. Nobody wanted to believe it was necessary. The implementation of the policy was chaotic and raised more questions than answers. And Trump was still downplaying the severity of the risk, which made the China travel ban seem even more aggressive at the time.

On February 1, the day after Trump announced a ban on all travelers save for American citizens who had been to China within the last fourteen days, one of the Democratic presidential primary contenders sent out a tweet. "We need to lead the way with science — not Donald Trump's record of hysteria, xenophobia, and fear-mongering," wrote Joe Biden, the former vice president under Barack Obama and a longtime presidential hopeful. Later, the Biden campaign would say Biden was not calling Trump's decision to ban travel from China "xenophobic," but rather referring to Trump's use of the term "China virus." But the timing of Biden's tweet shows that it was very likely a response to the travel ban decision. The Biden campaign didn't say that their candidate supported the China travel ban until early April.

Concerned about the political implications, Mulvaney tried to rein in Pottinger. He took O'Brien aside and told him, "You've got to get Pottinger under control." Pottinger was too young, Mulvaney said, and too immature to be deputy national security adviser. Mulvaney was among the most skeptical of all the White House officials that the virus threat was real. In late February, as the markets tanked, Mulvaney said the media was exaggerating the threat in an effort to bring down President Trump, calling it the "hoax of the day." As he prepared the White House's first budget to respond to the emerging crisis, Mulvaney pegged the total cost at $800 million. (Mulvaney was pushed out in early March.)

O'Brien ignored Mulvaney's order to get Pottinger under control. He called Ambassador Deborah Birx, the State Department's global AIDS coordinator, to come home early from a conference in Africa. She was tasked to the NSC and assigned directly to the office of Vice President Pence, who was put in charge of the newly created coronavirus task force at the end of February.

Pottinger, meanwhile, continued to organize and chair the interagency meetings on the crisis because—until the Pence-led task force was stood up—nobody else wanted to do it. "He just made himself in charge," a White House official told me. "He was warning about this shit in mid-January. We were all focusing on [the US killing of Iranian military leader Qasem] Soleimani and he's talking to doctors in China in Mandarin who were seeing this firsthand."

Still, there was widespread resistance across the government to taking stronger measures to respond. When O'Brien proposed sending two military hospital ships to New York and LA to support their health systems, Defense Secretary Mark Esper raised concerns.

Esper believed the White House was rushing and failing to properly think through how the ships would be used. When Trump went ahead anyway, Esper showed up in Norfolk, Virginia, with Trump to praise the idea and wish bon voyage to the USNS *Comfort* as it departed for New York City.

Trump was downplaying the threat from the virus publicly, in part because that was in his political interest and in part because at times he believed the rosy prognostications of his staff. But most of the staff didn't understand and couldn't believe that Beijing would handle such a serious issue with so much secrecy and misinformation. In one of the earliest meetings chaired by Pottinger, Azar said, "Well, we are relying on the Chinese authorities to handle this." The hardliners knew the Chinese Communist Party (CCP) better than the health secretary did, and they assumed the Chinese authorities would act the way they always do. They turned out to be right.

The only other senior official to sound the early warning alarm was Peter Navarro. He wrote a series of memos to Trump beginning on January 29, urging the president to consider the possibility that the 2020 outbreak was a 1918-like pandemic, and that this worst-case scenario must not be discounted. If the United States didn't move quickly to contain the spread and mitigate the damage, Navarro predicted the virus could infect up to one hundred million Americans, cause one to two million deaths, and cost up to $3.8 trillion. The coronavirus pandemic would turn out to be even costlier — but Navarro was closer than most.

The Cover-Up

Beijing's efforts from the very start of the coronavirus crisis to hide information, silence whistleblowers, put out false data, and thwart any real outside investigation are too extensive to recount. But the highlights of Beijing's early mishandling of the crisis are enough to show that the Chinese government's actions were both reckless and deliberate — and exacerbated the situation considerably in those early weeks, not least by causing misunderstandings about the outbreak that fueled confusion and hurt responses in countries around the world.

Chinese authorities first alerted the WHO on December 31 that an unidentified pneumonia was spreading in Wuhan, but they said that "the disease is preventable and controllable." This was the same day that Taiwanese officials alerted the WHO about reports of "atypical pneumonia cases" in Wuhan and noted that Chinese health authorities were saying it was not believed to be SARS. Also that same day, Chinese social media censors starting erasing from the Chinese internet any references to "Wuhan unknown pneumonia," "SARS variation," "Wuhan Seafood Market," or anything critical of the government's response. But publicly, Chinese officials were still mum. The next day, Li Wenliang, a doctor in Wuhan, was summoned to the Public Security Bureau and forced to sign an apology for making false statements and disturbing the public order by sending a warning about the new SARS-like virus in Wuhan to seven other doctors inside a WeChat group.

The original government story was that the new virus had originated in the Huanan seafood market in Wuhan, which had been connected to some of the early cases. Authorities started establishing this story early on, while at the same time ensuring that it could never fully be either proven or disproven. There were early signs the officials in Wuhan were focused on the market, even as public information about the emerging outbreak was still being suppressed. On January 1, Wuhan authorities completely emptied and then sanitized the Huanan market. But they didn't take blood or other fluid samples from the animals or workers, meaning any evidence that might tie the origin of the virus to the market was destroyed. A study by Chinese researchers published in the prestigious medical journal the *Lancet* would later find that the earliest known case, identified on December 1 — and over a third of the cases in the first large cluster — had no connection to the market, making it unlikely that the virus had originated there. But at first, Beijing pointed to the seafood market as the source of the outbreak — while simultaneously making sure that later investigators would never be able to prove or disprove the link.

Chinese authorities would later reveal that the Wuhan Institute of Virology (WIV), the world's leading research center for bat coronaviruses, had mapped out the genome by January 2. They had determined from samples collected that the virus was a SARS-like coronavirus, which plainly meant that they were dealing with a pathogen that was dangerous, was highly contagious, and had no known vaccine.

Any information about the virus's genome would be critical to containing its spread and starting the research for a cure — but the Chinese authorities had sat on that vital information as the virus spread. On January 5, the Shanghai Public Health Clinical Center alerted Chinese authorities that it had also successfully identified and mapped the genome of the new virus. The government forbade them from sharing that information. Six days later, the researchers defied that order and released the genome publicly. The lab was shut down the next day for "rectification."

The WHO began regurgitating Beijing's bad information about the virus from the very start. On January 14, the organization tweeted, "Preliminary investigations conducted by the Chinese authorities have found no clear evidence of human-to-human transmission of the novel #coronavirus (2019-nCov) identified in #Wuhan, China." That same day, talking on an internal conference call with provincial officials, National Health Commission chief Ma Xiaowei reportedly called the virus "the most severe challenge since SARS in 2003" and said that "clustered cases suggest that human-to-human transmission is possible." Beijing didn't communicate that urgent update to anyone outside official Chinese government channels for another six days. In the meantime, millions of Chinese citizens traveled around the country for the Lunar New Year festivities, including in Wuhan, fueling the outbreak.

It was January 21 when a WHO delegation was allowed into Wuhan and found that in fact there was evidence of human-to-human transmission, confirming the comments of Zhong Nanshan, the scientist at the head of Beijing's response effort, the day prior. Still, the WHO declined to name the crisis a "public health emergency of international concern." Two days later, Chinese authorities locked down the entire city of Wuhan. On January 30, the International Health Regulations Emergency Committee (a WHO body) praised the Chinese government's "commitment to transparency" in a statement. On February 3, WHO director-general Tedros Adhanom Ghebreyesus praised China's strategy and credited Beijing for preventing even more cases.

The WIV, just a few miles from the seafood market, was ordered to destroy its samples of the virus and not to share them with American researchers from a Texas lab they had been working with. Major General Chen Wei, the Chinese military's top epidemiologist and virologist, was sent to take over the lab. Researchers, journalists, and doctors who posted nonapproved information about the virus were rounded up and disappeared.

Meanwhile, the virus kept spreading. Li—one of the original "gang of eight" who had posted about the disease on social media and were detained for their trouble—contracted the disease from a patient he was treating; from his hospital bed, the doctor told the *New York Times,* "If the officials had disclosed information about the epidemic earlier, I think it would have been a lot better. There should be more openness and transparency." On February 7, he died.

Just as they had done during the SARS campaign, during the early days of this new coronavirus epidemic, the Chinese authorities mounted a concerted effort to present a false picture to the world. They also missed key opportunities to stop the outbreak early in its tracks, by warning the public about human-to-human transmission, stopping travel out of Wuhan earlier, and sharing the information they had with international scientists and foreign governments.

For those who had studied the Chinese government's actions during the SARS crisis, these tactics were no surprise—in fact, they were predictable. The CCP's paranoia, defensiveness, and overall lack of concern for things like truth and transparency are part of its character. But now, for the first time, those deficiencies threatened to kill thousands of Americans.

The Propaganda War

For the first few weeks of the crisis, the State Department maintained fairly good and constructive communication with their Chinese counterparts. The State Department needed to keep close watch on American diplomats and their families and eventually sent planes to Wuhan to extract them. Those planes brought crucial medical equipment for Wuhan hospitals in their time of need. China mounted its own aid offensive as well. By the end of March, China had delivered aid to 120 countries, a massive "mask diplomacy" effort. Early on, these Chinese efforts were widely welcomed — but later, "mask diplomacy" would become synonymous with China's use of aid as a means of leverage over countries that might want to criticize it or its handling of the coronavirus outbreak that had begun within its borders.

The cooperation between the US government and Chinese authorities largely ended after Trump announced the China travel ban. The Chinese government feared that other countries would follow suit, casting blame on China and potentially hurting the Chinese economy. So Beijing launched a worldwide campaign to deter other countries that were thinking about banning travel from China. Foreign Minister Wang Yi told his Indian counterpart on February 1 that China "opposes certain countries' actions that are creating tension and causing panic."

As the United States began to deal with its own outbreak, Trump continued to downplay the virus's severity. Pottinger's and Navarro's pleas to Trump to take the pandemic more seriously might have had more effect, if it were not for another voice countering their message in Trump's ear — that of Xi Jinping.

Trump and Xi had a lengthy telephone conversation that was presented as evidence to Americans that the outbreak was under control in China and that the trade deal was intact. "President Trump expressed confidence in China's strength and resilience in confronting the challenge of the 2019 novel coronavirus outbreak," the White House said in a statement after the call, adding, "The two leaders agreed to continue extensive communication and cooperation between both sides. They also noted the great achievement of the recent United States–China Phase One Trade Deal and reaffirmed their commitment to its implementation.

But in fact, Xi worked hard to ply Trump with misinformation on February 6, according to a senior administration official who was on the call. And Trump had come away from it with a decidedly warped view of the threat.

In their conversation, the official said, Xi told Trump he opposed the decision to close US borders to flights from China. Trump asked Xi to allow US CDC officials into Wuhan, which by that point had been locked down. Xi demurred and asked Trump not to take any more excessive actions that would create further panic, in essence asking him to downplay the threat. Xi also told Trump that China had the coronavirus outbreak under control, that the virus was not a threat to the outside world, and that it was sensitive to temperature and therefore would likely go away when the weather got warmer. None of these things were true, but Trump believed them — or wanted to believe them — enough to start saying them out loud, both internally and otherwise. "That was a soothing call," said the official, who paraphrased Xi's message as *Nothing to see here, we've got this handled, don't overreact.* "Xi was downplaying the whole thing." It was a message that Americans would soon be hearing directly from the mouth of their own president.

"Now, the virus that we're talking about having to do — you know, a lot of people think that goes away in April with the heat — as the heat comes in," Trump said on February 10 at a White House meeting with state governors, not revealing that when he said, "a lot of people," he was referring to the Chinese president. As the staff battled among itself about how to deal with the emerging crisis, Xi's assurances had helped to convince the US president to misrepresent the danger — and helped convince many Americans that the pandemic would be, at most, a short-lived threat.

All the while, scientists and government officials the world over were racing to get a clearer sense of what they were truly dealing with. The day after Trump spoke those words to governors making response policy for states all across the country, the international committee tasked with naming new viruses announced that it had dubbed the novel coronavirus "severe acute respiratory syndrome coronavirus 2 (SARS-CoV-2)," a nod to its genetic similarities to the original SARS virus. At the same time, the WHO named the disease caused by the new virus: COVID-19.

As COVID-19 cases in the United States mounted, the Trump team seemed to realize that they had been duped and began increasingly to point their fingers at China. It was important to make the origin of the outbreak clear, they reasoned. But at this stage, the State Department wanted to blame China without setting themselves up for accusations that they were stoking racism against Asians or Asian Americans. So after some deliberations among government agencies, it was determined that Mike Pompeo would use the term "Wuhan virus," which was determined to be strong but not too inflammatory.

But all bets were off after Chinese diplomat Zhao Lijian, a particularly aggressive foreign ministry spokesman, tweeted on March 12 that perhaps the US Army had brought the virus into Wuhan. In his press conference on the pandemic on March 18 at the White House, Trump ignored the cautions of his staff and called COVID-19 "the Chinese virus," something he would go on to do over two dozen times. The propaganda war was on, with the two countries' officials insulting each other in public and private.

Privately but explicitly, Chinese diplomats threatened US State Department officials that they would cut off their exports of medical supplies to the United States if Washington wasn't careful about the charges that it leveled against Beijing in this war of words. This was a threat the Trump administration had to take seriously. Beijing already had shown that it was willing to use medical supplies to reward or punish countries based on how willing they were to shield China from criticism—effectively blackmailing other governments by threatening to leave their citizens to suffer. Beijing was seeking to snuff out any discussion of the virus's origins that put any responsibility on China, along with any criticism of its domestic response and any allegation that it was hiding or misrepresenting information about the virus. In a move that US officials saw as punitive, Beijing had halted exports of items like face masks, even when they were made by American companies like 3M, which had factories inside China—prompting Navarro to comment on Fox Business that China had moved to "nationalize effectively 3M, our company." The Trump administration had to tread carefully, negotiating behind the scenes rather than calling out Beijing at the cost of American lives.

The staff set up another call between Trump and Xi for March 26. In this call, Xi told Trump that China was now on the other side of the peak and case numbers were dropping significantly. He claimed that new cases in China were only from people who imported the virus from other countries. Xi didn't directly threaten to hold back personal protective equipment if Trump continued to criticize China, but he said it obliquely, telling the US president there was a cause and effect between the tone of US statements and Chinese cooperation. Xi also claimed that herbal medicine was very effective against the virus.

The two leaders agreed to a truce. They would tell their officials to halt the blame game and focus on cooperation to fight the virus. But the fact that Beijing had made the threat, and the grim reality of the controls that China was already putting on American companies' factories there, convinced everyone in the White House that US dependence on critical supply chains in China was a huge problem. "We've got to keep our mouths shut until the planes from China get here," a senior official told me at the time. "But let me tell you, after this is over we are going to make sure we never find ourselves in this situation again."

The truce lasted for about two weeks. Without intending to, I would help to hasten its demise.

The Wuhan Cables

In late 2017, top health and science officials at the US embassy in Beijing had attended a conference in the Chinese capital. There, they saw a presentation on a new study put out by a group of Chinese scientists, including several from the WIV, in conjunction with the US National Institutes of Health. The NIH had funded a number of projects that involved the WIV scientists, including much of the Wuhan lab's work with bat coronaviruses, as part of the international effort to prevent the next SARS-like pandemic by predicting how it might emerge. The new study was entitled "Discovery of a Rich Gene Pool of Bat SARS-Related Coronaviruses Provides New Insights into the Origin of SARS Coronavirus."

These researchers, the American officials learned, had found a population of bats from caves in Yunnan Province that gave them insight into how SARS coronaviruses originated and spread. But what caught the eye of the US officials was this line: "Cell entry studies demonstrated that three newly identified SARSr-CoVs with different S protein sequences are all able to use human ACE2 as the receptor, further exhibiting the close relationship between strains in this cave and [the original 2002–3] SARS-CoV."

The ACE2 receptor is an enzyme attached to the cell membranes in the lungs, heart, arteries, kidneys, and intestines. It was the primary entry point for the original SARS coronavirus when infecting human lungs, because of a rare, simple, and exquisitely effective compatibility between the virus and the human body: the S protein in the virus linked with the ACE2 receptor in the lung cells of the human victims, allowing the virus to inject genetic material into the host cell, where the DNA replicates and then moves on to infect other cells. Now, these Wuhan scientists presented a paper showing they had found three new viruses that could do the same thing. The researchers boasted that they may have found the cave where the original SARS coronavirus originated. But all the US diplomats cared about was that three new viruses had been discovered that had been found to be potentially dangerous for humans—and that these viruses were now in a lab with which they were largely unfamiliar.

Knowing the significance of the Wuhan virologists' discovery, and knowing that the WIV's top-level biosafety laboratory (BSL-4) was relatively new, the US embassy health and science officials in Beijing decided to go to Wuhan and check it out. In total, the embassy sent three teams of experts in late 2017 and early 2018 to meet with the WIV scientists, among them Shi Zhengli, often referred to as the "bat woman," because of her extensive experience studying coronaviruses found in bats.

The American diplomats were also concerned about the WIV lab because of its involvement in what are known as "gain of function" experiments, whereby the transmissibility or pathogenicity of dangerous pathogens is deliberately increased. The idea is to predict how viruses might evolve in ways that hurt humans before it happens in nature. But by bypassing pathogens' natural evolutionary cycles, these experiments create risks of a human-made outbreak if a lab accident were to occur. It was for this very reason the Obama administration issued a moratorium on gain-of-function experiments in October 2014. One such study at the University of North Carolina continued with permission despite the moratorium. Shi Zhengli was a contributor to that study, which used gain-of-function research to create a novel chimeric bat coronavirus that could more easily infect human cells. In late 2015, an article in *Nature* warned that it was too risky.

When they sat down with the scientists at the WIV, the American diplomats were shocked by what they heard. The Chinese researchers told them they didn't have enough properly trained technicians to safely operate their BSL-4 lab. The Wuhan scientists were asking for more support to get the lab up to top standards. The first two delegations were made up of technical experts and lower-level officials, but the final delegation of US officials, in March 2018, was the most senior group and was led by Jamison Fouss, the consul general in Wuhan, and Rick Switzer, the embassy's counselor on the environment, science, technology, and health.

The diplomats wrote two diplomatic cables back to Washington reporting on their visits to the Wuhan lab. More should be done to help the lab meet top safety standards, they said, and they urged Washington to get on it. They also warned that the WIV researchers had demonstrated that bat coronaviruses could more easily infect human cells than previously thought, through the same cell receptor (ACE2) that had been used by the original SARS coronavirus. "This finding strongly suggests that SARS-like coronaviruses from bats can be transmitted to humans to cause SARS-like diseases," the cable stated. "From a public health perspective, this makes the continued surveillance of SARS-like coronaviruses in bats and study of the animal-human interface critical to future emerging coronavirus outbreak prediction and prevention."

The US diplomats were warning their colleagues back in Washington that the research being done at the WIV lab was in danger of causing a public health crisis. They kept the cables unclassified because they wanted more people back home to be able to read and share them. But there was no response from State Department headquarters. And as US-China tensions rose over the course of 2018, American diplomats lost access to labs such as the one at the WIV — and therefore lost visibility into the very issue to which they were trying to draw the attention of the US government.

"The cable was a warning shot," one US official said. "They were begging people to pay attention to what was going on." The world would be paying attention soon enough — but by then, it would be too late.

Origins

When a source tipped me off to the existence of the cables in early March, I tried everything I could think of to get my hands on them. I even went to Pompeo's senior staff directly to try to convince them to hand them over. Pompeo thought about it but refused. He needed to keep up the veneer of good relations with China, and these revelations would make that job more difficult. The cables were not leaked by any Trump administration political official, as many in the media wrongly assumed. In fact, Pompeo was very angry when he found out about the leak.

Eventually I found a source who had the cables and shared them with me, without any authorization. I called around to get reactions from scientists and other American officials I trusted. What I found was that, just months into the pandemic, a large swath of the government already believed the virus had escaped from the WIV lab, rather than having leapt from an animal to a human at the Wuhan seafood market or some other random natural setting, as the Chinese government had initially claimed.

The hypothesis that the virus had emerged naturally, without any connection to the WIV lab, rested entirely on circumstantial evidence. Most previous virus outbreaks had been the result of what's called a "natural spillover," and the US scientists who worked with the WIV scientists were publicly telling anyone and everyone that this had to be the case again — because, they claimed, there was just no way that the new coronavirus could have come from the lab. Shi, the "bat woman," released a statement on February 3 asserting that the WIV had searched its databases and not found any evidence that it previously had the new virus.

The WIV *did* have in its files a virus that was 96.2 percent similar genetically to the new coronavirus, Shi claimed in a February 3 scientific paper in *Nature*. It was called RaTG13 and its genome was the most similar known in the world to that of SARS-CoV-2 (which scientists at that time were also referring to as 2019-nCoV, for "2019 novel coronavirus"). Shi's paper noted that "RaTG13 is the closest relative of 2019-nCoV and they form a distinct lineage from other SARSr-CoVs." This made it possible that RaTG13 not only was a close relative of SARS-CoV-2 but also was its direct ancestor: that the new coronavirus had actually descended from this closely related pathogen, which had been discovered in the wild and brought to the Wuhan lab. But since SARS-CoV-2 had not been found in her files, Shi was arguing, it could not possibly have escaped the lab.

Even the closest of kin still have different genomes — and in this case, the genetic differences between these coronaviruses were considerable, despite their similarities. According to one researcher, these differences represented between twenty and fifty years of evolutionary changes caused by random mutations, although other researchers say that timeline may be overestimated. Some researchers conjecture that the evolution of SARS-CoV-2 likely happened outside the lab, and that it jumped to humans via an intermediate host animal, such as a pangolin, which could be found in an animal market, and in which a different, less closely similar relative of SARS-CoV-2 had indeed been found. Other researchers conjecture that there's no evidence that both SARS-CoV-2 and the virus found in pangolins may come directly from bats. The bottom line is that the direct link between RaTG13 and SARS-CoV-2 has not been found.

The similarities between RaTG13 and SARS-CoV-2 nevertheless drew attention, and presented a challenge for defenders of the circumstantial case for the natural-spillover theory, because it suggested that SARS-CoV-2 likely came from bats in Yunnan, which was more than one thousand kilometers away from Wuhan. So too did the fact that the Chinese government had destroyed the evidence at the Wuhan market—and that the first known case had not even been traced to there, according to the *Lancet* study, which was published on February 15.

What's more, it soon emerged that RaTG13 may have been a virus that had already been proved to be deadly to humans. Shi, in response to repeated queries, stated that RaTG13 had previously been named BtCoV/4991 and had been found by her lab in 2013 in bat feces collected from a mine in the Mojiang area of Yunnan Province—the same province where, in a cave, WIV researchers had discovered the three supercontagious coronaviruses that had inspired the Wuhan cables. Shortly before BtCoV/4991 was discovered, six miners had been cleaning bat feces there when they came down with a mysterious illness. They were taken to Wuhan, where three of them died. The symptoms those miners displayed were eerily similar to the symptoms caused in 2020 by the new SARS-CoV-2 virus, according to a master's thesis written by a doctor who oversaw the miners' treatment at the time. The thesis subsequently was translated into English and published by Western researchers in July 2020.

In an interview in March 2020, Shi remembered going to the mine where the miners got sick, but she claimed that the Wuhan researchers discovered that the cause was a fungal infection, not a virus. Nevertheless, the WIV sent four separate missions to that Yunnan mine in 2012 and 2013 to search for bat coronaviruses, not fungi. The trips to Yunnan took place while some of the miners were still in the hospital. When Shi published a paper in 2016 about what the WIV had found on these missions, she referred to one of the new viruses that had been collected in the Yunnan mines as BtCoV/4991. As noted previously, she later admitted this was the same exact virus she later called RaTG13.

These revelations were significant for several reasons. For one thing, they suggest that the WIV had known, or had reason to know, for six years that RaTG13 was capable of infecting humans. For another thing, they made clear that the closest known relative (and possible ancestor) of SARS-CoV-2 had been discovered far, far away from Wuhan — the city where they both eventually gained such notoriety.

Any theory of the pandemic's origins therefore had to account for the fact that the SARS-CoV-2 outbreak first appeared in Wuhan, on the doorstep of the lab that possessed the world's largest collections of bat coronaviruses and that possessed the closest known relative of SARS-CoV-2, RaTG13. If SARS-CoV-2 had emerged naturally in bats from caves in Yunnan Province, then the only possible explanation of its appearance in Wuhan, over one thousand miles away, was that SARS-CoV-2 or an immediate predecessor somehow had traveled with an animal for one thousand miles — only to spill over ten miles from the WIV and less than one thousand feet from the Wuhan Center for Disease Control lab.

The natural-spillover theory looked even more improbable in light of the strong probability that, if the virus had indeed made a "natural" one-thousand-mile journey from Yunnan to Wuhan, there likely would have been signs of smaller outbreaks along the way. RaTG13 had been transported to Wuhan by trained researchers, but if the natural-spillover theory was correct, SARS-CoV-2 or its immediate ancestor had traveled to Wuhan by hitching a ride with an animal host. This would mean that these highly infectious coronaviruses somehow stayed perfectly benign until they got to Wuhan, and only at that moment began to infect humans.

Even Shi admitted in her March interview that when she was first told about the virus outbreak in her town, she thought the officials had gotten it wrong, because she would have guessed that such a virus would break out in southern China, where most of the bats live. "I had never expected this kind of thing to happen in Wuhan, in central China," she said.

The spillover theory, in short, had huge holes in it. And its shakiness invited alternate hypotheses, including one that, at first glance, seemed beyond the pale to many observers in the United States. Many — but not all.

The Lab Accident Theory

By April, US officials at the NSC and the State Department had begun to compile another set of circumstantial evidence, one supporting a different theory: that the WIV lab was actually the source of the virus, not the seafood market. The former explanation for the outbreak was entirely plausible, they felt, whereas the latter would be the greatest coincidence in the history of the world. But the officials couldn't say that out loud because there wasn't firm proof either way. And if the US government accused China of lying about the outbreak without firm evidence, Beijing would surely escalate tensions even more, which meant that Americans might not get the medical supplies that were desperately needed to combat the rapid spread of SARS-CoV-2 in the United States.

Arkansas senator Tom Cotton seemed not to have been concerned about any of those considerations. On February 16, he had said on Fox News that the virus might have come from China's biowarfare program—suggesting, in other words, that it had been engineered deliberately to kill humans. He also had criticized the Chinese government's lack of transparency and called for more evidence: two points that were entirely deserved but that were undermined by Cotton's thinly veiled and unsubstantiated accusation that the Chinese government had deliberately engineered SARS-CoV-2.

By invoking the notion of a bioweapon, Cotton had left himself open for criticism and was immediately tarred as a conspiracy theorist. Scientists largely agree that the virus was not "engineered" to be deadly; SARS-CoV-2 showed no evidence of direct genetic manipulation. Furthermore, the WIV lab had published their research about bat coronaviruses that can infect humans—not exactly the level of secrecy you would expect for a secret weapons program.

But Cotton hadn't only done himself a disservice; he also had undermined the ongoing effort in other parts of the US government to pinpoint the exact origins and nature of the coronavirus pandemic. From then on, journalists and politicians alike would conflate the false idea of the coronavirus being a Chinese bioweapon with the plausible idea that the virus was the product of a gain-of-function experiment and accidentally had been released from the WIV lab.

At first, many scientists and officials were reluctant to speak publicly about the lab accident theory, lest they be attacked in the way Cotton was, as a conspiracy theorist or worse. But after I published a *Washington Post* column on the Wuhan cables on April 14, a more open discussion began about whether the natural-spillover theory or the lab accident theory more likely explained the origin of the pandemic.

Many people in and around the Trump administration came out of the woodwork to express their long-held skepticism of the natural-spillover theory. For instance, Pompeo, who had refused to share the cables with me but who had always believed the lab accident was more likely than a natural spillover, publicly declared there was "enormous evidence" to that effect beyond the Wuhan cables themselves. But he refused to produce any other proof.

At the same time, some members of the intelligence community leaked to my *Washington Post* colleagues that they had discovered "no firm evidence" that the outbreak originated in the lab. That was true in a sense. Pottinger had asked the intelligence community to look for evidence of all possible scenarios for the outbreak, including a lab accident, but they hadn't found any firm links. But absence of evidence is not evidence of absence. There was a gap in the intelligence. The insiders who had tried to sow doubt about the cables with my *Post* colleagues didn't know either way. They could have just as easily leaked that there was "no firm evidence" that the pandemic had originated in the seafood market, which also would have been technically accurate while likewise revealing nothing new.

Large parts of the scientific community also decried my report, pointing to the fact that natural spillovers have been the cause of other viral outbreaks, and that they were the culprit more often than accidents. But many of the scientists who spoke out to defend the WIV lab were Shi's research partners and funders, like the head of the global public health nonprofit EcoHealth Alliance, Peter Daszak; their research was tied to hers, and if the Wuhan lab were implicated in the pandemic, they would have to answer a lot of tough questions.

Likewise, the American scientists who knew and worked with Shi could not say for sure her lab was innocent, because there's no way they could know exactly what the WIV lab was doing outside their cooperative projects. Beijing threatened Australia and the EU for even suggesting an independent investigation into the origins of the virus.

Even Anthony Fauci, when asked, said there was "no scientific evidence" the virus had been engineered or manipulated in the lab. But he, too, was attacking a straw man. The virus didn't have to be engineered in order for it to have originated in the WIV lab. When pressed on whether it could have escaped from the lab by accident, Fauci said it was irrelevant because until that scenario, it had been of natural origin anyway. He was never asked directly about the gain-of-function research the WIV lab was doing, which would explain how a "natural spillover" could happen in a lab setting (given that the lab was essentially taking the same evolutionary processes that could lead to a natural spillover and speeding them up over and over and over again). Like Daszak, Fauci also had a conflict of interest: he was the head of the National Institute of Allergy and Infectious Diseases, which backed the NIH in its support of the gain-of-function research at the WIV lab. (The Trump administration suspended the US government funding for that program in April.)

In May, Chinese CDC officials declared on Chinese state media that they had ruled out the possibility that the seafood market was the origin of the virus, completely abandoning the original official story. But Beijing now claimed that neither the market nor the lab was the source. At the time of this writing, that is still their official position.

As for the "bat woman" herself, Shi didn't think the lab accident theory was so crazy. In her March interview, she described frantically searching her own lab's records after learning of the coronavirus outbreak in Wuhan. "Could they have come from our lab?" she recalled asking herself.

Shi said that she was relieved when she didn't find the new coronavirus in her files. "That really took a load off my mind," she said. "I had not slept a wink in days." Of course, if she had found the virus, she likely would not have been able to admit it, given that the Chinese government was going around the world insisting the lab had not been involved in the outbreak.

Playing with Fire

A key argument of those Chinese and American scientists disputing the lab accident theory is that Chinese researchers had performed their work out in the open and had disclosed the coronavirus research they were performing. This argument was used to attack anyone who didn't believe the Chinese scientists' firm denials their labs could possibly have been responsible for the outbreak. But one senior administration official told me that many officials in various parts of the US government, especially the NSC and the State Department, came to believe that these researchers had not been as forthcoming as had been claimed. They had evidence that Chinese labs were performing gain-of-function research on a much larger scale than was publicly disclosed, meaning they were taking more risks in more labs than anyone outside China was aware of. This insight, in turn, fed into the lab accident hypothesis in a new and troubling way.

A little-noticed study was released in early July 2020 by a group of Chinese researchers in Beijing, including several affiliated with the Academy of Military Medical Science. These scientists said that they had created a new model for studying SARS-CoV-2 by creating mice with humanlike lung characteristics by using the CRISPR gene-editing technology to give the mice lung cells with the human ACE2 receptor — the cell receptor that allowed coronaviruses to so easily infect human lungs. The paper noted that "the lack of vaccine and antivirals has brought an urgent need for an animal model," and recorded that — although none of the animals died during the study — the mice displayed signs of infection similar to those seen in human victims of COVID-19. The researchers therefore asserted that their mice model was "a useful tool" for research into the virus, the disease it causes, and its potential cures.

Buried in the Chinese report was a huge clue that these scientists were hiding information about their past work on the issue, the senior official told me. The Beijing scientists had studied some mice that were thirty weeks old at the time they were infected with SARS-CoV-2, according to the paper; as would be expected, these older mice suffered worse symptoms from COVID-19 than their baby mice counterparts. But in order for the mice to be thirty weeks old at the time of infection, the mouse model the scientists said they created would have had to been developed months before the SARS-CoV-2 virus was ever publicly identified.

Senior US officials who were briefed on this study were puzzled. Creating mice models to use for coronavirus testing was a fairly common practice, even mice that were "humanized" by giving them the ACE2 receptor. But these Chinese scientists didn't report that they had been developing such mouse models for studying SARS-like coronaviruses before the SARS-CoV-2 outbreak. Considering that human ACE2 mouse models had been in use in coronavirus research for many years, the Chinese scientists may have had such models already in use. But their lack of such an explanation suggested they weren't being transparent about their prior research. "It's plausible they would have these mice already kicking around, but it's not what they say. It may be true, but it's not what they say," the senior administration official told me. "So what's going on here? Why wouldn't they have just said, we are using these mice for other things we are looking at?"

After consultations with experts, some US officials came to believe that this Beijing lab was likely conducting coronavirus experiments on mice fitted with ACE2 receptors well before the coronavirus outbreak — research that they hadn't disclosed and continued not to admit to. That, by itself, did not help to explain how SARS-CoV-2 originated. But it did make clear to US officials that there was a lot of risky coronavirus research going on in Chinese labs that the rest of the world was simply not aware of. "This was just a peek under a curtain of an entire galaxy of activity, including labs in Beijing and Wuhan playing around with coronaviruses in ACE2 mice in unsafe labs," the senior administration official said. "It suggests we are getting a peek at a body of activity that isn't understood in the West or even has precedent here."

The Beijing study further reinforced the suspicions of many people inside the US government that the pandemic resulted in part due to the actions of humans, specifically Chinese researchers. The virus itself may not have been engineered, but the animal hosts that were being used to test it *were* engineered, which could explain how the virus might have evolved over a short period of time from something found in nature to something so deadly to humans that it would cause the worst pandemic in modern history. "If SARS-CoV-2 arose from gain-of-function research in a lab, it is entirely plausible, even likely, that an animal model involved in that work would have been humanized ACE2 mice," said Richard H. Ebright, a microbiologist and biosafety expert at Rutgers University. "There is clear plausibility, there is not evidence. To get evidence would require either a confession or an investigation."

There was, at least, evidence that the Wuhan scientists were using mice with the same engineered mutations as the Beijing scientists. According to Ebright, EcoHealth Alliance and its subcontractor WIV explicitly had proposed using humanized ACE2 mice in the proposal for a grant they received from the NIH in 2014, which was granted through the EcoHealth Alliance, run by Peter Daszak. In June 2020, Shi's lab released its own study of SARS-CoV-2 using humanized ACE2 mice, which Shi said she obtained from the lab of Ralph S. Baric, a researcher at the University of North Carolina who had worked with the WIV on bat coronaviruses and gain-of-function research for several years.

If the Wuhan researchers were using humanized mice models with the ACE2 receptor to study coronaviruses for years before the 2020 outbreak, it would raise the distinct possibility that they had included in their studies one virus in particular: BtCoV/4991, also known as

RaTG13—the closest known relative to SARS-CoV-2. It is not hard to imagine how a combination of gene-edited hosts and gain-of-function research methods could have resulted in a novel coronavirus that was uniquely adapted to infect human cells through the human ACE2. But the WIV never published any research on its work with RaTG13, which struck many scientists as odd, considering it was found in the same general location as where the miners got sick.

Consider, too, that during much of the period the WIV scientists did most of their coronavirus research in labs that did not have the most stringent safety standards. The WIV had seventeen BSL-2 labs and only two BSL-3 labs, information the institute later tried to erase off its website. Their BSL-4 lab, the highest level of biosafety, wasn't open for business until 2017.

Moreover, in June, two Chinese researchers living in the United States published a paper raising "major concerns" with the information that Shi had published about RaTG13 in her February 3 article in *Nature,* where she had first identified the virus that she claimed was the link between SARS-CoV-2 and bats. Shi's paper on RaTG13, they noted, was missing key details about how RaTG13 was discovered and what its relationship was to BtCoV/4991 (the virus that killed the miners). Also, the WIV provided no source data and claimed they no longer possessed any actual samples of RaTG13 that they could hand over to other scientists to study. In other words, aspects of Shi's first article on the new coronavirus were not standing up to scientific scrutiny. Other scientists concurred. "There are clear problems with how RaTG13 was described in Shi's 2020 paper. There were material omissions and material misstatements," Ebright told me.

The June paper's authors hypothesized that the WIV may have fabricated the information to bolster the natural-spillover theory. Shi's paper "was rushed to make a premature connection between bat coronavirus and SARS-CoV-2, drawing a potential bat origin scenario to support SARS-CoV-2 zoonotic transmission from bat to human," they wrote. "However, this connection was based on a potential bat coronavirus strain RaTG13, that may not truly exist, considering its key information [is] missing . . ."

This pattern of deception and obfuscation, combined with the new revelations about how Chinese labs were handling dangerous coronaviruses in ways their Western counterparts didn't know about, led some US officials to become increasingly convinced Chinese authorities were manipulating scientific information to fit their narrative. But there was so little transparency, it was impossible for the US government to prove, one way or the other. "If there was a smoking gun, the CCP buried it along with anyone who would dare speak up about it," one US official told me. "We'll probably never be able to prove it one way or the other, which was Beijing's goal all along."

Back in 2017, the US diplomats who had visited the lab in Wuhan had foreseen these very events, but nobody had listened and nothing had been done. "We were trying to warn that that lab was a serious danger," one of the cable writers who had visited the lab told me. "I have to admit, I thought it would be maybe a SARS-like outbreak again. If I knew it would turn out to be the greatest pandemic in human history, I would have made a bigger stink about it."

The Gloves Come Off

Throughout the summer of 2020, as the virus raged across the United States and Trump's election prospects looked increasingly dim, the president gave the green light for his national security team to take whatever policies to push back on China's malign behavior they had sitting on the shelf and let them fly. The Phase One trade deal was in limbo, and anyway, $50 billion in soybean sales seemed less consequential when the economy was losing trillions, and when millions of Americans were out of work. Besides, there was no longer much of a relationship to save.

The Justice Department continued arresting and charging Chinese scientists who were found to have lied about their pasts or to have stolen research. The US Navy ramped up its missions reinforcing the US right to sail through waters claimed by China in the South China Sea and near Taiwan. In May, the State Department issued a rule limiting

Chinese media visas to ninety days, whereas previously their duration had been unlimited. The Commerce Department sanctioned dozens of Chinese companies for proliferation and human rights abuses. Even the Treasury Department, for the first time, used its sanctions power against China in a real way, by applying the Global Magnitsky Act, a powerful law that could be invoked against officials in any country, to punish some Chinese human rights abusers.

The Trump administration slowly but surely began taking away all of the special economic and trade benefits afforded to Hong Kong, nominally as a response to Beijing's crackdown there. First, the administration ended Hong Kong's right to import sensitive US technologies. Then, it ended Hong Kong's special economic status altogether, promising to treat Hong Kong like any other Chinese city for the purposes of investments and trade. This was a drastic move, to be sure—akin to saving a drowning friend by pushing their head underwater. But the Hong Kong democracy leaders urged the Trump administration to take these moves, because they believed Beijing must not be allowed to crush Hong Kong's freedom while still profiting off the island's special status.

Top Trump officials also gave a series of tough-on-China speeches. Pompeo, Attorney General William Barr, FBI director Christopher Wray, and National Security Adviser Robert O'Brien each made their final public case for an approach to China that viewed the CCP as a malign actor and called on Americans and citizens of other democracies to wake up to what these officials saw as the urgent need to confront the Chinese government's threats across the board.

In early July, I traveled with O'Brien to Scottsdale, Arizona, an increasingly competitive 2020 battleground state, to watch him deliver his remarks on the CCP's global ambitions and their influence operations inside the United States. "America, under President Trump's leadership, has finally awoken to the threat the Chinese Communist Party's actions pose to our way of life," he told a room of about three dozen socially distanced audience members.

On the plane ride home, I asked him how the pandemic had altered the overall relationship with China. "We had hoped with the tariffs and the Phase One deal that China's behavior would change, that it would be modified," the national security adviser said. "It became very clear to the American people with the Wuhan virus outbreak that China is not going to change its behavior. The Chinese have weaponized COVID, they are trying to take advantage of this crisis to displace the United States as a global power."

Two weeks later, O'Brien was diagnosed with COVID-19.

Total Chaos

Beijing saw in the coronavirus pandemic both a challenge and an opportunity. This was China's chance to demonstrate that its model was more efficient and effective than the messy Western democracies. Because China was the first country to get hit by the virus, it was also the first country to deal with the consequences and come out on the other side. Its first-mover status gave Beijing an advantage. But the ways that the CCP decided to use that advantage ended up turning even more countries against it.

Rather than pursue open collaboration with the world's scientists by making available all the experts and information they had accumulated, Chinese authorities banned all Chinese researchers from sharing coronavirus research without explicit government approval. When the US company Gilead sent Chinese researchers samples of their antiviral drug remdesivir for clinical trials using Chinese patients, the WIV tried to patent it. The US government also publicly accused the Chinese government of trying to steal vaccine and therapeutic research from US labs through cyber hacking and other means of intelligence collection.

While Chinese scientists tried to win the race for the cure, Chinese officials and experts began planning early on to capitalize on the crisis by expanding China's economic reach and influence, especially in high-tech areas like 5G. "It is possible to turn the crisis into an opportunity—to increase the trust and the dependence of all countries around the world of 'Made in China,'" Han Jian, of the Chinese Academy of Sciences and director of the Ministry of Civil Affairs' China Industrial Economics Association, wrote on March 4.

Around the region, China flexed its muscles at the very moment its neighbors were most vulnerable. Chinese troops crossed into India over the Himalayan border, provoking armed confrontations. The CCP's rubber-stamp legislature passed a new national security law for Hong Kong, destroying the concept of "One Country, Two Systems" that Hong Kongers had depended on to maintain their freedom of speech and limited autonomy from Beijing. Immediately after passing the law, Hong Kong police began arresting high-profile members of the prodemocracy movement and raiding independent media organizations. China's threats against Taiwan, its provocations in the South China Sea, and its repression of the Uyghurs all increased, too. The rest of the world was too distracted to object.

But China's behavior did not go unnoticed. The Chinese government was simultaneously presenting itself as the global protector—the country to which other nations could turn for help—while also threatening to withhold that help unless countries agreed to avoid criticizing Beijing. Its coercive, strong-arm tactics demonstrated that China would not be a benevolent global superpower. They also turned domestic populations in countries around the world against China. In democracies, governments had to respond to their people's demands. When the people in Europe and Australia, for example, demanded investigations into the origins of the virus, Beijing threatened their governments. These governments realized—many for the first time—that their dependence on China was a political vulnerability.

Every country in the world was now waking up to the reality of dealing with the CCP; many shifted their strategic calculus as a result of this awakening. The UK government, for instance, reversed its earlier decision and decided to ban Huawei from its networks. (Pompeo traveled to

London to celebrate.) After the Netherlands recalled thousands of defective masks sent from China, Beijing threatened the country, angering its people. The Dutch government responded by gently asserting its independence and upgrading the name of its representative office in Taiwan, a symbolic gesture of support. The Chinese government threatened to hold back medical aid as punishment. Similarly, after the Australian government called for an investigation into the origins of the virus, China punished the country economically by boycotting beef imports, a gut punch to the Australian economy in the middle of the pandemic crisis.

For those in the American government who had yearned for an aggressive, US-led counterattack to China's assault on the world order, this was nothing short of a godsend. But the United States was not fully able to take advantage of the bad will that China was building around the world — because back home, the Trump White House was creating too much bad will of its own.

"Beijing Biden"

If Beijing's instinct was to make the best of a bad situation, Washington's seemed to be to make it worse. President Trump insisted on suspending US contributions to the WHO as punishment for its perceived pro-Beijing stance and then withdrawing the United States from the organization altogether — not a good look during such an acute international health crisis. Pompeo refused to sign off on a G7 statement regarding the pandemic in part because the other G7 countries refused to call it the "Wuhan virus." Trump, who was supposed to host the 2020 G7 meeting in June, delayed it first until September and then canceled it outright. "It's a very outdated group of countries," he said, insulting America's allies for no discernible reason.

Over the summer of 2020, the polls in the United States showed clearly that Americans in both parties were souring on China due to the pandemic and calling for a tougher US policy toward Beijing. For the Democrats, this was a problem; they wanted to take a tougher stance on China but didn't want to appear to be punishing it for the pandemic, because that could be seen as validating Trump's efforts to deflect blame for his own domestic failures in dealing with the crisis. Also, there were real concerns that Trump's anti-China rhetoric was fueling an increase of attacks on Asians and Asian Americans. To show they were active on China, during the pandemic the Democrat-led House passed several bills on Tibet, the Uyghurs, and Hong Kong, which all went through with strong bipartisan support. But when the Republicans put forth bills that sought to assign blame for the outbreak to China or call for investigations into the virus's origins, House Speaker Nancy Pelosi ordered her caucus not to cooperate with the Republicans.

When Indiana GOP congressman Jim Banks put forward a resolution calling for an investigation into the virus's origin, Representative Seth Moulton was the only Democrat to sign on. His fellow House member Democrat Judy Chu called Moulton and told him he was supporting racism. He took his name off the bill. There were other signs that the coronavirus pandemic was destroying the budding bipartisanship in Congress on the China issue. The two parties had been working for over a year to plan a new China task force to coordinate policy and move important legislation. But the Democrats pulled out the night before the task force was set to be announced.

Trump exacerbated this break in bipartisanship by actually ramping up the racism, using terms like "Kung Flu" at rallies. The Biden campaign switched from accusing Trump of being too tough on China to accusing him of being too deferential to Xi in the early stages of the pandemic. At the Democratic National Convention in early August, China was hardly mentioned. But when it came time for the Republicans to hold their convention, China was the featured villain. Trump brought up the "China virus" several times in his convention appearances. Donald Trump Jr. focused on a statement put forth by senior intelligence official William Evanina that suggested the leadership in Beijing wanted Trump to lose because he was so "unpredictable." "Beijing Biden is so weak on China that the intelligence community recently assessed that the Chinese Communist Party favors Biden," the president's eldest son said. Nikki Haley declared that Biden is "great for Communist China," while Trump is "tough on China." Campaign adviser Kimberly Guilfoyle said Democrats "will selfishly send your jobs back to China while they get rich."

As the United States headed into the November 2020 presidential election, the US-China relationship was essentially frozen. There were no more Trump-Xi phone calls. Trump joked that Xi probably didn't like him anymore. Knowing that their time in power might be short, Trump officials raced to put in place as many new China policies as they could manage before the end of the year: The State Department declared Chinese state media outlets and the Confucius Institute headquarters in the United States to be "foreign missions," meaning they had to report on their activities to the federal government, as did their hired lobbyists. A presidential proclamation was issued banning researchers from China in STEM fields if they had any association with the Chinese military. The Trump administration ordered the closure of the Chinese consulate in Houston, which was suspected of running extensive spying and research theft operations. The FCC named Huawei and ZTE as national security threats, banning the use of federal funds to purchase their equipment.

The Chinese leadership, meanwhile, seemed content to wait for the election result before trying to reengage with Washington in a serious way. Pompeo traveled once to Hawaii to meet with Yang Jiechi, the Politburo member who first visited Trump Tower after the election. But despite the long trip for both sides, neither arrived with any substantive ideas for how to move the relationship forward and they left having made no progress.

Both sides realized that no matter who won the 2020 election, the US-China relationship would be forever changed and the new normal was no longer going to be a relationship based on engagement and "win-win cooperation." All indications were that the Xi regime would continue its trend of ever-increasing economic aggression, military expansion, internal repression, and interference in democratic societies. The Biden campaign was advertising a China policy that would retain some elements of Trump's competitive approach. They promised to focus more on multilateral strategies and alliances, and consider getting rid of Trump's tariffs. But there was no going back to the stance that the Obama administration had taken toward China in 2016, when Susan Rice and John Kerry had attempted to shape the US-China relationship into one where any opportunity for cooperation took priority, and where most uncomfortable issues were swept under the rug.

Inside the Biden campaign, tensions were brewing over China. Some of the old Obama crew who still preferred engagement, such as Obama's former top Asia adviser, Jeffrey Bader, were still around. Some of the more CCP-skeptic Democrats around Biden, such as Kurt Campbell, formerly Hillary Clinton's top Asia official, were internally pushing a harder line. But that was a fight that would have to play out if and when Biden actually won.

And even if Biden's most pro-engagement, pro-Beijing advisers ended up with the key jobs, they would not be able to stop the greater awakening to the China challenge that was now well under way in Congress, academia, the tech industry, Wall Street, and the US media. The trends of rising tension, pressure toward decoupling, and politicization of the China issue in Washington were speeding up. The mission of the next administration would be to manage those trends in a way that avoided the outright conflict that neither side wanted.

"As Napoleon warned, don't rouse a sleeping giant," said Harvard professor Joseph Nye at the (virtual) Aspen Security Forum in August 2020. "But he was talking about China. We're talking about the United States."

Epilogue

On the evening of November 3, 2020, Steve Bannon sat on the rooftop of 101 Constitution Avenue NW, an office building just a quarter of a mile from the United States Capitol. He had erected a makeshift broadcasting set on the roof's terrace, with the camera positioned so that the Capitol Building was in the background. It was the same rooftop CNN had broadcast from on election night in 2016, but this time the set was adorned with Make America Great Again swag. Bannon was anchoring his own live coverage of election night — the premier event of the year for his *War Room: Pandemic* YouTube show and podcast, which provided alternative news for the alt-right.

Bannon's election-night event was also the culmination of a growing, troubling trend of Trump-world figures mixing US politics with Chinese politics. Standing next to Bannon as the show started was Lu De, also known as Wang Dinggang, the corporate lieutenant and propaganda chief for Chinese billionaire fugitive Guo Wengui. Bannon's *War Room: Pandemic* franchise was partnered with Guo's own expansive media enterprise, called the GTV Media Group, which operated a network of websites, including GNews. The GTV Media Group reportedly was under FBI and Securities and Exchange Commission investigation at the time of the election for fund-raising irregularities. Bannon had been a company director of the GTV Media Group until his arrest, and he clearly had no intention of abandoning Guo's substantial media platform while he was out on bail and awaiting trial on charges of fraud and embezzlement.

Guo claimed to lead a movement called the New Federal State of China, which was dedicated to taking down the Chinese Communist Party (CCP). His movement certainly had followers, fueled by Guo's media machine and endless supply of cash. And now, that entire organizational apparatus was working with Bannon and the president's lawyer Rudy Giuliani against Trump's electoral opponent.

For weeks, GNews and its army of social media accounts had been posting the most salacious content from a trove of documents and videos that appeared to have belonged to Joe Biden's youngest and only surviving son, Hunter. Bannon and Giuliani had begun releasing the content, which included documents alleging shady deals between Biden family members and several Chinese entities, three weeks before the vote. They said the material was found on a laptop Hunter Biden had abandoned at a Delaware computer repair store run by a mostly blind Trump supporter.

The most salacious material on the laptop — videos of Hunter Biden doing drugs and having sex — were leaked mostly through the GNews website and social media accounts associated with Guo and his "whistleblower movement." Those same social media accounts advertised the cooperation between the Trump team and Guo by posting photos of Guo, Lu De, Bannon, and Giuliani hanging out at Guo's apartment, smoking cigars. At the top of his election-night broadcast, Bannon actually thanked Lu De for his help spreading the word about "the hard drive from hell." Lu De couldn't stay long; he was anchoring his own Chinese-language GNews broadcast from a set nearby.

The Hunter Biden material was Bannon and Giuliani's "October surprise" — their attempt to introduce new information to the presidential contest that would tip the scales toward Trump, as they believed that FBI director James Comey's revelation about Anthony Weiner's laptop (and its hard drive containing Hillary Clinton's emails) had done in the run-up to the 2016 election. But this latest laptop gambit ended up falling flat because most of the mainstream media refused to cover it, still feeling burned after being used as a tool of Russian email hacking and dumping during the 2016 election cycle. What's more, Giuliani refused to allow most news organizations to view the hard drive, so the content couldn't be verified. Therefore, although the official story about the laptop's provenance—its discovery at a Delaware computer repair shop—was full of holes, at the time of this writing no credible alternative explanation has emerged.

In some ways, the laptop release had all the hallmarks of a foreign influence operation. Privately, the Biden campaign never believed the Delaware repair shop story and suspected Russian involvement, but they refused to talk publicly about the laptop for fear of giving the story more oxygen. And anyway, there was no real evidence the Hunter Biden material was the result of foreign hacking, just vague suspicion.

No evidence of foreign hacking—yet here was a foreign billionaire directly involved in the distribution of the materials from the laptop. And not just any foreign billionaire, but one who had been a controversial figure at various points in the Trump administration's relationship not with Russia but rather with China.

Certainly this was not the Chinese election interference that the Office of the Director of National Intelligence had warned about when it issued a statement on August 7 assessing that "China prefers President Trump—whom Beijing sees as unpredictable—not win re-election." That statement had focused on interference efforts by the Chinese government that had been fairly overt and appeared to be intended to benefit Biden and hurt Trump: Chinese state-affiliated media organizations had been harshly criticizing the Trump administration and lambasting American democracy as an inferior system, while armies of social media accounts and bots churned out disinformation sometimes aimed at Trump and sometimes designed simply to sow more chaos into the US political discussion.

No—this was interference on behalf of Trump, against the Bidens, performed by a self-proclaimed Chinese dissident. But Guo's actions in late 2020 indicated that his relationship with the CCP was more complicated than it seemed. Despite being publicly committed to taking down the CCP, his other main project was directly to the benefit of one of the CCP's main goals: silencing dissidents living inside the United States.

Guo had been sending legions of his followers to stalk, harass, and threaten several leading Chinese American dissidents all over the United States, including Pastor Bob Fu, the same activist who had helped free Washington University student Vera Zhou. On YouTube, Guo said Fu and other human rights and democracy activists were all CCP spies and called on his followers to "eliminate" them. Fu had to take his family into hiding under police protection as New Federal State of China followers "protested" outside his house, waving signs threatening his life and calling him a "fake pastor and CCP spy." On social media, Guo's followers spread posters of Fu beaten and bloodied. At the same time, Chinese state-affiliated propaganda outlets like the *Global Times* were also attacking US dissidents and activists, including Fu.

Fu told me Guo was a dissident hunter masquerading as a dissident. When I asked Guo about his actions against other dissidents, he claimed he was rooting out CCP spies inside the United States and referred me back to the story of how Beijing had worked so hard to convince Trump to extradite him. "If I had ties to the CCP, why would the CCP pay $8 million to Elliott Broidy and offer him a significantly larger success fee to have me deported back to China?" Guo asked me, rhetorically. "This is classic CCP disinformation 101, and Bob Fu and his friends seem to have a master's degree in it."

A senior administration official told me that many people inside the intelligence community believed that Guo was still working with one faction inside the CCP, as part of an interfactional competition within the CCP system, while using his US platform as a purported dissident to attack a different faction. Dueling interference efforts by dueling factions in an adversary government was not something the United States had seen before—but this scenario could well explain why the US intelligence community assessed China to be interfering in the presidential election in support of Joe Biden, even as a billionaire with a suspicious history of taking steps that benefited the CCP appeared to be interfering in the same election in support of Biden's opponent.

There is another possible explanation for Guo's involvement in the laptop story, however—an explanation that is, if anything, more disturbing than the scenario involving factional infighting within the CCP.

It was clear that GNews's involvement in the Hunter Biden story was harming the story's credibility. GNews users spliced the Hunter Biden videos with messages claiming that the compromising information came from the CCP in Beijing, not a blind computer repair shop owner in Delaware, as Bannon and Giuliani claimed. GNews also spliced the content with easily provable false information, such as crudely faked videos purporting to show that Hunter Biden had been caught in compromising positions with Lady Gaga, Malia Obama, and the actress from Disney's *Mulan*. These were so ridiculous that they made the rest of the information more suspect—a fact that would actually hurt Trump's cause, which would advance Beijing's interests, if indeed it did want to see Biden elected over Trump.

Guo's true motivations are unknowable, but his direct involvement in the laptop scandal, regardless of his aims, constitutes Chinese interference of a different nature, aided and abetted by the president's lawyer and former chief strategist. Bannon's partnership with Guo effectively was funneling Chinese money into an effort to smear the family of Trump's opponent just before the election.

When I pressed Bannon on why Guo was doing things that seemed to benefit the CCP he was promising to destroy, Bannon insisted to me that Guo was a dissident but admitted he didn't truly understand internal Chinese politics. "Forget it, Jake, it's Chinatown," Bannon told me, quoting the last line of the famous Roman Polanski movie. In the end, he didn't care. He was using Guo to further his agenda, and for money. And Guo was using Bannon for his own, still-murky purposes. In the process, Chinese politics and US politics were becoming intertwined in ways that Washington couldn't entirely understand, but which were surely bad for American democracy.

An additional, troubling consequence of the fact that China was interfering in the US electoral process was that it exacerbated the effect of the China issue becoming a political football in the scrum of US domestic partisan politics. The possibility of a real, national, and bipartisan conversation about confronting the challenge of a rising China was shrinking — and the election, whatever its outcome, did not seem likely to change that.

Full Circle

In the preceding months, as the election had closed in, President Trump had abandoned all talk of his trade deal and previously close friendship with President Xi Jinping, and had reverted to bashing China at every opportunity. Trump's closing argument to his voters had been to blame China for the coronavirus pandemic and its effect on the US economy, while accusing Joe Biden of being corruptly compromised by the CCP. At rallies and in debates, Trump pointed to the Hunter Biden laptop material as evidence for his case that Joe Biden was not to be trusted to handle the US-China relationship because his family had been bought off by the Chinese government.

To be fair, neither Trump nor Biden had been interested in discussing China in depth during the campaign. Biden had made some mistakes early on, including criticizing Trump for being "xenophobic," on the same day Trump had instituted a travel ban on China. Later, when it had become clear the travel ban was a prudent, albeit insufficient, step, Biden pivoted to criticizing Trump for being too weak on China, for praising Xi's response in those early days of the crisis. The Biden team was coming to realize that the politics of this particular issue had shifted since their candidate had last occupied the White House, and that voters in both parties were calling for a tougher approach to China.

In an interview with *60 Minutes* just before the election, Biden had been asked which country posed the greatest threat to the United States. The candidate had said Russia, but then volunteered that China was America's greatest "competitor." He was clearly leaving the door open for a good relationship with Xi, with whom he had spent over twenty-five hours having dinner over his years as vice president, according to his own informal tally.

At their final debate on October 23, Trump and Biden each accused the other of being beholden to China. But both of them got the facts wrong. Biden denied that his son Hunter had made any money in China, when in fact the Bidens have never directly answered allegations that he had—both through his participation in joint ventures with state-connected Chinese firms and through his admitted personal representation of a Chinese businessman who was later convicted of corruption. But Trump said that Hunter had taken $1.5 billion out of China, totally exaggerating his stakes there. When pressed on how they would get China to play by the rules, the two candidates both equivocated: Biden bragged about the tariffs that the Obama administration had used, while criticizing Trump's tariff-based trade war; for his part, Trump claimed incorrectly that China was paying billions in extra fees to the US Treasury. The whole discussion about US-China relations was a garbled mess of poorly delivered attack lines.

There's great irony in the fact that Trump credits his approach to China with his election and also blames it for his subsequent defeat. And while he is not completely wrong that China was the key to his rise and fall, neither is he completely right.

Trump's populist, nationalist, protectionist campaign stance, promising to fix decades of neglect of how China was screwing over America, had been one of many factors that made his message attractive to blue-collar workers in swing states in 2016, who were crucial to his narrow victory. China's mishandling of the coronavirus outbreak and the subsequent damage it did to the US economy (exacerbated by Trump's own failed pandemic response) would prove to be one of many factors that drove away independent voters, who would prove crucial to Biden's eventual victory in the 2020 presidential election.

Nevertheless, Trump finished out his campaign blaming the "plague from China" for foiling his reelection prospects at nearly every rally. Even the head of the Republican National Committee, Ronna Romney

McDaniel, was warning before Election Day that "if he loses, it's going to be because of covid." Of course, there is never only one reason for the result of a presidential election. Struggles over social justice, race relations, the future of health care, and the makeup of the Supreme Court were also core election issues. But the president believed the pandemic did him in. And as it became clear how much the SARS-CoV2 pandemic was costing him politically, his relationship with his Chinese counterpart gradually iced over. As of this writing, his last call with his "great friend" President Xi was in late March, nearly ten months before he left office.

In a way, Trump ended up where he started, earnestly blaming China for most of America's ills while politicizing the issue as much as possible for his own benefit. But getting back to square one was an epic journey. Trump angered Xi right off the bat, then built a relationship with him, then tested that relationship through a trade war, then declared a deal and a truce, only to have that all blow up when the pandemic hit. Trump had come full circle — but what a long, strange trip it had been.

Final Battles

As the Trump administration had braced for the election, only a smattering of battle-hardened veterans were on hand to see the full evolution of the relationship from 2016 through 2020. The only officials from Trump's original China team to have survived the president's entire term were Matthew Pottinger, Peter Navarro, Robert Lighthizer, Wilbur Ross, and Steve Mnuchin. The coterie of former Goldman Sachs billionaires and other Wall Street Illuminati had faded away as Trump stopped valuing their ability to backchannel to Beijing. Michael Pillsbury never did get an administration job, but he surely took solace in the fact that all the China experts who had long seen him as the oddball now had to acknowledge he was probably the China hand closest to the president of the United States.

The internal administration struggles over China policy played out right until the end, along well-established lines. The national security team, taking advantage of Trump's sour attitude toward Xi, were able to convince the president to sign off on new Taiwan arms sales, broad sanctions on companies that abused Uyghurs, an executive order banning TikTok and WeChat, and new regulations restricting US capital market access to companies linked to China's military. But Mnuchin opposed each of these moves and continued to defend Wall Street's practice of funneling US investors' money into Chinese companies of all kinds. The result was that the end of the Trump administration's approach to China appeared every bit as chaotic and confusing as had been its beginning.

A case in point was when, just months before the election, Trump had sided with his national security officials in signing the ban on TikTok and WeChat—but then had promptly handed the TikTok issue to Mnuchin, who quickly changed the priority from safeguarding national security to saving the company. Mnuchin tried to negotiate between TikTok's Chinese parent company, ByteDance, and Oracle, Trump's favorite tech company, to have Oracle take over TikTok's US operations in preparation for a Wall Street–supported IPO that would make everybody rich. The problem was, Beijing had no intention of letting ByteDance sell its intellectual property to the United States at the point of a gun. Now China was accusing the United States of forcing it into a joint venture in exchange for market access in a form of forced technology transfer. And they had a point. As if to accentuate the arbitrary nature of the arrangement, Trump was demanding the deal include a $5 billion payoff to the US government in what he called "key money." As of this writing, the TikTok and WeChat ban was held up in US courts. Pottinger was working to expand it over a dozen other Chinese apps in late 2020, but the ongoing court battles made additional bans too difficult.

As 2020 came to an end, the Wall Street firms were doubling down on their investments in China. Billions of US investor dollars were set to be used to support the IPO of Jack Ma's Ant Financial on the Hong Kong and Shanghai stock exchanges. This $35 billion deal, to be split between the two Chinese cities, was meant to prove that Hong Kong could still be a top financial hub even after the crackdowns on freedom and democracy.

Trump's national security officials were contemplating how to throw a wrench into the deal, even as they knew that the approaching election meant that their time for subterfuge might be limited. But Beijing could not be allowed to crush Hong Kong's autonomy and still use the region to milk the West for money.

Then Xi solved the problem himself. Chinese authorities killed the Ant Financial IPO in early November. It was widely reported that Xi was crushing Ma for becoming too rich, too powerful, and too outspoken. Although the Chinese government had a real interest in proving that its huge tech and financial companies were world class, Xi completely undermined that argument by accusing Ma's company of not being suitable for a public offering. For Xi, the political goal was more important than the economic goal. The CCP was truly, and nakedly, putting politics and ideology above all else.

For the Trump national security officials, this was a clear vindication of the argument they had been making the entire time—that US investors bet on Chinese companies at great risk—because Chinese companies and their leaders can be squashed by the Beijing leadership at any time without warning. Xi was doing the opposite of what would promote the stable and safe corporate image Chinese companies depended on, because he needed to demonstrate total political control. It was now crystal clear there was no such thing as a Chinese company that didn't have to answer to the CCP. Wall Street could no longer pretend otherwise.

Pottinger's Last Play

In the final weeks before the 2020 election, the US-China relationship objectively had reached a historic low. Inside the United States, the China issue had become so politicized and polarized that the room for constructive discussion had all but evaporated and each side invoked China to accuse the other of every sin from greed to treason. Trump's national security officials toured the country making harshly critical (and largely accurate) speeches railing against the CCP. They were engaging in policy and politics at once — for the hardline approach was now the politically smart approach as well.

As Trump's national security officials, led by Pottinger, contemplated a Biden victory and the end of their time in government, they worked to cement as many wins as possible in the US-China competition before a new administration might come in and change the rules of engagement. The Justice Department announced the arrest of a network of Chinese intelligence agents who had been illegally kidnapping dissidents and smuggling them out of the United States — what prosecutors called Operation Fox Hunt. The State Department continued naming Chinese media and influence organizations as foreign agents, to put in place reporting requirements a new administration would have a hard time arguing to remove.

Pottinger began organizing briefings over video teleconference with huge teams of officials from foreign governments, to lay out for them the competition framework he had helped put in place. He focused on engaging allied countries like Canada, India, and the United Kingdom. He wanted to institutionalize the shift in strategy and pass along to a Biden administration as much of it as they were willing to preserve.

Two weeks before the election, Pottinger laid out his closing argument in a video conference hosted by the Policy Exchange of London. In reasonably competent Mandarin, he said that the whole world was now, finally, having a long-overdue conversation about how China was acting outside its borders. He summed up the accomplishments of Trump's policy as incorporating two principles into the bilateral relationship, reciprocity and candor. He warned of returning to the prevailing conventional wisdom of the past, which was to downplay the threat of the CCP's strategy and at the same time declare there is nothing we can do about it. He called on Chinese listeners to his speech to confront their leaders about the crimes against humanity the Chinese government is perpetrating in Xinjiang. "It is in a spirit of friendship, reflection, and, yes, candor, that I ask friends in China to research the truth about your government's policies toward the Uyghur people and other religious minorities," he said. "There is no credible justification I can find in Chinese philosophy, religion, or moral law for the concentration camps inside your borders."

Pottinger also argued that the CCP's efforts to shape the politics and information environments in democratic countries, all while collecting as much data on citizens of those countries as possible, represent a new kind of digital authoritarianism that all free and democratic societies must confront. "The smart phones we use all day to chat, search, buy, view, bank, navigate, worship and confide make our thoughts and actions as plain to cyber spooks as the plumes of exhaust from a vintage double-decker bus. Chinese Communist Party has reorganized its national strategy around harnessing that digital exhaust to expand the party's power and reach," Pottinger said. "The party's goal, in short, is to co-opt or bully people — and even nations — into a particular frame of mind that's conducive to Beijing's grand ambitions."

"We Laid a Trap for Them"

Throughout the Trump years, the conventional wisdom in Washington was that the administration had no real strategy for China. But it would be more accurate to say that the administration had *several* strategies, between which Trump wandered with varying levels of awareness or intentionality. Trump's commitment to trusting his own gut instincts, which followed no discernible pattern, guided the course of the US-China relationship during this fateful period — and determined the relative success of the different factions' strategies, and their rise and fall over time.

The hardliners based their strategy on their bet that they understood the CCP better than did the Wall Street clique. They predicted (correctly) that Trump would fail in his mission to set the US-China relationship on a new, fairer economic footing — not for want of trying, but because the CCP under Xi had no intention of changing its strategy to accommodate the demands of the United States. But the hardliners also knew that Trump would have to come to that realization himself. That awareness did seem to dawn on the American president, albeit very slowly.

To be sure, Trump at many points misunderstood China—just as, at many points, China totally misread the Trump administration. In the first year of his presidency, for instance, Trump, Ross, and Mnuchin didn't understand how the CCP really viewed the US-China relationship. They believed that Xi was genuinely most interested in business, and that as a result the two sides would be able to forge a speedy and conclusive trade deal. Those pesky national security folks were mostly getting in the way, in the eyes of Trump and his top economic officials. But as they engaged with Beijing, the Trump officials in charge of those negotiations slowly learned that the CCP is primarily motivated not by business but by the interests of the party. Everyone came to understand that the security apparatus exerts the most power within the Chinese system, not the foreign ministry or economic teams.

The hardliners in the Trump administration ultimately succeeded in moving the government closer to a competitive stance vis-à-vis China than any administration that had come before. But that success was not because they had the best strategy documents or because the hardliners played their Machiavellian games more skillfully than the Wall Street clique or the engagement crowd. The hardliners came out on top because the CCP proved them right. Xi never gave the pro-engagement officials and businesspeople in Trump's orbit any real proof that Beijing was willing to change its approach to trade, technology, or ideology one bit.

As Trump neared his referendum at the polls, Xi seemed more firmly in power than ever before and more dedicated to his mission of restoring the "China dream." In a late October speech at the CCP's Fifth Plenum, Xi projected confidence, preached self-reliance, and promised to speed up China's technological, industrial, and military expansion. The official communiqué from the meeting declared, "We will surely overcome all kinds of difficulties and hindrances on the road ahead and push forward socialism with Chinese characteristics even more vigorously in the new era."

China scholars will debate whether Xi's confidence was genuine, much less justified. The internal dynamics at the top of the CCP are unknowable. Pottinger came to believe that the Trump administration had forced the CCP to speed up its plans, causing it to make mistakes like overreaching and bullying. The pressure the Trump administration was applying was keeping Xi on his back foot.

Still, looking back, it seems clear Beijing would have been better off if it had just made a deal in 2018 that would have satisfied Trump. The Chinese leadership would have stopped the hardliners and hawks from succeeding in their plan to turn the government and US foreign policy away from engagement and toward competition and pressure. Instead, China now faces a situation where its industrial policy is under permanent attack and the tariffs have become a fact of life. This will, over time, push the cost of manufacturing in China up at the same time Chinese workers are demanding a better lifestyle and more pay. This could result in China falling into what's called the "middle-income trap," a theory of economic development that warns of a situation where wages in a country rise too high to support low-end manufacturing before that country is developed enough to compete in the higher-end industries.

Since the hardliners never believed China would change its economic policies, they designed the tariffs to create ongoing pain for China's economic abuses and slow their technological advance at the same time. The tariffs could push China into the middle-income trap and thereby dump sand into the Chinese economic machine, the theory went, although that was not the goal of the tariffs that was presented in public.

"We laid a trap for them and they walked into it," one former White House China official told me. "You couldn't have designed a better way to get them to initiate how this happens."

The real significance of Trump's Phase One deal with China is not the agricultural export commitments or the promises of intellectual property protections that Beijing will never honor. The significance is that the Phase One deal left most of the tariffs in place, raising the costs and risks of doing business with China at the same time that Xi is making his economic situation worse by exerting more party control over the economy and quashing free market reforms. That was all part of one of the Trump administration's strategies, one that some members of the administration were more aware of than others.

"There was a design for this," the former White House official said. "It's just that Trump wasn't in on it."

A New Dawn

Starting well before November 3, 2020, journalists, think tankers, and diplomats all over Washington had devoted endless hours to speculating about what a Biden administration foreign policy might look like, especially with regard to China.

Inside the Biden campaign, there were hundreds of informal advisers assembled into dozens of policy teams before the election. These teams were meant to keep think tankers plied with busywork, filing memos to each other while they jockeyed for potential administration jobs. There were only a few campaign officials on foreign policy who really mattered. At the top of the list was former deputy secretary of state Antony Blinken.

In a series of public events during the campaign, Blinken said a Biden administration would fix what he called a failed Trump approach to China. "Right now, by every key metric, China's strategic position is stronger and America's strategic position is weaker," he told the US Chamber of Commerce in September, promising that a Biden administration would fix the structural issues in the trade relationship where Trump's trade deal failed.

One leading adviser and potential cabinet member before the election was Delaware senator Chris Coons, who told me during the campaign that a Biden administration would convene the free and open societies of the world, perhaps in a formal manner under the banner of a community of democracies, to rally allies around the common cause of confronting China's malign behavior and pushing back on rising digital authoritarianism around the world. The Biden team would focus on "confronting China in a way that offers the opportunity for a partnership where appropriate and standing up to their human rights violations domestically and their assertiveness, even aggressiveness, regionally," Coons said.

Inside Biden World, this competition-focused view was shared by many. But other senior officials who had resisted this view at the end of the Obama administration were still around. They included Susan Rice, who led the last meeting between the Obama administration and the Chinese leadership before the 2016 election in New York, and former national security adviser Tom Donilon, who chairs the Blackrock Investment Institute, one of the Wall Street companies most deeply invested in China.

The question of how Biden would engage with China became a lot more pressing on Saturday, November 7, when the former vice president's lead in Pennsylvania became great enough for news networks to declare him the winner of the 2020 presidential contest. In the days that followed, as Biden set about organizing his transition and Trump did everything in his power to deny the reality of his defeat, China remained eerily silent. There was little doubt that the Chinese leadership preferred the establishment candidate to the disruptor. But at a time when other nations were hastening to congratulate President-Elect Biden, China's careful statement finally issued on November 13, hedged by saying the Chinese government congratulated Biden but understood the result "will be ascertained in accordance with U.S. laws and procedures." This was a sure sign the Beijing leadership was itself unsure what the next phase of the relationship would look like.

Like the Trump administration, the Biden administration would come to have different factions competing for control and influence over the China issue, and vying to push it toward competition or engagement. As of this writing, those fights are just beginning. The main indicators of which side is winning will be who gets key positions in the new administration, as well as how Biden reacts the first time Xi tries to lull him back into familiar patterns of soothing language meant to obscure serious concerns. But it will also be telling to see which policies from Biden's predecessor are carried over into the new administration.

There will be certain elements of Trump's China policy that the Biden team would be foolish to toss aside. The tariffs, no matter how they got there, represent real leverage that Biden would be smart to use rather than just give away in order to start negotiations afresh. The Justice Department's efforts to enforce laws to counter Chinese espionage should continue, albeit with careful watch to make sure the sensitivities and rights of the Asian American community are protected. The drive to force transparency in foreign funding of US institutions and seek reciprocity from Beijing in its treatment of Americans should be bipartisan. The Biden campaign had criticized Trump for not standing up to Beijing's human rights violations, but the incoming administration will find that a lot of work has already begun — and deserves to be continued.

As with the Trump administration, the Biden administration will find that conflicts of interest, too, will remain a defining feature of the US-China relationship. During the campaign, the Biden team refused to even comment on Hunter Biden's long record of working with Chinese state-affiliated companies and shady Chinese executives. After the election, however, Biden won't be able to use "election interference" as an excuse for dodging legitimate questions about his family's connections to America's most serious geostrategic competitor. In fact, before it became a taboo subject, Hunter's dealings with several Chinese companies had already been widely reported: in a long piece in 2018 by the *New York Times,* in Peter Schweizer's 2018 book *Secret Empires* (which was funded by a Bannon-connected organization), and in a 2019 *New Yorker* profile in which Hunter Biden admitted he tried to negotiate a Louisiana deal for a Chinese energy company and became the personal lawyer for a Chinese businessman who was later convicted of bribery. After one meeting in Miami, the energy company's chairman gifted Biden with a 2.8-carat diamond Hunter says he gave to his business partner. "What would they be bribing me for?" Hunter told the *New Yorker.* "My dad wasn't in office."

Joe Biden's younger brother James has also refused to answer basic questions about his involvement in business dealings with China. Hunter and James Biden were both partners in a company called Sinohawk Holdings, which was a joint venture with CEFC, the same Chinese energy company whose chairman, Ye Jianming, gave Hunter the diamond in Miami. Ye, who had previous ties to Chinese military intelligence, was arrested by Chinese authorities in 2018 under suspicion of corruption and hasn't been heard from since.

Hunter Biden's defense is either disingenuous or naïve. The CCP doesn't only bribe officials when they are in power. They invest in these relationships over time and try to compromise officials and their family members in both parties. In order to truly end this pattern of corruption, President Biden will have to answer valid questions about his brother and his son, who were clearly trading on the family name to make money in China for several years.

How Does This End?

The late senator John S. McCain would often quote Mao Zedong as saying, "It's always darkest before it goes completely black." There's no evidence Mao ever said such a thing. In fact, it's extremely unlikely Mao would have been familiar with the reference (a quote from seventeenth-century English theologian Thomas Fuller), much less adapted it for comedic effect. That's why McCain repeated the quote so often; he thought it was funny. But spurious or not, the quote aptly captures the mood in Washington, DC, at the end of Trump's presidency. The fact that McCain — no great admirer of the CCP or Trump — was not around to appreciate the irony makes it even more fitting.

The series of events that brought US-China relations to where they sat at the end of the Trump presidency was far from predictable, much less inevitable. No one in the United States or China could have foreseen Trump, a president who was not beholden to any form of conventional wisdom and was driven by his own instincts in a way that made a range of new policies suddenly possible, but simultaneously running a government so dysfunctional that implementing those policies was near impossible.

Trump was great at flipping over the chess board, but he couldn't set the board back up again. Nevertheless, he shifted the conversation about

China in a way that cannot be undone. This shift was fueled by the slow but steady awakening of various parts of American society to the scope and scale of the China challenge. And it was accompanied by a parallel awakening around the world to the character of the CCP and its broad efforts to both reshape the global order to its advantage and interfere in free and open societies.

Part of what the CCP has done is to disable the antibodies in healthy democracies, through a mix of capturing elites and creating dependencies in all of the institutions that make up the infrastructure of Western democracies, through intelligence and influence efforts of all kinds. Making the US public aware of this challenge is the first step to confronting it, and the Trump presidency forced all Americans to have that conversation, most for the first time.

The coronavirus pandemic has become the lightning rod for discussing previously understood but undiscussed problems every country has had with China's role in the world. Governments in countries all over are waking up to the difficulties they face as their populations press them to rise to the China challenge. The game is on, whether you like the way the Trump administration played the first inning or not.

Is the United States in a cold war with China? That's the wrong question, because it doesn't provide a useful answer. The historical analogy is too imperfect. But the one part of the analogy that holds is that the CCP under Xi sees itself as being locked in an existential ideological and political struggle with the West. Some may argue that ideology doesn't matter, but the sheer amount of time and effort Xi spends enforcing it shows that it does, to China. Some may argue that America and its allies should avoid casting the US-China competition as a battle between ideologies, but that ship has sailed. Xi is waging an ideological battle, and the West can either engage in it or lose it.

There is no telling what the end game will look like. The United States and its allies must avoid the hubristic idea that the Western world can force on China a political, social, or economic system identical to its own. China's development will certainly be driven by the Chinese people. But

China's development cannot be allowed to come at the expense of the security, prosperity, freedom, and public health of citizens in free and open societies. And while all people who believe in human dignity want the Chinese government to change its behavior inside its borders, especially as it commits mass atrocities against its own people, the more important task than changing China is changing what China is doing around the world.

The first step for all like-minded countries facing the China challenge is to shore up the world's democracies by reforming democratic institutions, addressing gaps in national security, strengthening their economies, and protecting their citizens' public health. The US government can't compete while mired in the dysfunction wrought by Trump's mismanagement. America can't lead a push to defend core values like the rule of law, human rights, political pluralism, and freedom of speech abroad if it doesn't uphold those values at home. US politicians on both sides must stop using China as a domestic political weapon. And policy makers must start recognizing China as the top priority in our foreign policy, not to be subjugated for the benefit of any other issue. The US government must also be organized around the task. All of the tools of US policy must be put on the table.

The values on which the US system is built—democracy, rule of law, human rights, freedom of speech, freedom of religion, and freedom of thought—are not only the way that humans ought to treat one another. They also are America's competitive advantage over the authoritarian model that China is putting forth.

America can't out-China China—and it shouldn't try. The United States must avoid policies that disproportionately target Chinese and Chinese Americans, who are not responsible for the actions of the Chinese government and contribute greatly to American society. America must not become inhospitable to Chinese visitors in the way China has become for Americans. When it comes to liberal democratic values, America must lead by example and practice what it preaches. If the competition devolves into a race to the bottom, the free and open societies will lose. But in a race to the top, they will win.

Make no mistake, the China challenge will last a generation. It will require free and open governments and societies to grapple with a set of problems that often places various domestic interests in conflict with each other. The economic lure of China will always tempt governments to look away from the national security threats. The available solutions will all be imperfect and come with costs, risks, and trade-offs. All of this will play out over the next few years in a world where the coronavirus pandemic has crushed economies and brought societal and political tensions to a boil.

The goal of the United States and all other like-minded countries should be to establish a relationship between China and the rest of the world that both sides can live with, to avoid the conflict that neither side seeks. The Biden administration has an opportunity to lead the world in getting closer to that goal, but it must move forward, not backward. There will always be pressure from Beijing and aligned forces inside the United States to return to the pre–Trump era patterns of engagement mixed with hope that the problem will somehow go away. But hope is not a strategy.

The precondition for grappling with the China challenge is admitting that the old policies have failed and the CCP's actions under Xi require a new response. All Americans should work to put aside their differences and come together with allies and partners to craft and mount that new response. Until that happens, the chaos under heaven is likely to only continue.

Afterword

Hey, Josh. How are you?"

Donald Trump sounded upbeat, rested, and ready to talk. It was October 4, 2021, and the former president had been out of office for more than nine months. I had been trying to get him to sit down for an interview for many times longer than that. And although I had no idea what to expect from the conversation that was now starting, I knew that my telling of the story of US-China relations during the Trump presidency would not be complete until I had spoken to Trump himself.

After years of interviews with Trump, reporters have a well-understood playbook for getting the most substance out of any conversation with him. The advice from journalist friends and officials who talked with him regularly was consistent: Don't let him trail off into his stump speech. Don't try to argue the fine points of policy. Don't even argue factual details. Any of that would be a waste of time. Instead, try to craft questions that make him stop and think, after which Trump often provides genuine insight. If you want new, revealing information, ask him the same question over and over again; sometimes he eventually gives in and answers it.

As expected, I spent most of my forty-five-minute interview trying to get a word in edgewise. But I also learned a thing or two that have helped to sharpen my understanding of what Trump was really all about when it came to his relations with Beijing — and that have deepened my conviction that, when it comes to US-China relations, at least, the chaos of the Trump years is going to long outlast the forty-fifth American presidency.

Just to get the ball rolling, I asked Trump what he thought were his main accomplishments on China.

"Well, I think China respected us again, which they haven't for years, as you know," Trump said, launching into a monologue about how China had been taking advantage of the United States on trade — until he started the trade war that brought them to heel.

"And we hit them very hard with taxes and with tariffs and they were paying tens of billions of dollars to us," he said. "And our farmers, as you know, I made a great trade deal with them, which is why our farmers are doing so well. And they adhered to the deal, which some people are surprised at. I'm not."

Fact-checking each of these characterizations and claims would be excruciating and of little probative value. Suffice to say, without relying on any specific data, President Trump still believes his tariff-based trade war, which culminated with the Phase One trade deal in January 2020, was a stunning success.

I informed Trump that the Biden administration had that very morning announced China was no longer adhering to the requirements of the Phase One trade deal. Admitting he had not known that, Trump immediately pointed to China's noncompliance as evidence that Biden was weak on China.

"Well, I thought that would happen, because they have to respect you," Trump said. "In fact, during my term, after they made the deal, they did more than they were supposed to because they wanted me to be happy . . . They wanted no problems with me. They respected our country again. As you know, they did more than they were obligated to under the deal."

The human memory is an imperfect narrator, but Trump's takes imperfection to a whole new level. He claimed American farmers had such a great year in 2020 that they had to buy more land and bigger tractors. He referred back to his prediction that this would happen and then took credit for the prediction coming true, even though that was not the case.

"Remember after the deal I said, 'You're gonna need more tractors and more land.' And that's what they did, Josh . . . They got more land and bigger tractors."

At the same time, Trump said that any economic benefit his trade policies might have brought was spoiled by the pandemic that came out of China soon thereafter. The scope and scale of the COVID crisis overshadowed his greatest accomplishment, in his view.

"You couldn't take that and say, 'Oh, what a great trade deal I made,' because this is many times bigger, what happened to the country and what happened to the world because of what came out of probably the Wuhan lab," he said.

What did Trump think were his main accomplishments vis-à-vis China? The subtext of the ex-president's remarks was clear. He claimed, contrary to the facts, that he had kept his original 2016 campaign promise, which was to fundamentally reset the US-China economic relationship. But then, he said, his Democratic successor and China itself had come along and ruined everything.

It was a message we could expect to hear a lot more of in the years ahead.

Reparations and 2024

Throughout our conversation, Trump gave the clear impression he was running for president again in 2024, without confirming it explicitly. He talked about how the country would look by the end of Biden's first term and the things he planned to do in a second term. One of these agenda items was to make China pay the price—literally—for their responsibility for the SARS-CoV-2 outbreak and spread of the COVID-19 pandemic.

By Trump's thinking, China's actions during the initial stages of the outbreak, including concealing it for months while it spread worldwide, render Beijing liable for reimbursing the world for the subsequent economic damage. Trump told me he would insist on China paying COVID reparations if he was elected to a second term in 2024.

"I was doing some math, you are probably talking about $40 trillion around the world, $40 trillion and massive death," he said. "They can never pay the full amount . . . They don't have the money to do that, but they do have the money to do something significant and I think it's something that should be discussed . . . That should be the request of the world."

Trump repeatedly said he believed the outbreak of COVID-19 was the result of an accident at a lab in Wuhan, China—not an intentional act, but not a naturally occurring spillover. I pressed him several times, unsuccessfully, to reveal the details of what convinced him this was true.

"As president, I had access to certain things that other people perhaps didn't," said Trump. "But maybe equally important is common sense. You see where it is. You see what was happening around the Wuhan lab when this was happening. Were there indeed body bags around the lab? Check that, you'll find out. There were many, many body bags. And why was it that it started from that area? It came from the Wuhan lab."

Later, after our conversation had ended, I checked out the body bags claim. According to multiple former senior Trump officials, Trump was likely referring to open-source information his officials showed him in early 2020, which indicated that Chinese officials were underreporting the scale of the outbreak and the deaths in Wuhan. One piece of evidence that officials showed to Trump was that, according to local reports, Wuhan crematoriums were working overtime and churning out urns by the thousands.

This wasn't secret intelligence. More importantly, even if the reports were true, underreported deaths in Wuhan didn't have any bearing on the question of whether the virus emerged from a natural spillover in nature or after existing in a Wuhan lab. But that was all Trump could remember about the case. His belief that the labs must have been involved was based largely on Occam's razor and public reporting. He really didn't know either way.

Taiwan Tensions

At the time of this writing, the most heated and dramatic issue in US-China relations is increased tensions between China and Taiwan, caused primarily by Beijing's increased military aggression. The Taiwan issue, according to my reporting, was one that Trump had strong feelings about. As I described in chapter 2, I had been told by a GOP senator that Trump once admitted he had no intention of intervening to save Taiwan in the case of a Chinese military attack. ("If they invade," he said, memorably, "there isn't a fucking thing we can do about it.")

Trump declined to confirm those remarks during our interview, insisting that he never talks publicly about whether he would have sent American soldiers to defend Taiwan. He seemed to be aware of and adhering faithfully to the four-decade US policy of "strategic ambiguity," a compromise position meant to maintain the status quo across the Taiwan Strait.

"That really is a big question. What do you do?" Trump asked, rhetorically. "Do you do it, 9,000 miles away? Or do you not do it? So that is a big question and I'll comment at the right time. But I have never commented on that," he said.

"But I did support Taiwan," he continued. "I sold them about two billion dollars a year on equipment. That's like a matchstick for China; it's not a big deal. But still, it's two billion a year, and I took a lot of heat for it . . . because China wasn't happy about that."

I pressed Trump again for an answer. He said he would be writing his own book, in which he planned to make a statement about his secretly held position on defending Taiwan. Trump encouraged me to wait for the revelation there.

I pressed him again.

"Let me put it a different way. I had a relationship that was a very good one with Xi. They never would have attacked Taiwan if I were president. As to what I would have done, I never say, one way or the other, I never said. But if you look at what's happening now, it looks to me like it's inevitable. But they would have never attacked while I was president," he said. "They never would have attacked during that eight-year period. I had assurances. That would have never happened."

His mention of "assurances" was intriguing. I pressed again.

"I had absolute assurances, which I believed in," Trump said.

Assurances from whom, I asked. Xi Jinping?

"I don't want to comment on that," Trump responded. "But, the answer is . . . yes."

On the fifth answer to the same question, Trump had told me something new. The president of China had promised him directly that China would not invade Taiwan while he was in office. And Trump had believed him. Given Xi's record of making and then breaking promises to American presidents, Trump's trust in his "friend" was both misplaced and dangerous.

This was not the only time Trump had put his trust in Xi when making a crucial national security decision. But this was perhaps the most serious. Xi was simultaneously building up China's military capability to invade Taiwan while placating Trump by telling him the invasion would not happen on his watch. By telling Trump what he wanted to hear, Xi defanged what would otherwise have been a more robust US response to Beijing's increasing aggression and intimidation of Taiwan. By the time Xi's promises are revealed to be worthless, it may be too late to stop his plans. But Trump's main concern was that he not be the one who got the blame.

The Trump-Xi Bromance

Trump always believed—and still does—that he and Xi Jinping were genuine friends for most of his presidency. For instance, as with the trade issue, Trump pointed to China's increased aggression toward Taiwan as evidence that Xi had respected him but now does not respect Biden. ("You didn't see planes flying over Taiwan when I was president," Trump said, incorrectly. "Look at what's going on, you have, like, an entire air force flying over Taiwan. It's terrible. What's happening now is a lack of respect for our country.")

The Trump-Xi relationship was often seen by Trump's officials as problematic, because Xi would constantly leverage his "friendship" with Trump to elicit favors, which Trump almost always granted. Sometimes, the bromance had deadly consequences.

As I reported, in two early 2020 phone calls, Xi told Trump several lies about the emerging COVID-19 outbreak in China. The Chinese president told the US president it would go away in warm weather, that herbal medicine could treat it, and that China had the outbreak under control. Trump began repeating those lies in public and in private, feeding them into the already garbled US government reaction to the pandemic in those early months.

Looking back, Trump said he didn't blame Xi for these claims, arguing that many others also underestimated the virus's deadliness and the scale of the damage. In fact, during our interview, Trump lamented that he and Xi had stopped talking after the pandemic took hold.

"I had a great relationship with President Xi—a really great relationship for a long time, until the virus came," he said. "And once the virus came, it was so big and so furious . . . that it obviously affected the relationship. And the relationship went downhill, unfortunately. We had a very good relationship. I respect him a lot."

If Trump is elected president again in 2024, there's a strong chance that Xi will still be his counterpart across the Pacific. There is a good chance, too, that the dynamics of their relationship would continue unchanged in such a scenario. That means US-China relations would once again be overseen by a president of the United States who is vulnerable to manipulation by the president of China.

I asked Trump if he thought the United States and China were headed into, or perhaps already fighting, a cold war. Trump said a larger US-China confrontation was exactly the thing he had been trying to avoid before he lost the election — a fact he still does not acknowledge at the time of this writing, and which he pointedly denied during our phone call.

"Had the election not been rigged, had the result been what it should have been, we were very close to solving the China problem. Now the China problem will get worse than it ever was," he said. "On top of that, they don't respect us at all."

Trump was dismissive of my suggestion that Xi Jinping is taking China backward through his drastic crackdowns on various domestic industries and worsening treatment of Hong Kongers, Uyghurs, and many others inside China's borders.

"Maybe they are having problems. Maybe they're not having problems. Maybe they just don't like capitalism. Maybe they don't want anything to do with capitalism," Trump said. "Maybe they see what's happening in our country and they don't like what's happening in our country. Maybe they don't want to see riots. Maybe they don't want to see their cities burned down. Maybe they are looking at our borders and they don't want to have borders like that."

Listening to the former president of the United States draw a false equivalence between the Chinese government's crackdowns and the unrest in American cities in 2020 was chilling. It seemed to me that Trump was envious of Xi's power inside his own system. At the very least, Trump did not make any particular value judgment about the atrocities that Xi was committing.

As the interview ended, I realized my mission to understand Trump's strategic view of the US-China relationship had failed, because he didn't seem to have one. He was only capable of processing the issue through the lens of his own reputation. "Nobody's been tougher on China than me, and yet I got along with them very well and had a great relationship with the president and would have, until COVID came in, and then I took a different view," Trump said before hanging up the phone. As I did the same, I had the distinct feeling that I had just sat through a rehearsal for campaign speeches yet to come.

If this was Trump's platform, I thought, it was as outlandish and politically opportunist as his last one. He was betting the US-China relationship would be in a worse place by the end of Biden's term, which would give him the opening he craved. It's a pretty good bet, actually, but not for the reasons Trump is preparing to claim.

Biden's Pivot

The Biden administration spent its first year taking the US-China relationship down from a rolling boil to a steady simmer. Focusing on repairing relationships with allies, Biden's foreign policy team had almost no substantive interaction with the Chinese leadership during his first several months in office. The idea was to corral partners to reengage with China from a position of renewed multilateral strength.

Beijing, on the other hand, decided to test the Biden team right out of the gate. At their first meeting with Chinese officials in Anchorage, Alaska, in March 2021, Biden's national security officials found themselves across the table from Yang Jiechi, the same Chinese official who had lectured the incoming Trump officials in 2016 at a secret meeting inside Jared Kushner's Manhattan high-rise. But this time, Yang lectured the Biden officials in public, haranguing them about Black Lives Matter as a way to accuse the United States of being hypocritical on human rights.

In public, Biden's officials talked tough, keeping Trump's "strategic competition" framework and preserving many aspects of Trump's policy. The Biden administration reaffirmed the designation of genocide to describe Beijing's attacks on its Uyghur Muslim citizens, kept the Trump tariffs in place, and even added some new sanctions. Secretary of State Antony Blinken stated that US policy toward China would consist of equal parts competition, cooperation, and confrontation, all of which should coexist. He was trying to convince China's leadership to compartmentalize areas of overlapping interests (climate change) with subjects where tensions were sure to remain or increase (human rights), while competing in the economic sphere more or less fairly.

While maintaining a public stance of continuity, however, in private, the Biden team quietly rolled back several of the Trump team's initiatives and reached out to Beijing for cooperation on matters including Iran, climate change, and a prisoner swap to trade the chief financial officer of Huawei, who was fighting extradition to the United States on charges of sanctions busting, for two Canadian citizens who had been arrested in China in retaliation. The goal was to entice Beijing to reset relations by granting small concessions, but without saying as much. For example, Justice Department efforts to prosecute US-based researchers accused of hiding their affiliations with the Chinese military were dropped without comment. The State Department softened its language regarding the crackdown in Hong Kong. And the Biden administration all but abandoned the push to discover the origin of the outbreak, not wanting to further irritate the US-China relationship. These moves also represented small early victories for pro-engagement officials in a Biden foreign policy team that was largely hawkish when it came to China.

Biden did initiate a new review of intelligence related to the origins of COVID-19 in April 2021, publicly stating that both the natural spillover and lab accident theories should be investigated. This ended the ability of lab leak skeptics to portray that hypothesis as a conspiracy theory. But after three months of work, the intelligence community came up empty, declaring that it had no idea how the pandemic had started. The Biden

White House punted the responsibility to the World Health Organization, despite knowing that the organization had no leverage and therefore no ability to conduct a real investigation. Meanwhile, new evidence supporting the lab accident theory continued to emerge throughout the year, with little to no acknowledgment by the administration.

In the first months of the Biden administration, the China portfolio—like most foreign policy files—was managed jointly by the National Security Council and the State Department. The policy was largely controlled by the more competition-minded officials, such as National Security Adviser Jake Sullivan, who held the first set of genuinely constructive meetings between the two governments, sitting opposite Yang Jiechi in Zurich in October 2021. Outreach by more dovish officials like Special Envoy for Climate John Kerry was rebuffed by Beijing. The tariffs and sanctions remained in place. Congress kept up its hawkish rhetoric on a bipartisan basis, while doing little if anything to address the Chinese challenge legislatively.

But the push inside the government for one more stab at engagement and cooperation with Beijing as a means of avoiding a long-term strategic competition was not over. Inside parts of the State, Treasury, and Commerce Departments, officials with competing views were slowly taking up their posts. Inside the bureaucracy, there was still deep skepticism about any measures seen as protectionist or provocative or—even worse—Trumpian. The business community and Wall Street began mounting their own lobbying campaigns to advocate a return to a time when the United States and China were focused on doing business with each other, not locked in a generational battle. Many inside the system refused to acknowledge that the era of engagement was over.

The Great Leap Backward

While the US government pulled back from the brink of confrontation, Xi Jinping barreled forward. By the end of 2021, China was expanding its military aggression and internal repression while doing everything possible to take advantage of its privileged economic position coming out of the global pandemic, which had emerged from its own territory. By abusing their manufacturing monopolies and first-mover advantage, China used everything from masks to vaccines to gouge the suffering for hefty profits. Meanwhile the CCP used blackmail, bribery, and coercion to compel countries across the globe to do Beijing's political bidding on issues like Taiwan or suppressing investigations into the origins of the virus.

Domestically, Xi was leading an ever-expanding crackdown on Chinese companies and industries as part of the Chinese Communist Party's broad consolidation of power over the entire economy. The party moved to reign in China's tech, education, financial services, online gaming, and real estate industries, to name a few. In the second half of 2021, Chinese corporations lost more than $1 trillion worth of market value due to the government's actions. The CCP is willing to pay any price to assert total control.

Beijing's foreign policy in 2021 was an outgrowth of its domestic policy: aggressive, totalitarian, and unabashedly dedicated to Chinese Communist Party ideology above all else. China replaced its Washington ambassador Cui Tiankai, a skilled, statesmanlike diplomat, with a representative dedicated to China's new "Wolf Warrior," style, named after a 2015 film — a terrible *Rambo* rip-off — about a Chinese vigilante who saves Africa from the evil United States. China's interactions with countries from Australia to Lithuania worsened as Beijing's strong-arm tactics backfired, turning off people in free and open societies. Nevertheless, the Chinese leadership showed no signs of slowing down its steady military modernization and build-up, while expanding its tech-enabled atrocities against its own minorities, as well.

As 2021 came to a close, Beijing seemed to be rejecting Biden's plan to reduce tensions and sequester areas of cooperation. China offered Biden no help on Iran or climate change or North Korea, for that matter. Chinese jets menaced Taiwan constantly. The atrocities in Xinjiang and elsewhere inside China expanded apace. If anything, Xi was speeding up his plans to place China atop a new world order, now that the West seemed to have awakened to the scheme. China was still decrying the idea of a cold war, while doing everything possible to prepare to wage one.

Meanwhile, Biden pressed gamely ahead with a US foreign policy script whose language on China was by now looking painfully familiar. At his first speech to the United Nations General Assembly in September 2021, Biden said, "We are not seeking a new cold war or a world divided into rigid blocs," without ever mentioning China by name. The goal of Biden's strategy was to avoid conflict with China, rather than to solve the problems caused by China's actions. Making matters worse, Biden seemed to think that the secret to keeping US-China relations steady was to bolster what he believed to be his close, trusted relationship with the Chinese president.

On October 5, 2021, the day after my interview with his predecessor, Biden told reporters that he had "spoken with Xi about Taiwan," and that Xi had given him personal assurances everything would be fine. "We agree we will abide by the Taiwan agreement," Biden said, apparently referring to the set of understandings between Washington and Beijing that underpins the fragile status quo.

It seemed never to have occurred to President Biden that Xi might be lying to him, as he had lied to President Obama when promising not to militarize the South China Sea, and as he had lied to President Trump about the coronavirus being under control. Biden is overly enamored with his own diplomatic skill and overly trusting of the dictator who runs the country that represents our greatest twenty-first-century adversary. In this way, he and Trump are not so different after all.

The End of the Beginning

A new cold war with China would bring with it enormous costs, risks, and complications for our country, our allies, and the international system writ large. But avoiding a cold war is not the primary goal of US foreign policy; rather, the government's mandate is to advance America's values and interests while protecting the country and its citizens. That requires actively defending our democratic system from the threat China presents.

In the year since President Trump left office, the cause of democracy and human rights continued to suffer greatly around the world. Despite talking big about the battle between democracies and autocracies, the Biden administration did very little to halt the fall of democracies in several countries in 2021, including Burma, Tunisia, Nicaragua, and Afghanistan, among others. While Western nations focused inwardly on their own pandemic crises, autocrats on several continents ramped up their abuses. Multilateral organizations proved ineffective in mitigating the disparity of suffering between rich and poor countries, further losing the trust of people in the developing world.

Democracy also continued to erode here at home. Large parts of the Republican Party continue to support the false notion that the 2020 presidential election was not free and fair. Republicans in several states worked to change laws to weaken the rights of voters ahead of the next contest. Democrats are focused on the perpetrators and instigators of the riot at the Capitol Building on January 6, who deserve punishment under the law. But the Democratic Party struggled mightily to even agree among itself on an economic package to modernize the US economy and guide the post-pandemic recovery. On a bipartisan basis, Congress failed in 2021 to address the China challenge in any serious way.

Meanwhile, in the family of democracies, bickering abounded. The Biden team's bungled withdrawal from Afghanistan, while politically popular at home, eroded confidence in the competence of the United States in the minds of our European allies. In the region, Biden officials showed up and talked big about working together on competing with

China. But while Asian allies welcomed the tone change of a Biden administration that would no longer attack them publicly, many regional partners didn't see much new substance in the latest US pivot to Asia. The United States would not join the Trans-Pacific Partnership. There was no real plan to address the North Korea nuclear crisis. Biden had declared "America is back." But foreign governments could see the Biden team pursuing a realist, pragmatic approach, not an idealist push for the expansion of values like freedom, democracy, and human rights.

When these observations are pointed out to senior Biden officials, they often point back to the Trump administration as the cause of this downslide in democratic progress and American prestige. To be sure, Trump and his officials dropped several balls on this front. And Trump's personal disregard for these issues was tragic. But to blame Trump for the backslide of democracy at home and abroad misses the point. Democratic institutions have failed to keep up with the times. Citizens in democracies have lost faith in those institutions. Trump's popularity is a symptom of these circumstances, not the cause. Still, if he manages to regain the White House, his efforts to further weaken those institutions could be calamitous. Both domestically and in regard to our foreign policy, the chaos of a second Trump administration promises to be even worse than the first.

One unfortunate consequence of the Trump era is that many now frame the issue narrowly as a US-China superpower showdown, rather than an international response to China's actions as it rises. By focusing only on Washington and Beijing, what's missed is that the China challenge is inextricably linked to the larger struggle between democracies and autocracies. This is proven by the fact that the CCP believes Western liberal values and institutions represent a threat to its survival. China's strategy is to shape a world order safe for autocracy and repression. That would be horrific not just for Americans, but for free people and people yearning for freedom everywhere.

The democratic model is more attractive than the autocratic one, but only if it functions to provide people in democracies with the dignity, agency, and prosperity all humans want and deserve. This work begins at home, and the stakes could not be higher. The battle for the twenty-first century has only just begun.

Acknowledgments

This book is rooted in four years of my reporting on the Trump administration's approach to US-China relations, supplemented by more than three hundred additional interviews with officials, lawmakers, experts, scholars, scientists, activists, diplomats, and staffers from government, Congress, academia, nonprofit organizations, think tanks, and corporations, each of whom brought a unique perspective to the book and contributed a piece of the puzzle that I have aimed to assemble.

There were dozens of people inside the Trump administration and throughout the US government, from Cabinet members down to staff assistants, who went out of their way to sit for interviews, provide me with documents, and otherwise help me understand the internal workings of the Trump administration and the government as they battled over the US approach to China. In an era when the administration's relationship with the press was under great strain, these officials took the personal and professional risk of helping me because they believed it was important that the American people understand what had happened inside the US government on this vital issue during this crucial period. I was fortunate to gain insight and knowledge from several Obama administration senior national security officials as well.

Many of the officials who provided firsthand accounts of specific events described in the book were willing to be named and quoted on the record. Many others were willing to be identified on background, meaning not by name, because they were still working in sensitive government positions at the time of this writing. Some officials and sources were not willing to be identified at all, given the nature of their government positions or because they were disclosing sensitive or classified internal government information without official authorization. I have attempted to be as transparent as possible with sourcing information in this book, applying similar sourcing and reporting standards as would apply to my work at the *Washington Post.*

Sincere thanks go to the people who spoke for this book at great personal risk, including dozens of brave Uyghurs, Tibetans, Hong Kongers, and Chinese dissidents who know that when they exercise their right to free speech in the United States, their family members inside China could bear the brunt of the Chinese government's retaliation. These sources took this risk in the hope that by telling their stories, people around the world might understand — and then act to stop — the suffering of their families and friends undergoing severe repression at the hands of the Chinese Communist Party. I thank them for trusting me with these stories, and I only hope I did those stories justice.

The credit for inspiring this book and coming up with the title belongs to Peter Mattis, an old friend and a true patriot. I thank him, along with dozens of other Americans serving their country inside and outside government, for helping bring the story of China's influence operations inside the United States out of the shadows and for helping me tell these parts of it. A group of Australian scholars and journalists paved the way for this genre of reporting and helped me immensely as I delved into it, including John Garnaut, John Fitzgerald, Clive Hamilton, and Alex Joske. Joske and Hana Meihan Davis were the researchers for this book, and they represent the best and brightest of the next generation of China scholars. They both have long and bright professional futures ahead of them.

Thanks to my super-agents, Keith Urbahn and Matt Latimer at Javelin, for guiding me through every step of this process, beginning with the concept and the proposal. And thanks to the entire team at Houghton Mifflin Harcourt for their excellence and professionalism throughout, including former publisher Bruce Nichols, current publisher Deb Brody,

Laura Brady, Lori Glazer, Megan Wilson, Michael Dudding, Andrea DeWerd, Olivia Bartz, Tommy Harron, Brian Moore, Wendy Muto, and David Eber. Special thanks to my editor Alex Littlefield, whose ability to make hundreds of small improvements in the manuscript while seamlessly and steadily guiding the larger vision was invaluable. He eclipsed the role of editor and became a true partner in this project.

This book would not have been possible without the help and support of my colleagues at the *Washington Post,* especially Editorial Page Editor Fred Hiatt and Deputy Editorial Page Editor Jackson Diehl. They trusted me, in 2016, when I told them the China story was worth the significant time and investment I wished to devote to it, despite that other issues may have seemed more newsy. I owe thanks and appreciation to the other leaders of the Editorial section, including Ruth Marcus, Jo-Ann Armao, Michael Duffy, Michael Larabee, Mark Lasswell, Trey Johnson, Eli Lopez, Christian Caryl, Mili Mitra, James Downie, Becca Clemons, and others, along with *Washington Post* columnists who set the gold standard by their examples, including David Hoffman, Robert Samuelson, Charles Lane, David Ignatius, and many more. I must also thank *Washington Post* owner Jeff Bezos and Publisher Fred Ryan for building an organization that supports great journalism and has kept the highest standards of integrity and quality during this tumultuous period in both journalism and politics.

I am also very appreciative of the chance to work with great journalists and executives at CNN, including Jeff Zucker, Sam Feist, Rebecca Kutler, Wolf Blitzer, Jake Tapper, Chris Cuomo, Anderson Cooper, Brooke Baldwin, Brianna Keilar, Kate Bolduan, John Berman, Alisyn Camerota, Jim Sciutto, Poppy Harlow, Erin Burnett, Dana Bash, and the army of producers, bookers, news assistants, cameramen, makeup artists, and technicians who make quality news production on cable television possible.

Any success I have had in journalism would not have been possible without the help of many great journalists who hired or mentored me throughout my career. They include my former editors at *Bloomberg,* David Shipley, Tim O'Brien, and Toby Harshaw; my former editors at the *Daily Beast*, John Avlon and Noah Shachtman; my former editors at *Foreign Policy* magazine, Moises Naim, Susan Glasser, and Blake Hounshell; my former editors at *Congressional Quarterly,* Jonathan Broder, Frank Oliveri, and Jeff Stein; the former editor in chief at *Federal Computer Week* magazine, Chris Dorobek; and my former bosses at the *Asahi Shimbun,* Nishimura Yoichi, Sakajiri Nobuyoshi, and Ishiai Tsutomu.

I owe special thanks to *Washington Post* columnist E. J. Dionne, who hired me as an undergrad with no experience for my first Washington internship at the Brookings Institution and gave me the best advice I've received for journalism and life: always treat people with kindness and good things will happen. I also owe a debt of gratitude to my former writing partner Eli Lake, who helped me navigate both Washington and the journalism business when I was a younger reporter.

Reporting on the Trump administration's approach to China is akin to the fable of the blind men and the elephant. In the story, a group of blind men are arguing as they describe an elephant based on touching it. One is touching the tusk, another is touching the tail, another is touching the leg, et cetera, and so they all have different, competing accounts. Only when the wise man comes to tell them they are all touching different parts of the same elephant do they realize they are all telling the truth, just from the perspective of their subjective experiences. I've tried to touch as many parts of the elephant as possible in my own reporting. But I could not have assembled this more comprehensive account without relying on the work of many other journalists who were covering this issue at the same time for various publications. I've endeavored to credit as many of them as possible in the text and endnotes, and I especially valued the work of Bethany Allen-Ebrahimian, Bill Bishop, Chris Buckley, Bob Davis, Ana Fifield, Mike Forsythe, Joshua Kurlantzick, David Nakamura, Kate O'Keefe, Evan Osnos, John Pomfret, Austin Ramzy, Emily Rauhala, Gerry Shih, Isaac Stone-Fish, Nahal Toosi, Aruna Viswanatha, Lingling Wei, and Bob Woodward.

I would like to thank my parents, Michael and Sharon Rogin, to whom this book is dedicated; my sister Naomi Kaplan; my in-laws, Max and Rebecca Weinberg; and my siblings-in-law, Barry Kaplan and Jay and Chloe Weinberg, for putting up with me all these years. And last but not least, I am thankful each and every day for the love and support of my "elegant, talented, and pugnacious" wife, Ali. When asked at our wedding to describe her in three words, these were the ones I chose, and so they remain. I love you.

Notes

PROLOGUE

page

xiii *at his Boston home:* "John Kerry Hosts Yang Jiechi for 'Frank' Talks at His Boston Home," *South China Morning Post,* October 19, 2014, https://www.scmp.com/news/china/article/1619633/john-kerry-hosts-yang-jiechi-frank-talks-his-boston-home.

"important consensus": "Yang Jiechi Holds Working Meeting with US Side," Chinese Embassy, November 2, 2016, http://no.china-embassy.org/eng/zyxw/t1412858.htm.

White House's readout: "Statement by NSC Spokesperson Ned Price on National Security Advisor Susan E. Rice's Meeting with State Councilor Yang Jiechi of China," White House, November 1, 2016, https://obamawhitehouse.archives.gov/the-press-office/2016/11/01/statement-nsc-spokesperson-ned-price-national-security-advisor-susan-e.

pitched directly to Obama: "Remarks by President Obama and President Xi Jinping of the People's Republic of China After Bilateral Meeting," White House, June 8, 2013, https://obamawhitehouse.archives.gov/the-press-office/2013/06/08/remarks-president-obama-and-president-xi-jinping-peoples-republic-china-.

xiv *Rice herself:* David Feith, "The Great American Rethink on China," *Wall Street Journal,* May 28, 2015, https://www.wsj.com/articles/the-great-american-rethink-on-china-1432832888.

xv *Xi had referred:* "Xi Jinping Meets with President Barack Obama of US," Ministry of Foreign Affairs of the People's Republic of China, September 3, 2016, https://www.fmprc.gov.cn/mfa_eng/topics_665678/XJPCXBZCESGJTLDRDSYCFHJCXYGHD/t1395073.shtml.

xvi *a firm that has made history:* Having helped pioneer the use of plaintiffs' class action litigation to sue foreign entities in US courts, Berger Montague counted among its wins a leading role in securing a $1.25 billion settlement for Holocaust survivors from the Swiss banks. "Holocaust Victim Asset Litigation," Berger Montague, accessed September 21, 2020, https://bergermontague.com/cases/holocaust-victim-asset-litigation/.

Joshua Eisenman: Eisenman would go on to write two influential books on China's diplomacy in Africa and around the world. He is also mentioned in chapter 6, on Chinese infiltration of US academia. He is now an associate professor of China policy at Notre Dame University.

xvii *We coauthored an op-ed:* Joshua Rogin and Joshua Eisenman, "China Must Play by the Rules in Oil-Rich Sudan," Alexander's Gas and Oil Connections: An Institute for Global Energy Research, accessed September 1, 2020, http://www.gasandoil.com/news/africa/d776167ab2c93b59d67da62becc94122.

The first article: Joshua Rogin, "DOD: China Fielding Cyberattack Units," *FCW: The Business of Federal Technology,* May 25, 2006, https://fcw.com/articles/2006/05/25/dod-china-fielding-cyberattack-units.aspx.

"everything and anything": Josh Rogin, "Cyber Officials: Chinese Hackers Attack 'Anything and Everything,'" *FCW: The Business of Federal Technology,* February 13, 2007, https://fcw.com/articles/2007/02/13/cyber-officials-chinese-hackers-attack-anything-and-everything.aspx.

xx *Graham Allison wrote:* Graham Allison, "The Thucydides Trap: Are the U.S. and China Headed for War?," *Atlantic,* September 24, 2015, https://www.theatlantic.com/international/archive/2015/09/united-states-china-war-thucydides-trap/406756/.

I. THE TRANSITION

3 *often reported version:* Julie Hirschfeld Davis and Eric Lipton, "Bob Dole Worked Behind the Scenes on Trump-Taiwan Call," *New York Times,* December 6, 2016, https://www.nytimes.com/2016/12/06/us/politics/bob-dole-taiwan-lobby-trump.html.

as reported by: Davis and Lipton, "Bob Dole."

5 *when he tweeted:* Donald J. Trump (@realDonaldTrump), "The President of Taiwan CALLED ME today to wish me congratulations on winning the Presidency. Thank You!," Twitter, December 2, 2016, 4:44 p.m., https://twitter.com/realDonaldTrump/status/804848711599882240.

was in Beijing: Elizabeth Shim, "Henry Kissinger Visits China to Ease Concerns amid Trump Transition," UPI, December 2, 2016, https://www.upi.com/Top_News/World-News/2016/12/02/Henry-Kissinger-visits-China-to-ease-concerns-amid-Trump-transition/3041480733459/.

6 *in its brochure:* John Fialka, "Mr. Kissinger Has Opinions on China—and Business Ties," *Wall Street Journal,* September 15, 1989.

China's state media outlet: "Kissinger Against Politicizing Olympics," Xinhua News Agency, April 9, 2008.

7 *campaign speech:* "Full Transcript: Donald Trump's Jobs Plan Speech," Politico, June 28, 2016, https://www.politico.com/story/2016/06/full-transcript-trump-job-plan-speech-224891.

8 *slowest growth year:* "China's Economy Grows 6.7% in 2016," BBC News, January 20, 2017, https://www.bbc.com/news/business-38686568.

9 *profile by* Vanity Fair: Marie Brenner, "After the Gold Rush," *Vanity Fair,* September 1990, https://archive.vanityfair.com/article/share/e515a2cd-a51b-4f83-8d61-6ebb9a104e0a.

"hands of a dealmaker": Donald Trump, *The America We Deserve* (New York: St. Martin's, 2013), 104.

"our biggest long-term challenge": Trump, *America We Deserve,* 110.

"it could happen": Trump, *America We Deserve,* 111.

10 *"viewed that way"*: Trump, *America We Deserve,* 112.

it claimed that: Donald Trump, *Time to Get Tough: Making America Great Again!* (New York: Regnery, 2015), 162.

"not bow down to China": Trump, *Time to Get Tough,* 164.

"I'm a competitor": Donald J. Trump, *Crippled America: How to Make America Great Again* (New York: Threshold Editions, 2015), 102.

"more equitable relationship": Trump, *Crippled America,* 63.

"exactly what they are": Trump, *Crippled America,* 59.

11 *crowed in late 2014:* Fangbin Gong, "Mao Made the Chinese Nation Stand Up, Deng Made the People of China Grow Rich, Xi Jinping Will Make the People of China Grow Powerful" [in Chinese], Chinese Communist Party News, October 21, 2014, http://theory.people.com.cn/n/2014/1021/c49150-25876113.html. Unless otherwise noted, all translations are my own.

Xi's first major speech: "Full Text: China's New Party Chief Xi Jinping's Speech," BBC News, November 15, 2012, https://www.bbc.com/news/world-asia-china-20338586.

12 *memo called Document 9:* "Document 9: A ChinaFile Translation," ChinaFile, November 8, 2013, https://www.chinafile.com/document-9-chinafile-translation.

reportedly was directly approved by Xi: Chris Buckley, "China Takes Aim at Western Ideas," *New York Times,* August 19, 2013, https://www.nytimes.com/2013/08/20/world/asia/chinas-new-leadership-takes-hard-line-in-secret-memo.html.
signed an agreement: John W. Rollins et al., "U.S.–China Cyber Agreement," CRS Insight, October 16, 2015, https://fas.org/sgp/crs/row/IN10376.pdf.
did "not intend to": "Remarks by President Obama and President Xi of the People's Republic of China in Joint Press Conference," White House, September 25, 2015, https://obamawhitehouse.archives.gov/the-press-office/2015/09/25/remarks-president-obama-and-president-xi-peoples-republic-china-joint.

13 *his book, which was titled* The Pivot: Kurt Campbell, *The Pivot: The Future of American Statecraft in Asia* (Boston: Grand Central, 2016).
it never went anywhere: Josh Rogin, "The End of the Concept of 'Strategic Reassurance'?," *Foreign Policy,* November 6, 2009, https://foreignpolicy.com/2009/11/06/the-end-of-the-concept-of-strategic-reassurance/.

14 *instruct the Pentagon:* David B. Larter, "White House Tells the Pentagon to Quit Talking About 'Competition' with China," *Navy Times,* September 26, 2016, https://www.navytimes.com/news/your-navy/2016/09/26/white-house-tells-the-pentagon-to-quit-talking-about-competition-with-china/.
the New York Times *reported:* Mark Landler, "Confrontations Flare as Obama's Traveling Party Reaches China," *New York Times,* September 3, 2006, https://www.nytimes.com/2016/09/04/world/asia/obama-xi-staff-shouting-match.html.

15 *reached out to Jared Kushner:* Adam Entous and Evan Osnos, "Jared Kushner Is China's Trump Card," *New Yorker,* January 20, 2018, https://www.newyorker.com/magazine/2018/01/29/jared-kushner-is-chinas-trump-card.
write his biography: Henry Kissinger, "Jared Kushner: The World's 100 Most Influential People," *Time,* April 20, 2017, https://time.com/collection/2017-time-100/4742700/jared-kushner/.

16 *very public walk:* Politico Staff, "Kushner Takes a Walk with McDonough, Stoking Chief of Staff Speculation," Politico, July 29, 2020, https://www.politico.com/story/2016/11/jared-kushner-chief-of-staff-trump-cabinet-231182.

17 *joining the Marines:* John Avlon, "Gen Xer Joins the U.S. Marines," *New York Sun,* December 27, 2005, https://www.nysun.com/opinion/gen-xer-joins-the-usmarines/24995/.
think tank report: Matthew Pottinger, Michael T. Flynn, and Paul D. Batchelor, "Fixing Intel: A Blueprint for Making Intelligence Relevant in Afghanistan," Center for a New American Security, January 4, 2005, https://www.cnas.org/publications/reports/fixing-intel-a-blueprint-for-making-intelligence-relevant.

21 *behind the 2012 attack:* Matthew Rosenberg, Mark Mazzetti, and Eric Schmitt, "In Trump's Security Pick, Michael Flynn, 'Sharp Elbows' and No Dissent (Published 2016)," *New York Times,* December 3, 2016, sec. U.S., https://www.nytimes.com/2016/12/03/us/politics/in-national-security-adviser-michael-flynn-experience-meets-a-prickly-past.html.

22 *Rice testified:* US Congress, Executive Session of the Permanent Select Committee on Intelligence, interview of Susan Rice, September 8, 2017, 46–47, https://intelligence.house.gov/uploadedfiles/sr44.pdf.

2. ALL ABOARD

27 *withdrew the United States:* "Presidential Memorandum Regarding Withdrawal of the United States from the Trans-Pacific Partnership Negotiations and Agreement," White House, January 23, 2017, https://www.whitehouse.gov/presidential-actions/presidential-memorandum-regarding-withdrawal-united-states-trans-pacific-partnership-negotiations-agreement/.
national security decision-making: Glenn Thrush and Maggie Haberman, "Bannon Is Given Security Role Usually Held for Generals," *New York Times,* January 29, 2017, https://www

.nytimes.com/2017/01/29/us/stephen-bannon-donald-trump-national-security-council .html.

28 *cheap labor in China:* Shawn Boburg and Emily Rauhala, "Stephen K. Bannon Once Guided a Global Firm That Made Millions Helping Gamers Cheat," *Washington Post,* August 4, 2017, https://www.washingtonpost.com/investigations/steve-bannon-once-guided-a-global -firm-that-made-millions-helping-gamers-cheat/2017/08/04/ef7ae442-76c8-11e7-803f -a6c989606ac7_story.html.

29 *emails surfaced:* Michael S. Schmidt, Sharon LaFraniere, and Scott Shane, "Emails Dispute White House Claims That Flynn Acted Independently on Russia," *New York Times,* December 2, 2017, https://www.nytimes.com/2017/12/02/us/russia-mcfarland-flynn-trump-emails.html.

32 *a huge argument with Cohn:* Demetri Sevastopulo and Shawn Donnan, "White House Civil War Breaks Out over Trade," *Financial Times,* March 10, 2017, https://www.ft.com/content/ badd42ce-05b8-11e7-ace0-1ce02ef0def9.

two-page memo: Bob Woodward, *Fear: Trump in the White House* (New York: Simon and Schuster, 2018), 165.

38 *"said in 2001":* "Zhu Rongji on Sino-US Relations," *China Daily,* October 4, 2001, http:// www.china.org.cn/english/2001/Oct/20021.htm.

39 *it had been revealed:* Suzanne Craig, "Jared Kushner, a Trump In-Law and Adviser, Chases a Chinese Deal," *New York Times,* January 7, 2017, https://www.nytimes.com/2017/01/07/us/ politics/jared-kushner-trump-business.html.

41 *several years later:* "The Aspen Strategy Group Presents: The Struggle for Power: U.S.-China Relations in the 21st Century," Aspen Institute, January 13, 2020, https://www.aspeninstitute .org/events/the-struggle-for-power-u-s-china-relations-in-the-21st-century/.

official White House statement: "Readout of the President's Call with President Xi Jinping of China," White House, February 9, 2017, https://www.whitehouse.gov/briefings-statements/ readout-presidents-call-president-xi-jinping-china/.

42 *give a speech:* "Remarks by Deputy Assistant Secretary of State Alex Wong at the American Chamber of Commerce in Taipei Hsieh Nien Fan," American Institute in Taiwan, March 21, 2018, https://www.ait.org.tw/remarks-deputy-assistant-secretary-state-alex-wong-american -chamber-commerce-taipei-hsieh-nien-fan/.

3. MAR-A-LAGO AND BEYOND

48 *he made news:* Michael Kranish, "Trump's China Whisperer: How Billionaire Stephen Schwarzman Has Sought to Keep the President Close to Beijing," *Washington Post,* March 12, 2018, https://www.washingtonpost.com/politics/trumps-china-whisperer-how -billionaire-stephen-schwarzman-has-sought-to-keep-the-president-close-to-beijing/ 2018/03/11/67e369a8-0c2f-11e8-95a5-c396801049ef_story.html.

When asked later: Jason Kelly, "How Blackstone's CEO Made It Through Wall Street's Most Turbulent Decade," Bloomberg, June 6, 2017, https://www.bloomberg.com/features/2017 -blackstone-steve-schwarzman-interview/.

liked to brag: Kranish, "Trump's China Whisperer."

in his own book: Stephen A. Schwarzman, *What It Takes: Lessons in the Pursuit of Excellence* (New York: Avid Reader Press / Simon and Schuster, 2019).

50 *told the* Wall Street Journal: Gerard Baker, Carol E. Lee, and Michael C. Bender, "Trump Says He Offered China Better Trade Terms in Exchange for Help on North Korea," *Wall Street Journal,* April 12, 2017, https://www.wsj.com/articles/trump-says-he-offered-china -better-trade-terms-in-exchange-for-help-on-north-korea-1492027556.

51 *tweeted out a video:* Ivanka Trump (@IvankaTrump), "Very proud of Arabella and Joseph for their performance in honor of President Xi Jinping and Madame Peng Liyuan's official visit to the US!," Twitter video, April 7, 2017, 4:20 p.m., https://twitter.com/IvankaTrump/ status/850488492828360704.

approved three provisional trademarks: Associated Press, "Ivanka Trump Won Chinese Trademarks the Same Day She Dined with China's President," *Los Angeles Times*, April 18, 2017, https://www.latimes.com/business/la-fi-ivanka-trump-brand-20170418-story.html.

52 *often would approve:* Bob Davis and Lingling Wei, "Superpower Showdown: How the Battle between Trump and Xi Threatens a New Cold War," June 2020, 157.

statement released later by the White House: "Statement from the Press Secretary on the United States-China Visit," White House, April 7, 2017, https://www.whitehouse.gov/briefings-statements/statement-press-secretary-united-states-china-visit/.

54 *Chinese food export scandals:* Maria Godoy, "Chinese Chicken Is Headed to America, but It's Really All About the Beef," NPR, May 12, 2017, https://www.npr.org/sections/thesalt/2017/05/12/528139468/chinese-chicken-is-headed-to-america-but-its-really-all-about-beef.

55 *told reporters on May 12:* Martin Crutsinger, "China, U.S. Reach Agreement on Beef, Poultry and Natural Gas," *Chicago Tribune*, May 12, 2017, https://www.chicagotribune.com/business/ct-china-us-trade-agreement-beef-poultry-natural-gas-20170512-story.html.

entered into a joint venture: Ben Schreckinger, "Wilbur Ross's Chinese Love Affair," *Politico*, January 2, 2017, https://www.politico.com/magazine/story/2017/01/wilbur-rosss-chinese-love-affair-214590.

the campaign on trade: Peter Navarro and Wilbur Ross, *Scoring the Trump Economic Plan: Trade, Regulatory, & Energy Policy Impacts*, September 29, 2016, https://assets.donaldjtrump.com/Trump_Economic_Plan.pdf.

56 *impose tariffs was in 1986:* Rachel F. Fefer and Vivian C. Jones, *Section 232 of the Trade Expansion Act of 1962*, In Focus IF10667 (Congressional Research Service, 2020), https://fas.org/sgp/crs/misc/IF10667.pdf.

58 *reported it:* Kate O'Keeffe, Aruna Viswanatha, and Cezary Podkul, "China's Pursuit of Fugitive Businessman Guo Wengui Kicks Off Manhattan Caper Worthy of Spy Thriller," *Wall Street Journal*, October 23, 2017, https://www.wsj.com/articles/chinas-hunt-for-guo-wengui-a-fugitive-businessman-kicks-off-manhattan-caper-worthy-of-spy-thriller-1508717977.

61 *as Business Insider reported:* Linette Lopez, "And Now It's Clear How China Will Exploit Steve Wynn's Moment of Weakness," Business Insider, January 20, 2018, https://www.businessinsider.com.au/how-china-responds-to-steve-wynn-allegations-2018-1.

he told shareholders: Linette Lopez, "STEVE WYNN: 'In My 45 Years of Experience I've Never Seen Anything like This Before,'" Business Insider, October 15, 2016, https://www.businessinsider.in/steve-wynn-in-my-45-years-of-experience-ive-never-seen-anything-like-this-before/articleshow/49396379.cms.

in a call with shareholders: Bob Bryan, "STEVE WYNN: China's Economic Policies Have Done Something 'Unequaled in the History of Civilisation,'" Business Insider, February 17, 2016, https://www.businessinsider.com.au/wynn-chinese-economic-policies-unequaled-in-history-2016-2?r=US&IR=T.

62 *share price jumped:* Bryan, "STEVE WYNN."

engage in sexual acts: Jane Li, "Billionaire Steve Wynn Resigns as Chairman of Wynn Macau, Shares to Resume Trading on Thursday," *South China Morning Post*, February 7, 2018, https://www.scmp.com/business/china-business/article/2132372/billionaire-steve-wynn-steps-down-ceo-wynn-resorts-wynn.

received at least $400,000: Alex Isenstadt, "Republicans Take $400k from Casino Mogul Accused of Sexual Assault," *Politico*, May 17, 2019, https://www.politico.com/story/2019/05/17/republicans-steve-wynn-sexual-assault-1331479.

Guo hired Bannon: Jonathan Swan and Erica Pandey, "Exclusive: Steve Bannon's $1 Million Deal Linked to a Chinese Billionaire," Axios, October 29, 2019, https://www.axios.com/steve-bannon-contract-chinese-billionaire-guo-media-fa6bc244-6d7a-4a53-9f03-1296d4fae5aa.html.

hired a private intelligence firm: Aruna Viswanatha and Kate O'Keeffe, "Chinese Tycoon Holed Up in Manhattan Hotel Is Accused of Spying for Beijing," *Wall Street Journal*, July 22, 2019, https://www.wsj.com/articles/chinese-tycoon-holed-up-in-manhattan-hotel-is-accused-of-spying-for-beijing-11563810726.

64 *Pras Michel:* Dan Friedman, "How a Member of the Fugees Got Caught Up in Pro-China Lobbying," *Mother Jones,* December 2018, https://www.motherjones.com/politics/2018/12/how-fugees-pras-michel-got-caught-up-in-pro-china-lobbying-elliott-broidy/.

Justice Department released: Matt Zapotosky, "Longtime GOP Fundraiser Elliott Broidy Charged with Acting as a Foreign Agent, Is Likely to Plead Guilty," *Washington Post,* October 8, 2020, https://www.washingtonpost.com/national-security/trump-fundraiser-broidy-charged/2020/10/08/f2640488-f1f7-11ea-b796-2dd09962649c_story.html.

65 *Navarro said:* Peter Navarro, "Economic Security as National Security: A Discussion with Dr. Peter Navarro," Center for Strategic and International Studies, November 13, 2018, https://www.csis.org/analysis/economic-security-national-security-discussion-dr-peter-navarro.

on the advisory board: Matt Schrader (@MattSchrader_DC), "He's on the international advisory board of China Investment Corporation, the PRC's sovereign wealth fund," Twitter, January 12, 2019, 12:52 p.m., https://twitter.com/MattSchrader_DC/status/1084191345135271938.

66 *an essay in* Foreign Affairs: John L. Thornton, "Long Time Coming," *Foreign Affairs,* January 2008, https://web.archive.org/web/20150822083851/https://www.foreignaffairs.com/articles/asia/2008-01-01/long-time-coming.

In 2013 he predicted: Brookings Institution, "John Thornton: Chinese Need Advice, Not Help on Concepts," YouTube video, March 25, 2013, 3:45, https://www.youtube.com/watch?v=MjhoOHsfbhg.

4. THE ROAD TO WAR

75 *famously reported:* Philip Rucker and Robert Costa, "Bob Woodward's New Book Reveals a 'Nervous Breakdown' of Trump's Presidency," *Washington Post,* September 4, 2018, https://www.washingtonpost.com/politics/bob-woodwards-new-book-reveals-a-nervous-breakdown-of-trumps-presidency/2018/09/04/b27a389e-ac60-11e8-a8d7-0f63ab8b1370_story.html.

81 *Mao wrote in 1939:* Mao Tse-tung, "Introducing the Communist," Marxists, October 4, 1939, https://www.marxists.org/reference/archive/mao/selected-works/volume-2/mswv2_20.htm.

82 *when he said:* Alex Joske, "The Party Speaks for You: Foreign Interference and the Chinese Communist Party's United Front System," Strategist, June 9, 2020, https://www.aspistrategist.org.au/the-party-speaks-for-you-foreign-interference-and-the-chinese-communist-partys-united-front-system/.

Central Intelligence Agency defined: "The United Front in Communist China," Central Intelligence Agency, May 1957, https://www.cia.gov/library/readingroom/docs/CIA-RDP78-00915R000600210003-9.pdf.

in a report: Alex Joske, "The Party Speaks for You," Australian Strategic Policy Institute, June 9, 2020, https://www.aspi.org.au/report/party-speaks-you.

86 *Japanese "blood":* Josh Rogin, "China's Smear Campaign Against a U.S. Admiral Backfires," *Washington Post,* May 8, 2017, https://www.washingtonpost.com/news/josh-rogin/wp/2017/05/08/chinas-smear-campaign-against-a-u-s-admiral-backfires/.

87 *news reports at the time:* David Nakamura and Anne Gearan, "Disagreement on North Korea Policy Derails White House Choice for Ambassador to South Korea," *Washington Post,* January 30, 2018, https://www.washingtonpost.com/politics/disagreement-on-north-korea-policy-could-derail-white-house-choice-for-ambassador-to-south-korea/2018/01/30/3a21191c-05da-11e8-94e8-e8b8600ade23_story.html.

he lost the gig: Victor Cha, "Giving North Korea a 'Bloody Nose' Carries a Huge Risk to Americans," *Washington Post,* January 30, 2018, https://www.washingtonpost.com/opinions/

victor-cha-giving-north-korea-a-bloody-nose-carries-a-huge-risk-to-americans/2018/01/30/43981c94-05f7-11e8-8777-2a059f168dd2_story.html.

88 *launch a public attack:* Josh Rogin, "Bannon's Departure Has Huge Implications for the U.S.-China Relationship," *Washington Post,* August 18, 2017, https://www.washingtonpost.com/news/josh-rogin/wp/2017/08/18/bannons-departure-has-huge-implications-for-the-u-s-china-relationship/.
Rubio announced: Josh Rogin, "Without Rex Tillerson's Protection, a Top State Department Asia Nominee Is in Trouble," *Washington Post,* March 15, 2018, https://www.washingtonpost.com/news/josh-rogin/wp/2018/03/15/without-rex-tillersons-protection-a-top-state-department-nominee-is-in-trouble/.

89 *BuzzFeed reported:* Joseph Bernstein, "Sources: McMaster Mocked Trump's Intelligence at a Private Dinner," BuzzFeed News, November 20, 2017, https://www.buzzfeednews.com/article/josephbernstein/sources-mcmaster-mocked-trumps-intelligence-in-a-private.

5. THE TRUMPS GO TO ASIA

91 *issue a joint statement:* "Remarks by President Trump and President Xi of China in Joint Press Statement—Beijing, China," White House, July 30, 2020, https://www.whitehouse.gov/briefings-statements/remarks-president-trump-president-xi-china-joint-press-statement-beijing-china/.
has been held up: Kayla Tausche, "West Virginia Is Still Waiting on a Game-Changing $84 Billion Investment from China That Was Promised in 2017," CNBC, June 21, 2019, https://www.cnbc.com/2019/06/20/west-virginia-still-waiting-on-84-billion-investment-from-china.html.

92 *major speech on economics:* "Remarks by President Trump at APEC CEO Summit—Da Nang, Vietnam," White House, November 10, 2017, https://www.whitehouse.gov/briefings-statements/remarks-president-trump-apec-ceo-summit-da-nang-vietnam/.

93 *I wrote a column:* Josh Rogin, "Trump to Skip Key Asia Summit in Philippines to Go Home Earlier," *Washington Post,* July 30, 2020, https://www.washingtonpost.com/news/josh-rogin/wp/2017/10/24/trump-to-skip-key-asia-summit-in-philippines-to-go-home-earlier/.
I wrote another column: Josh Rogin, "Trump Reverses Course, Decides to Attend the East Asia Summit," *Washington Post,* November 3, 2017, https://www.washingtonpost.com/news/josh-rogin/wp/2017/11/03/trump-reverses-course-decides-to-attend-the-east-asia-summit/.

94 *Trump recounted:* Ben Wescott, "US President Trump Says He Called Xi Jinping the 'King' of China," CNN, April 2, 2019, https://www.cnn.com/2019/04/02/politics/trump-xi-king-of-china-intl/index.html.
confirmed his attendance: Kayla Tausche, "Trump Administration Has Yet to Reveal Details of Jared Kushner's Secretive 2017 Meeting in China," CNBC, January 30, 2020, https://www.cnbc.com/2020/01/30/trump-administration-mum-on-secretive-kushner-meeting-in-china-in-2017.html.
had revealed: Emily Rauhala and William Wan, "In a Beijing Ballroom, Kushner Family Pushes $500,000 'Investor Visa' to Wealthy Chinese," *Washington Post,* May 6, 2017, https://www.washingtonpost.com/world/in-a-beijing-ballroom-kushner-family-flogs-500000-investor-visa-to-wealthy-chinese/2017/05/06/cf711e53-eb49-4f9a-8dea-3cd836fcf287_story.html.

95 *opened an investigation:* Brennan Weiss, "The SEC Is Investigating the Kushner Family's Company over Its Use of a Controversial Visa Program," Business Insider, January 6, 2018, https://www.businessinsider.com/sec-launches-probe-into-kushner-companies-for-use-of-eb-5-visa-program-2018-1.
licensed his name: Chris Isidore, "Trump Tower's Chinese Investors Buy a Path to U.S. Citizenship," CNNMoney, March 8, 2016, https://money.cnn.com/2016/03/08/news/companies/donald-trump-wealthy-chinese-visas/index.html.

said to the Wall Street Journal: Julianna Goldman, "Trump's Rhetoric and Financial Interests in China Present Conflicts of Interest," CBS News, November 16, 2016, https://www.cbsnews.com/news/donald-trump-rhetoric-financial-interests-in-china-present-conflicts-of-interest/.
according to PBS: Robert Lawrence, "Column: Trump's Outrage over Outsourcing Doesn't Apply to His Own Merchandise," *PBS NewsHour,* March 8, 2016, https://www.pbs.org/newshour/economy/column-trumps-outrage-over-outsourcing-doesnt-apply-to-his-own-merchandise.
also spotted dining: Josh Rogin, "China's Jack Ma Has Penetrated the Trump Administration — and He Knows What He Wants," *Washington Post,* July 19, 2017, https://www.washingtonpost.com/news/josh-rogin/wp/2017/07/19/chinas-jack-ma-has-penetrated-the-trump-administration-and-he-knows-what-he-wants/.

96 *had reportedly been arranged:* Kayla Tausche, "Trump Administration Has Yet to Reveal Details of Jared Kushner's Secretive 2017 Meeting in China," CNBC, January 30, 2020, https://www.cnbc.com/2020/01/30/trump-administration-mum-on-secretive-kushner-meeting-in-china-in-2017.html.
born at the movement's height: "The Fabulous Life of Wendi Deng Murdoch, a Close Friend of Ivanka Trump Whom Jared Kushner Was Reportedly Warned May Be a Chinese Spy," Business Insider, July 30, 2020, https://www.businessinsider.com.au/fabulous-life-of-wendi-deng-murdoch-2017-12?r=US&IR=T.
her parents were engineers: Eric Ellis, "Wendi Deng Murdoch," *The Monthly,* June 6, 2007, https://www.themonthly.com.au/issue/2007/june/1311127304/eric-ellis/wendi-deng-murdoch.
Jake and Joyce Cherry: John Lippman, "Rupert Murdoch's Wife Wendi Wields Influence at News Corp.," *Wall Street Journal,* November 1, 2000, https://www.wsj.com/articles/SB973040597961471219.

97 *Ken Chapman would later reflect:* "Rupert and Wendi on Their Chinese Joyride," Crikey, May 6, 2000, https://www.crikey.com.au/2000/05/07/rupert-and-wendi-on-their-chinese-joyride/.
Murdoch has implied: Roy Greenslade, "Rupert Murdoch on His Divorce from Wendi, His Sons and His Accident," *Guardian,* April 10, 2014, https://www.theguardian.com/media/greenslade/2014/apr/10/rupert-murdoch-lachlan-murdoch.
text of a diary entry: "Read Wendi Deng Murdoch's Mash Note Allegedly About Tony Blair: 'He Has Such Good Body,'" *Vanity Fair,* March 1, 2014, https://www.vanityfair.com/style/2014/03/wendi-deng-note-tony-blair.
a Chinese blog claimed: "Deng Wendi Is the Leading Spy of the Chinese Communist Party" [in Chinese], Aboluowang.com, June 19, 2013, http://archive.vn/4pR77.

98 *brief Jared:* Kate O'Keefe and Aruna Viswanatha, "U.S. Warned Jared Kushner About Wendi Deng Murdoch," *Wall Street Journal,* January 15, 2018, https://www.wsj.com/articles/u-s-warned-jared-kushner-about-wendi-deng-murdoch-1516052072.
Deng denied: O'Keeffe and Viswanatha, "U.S. Warned Jared Kushner."

99 *Ivanka first revealed:* Doretta Lau, "My Life: Ivanka Trump Talks Family, Branding and China," *South China Morning Post,* November 11, 2012, https://www.scmp.com/magazines/post-magazine/article/1077792/my-life-ivanka-trump.
played a video: Simon Denyer, "Trump's Granddaughter Gets Praise and Sympathy for Singing for Chinese President," *Washington Post,* November 9, 2017, https://www.washingtonpost.com/news/worldviews/wp/2017/11/09/trumps-granddaughter-gets-praise-and-sympathy-for-singing-for-chinese-president/.
Global Times *defended her:* Sidney Leng, "Was Wendi Deng a Spy? Claims Fuel Debate in China," *South China Morning Post,* January 18, 2018, https://www.scmp.com/news/china/society/article/2129581/report-wendi-deng-murdoch-could-be-spy-fuels-debate-china.

100 *tweeted in response:* Michael Wolff (@MichaelWolfNYC), "Since their divorce, Murdoch has been telling anybody who would listen that Wendi is a Chinese spy — and had been throughout the marriage," Twitter, January 15, 2018, 4:01 p.m., https://twitter.com/MichaelWolffNYC/status/953054474532261888.

had been circumspect: Derek Hawkins, "Dalai Lama, Long Friendly with U.S. Presidents, Says He Has 'No Worries' About Trump," *Washington Post,* November 23, 2016, https://www.washingtonpost.com/news/morning-mix/wp/2016/11/23/dalai-lama-long-friendly-with-u-s-presidents-says-he-has-no-worries-about-trump/.

104 *Freedom House scored Tibet:* "Countries and Territories," Freedom House, accessed July 30, 2020, https://freedomhouse.org/countries/freedom-world/scores.

Xi Jinping promised: "China to 'Smash' Tibet Separatism," BBC News, July 19, 2011, https://www.bbc.com/news/world-asia-pacific-14205998.

6. THE BINGO CLUB

114 *and was arrested:* "Read the Criminal Complaint: United States of America v. Yujing Zhang," *Washington Post,* April 2, 2019, https://www.washingtonpost.com/context/read-the-criminal-complaint-united-states-of-america-v-yujing-zhang/0cda8f8c-a523-4c40-8afd-036036b99eb3/.

who founded and runs: Anna Fifield, "How China's 'Dr. Charles' Claims to Have a Pipeline to U.S. Power. The Reality Appears Far More Murky," *Washington Post,* April 3, 2019, https://www.washingtonpost.com/world/asia_pacific/how-chinas-dr-charles-peddles-claims-of-access-to-us-power/2019/04/03/516a792c-5617-11e9-aa83-504f086bf5d6_story.html.

statement posted on Business Wire: "UNCFA's New Year Greetings and Overview of Key Activities," Business Wire China, January 16, 2012, http://www.businesswirechina.com/en/news/12383.html.

Washington Post *reported:* Fifield, "How China's 'Dr. Charles.'"

115 Wall Street Journal *reported:* Brian Spegele, "Political Donors Linked to China Won Access to Trump, GOP," *Wall Street Journal,* June 23, 2020, https://www.wsj.com/articles/political-donors-linked-to-china-won-access-to-trump-gop-11592925569.

Mother Jones *reported:* Daniel Schulman, David Corn, and Dan Friedman, "The Massage Parlor Owner Peddling Access to Trump Has Ties to Chinese Government-Linked Groups," *Mother Jones,* March 10, 2019, https://www.motherjones.com/politics/2019/03/the-massage-parlor-owner-peddling-access-to-trump-has-ties-to-chinese-government-linked-groups-cindy-yang/.

116 *Joske wrote:* Alex Joske, "The Party Speaks for You," Australian Strategic Policy Institute, June 9, 2020, https://www.aspi.org.au/report/party-speaks-you.

117 *given money or sponsored research:* Bethany Allen-Ebrahimian, "This Beijing-Linked Billionaire Is Funding Policy Research at Washington's Most Influential Institutions," *Foreign Policy,* November 28, 2017, https://foreignpolicy.com/2017/11/28/this-beijing-linked-billionaire-is-funding-policy-research-at-washingtons-most-influential-institutions-china-dc/.

in his book: Jeffrey A. Bader, *Obama and China's Rise: An Insider's Account of America's Asia Strategy* (Washington, DC: Brookings Institution, 2013).

119 *starting with the document:* "Nature and Position," National Committee of the Chinese People's Political Consultative Conference, July 3, 2012, http://www.cppcc.gov.cn/zxww/2012/07/03/ARTI1341301557187103.shtml.

held an event: "U.S.-China Forum: Prospects for U.S.-China Relations," Eventbrite, November 16, 2017, https://www.eventbrite.com/e/39514232132?aff=efbneb.

affiliated with the Ministry of State Security: Michael D. Swaine and National Defense Research Institute, *The Role of the Chinese Military in National Security Policymaking,* rev. ed. (Santa Monica, CA: RAND, 1998).

121 *He pushed:* Gao Lu, "Economic Collaboration Driving Force in U.S.-China Relations: Neil Bush," Xinhua, November 8, 2017, http://www.xinhuanet.com/english/2017-11/08/c_136735014.htm.

blamed bad relations: May Zhou, "Neil Bush Urges Talks, Not Tariffs," *China Daily,* October 25, 2018, http://www.chinadaily.com.cn/a/201808/24/WS5b7f033ea310add14f387788.html.

122 *deposition for his divorce:* Reuters, "Bush Brother's Divorce Reveals Sex Romps," CNN, November 26, 2003, https://edition.cnn.com/2003/ALLPOLITICS/11/25/bush.brother.reut/.

the Charhar Institute: "Chronology: China Focus," Carter Center, accessed September 25, 2020, https://www.cartercenter.org/peace/china_elections/chronology.html.

forums on US-China relations: "China-U.S. Relations Held in Suzhou," China-United States Exchange Foundation, accessed September 10, 2020, http://archive.vn/EFth1.

a February 2020 speech: "U.S. States and the China Competition," US Department of State, February 8, 2020, https://www.state.gov/u-s-states-and-the-china-competition/.

an agreement with the Chinese government: "Strengthening U.S.-China Sub-national Cooperation: The U.S.-China Governors Forum," US Department of State, January 19, 2011, https://web.archive.org/web/20200428094212/https://2009-2017.state.gov/r/pa/prs/ps/2011/01/154874.htm.

124 *explosive investigation:* Michael Forsythe et al., "A 'Bridge' to China, and Her Family's Business, in the Trump Cabinet," *New York Times,* June 2, 2019, https://www.nytimes.com/2019/06/02/us/politics/elaine-chao-china.html.

125 *next to her father:* Tanya Snyder, "Did Elaine Chao's DOT Interviews Help Her Family's Business?," *Politico,* May 6, 2018, https://politi.co/2KHPhHe.

7. PLOUGHSHARES INTO SWORDS

128 *took a delegation to China:* "Daines Leads Congressional Delegation to China and Japan," Office of Senate Steve Daines, April 17, 2017, https://www.daines.senate.gov/news/press-releases/daines-leads-congressional-delegation-to-china-and-japan.

hosted the Chinese ambassador: Freddy Monares, "Daines, China Ambassador Discuss Future Trade Opportunities," *Bozeman Daily Chronicle,* September 9, 2017, https://www.bozemandailychronicle.com/news/daines-china-ambassador-discuss-future-trade-opportunities/article_32f8354d-33fa-5822-9c27-89aca614caf8.html.

China Daily *reported:* Zhao Huanxin, "Tibetans Invite US Lawmakers to Region," *China Daily,* December 7, 2017, http://www.chinadaily.com.cn/a/201712/07/WS5a28a4a2a310fcb6fafd2b25.html.

a column I wrote: Josh Rogin, "How China Got a U.S. Senator to Do Its Political Bidding," *Washington Post,* December 17, 2017, https://www.washingtonpost.com/opinions/global-opinions/how-china-got-a-us-senator-to-do-its-political-bidding/2017/12/17/8eee82c6-e1dc-11e7-8679-a9728984779c_story.html.

129 *Derek Mitchell told me:* Rogin, "How China."

134 *at the first hearing:* "CFIUS Reform: Examining the Essential Elements," United States Senate Committee on Banking, Housing, and Urban Affairs, January 18, 2018, https://www.banking.senate.gov/hearings/cfius-reform-examining-the-essential-elements.

135 *announced the results:* "Secretary Ross Releases Steel and Aluminum 232 Reports in Coordination with White House," US Department of Commerce, July 30, 2020, https://www.commerce.gov/news/press-releases/2018/02/secretary-ross-releases-steel-and-aluminum-232-reports-coordination.

138 *attended the public signing:* "GE and AVIC Sign Agreement for Integrated Avionics Joint Venture," GE Aviation, January 21, 2011, https://www.geaviation.com/press-release/systems/ge-and-avic-sign-agreement-integrated-avionics-joint-venture.

139 *according to a report:* Joel Hruska, "Report: China's New Comac C919 Jetliner Is Built with Stolen Technology," Extreme Tech, October 16, 2019, https://www.extremetech.com/extreme/300313-report-chinas-new-comac-c919-jetliner-is-built-with-stolen-technology.

blocked the acquisition: "Presidential Order Regarding the Proposed Takeover of Qualcomm Incorporated by Broadcom Limited," White House, March 12, 2018, https://www.whitehouse.gov/presidential-actions/presidential-order-regarding-proposed-takeover-qualcomm-incorporated-broadcom-limited/.

141 *HNA and SkyBridge announced:* Julie Steinberg, "HNA Scuttles Deal for Scaramucci's SkyBridge," *Wall Street Journal,* April 30, 2018, https://www.wsj.com/articles/hna-set-to-drop-acquisition-of-skybridge-capital-1525117804.

Scaramucci told CNBC: Evelyn Cheng, "Scaramucci Says SkyBridge Will Form Joint Venture with HNA to Tap Chinese Market," CNBC, May 1, 2018, https://www.cnbc.com/2018/05/01/scaramuccis-skybridge-forming-joint-venture-with-hna-to-tap-chinese-market.html.

142 *HNA acquiring:* "Ingram Micro and HNA Group Announce Completion of Acquisition," Ingram Micro, accessed September 2, 2020, https://ingrammicro.gcs-web.com/news-releases/news-release-details/ingram-micro-and-hna-group-announce-completion-acquisition.

Wall Street Journal *declared:* Charles Forelle and Dennis K. Berman, "In Davos, Anthony Scaramucci Translates Trump Message to Global Elite," *Wall Street Journal,* January 17, 2017, https://www.wsj.com/articles/trump-represents-last-great-hope-for-globalism-adviser-anthony-scaramucci-says-in-davos-1484671450.

front-page story: Sharon LaFraniere, Michael Forsythe, and Alexandra Stevenson, "Trump Aide's Deal with Chinese Firm Raises Fear of Tangled Interests," *New York Times,* January 31, 2017, https://www.nytimes.com/2017/01/31/us/anthony-scaramucci-business-white-house.html.

143 *backed out of negotiations:* Julie Steinberg, "HNA Group Questions Bank of America's Stance on Working with the Company," *Wall Street Journal,* July 24, 2017, https://www.wsj.com/articles/hna-group-questions-bank-of-americas-stance-on-working-with-the-company-1500901095.

8. THE BATTLE FOR THE FUTURE

146 *when he tweeted:* Donald J. Trump (@realDonaldTrump), "President Xi of China, and I, are working together to give massive Chinese phone company, ZTE, a way to get back into business, fast. Too many jobs in China lost. Commerce Department has been instructed to get it done!," Twitter, May 13, 2018, 8:01 a.m., https://twitter.com/realDonaldTrump/status/995680316458262533.

rare tweet clarification: Damian Paletta et al., "Penalties Against China Telecom Giant ZTE Become a Bargaining Chip as White House, Chinese Officials Discuss Potential Trade Deal," *Washington Post,* May 13, 2018, https://www.washingtonpost.com/news/the-switch/wp/2018/05/13/trump-pledges-to-help-chinese-phone-maker-zte-get-back-into-business/.

147 *"separate from trade":* Eli Okun, "Wilbur Ross: We're Exploring 'Alternative Remedies' for ZTE Ban," Politico, May 14, 2018, https://politi.co/2IHFq62.

"alternative remedies": Eli Okun, "Wilbur Ross: We're Exploring 'Alternative Remedies' for ZTE Ban," *Politico,* May 14, 2018, https://www.politico.com/story/2018/05/14/wilbur-ross-zte-ban-584713.

Trump just tweeted again: Donald J. Trump (@realDonaldTrump), Twitter, May 14, 2018, 1:06 p.m., https://twitter.com/realDonaldTrump/status/996119678551552000.

column I published: Josh Rogin, "China Gave Trump a List of Crazy Demands, and He Caved to One of Them," *Washington Post,* May 15, 2018, https://www.washingtonpost.com/news/josh-rogin/wp/2018/05/15/china-gave-trump-a-list-of-crazy-demands-and-he-caved-to-one-of-them/.

and tweeted: Donald J. Trump (@realDonaldTrump), "The Washington Post and CNN have typically written false stories about our trade negotiations with China. Nothing has happened with ZTE except as it pertains to the larger trade deal. Our country has been losing hundreds of billions of dollars a year with China . . . ," Twitter, May 16, 2018, 6:09 a.m., https://twitter.com/realDonaldTrump/status/996739372723638272.

148 *several stories started leaking*: Damian Paletta, "Top Trump Trade Officials Still at Odds After Profane Shouting Match in Beijing," *Washington Post*, May 16, 2018, https://www.washingtonpost.com/news/business/wp/2018/05/16/top-trump-trade-officials-still-at-odds-after-profane-shouting-match-in-beijing/.

Office of the US Trade Representative: "Statement from the President Regarding Trade with China," White House, June 18, 2018, https://www.whitehouse.gov/briefings-statements/statement-president-regarding-trade-china-2/.

149 *publicly threatening*: "CNBC Transcript: President Donald Trump Sits Down with CNBC's Joe Kernen," CNBC, July 20, 2018, https://www.cnbc.com/2018/07/20/cnbc-transcript-president-donald-trump-sits-down-with-cnbcs-joe-kern.html.

151 *"carried on to success"*: "The Analects Attributed to Confucius [Kongfuzi], 551–479 BCE by Lao-Tse [Lao Zi], Translated by James Legge (1815–1897)," US-China Institute, University of Southern California, Annenberg, accessed September 14, 2020, https://china.usc.edu/confucius-analects-13.

153 *"new Cold War"*: Jane Perlez, "Pence's China Speech Seen as Portent of 'New Cold War,'" *New York Times*, October 5, 2018, https://www.nytimes.com/2018/10/05/world/asia/pence-china-speech-cold-war.html.

the official said: Josh Rogin, "The Trump Administration Just 'Reset' the U.S.-China Relationship," *Washington Post*, October 4, 2020, https://www.washingtonpost.com/opinions/global-opinions/the-trump-administration-just-reset-the-us-china-relationship/2018/10/04/c727266e-c810-11e8-b2b5-79270f9cce17_story.html.

154 *Pence's speech*: "Remarks by Vice President Pence on the Administration's Policy Toward China," White House, October 4, 2018, https://www.whitehouse.gov/briefings-statements/remarks-vice-president-pence-administrations-policy-toward-china/.

155 *In a speech*: "Ambassador John Bolton: Foreign Policy Challenges for the Trump Administration," Daniel Morgan Graduate School of National Security, February 21, 2018, https://dmgs.org/foreign-policy-challenges-facing-the-trump-administration-presentation-by-ambassador-john-bolton/.

156 *Mira Ricardel*: Josh Rogin, "The White House Bickering Endangers National Security," *Washington Post*, November 15, 2018, https://www.washingtonpost.com/opinions/global-opinions/the-white-house-bickering-endangers-national-security/2018/11/15/a21371de-e8ef-11e8-bbdb-72fdbf9d4fed_story.html.

the White House: Josh Rogin, "John Bolton's New Deputy Is a Hawk with Sharp Elbows, Just like Him," *Washington Post*, April 23, 2018, https://www.washingtonpost.com/news/josh-rogin/wp/2018/04/23/john-boltons-new-deputy-is-a-hawk-with-sharp-elbows-just-like-him/.

159 *at the time*: Josh Rogin, "Inside China's 'Tantrum Diplomacy' at APEC," *Washington Post*, November 20, 2018, https://www.washingtonpost.com/news/josh-rogin/wp/2018/11/20/inside-chinas-tantrum-diplomacy-at-apec/.

161 *in the press*: Elise Viebeck, "Kudlow: Trump Didn't Know About Huawei Executive's Arrest Before Dining with Chinese Leader," *Washington Post*, December 9, 2018, https://www.washingtonpost.com/politics/kudlow-trump-didnt-know-about-huawei-executives-arrest-before-dining-with-chinese-leader/2018/12/09/da667a6c-fbc4-11e8-83c0-b06139e540e5_story.html.

162 *"fretted constantly"*: John R. Bolton, *The Room Where It Happened: A White House Memoir* (New York: Simon and Schuster, 2020), 277.

"on several occasions": Bolton, *Room Where It Happened*, 277.

163 *Lighthizer said*: Doina Chiacu and Jeff Mason, "U.S. Says China Reneged on Trade Commitments, Talks Continue," Reuters, May 6, 2019, https://www.reuters.com/article/us-usa-trade-china-talks-idUSKCN1SC247.

signed an executive order: "Executive Order on Securing the Information and Communications Technology and Services Supply Chain," White House, May 15, 2019, https://www.whitehouse.gov/presidential-actions/executive-order-securing-information-communications-technology-services-supply-chain/.
in the Oval Office: Jeanne Whalen and David J. Lynch, "Trump Calls Huawei 'Dangerous' but Says Dispute Could Be Resolved in Trade Deal," *Washington Post,* May 23, 2019, https://www.washingtonpost.com/business/economy/trump-calls-huawei-dangerous-but-says-dispute-could-be-resolved-in-trade-deal/2019/05/23/ed75c4a0-7da6-11e9-8ede-f4abf521ef17_story.html.

164 *Huawei tweeted out:* Huawei Facts (@HuaweiFacts), "U-turn? Donald Trump suggests he would allow #Huawei to once again purchase U.S. technology! #HuaweiFacts," Twitter, June 29, 2019, 1:17 a.m., https://twitter.com/HuaweiFacts/status/1144882620804689921.
Bolton wrote: Bolton, *Room Where It Happened,* 282.

9. NEW WORLD ORDER

165 *series of historic speeches:* Austin Ramzy and Chris Buckley, "'Absolutely No Mercy': Leaked Files Expose How China Organized Mass Detentions of Muslims," *New York Times,* November 16, 2019, https://www.nytimes.com/interactive/2019/11/16/world/asia/china-xinjiang-documents.html.

166 *blew themselves up:* Ramzy and Buckley, "'Absolutely No Mercy.'"
"the China Cables": Bethany Allen-Ebrahimian, "Exposed: China's Operating Manuals for Mass Internment and Arrest by Algorithm," International Consortium of Investigative Journalists, November 24, 2019, https://www.icij.org/investigations/china-cables/exposed-chinas-operating-manuals-for-mass-internment-and-arrest-by-algorithm/.

168 *called the program:* Adam Withnall, "China Sends State Spies to Live in Uighur Muslim Homes and Attend Private Family Weddings and Funerals," *The Independent,* November 30, 2018, https://www.independent.co.uk/news/world/asia/china-uighurs-muslim-xinjiang-weddings-minority-communist-party-a8661006.html.

169 *Indigenous Issues:* "Permanent Forum," United Nations Department of Economic and Social Affairs: Indigenous Peoples, accessed September 3, 2020, https://www.un.org/development/desa/indigenouspeoples/unpfii-sessions-2.html.

170 *heated exchange:* "17th Meeting, Committee on Non-governmental Organizations—2018 Resumed Session," United Nations Web TV, May 21, 2018, http://webtv.un.org/watch/17th-meeting-committee-on-non-governmental-organizations-2018-resumed-session/5787832316001/?term=.
introduced a resolution: Sophie Richardson, "Is China Winning Its Fight Against Rights at the UN?," Human Rights Watch, December 12, 2018, https://www.hrw.org/news/2018/12/12/china-winning-its-fight-against-rights-un.
Switzerland abstained: "Only US Rejects China's UN Human Rights Resolution," March 26, 2018, https://www.aljazeera.com/news/2018/03/rejects-chinas-human-rights-resolution-180326144912907.html.

172 *official took over:* "Dr. Fang Liu of China Becomes First-Ever Woman Appointed Secretary General of ICAO," Council of the International Civil Aviation Organization, March 11, 2015, https://www.icao.int/Newsroom/Pages/Dr-Fang-Liu-of-China-becomes-first-ever-woman-appointed-Secretary-General-of-ICAO.aspx.
stopped inviting: Reuters, "Sorry, You're Not Invited: UN Aviation Agency Snubs Taiwan in Sign of Pressure from Beijing," *South China Morning Post,* September 23, 2016, https://www.scmp.com/news/china/policies-politics/article/2021950/sorry-youre-not-invited-un-aviation-agency-snubs-taiwan.
hid for months: "UN Aviation Agency ICAO Was 'Hacked by Chinese Group' and Tried Conceal It, Report Claims," *South China Morning Post,* February 28, 2019, https://www

.scmp.com/news/world/united-states-canada/article/2188034/un-aviation-agency-icao-was-hacked-chinese-group-and.

then retaliated: Allison Lambert, "U.S. Withholds U.N. Aviation Dues, Calls for Immediate Whistleblower Protections," Reuters, October 12, 2019, https://www.reuters.com/article/us-un-aviation-us/u-s-withholds-u-n-aviation-dues-calls-for-immediate-whistleblower-protections-idUSKBN1WH2C1.

173 *increased cooperation with Beijing:* Kong Wenzheng, "ITU Vows to Join Hands with China," *China Daily,* April 24, 2019, http://global.chinadaily.com.cn/a/201904/24/WS5cbfbb1aa3104842260b7f2f.html.

telecom giant Huawei: "Huawei Allegations Driven by Politics Not Evidence: U.N. Telecoms Chief," Reuters, April 5, 2019, https://www.reuters.com/article/us-usa-china-huawei-tech-un-idUSKCN1RH1KN.

is pushing: Colum Lynch, "China Enlists U.N. to Promote Its Belt and Road Project," *Foreign Policy,* May 10, 2018, https://foreignpolicy.com/2018/05/10/china-enlists-u-n-to-promote-its-belt-and-road-project/.

"big data research institute": "UN DESA, China to Set Up Big Data Research Institute to Boost Statistical Capacity," *Global Times,* June 4, 2019, http://www.globaltimes.cn/content/1153151.shtml.

secretly sent back: Echo Huang, "A Knife Emoji, Then Silence: The Strange Story of How China Detained the Head of Interpol," Quartz, October 8, 2018, https://qz.com/1416651/the-strange-story-of-how-china-detained-interpol-head-meng-hongwei/.

174 *at the opening session:* Michael Igoe, "Will the World Bank Push China's Belt and Road Initiative in the Right Direction?," Devex, November 2, 2018, https://www.devex.com/news/sponsored/will-the-world-bank-push-china-s-belt-and-road-initiative-in-the-right-direction-93657.

In his speech: Jim Yong Kim, "World Bank Group President Jim Yong Kim's Remarks at the International Forum on China's Reform and Opening Up and Poverty Reduction," World Bank, November 1, 2018, https://www.worldbank.org/en/news/speech/2018/11/01/world-bank-group-president-jim-yong-kim-remarks-at-the-international-forum-on-chinas-reform-and-opening-up-and-poverty-reduction.

Yang Shaolin: "Shaolin Yang," World Bank, accessed September 28, 2020, https://www.worldbank.org/en/about/people/s/shaolin-yang.

175 *Elliot Wilson wrote:* Elliot Wilson, "Jin-Yong Cai: An Activist at the IFC," *Euromoney,* September 6, 2013, http://www.euromoney.com/article/b12kjwfn6f6k9p/jin-yong-cai-an-activist-at-the-ifc.

amid a scandal: Ian Talley, "World Bank Probes $1 Billion China Loan," *Wall Street Journal,* February 3, 2015, https://www.wsj.com/articles/world-bank-probes-1-billion-china-loan-1423012000.

the World Bank's development fund: Kim hired a law firm to investigate the donation, and the firm reported it found no evidence of malfeasance.

Global Infrastructure Partners hired: Gillian Tan and Andrew Mayeda, "GIP Hires Ex-TPG, World Bank Executive Jin-Yong Cai," BloombergQuint, May 2, 2019, https://www.bloombergquint.com/business/gip-is-said-to-hire-ex-tpg-world-bank-executive-jin-yong-cai.

10. COLD WAR REDUX

180 *"The Sources of Soviet Conduct":* X [George F. Kennan], "The Sources of Soviet Conduct," *Foreign Affairs,* July 1947, http://slantchev.ucsd.edu/courses/pdf/Kennan%20-%20The%20Sources%20of%20Soviet%20Conduct.pdf.

181 *called NSC 68: United States Objectives and Programs for National Security,* NSC 68, April 14, 1950, https://digitalarchive.wilsoncenter.org/document/116191.pdf?v=2699956db534c1821edefa61b8c13ffe.

and economic means: "NSC-68, 1950," Office of the Historian, Foreign Service Institute, accessed September 29, 2020, https://history.state.gov/milestones/1945-1952/NSC68.

183 *for a public event:* "Future Security Forum 2019," New America, April 29, 2019, http://newamerica.org/conference/future-security-forum-2019/.

185 *doctrine was racist:* Paul Musgrave, "The Slip That Revealed the Real Trump Doctrine," *Foreign Policy,* May 2, 2019, https://foreignpolicy.com/2019/05/02/the-slip-that-revealed-the-real-trump-doctrine/.

out of her depth: Daniel W. Drezner, "Let's Grade the State Department's Director of Policy Planning on Her Grand Strategy Musings!," *Washington Post,* May 1, 2019, https://www.washingtonpost.com/outlook/2019/05/02/lets-grade-state-departments-director-policy-planning-her-grand-strategy-musings/.

186 *she was fired:* Nahal Toosi and Eliana Johnson, "Top State Department Adviser Fired over 'Abusive' Management Style," *Politico,* August 2, 2019, https://politi.co/2MB2ip6.

read a commentary: Sheng Zhong, "'Clash of Civilizations' Theory Will Come to No Good End," *Global Times,* May 26, 2019, https://www.globaltimes.cn/content/1151639.shtml.

in his official speech: "Speech at the 18th Shangri-La Dialogue by Gen. Wei Fenghe, State Councilor and Minister of National Defense, PRC," Ministry of National Defense of the People's Republic of China, June 2, 2019, http://eng.mod.gov.cn/leadership/2019-06/02/content_4842884.htm.

187 *Shanahan said:* Paul McLeary, "Acting SecDef Shanahan's First Message: 'China, China, China,'" Breaking Defense, January 2, 2019, https://breakingdefense.com/2019/01/acting-secdef-shanahans-first-message-china-china-china/.

Indo-Pacific Strategy Report: *Indo-Pacific Strategy Report: Preparedness, Partnerships, and Promoting a Networked Region* (US Department of Defense, June 1, 2019), https://media.defense.gov/2019/Jul/01/2002152311/-1/-1/1/DEPARTMENT-OF-DEFENSE-INDO-PACIFIC-STRATEGY-REPORT-2019.PDF.

190 *Singapore in 2018:* Josh Rogin, "Pence: It's Up to China to Avoid a Cold War," *Washington Post,* November 13, 2018, https://www.washingtonpost.com/news/josh-rogin/wp/2018/11/13/pence-its-up-to-china-to-avoid-a-cold-war/.

a similar answer: Josh Rogin, "Esper: 'We're Not the Ones Looking for a Cold War' with China," *Washington Post,* November 19, 2019, https://www.washingtonpost.com/opinions/2019/11/19/esper-were-not-ones-looking-cold-war-with-china/.

191 *2018 Aspen Security Forum:* Josh Rogin, "Russia Fever Is Distracting the United States from the China Threat," *Washington Post,* June 25, 2017, https://www.washingtonpost.com/news/josh-rogin/wp/2018/07/25/russia-fever-is-distracting-the-united-states-from-the-china-threat/.

192 *"The China Challenge":* Michael Pompeo, "The China Challenge (Speech)," US Department of State, October 30, 2019, https://www.state.gov/the-china-challenge/.

"security as well": Michael Pompeo, "Silicon Valley and National Security," US Department of State, January 13, 2020, https://www.state.gov/silicon-valley-and-national-security/.

National Governors Association: Michael Pompeo, "U.S. States and the China Competition," US Department of State, February 8, 2020, https://www.state.gov/u-s-states-and-the-china-competition/.

Chinese think tank: Bethany Allen-Ebrahimian, "How a Chinese Think Tank Rates All 50 U.S. Governors," Axios, February 10, 2020, https://www.axios.com/china-rating-us-governors-bff6cc73-e485-44f2-98d0-b7639af3f0aa.html.

Allen-Ebrahimian, "How a Chinese Think Tank."

195 *"The Sources of CCP Conduct":* Mike Gallagher, "The Sources of CCP Conduct," *American Interest,* May 9, 2019, https://www.the-american-interest.com/2019/05/09/the-sources-of-ccp-conduct/.

196 *"The Sources of Chinese Conduct":* Odd Arne Westad, "The Sources of Chinese Conduct," *Foreign Affairs,* October 2019, https://www.foreignaffairs.com/articles/china/2019-08-12/sources-chinese-conduct.

197 People's Republic of China: *United States Strategic Approach to the People's Republic of China* (White House, May 2020), https://www.whitehouse.gov/wp-content/uploads/2020/05/U.S.-Strategic-Approach-to-The-Peoples-Republic-of-China-Report-5.20.20.pdf.
it states: United States Strategic Approach, 1.

11. THE BIG CHILL

201 *in 2018:* Samantha Hoffman, "Social Credit," Australian Strategic Policy Institute, June 28, 2018, https://www.aspi.org.au/report/social-credit.
The letter: "General Department of Civil Aviation Administration of China" [in Chinese], April 25, 2018, https://www.washingtonpost.com/r/2010-2019/WashingtonPost/2018/05/05/Editorial-Opinion/Graphics/AirlineLetter.pdf?itid=lk_inline_manual_4.

202 *issued a statement:* Sarah Huckabee Sanders, "Statement from the Press Secretary on China's Political Correctness," White House, May 5, 2018, https://www.whitehouse.gov/briefings-statements/statement-press-secretary-chinas-political-correctness/.

203 *Marriott Hotels:* Josh Rogin, "How China Forces American Companies to Do Its Political Bidding," *Washington Post,* January 21, 2018, https://www.washingtonpost.com/opinions/global-opinions/how-china-forces-american-companies-to-do-its-political-bidding/2018/01/21/52a1d5a0-fd63-11e7-8f66-2df0b94bb98a_story.html.
Mercedes-Benz: Pei Li, "Mercedes-Benz Apologizes to Chinese for Quoting Dalai Lama," Reuters, February 6, 2018, https://www.reuters.com/article/us-mercedes-benz-china-gaffe-idUSKBN1FQ1FJ.
even fired: Wayne Ma, "Marriott Employee Roy Jones Hit 'Like.' Then China Got Mad," *Wall Street Journal,* March 3, 2018, https://www.wsj.com/articles/marriott-employee-roy-jones-hit-like-then-china-got-mad-1520094910.

205 *claimed on Twitter:* Tilman Fertitta (@TilmanJFertitta), "Listen . . . @dmorey does NOT speak for the @HoustonRockets. Our presence in Tokyo is all about the promotion of the @NBA internationally and we are NOT a political organization. @espn," Twitter, October 4, 2019, 8:54 p.m., https://twitter.com/TilmanJFertitta/status/1180330287957495809.
Kanter tweeted: Enes Kanter (@EnesKanter), "The @NBA stands with me for freedom and democracy. It's made all the difference. I hope we can build bridges, instead of breaking them," Twitter, October 6, 2019, 7:37 p.m., https://twitter.com/EnesKanter/status/1181035791092465665.
Tsai posted: Joseph Tsai, "Open Letter to All NBA Fans," Facebook, October 6, 2019, https://www.facebook.com/joe.tsai.3781/posts/2653378931391524.

206 *Ted Cruz:* Ted Cruz (@tedcruz), "As a lifelong @HoustonRockets fan, I was proud to see @dmorey call out the Chinese Communist Party's repressive treatment of protestors in Hong Kong. Now, in pursuit of big $$, the @nba is shamefully retreating," Twitter, October 6, 2019, 7:16 p.m., https://twitter.com/tedcruz/status/1181030464661999616.
Beto O'Rourke: Beto O'Rourke (@BetoORourke), "The only thing the NBA should be apologizing for is their blatant prioritization of profits over human rights. What an embarrassment," Twitter, October 6, 2019, 8:22 p.m., https://twitter.com/BetoORourke/status/1181047092875157504.
lost hundreds of millions of dollars: Ben Cohen, "China Standoff Cost the NBA 'Hundreds of Millions,'" *Wall Street Journal,* February 16, 2020, https://www.wsj.com/articles/china-standoff-cost-the-nba-hundreds-of-millions-11581866522.
Commerce Department announced: "U.S. Department of Commerce Adds 28 Chinese Organizations to Its Entity List," US Department of Commerce, accessed September 4, 2020, https://www.commerce.gov/news/press-releases/2019/10/us-department-commerce-adds-28-chinese-organizations-its-entity-list.

207 *for defending:* Robert Silverman, "LeBron James' China Comments Aren't Unique. The Criticism He Received Is," NBC News, October 20, 2019, https://www.nbcnews.com/think/opinion/what-did-lebron-james-say-about-china-nearly-everyone-else-ncna1069131.

208 *he told me:* Josh Rogin, "Americans Must Search Their Conscience and 'Google Uyghurs,'" *Washington Post,* October 31, 2019, https://www.washingtonpost.com/opinions/global-opinions/americans-must-search-their-conscience-and-google-uyghurs/2019/10/31/7487fdf6-fc1d-11e9-8190-6be4deb56e01_story.html.

210 *at least fifty years:* John R. Bolton, *The Room Where It Happened: A White House Memoir* (New York: Simon and Schuster, 2020), 280.

in a June 18 phone call: Rogin, "Americans Must Search."

calling the protests "riots": "Trump Says It's Up to China to Deal with Hong Kong 'Riots,'" Reuters, August 2, 2019, https://www.reuters.com/article/us-hongkong-protests-trump/trump-says-its-up-to-china-to-deal-with-hong-kong-riots-idUSKCN1US0OR.

said the president: "Trump Says."

the news broke: Aime Williams and Sue-Lin Wong, "US Barred Hong Kong Consul from Giving Critical Speech on Protests," *Financial Times,* July 8, 2019, https://www.ft.com/content/ce55c3f8-a1d3-11e9-a282-2df48f366f7d.

211 *"do the right thing":* Kevin Cirilli and Nick Wadhams, "Pompeo Urges China to 'Do the Right Thing' in Hong Kong Protests," Bloomberg, July 25, 2019, https://www.bloomberg.com/graphics/2020-coronavirus-dash/.

he said: Vivian Salama, "White House Told Officials to Go Easy on China over Hong Kong," *Wall Street Journal,* July 31, 2019, https://www.wsj.com/articles/white-house-tells-officials-to-go-easy-on-china-over-hong-kong-11564607899.

massing thousands of police: Joe Tacopino, "US Monitoring Hong Kong as Chinese Forces Amass at Border," *New York Post,* July 30, 2019, https://nypost.com/2019/07/30/us-monitoring-hong-kong-border-as-chinese-forces-gather-en-masse/.

social media tagline: Global Times (@globaltimesnews), "A blunt warning for #HongKong secessionists and their foreign backers? First, the PLA's Hong Kong garrison commander vowed to safeguard Hong Kong's stability; then shortly after, the #garrison said it has the confidence to protect HK," Twitter, July 31, 2019, 9:27 a.m., https://twitter.com/globaltimesnews/status/1156602387835940864.

CCP rule by tweeting: Donald J. Trump (@realDonaldTrump), Twitter, October 1, 2019, 3:54 a.m., https://twitter.com/realDonaldTrump/status/1178986524630802432.

Hawley's statement: "Senator Hawley Statement on the 70th Anniversary of the People's Republic of China," Senator Josh Hawley, October 1, 2019, https://www.hawley.senate.gov/senator-hawley-statement-70th-anniversary-peoples-republic-china.

212 *wrote a story:* Josh Rogin, "Trump and McConnell Are Failing the People of Hong Kong," *Washington Post,* November 7, 2019, https://www.washingtonpost.com/opinions/global-opinions/trump-and-mcconnell-are-failing-the-people-of-hong-kong/2019/11/07/913af586-0193-11ea-8bab-0fc209e065a8_story.html.

op-ed in the Wall Street Journal: Mitch McConnell, "We Stand with Hong Kong," *Wall Street Journal,* August 20, 2019, https://www.wsj.com/articles/we-stand-with-hong-kong-11566341474.

12. WAKING UP

216 *established in 2004:* "Confucius Institutes Rebrand After Overseas Propaganda and Influence Rows," *South China Morning Post,* July 4, 2020, https://www.scmp.com/news/china/diplomacy/article/3091837/chinas-confucius-institutes-rebrand-after-overseas-propaganda.

217 *closed the institute:* Joseph Baucum, "UWF Cuts Ties with Controversial Chinese-Affiliated Confucius Institute," *Pensacola News Journal,* February 7, 2018, https://www.pnj.com/story/money/business/2018/02/07/uwf-cuts-ties-chinese-run-confucius-institute-criticized-controversial-chinese-government-affiliated/312966002/.

back and forth: "Florida-China Linkage Institute," University of West Florida, accessed September 30, 2020, https://uwf.edu/academic-engagement-and-student-affairs/departments/international-affairs/scholarships-and-linkages/florida-china-linkage-institute/.

bragged: Josh Rogin, "Pentagon Barred from Funding Confucius Institutes on American Campuses," *Washington Post,* August 14, 2018, https://www.washingtonpost.com/news/josh-rogin/wp/2018/08/14/pentagon-barred-from-funding-confucius-institutes-on-american-campuses/.

218 *closed their Confucius Institutes:* Hannah Critchfield, "ASU Joins 15 Other Universities in Closing Confucius Institute," *Phoenix New Times,* August 23, 2019, https://www.phoenixnewtimes.com/news/asu-joins-15-other-universities-in-closing-confucius-institute-11348296.

closed the institute: Josh Rogin, "America's Universities Are Finally Waking Up to the China Threat," *Washington Post,* April 4, 2019, https://www.washingtonpost.com/opinions/global-opinions/americas-universities-are-finally-waking-up-to-the-china-threat/2019/04/04/1b21e616-5716-11e9-9136-f8e636f1f6df_story.html.

According to a report: Rachelle Peterson, "Outsourced to China: Confucius Institutes and Soft Power in American Higher Education," National Association of Scholars, April 7, 2017, https://www.nas.org/reports/outsourced-to-china/full-report.

219 *"that is cowardice":* Confucius, *The Analects,* trans. Simon Leys (New York: W. W. Norton, 1997), xvii at 2.24.

used these student organizations: Bethany Allen-Ebrahimian, "China's Long Arm Reaches into American Campuses," *Foreign Policy,* March 7, 2018, https://foreignpolicy.com/2018/03/07/chinas-long-arm-reaches-into-american-campuses-chinese-students-scholars-association-university-communist-party/.

have increased vastly: Bethany Allen-Ebrahimian, "Chinese Government Gave Money to Georgetown Chinese Student Group," *Foreign Policy,* February 14, 2018, https://foreignpolicy.com/2018/02/14/exclusive-chinese-government-gave-money-to-georgetown-chinese-student-group-washington-china-communist-party-influence/.

a 2016 directive: Chris Buckley, "China Says Its Students, Even Those Abroad, Need More 'Patriotic Education,'" *New York Times,* February 10, 2016, https://www.nytimes.com/2016/02/11/world/asia/china-patriotic-education.html.

220 *told the* New York Times: Stephanie Saul, "On Campuses Far from China, Still Under Beijing's Watchful Eye," *New York Times,* May 4, 2017, https://www.nytimes.com/2017/05/04/us/chinese-students-western-campuses-china-influence.html.

University of California, San Diego, announced: Judy Piercey and Christine Clark, "Tenzin Gyatso, His Holiness the 14th Dalai Lama to Speak at UC San Diego Commencement," UC San Diego News Center, February 2, 2017, https://ucsdnews.ucsd.edu/feature/tenzin_gyatso_his_holiness_the_14th_dalai_lama_to_speak_at_uc_san_diego.

admitted they had spoken: "Chinese Student Organizations Denounce Dalai Lama as Commencement Speaker," *Triton,* February 3, 2017, https://triton.news/2017/02/chinese-student-organizations-denounce-dalai-lama-commencement-speaker/.

Chinese government retaliated: Larry Diamond and Orville Schell, eds., *China's Influence & American Interests: Promoting Constructive Vigilance*, Report of the Working Group on Chinese Influence Activities in the United States (Stanford, CA: Hoover Institution, Stanford University, November 29, 2018), https://www.hoover.org/sites/default/files/research/docs/diamond-schell_corrected-april2020finalfile.pdf.

gave a speech: Simon Denyer and Congcong Zhang, "A Chinese Student Praised the 'Fresh Air of Free Speech' at a U.S. College. Then Came the Backlash," *Washington Post,* May 23, 2017, https://www.washingtonpost.com/news/worldviews/wp/2017/05/23/a-chinese-student-praised-the-fresh-air-of-free-speech-at-a-u-s-college-then-came-the-backlash/.

221 *it uncovered:* "U.S. Department of Education Launches Investigation into Foreign Gifts Reporting at Ivy League Universities," press release, US Department of Education, February 12, 2020, https://www.ed.gov/news/press-releases/test-0.

A 2019 report: Rob Portman and Tom Carper, *China's Impact on the U.S. Education System,* staff report (Washington, DC: US Senate, Permanent Subcommittee on Investigations, 2019).

wrote to: Josh Rogin, "Congress Wants DeVos to Investigate Chinese Research Partnerships on American Campuses," *Washington Post,* June 20, 2018, https://www.washingtonpost.com/news/josh-rogin/wp/2018/06/20/congress-wants-devos-to-investigate-chinese-research-partnerships-on-american-campuses/.

222 *warned in 2015:* FBI, "FBI Counterintelligence Note: Chinese Talent Programs," Public Intelligence, September 2015, https://publicintelligence.net/fbi-chinese-talent-programs/.

raised concerns: Mihir Zaveri, "Wary of Chinese Espionage, Houston Cancer Center Chose to Fire 3 Scientists," *New York Times,* April 22, 2019, https://www.nytimes.com/2019/04/22/health/md-anderson-chinese-scientists.html.

223 *claimed ignorance:* Sui-Lee Wee, "China Uses DNA to Track Its People, with the Help of American Expertise," *New York Times,* February 21, 2019, https://www.nytimes.com/2019/02/21/business/china-xinjiang-uighur-dna-thermo-fisher.html.

MIT had announced: Adam Conner-Simons, "CSAIL Launches New Five-Year Collaboration with IFlyTek," MIT News, June 15, 2018, https://news.mit.edu/2018/csail-launches-five-year-collaboration-with-iflytek-0615.

after reports accused: Will Knight, "MIT Cuts Ties with a Chinese AI Firm amid Human Rights Concerns," *Wired,* April 21, 2020, https://www.wired.com/story/mit-cuts-ties-chinese-ai-firm-human-rights/.

is collaborating with: Madhumita Murgia and Christian Shepherd, "Western AI Researchers Partnered with Chinese Surveillance Firm," *Financial Times,* April 19, 2019, https://www.ft.com/content/41be9878-61d9-11e9-b285-3acd5d43599e.

working to automate: Paul Mozur, "One Month, 500,000 Face Scans: How China Is Using A.I. to Profile a Minority, *New York Times,* April 14, 2019, https://www.nytimes.com/2019/04/14/technology/china-surveillance-artificial-intelligence-racial-profiling.html.

224 *began a sweep:* Kate O'Keeffe and Aruna Viswanatha, "FBI Sweep of China Researchers Leads to Cat-and-Mouse Tactics," *Wall Street Journal,* September 7, 2020, https://www.wsj.com/articles/fbi-sweep-of-china-researchers-leads-to-cat-and-mouse-tactics-11599471001.

226 *Soon it leaked:* Paul Mozur and Jane Perlez, "China Bets on Sensitive U.S. Start-Ups, Worrying the Pentagon," *New York Times,* March 22, 2017, https://www.nytimes.com/2017/03/22/technology/china-defense-start-ups.html.

The full report: Michael Brown and Pavneet Singh, *China's Technology Transfer Strategy: How Chinese Investments in Emerging Technology Enable a Strategic Competitor to Access the Crown Jewels of U.S. Innovation* (Defense Innovation Unit Experimental, January 2018), 48.

227 *launched a public attack:* Peter Thiel, "Good for Google, Bad for America," *New York Times,* August 1, 2019, https://www.nytimes.com/2019/08/01/opinion/peter-thiel-google.html.

"take a look": "Remarks by President Trump in Cabinet Meeting," White House, July 16, 2019, https://www.whitehouse.gov/briefings-statements/remarks-president-trump-cabinet-meeting-14/.

Mnuchin announced: Bowdeya Tweh, "Treasury Secretary Finds No Security Concerns with Google Work in China," *Wall Street Journal,* July 24, 2019, https://www.wsj.com/articles/treasury-secretary-finds-no-security-concerns-with-google-work-in-china-11563976459.

Trump tweeted: Donald J. Trump (@realDonaldTrump), "@sundarpichai of Google was in the Oval Office working very hard to explain how much he liked me, what a great job the Administration is doing, that Google was not involved with China's military, that they didn't help Crooked Hillary over me in the 2016 Election, & that they . . . ," Twitter, August 6, 2019, 10:51 a.m., https://twitter.com/realDonaldTrump/status/1158797732821291018.

on multiple occasions: Alex Joske, "The Chinese Military's Exploitation of Western Tech Firms," *Strategist,* April 11, 2019, https://www.aspistrategist.org.au/the-chinese-militarys-exploitation-of-western-tech-firms/.

according to the testimony: Gordon G. Chang, "U.S. Must Put a Ban on Google Helping China Develop a Global Digital Dictatorship," Daily Beast, March 26, 2019, https://www.thedailybeast.com/google-snubbed-the-pentagonbut-not-the-chinese-military.

228 *reorient Facebook's approach:* Josh Rogin, "Facebook Wakes Up to the China Challenge," *Washington Post,* October 24, 2019, https://www.washingtonpost.com/opinions/facebook-wakes-up-to-the-china-challenge/2019/10/24/ae5b2fcc-f69f-11e9-8cf0-4cc99f74d127_story.html.

"to other countries": Tony Romm, "Zuckerberg: Standing for Voice and Free Expression," *Washington Post,* October 17, 2019, https://www.washingtonpost.com/technology/2019/10/17/zuckerberg-standing-voice-free-expression/.

229 *"key money":* Josh Rogin, "Trump's TikTok Deal Would Only Make the Problem Worse," *Washington Post,* September 24, 2020, https://www.washingtonpost.com/opinions/global-opinions/trumps-tiktok-deal-would-only-make-the-problem-worse/2020/09/24/3b418b7c-fe9f-11ea-8d05-9beaaa91c71f_story.html.

230 *move its data:* Nick Statt, "Apple's iCloud Partner in China Will Store User Data on Servers of State-Run Telecom," Verge, July 18, 2018, https://www.theverge.com/2018/7/18/17587304/apple-icloud-china-user-data-state-run-telecom-privacy-security.

granting Beijing's demands: Washington Post Editorial Board, "Apple Accedes to China's Despotic Demands," *Washington Post,* October, 15, 2019, https://www.washingtonpost.com/opinions/the-costs-of-apples-business-in-china/2019/10/15/8a038dde-ef85-11e9-89eb-ec56cd414732_story.html.

Global Times *would report:* Stephen Warwick, "China Threatens Apple with Investigations and Restrictions in Response to U.S. Treatment of Huawei," iMore, May 15, 2020, https://www.imore.com/china-threatens-companies-apple-investigations-and-restrictions-response-treatment-huawei.

231 *In its 2017 report: 2017 Report to Congress of the U.S.-China Economic and Security Review Commission* (Washington, DC: US Government Publishing Office, November 2017), 73. https://www.uscc.gov/sites/default/files/annual_reports/2017_Annual_Report_to_Congress.pdf.

that went bad: Walter Pavlo, "Fraud in Chinese Reverse Mergers on American Exchanges — and We're Surprised?," *Forbes,* April 8, 2011, https://www.forbes.com/sites/walterpavlo/2011/04/08/fraud-in-chinese-reverse-mergers-on-american-exchanges-and-were-surprised/.

memorandum of understanding: "PCAOB Enters into Enforcement Cooperation Agreement with Chinese Regulators," Public Company Accounting Oversight Board, May 24, 2013, https://pcaobus.org:443/News/Releases/Pages/05202013_ChinaMOU.aspx.

232 *raised $25 billion:* Aaron Timms, "Deals of the Year 2014: Alibaba Sets IPO Record with NYSE Debut," *Institutional Investor,* December 10, 2014, https://www.institutionalinvestor.com/article/b14zbh3xzm35m3/deals-of-the-year-2014-alibaba-sets-ipo-record-with-nyse-debut.

The China Hustle: Josh Rogin, "It's Time to End the 'China Hustle' on U.S. Stock Exchanges," *Washington Post,* August 30, 2018, https://www.washingtonpost.com/opinions/global-opinions/its-time-to-end-the-china-hustle-on-us-stock-exchanges/2018/08/30/50137c1a-ac8d-11e8-8a0c-70b618c98d3c_story.html.

233 *"Chinese government":* Mike Bird, "How China Pressured MSCI to Add Its Market to Major Benchmark," *Wall Street Journal,* February 3, 2019, https://www.wsj.com/articles/how-china-pressured-msci-to-add-its-market-to-major-benchmark-11549195201.

234 *MSCI quadrupled:* Asjylyn Loder, "Indexes to Unleash Flood of Money into Chinese Stocks," *Wall Street Journal,* May 16, 2019, https://www.wsj.com/articles/indexes-to-unleash-flood-of-money-into-chinese-stocks-11558006200.

sent about $80 billion: Michael Wursthorn and Shen Hong, "Chinese Shares Gain Global Sway Thanks to Index Firm's Move," *Wall Street Journal,* March 1, 2019, https://

www.wsj.com/articles/chinese-shares-gain-global-sway-thanks-to-index-firms-move-11551392626.

support 364 Chinese firms: Yen Nee Lee, "China's $13 Trillion Bond Market Marks a Milestone. Here's What It Means," CNBC, April 1, 2019, https://www.cnbc.com/2019/04/01/china-bonds-debut-on-bloomberg-barclays-global-aggregate-index.html.

237 *the letter stated:* Josh Rogin, "China's Infiltration of U.S. Capital Markets Is a National Security Concern," *Washington Post,* June 13, 2019, https://www.washingtonpost.com/opinions/2019/06/13/chinas-infiltration-us-capital-markets-is-national-security-concern/.

240 *Schwarzman told* Bloomberg News: John Gittlesohn, "Calpers Top Money Man Is Swept Up in Chinese Espionage Fears," Bloomberg, February 25, 2020, https://www.bloomberg.com/news/articles/2020-02-25/how-chinese-espionage-fears-ensnared-calpers-top-money-man.

resign from his position: Josh Rogin, "Americans Shouldn't Be Forced to Invest in China's Military," *Washington Post,* August 27, 2020, https://www.washingtonpost.com/opinions/global-opinions/americans-shouldnt-be-forced-to-invest-in-chinas-military/2020/08/27/e027b6f4-e89f-11ea-97e0-94d2e46e759b_story.html.

13. ENDGAME

244 *"in early September":* "Remarks by President Trump Before Marine One Departure," White House, August 1, 2019, https://www.whitehouse.gov/briefings-statements/remarks-president-trump-marine-one-departure-56/.

spooked the markets: Damian Paletta et al., "Treasury Dept. Designates China a 'Currency Manipulator,' a Major Escalation of the Trade War," *Washington Post,* August 5, 2019, https://www.washingtonpost.com/world/asia_pacific/china-lets-currency-plunge-below-7-a-decade-low-after-trump-adds-new-tariffs/2019/08/05/c7415db6-b754-11e9-8e83-4e6687e99814_story.html.

245 *met with Trump:* Todd Shriber, "Las Vegas Sands Boss Adelson Told Trump to Tread Carefully with China," Casino.org, September 23, 2019, https://www.casino.org/news/las-vegas-sands-adelson-told-trump-to-tread-carefully-with-china/.

released its plan: Jeff Stein et al., "Trump Retaliates in Trade War by Escalating Tariffs on Chinese Imports and Demanding Companies Cut Ties with China," *Washington Post,* August 23, 2019, https://www.washingtonpost.com/business/2019/08/23/china-hits-us-with-tariffs-billion-worth-goods-reinstates-auto-levies-state-media-report/.

promised on Twitter: Donald J. Trump (@realDonaldTrump), "For many years China (and many other countries) has been taking advantage of the United States on Trade, Intellectual Property Theft, and much more. Our Country has been losing HUNDREDS OF BILLIONS OF DOLLARS a year to China, with no end in sight . . . ," thread, Twitter, August 23, 2019, 2:00 p.m., https://twitter.com/realDonaldTrump/status/1165005927864512512.

Twitter rant: Donald J. Trump (@realDonaldTrump), "Our Country has lost, stupidly, Trillions of Dollars with China over many years. They have stolen our Intellectual Property at a rate of Hundreds of Billions of Dollars a Year, & they want to continue. I won't let that happen! We don't need China and, frankly, would be far . . . ," thread, Twitter, August 23, 2019, 7:59 a.m., https://twitter.com/realDonaldTrump/status/1164914959131848705.

246 *Bolton wrote:* John R. Bolton, *The Room Where It Happened: A White House Memoir* (New York: Simon and Schuster, 2020), 375.

Trump tweeted: Donald J. Trump (@realDonaldTrump), "For all of the Fake News Reporters that don't have a clue as to what the law is relative to Presidential powers, China, etc., try looking at the Emergency Economic Powers Act of 1977. Case closed!," Twitter, August 23, 2019, 8:58 p.m., https://twitter.com/realDonaldTrump/status/1165111122510237696.

249 *was asked again:* "Trump: No Deadline for China Trade Deal, Might Follow 2020 Election," Reuters, December 3, 2019, https://www.reuters.com/article/usa-china-trade-trump-idUSL9N27702H.

Trump commented: "Remarks by President Trump and Prime Minister Trudeau of Canada Before Bilateral Meeting — London, United Kingdom," White House, December 3, 2019, https://www.whitehouse.gov/briefings-statements/remarks-president-trump-prime-minister-trudeau-canada-bilateral-meeting-london-united-kingdom/.

largely conceded: Josh Rogin, "Trump Is Getting Played by China on Trade," *Washington Post,* December 12, 2019, https://www.washingtonpost.com/opinions/global-opinions/trump-is-getting-played-by-china-on-trade/2019/12/12/a8381362-1d2d-11ea-b4c1-fd0d91b60d9e_story.html.

reinvigorated his personal channel: Reuters, "Trump Son-in-Law Jared Kushner Takes a Bigger Role in China Trade Talks," CNBC, December 4, 2019, https://www.cnbc.com/2019/12/04/jared-kushner-trumps-son-in-law-takes-a-bigger-role-in-china-trade-talks.html.

The announcement: "United States and China Reach Phase One Trade Agreement," Office of the United States Trade Representative, December 13, 2019, https://ustr.gov/about-us/policy-offices/press-office/press-releases/2019/december/united-states-and-china-reach.

250 *"reformers":* Blair Shiff, "Robert Lighthizer on China Trade Deal: 'We Expect Them to Live Up' to It," Fox Business, January 13, 2020, https://www.foxbusiness.com/technology/robert-lighthizer-china-intellectual-property.

he wrote later: Robert Lighthizer, "The Case for the Trump Administration's Approach to Trade," *Foreign Affairs,* July/August 2020, https://www.foreignaffairs.com/articles/united-states/2020-06-09/how-make-trade-work-workers.

14. THE CORONAVIRUS

258 *sent out a tweet:* Joe Biden (@JoeBiden), "We are in the midst of a crisis with the coronavirus. We need to lead the way with science — not Donald Trump's record of hysteria, xenophobia, and fear-mongering. He is the worst possible person to lead our country through a global health emergency," Twitter, February 1, 2020, 2:01 p.m., https://twitter.com/JoeBiden/status/1223727977361338370.

until early April: Jake Tapper, "Biden Campaign Says He Backs Trump's China Travel Ban," CNN, April 3, 2020, https://www.cnn.com/2020/04/03/politics/joe-biden-trump-china-coronavirus/index.html.

259 *"hoax of the day":* Savannah Behrmann, "Mick Mulvaney Says Media Hopes Coronavirus Will 'Bring Down' Trump," *USA Today,* February 28, 2020, https://www.usatoday.com/story/news/politics/2020/02/28/mick-mulvaney-says-media-hopes-coronavirus-bring-down-trump/4907058002/.

Esper showed up: Philip Ewing, "Trump, Esper Wish Bon Voyage to Hospital Ship Bound for New York City," NPR, March 28, 2020, https://www.npr.org/sections/coronavirus-live-updates/2020/03/28/823268706/trump-esper-wish-bon-voyage-to-hospital-ship-bound-for-new-york-city.

260 *Taiwanese officials alerted:* Katrina Manson et al., "Taiwan Says WHO Failed to Act on Coronavirus Transmission Warning," March 20, 2020, https://www.ft.com/content/2a70a02a-644a-11ea-a6cd-df28cc3c6a68.

Chinese health authorities: Vandana Rambaran, "Taiwan Releases December Email to WHO Showing Unheeded Warning About Coronavirus," Fox News, April 13, 2020, https://www.foxnews.com/world/taiwan-releases-december-email-showing-unheeded-warning-to-who-about-coronavirus.

261 *forced to sign:* Andrew Green, "Li Wenliang," *Lancet* 395, no. 10225 (February 29, 2020): 682, https://doi.org/10.1016/S0140-6736(20)30382-2.
A study by Chinese researchers: Chaolin Huang et al., "Clinical Features of Patients Infected with 2019 Novel Coronavirus in Wuhan, China," *Lancet* 395, no. 10223 (February 15, 2020): 497–506, https://doi.org/10.1016/S0140-6736(20)30183-5.

262 *lab was shut down:* Zhuang Pinghui, "Lab That First Shared Coronavirus Sequence Closed for 'Rectification,'" *South China Morning Post,* February 28, 2020, https://www.scmp.com/news/china/society/article/3052966/chinese-laboratory-first-shared-coronavirus-genome-world-ordered.
organization tweeted: World Health Organization (@WHO), "Preliminary investigations conducted by the Chinese authorities have found no clear evidence of human-to-human transmission of the novel #coronavirus (2019-nCoV) identified in #Wuhan, #China," Twitter, January 14, 2020, 3:18 a.m., https://twitter.com/WHO/status/1217043229427761152.
in a statement: "Statement on the Second Meeting of the International Health Regulations (2005) Emergency Committee Regarding the Outbreak of Novel Coronavirus (2019-NCoV)," World Health Organization, January 30, 2020, https://www.who.int/news-room/detail/30-01-2020-statement-on-the-second-meeting-of-the-international-health-regulations-(2005)-emergency-committee-regarding-the-outbreak-of-novel-coronavirus-(2019-ncov).
praised China's strategy: "Report of the Director-General, 146th Meeting of the Executive Board," World Health Organization, February 3, 2020, https://www.who.int/dg/speeches/detail/report-of-the-director-general-146th-meeting-of-the-executive-board.

263 *told the* New York Times: "He Warned of Coronavirus. Here's What He Told Us Before He Died," *New York Times,* February 7, 2020, https://www.nytimes.com/2020/02/07/world/asia/Li-Wenliang-china-coronavirus.html.

264 *to 120 countries:* Ryo Nakamura, "US Counters China's 'Mask Diplomacy' with $225m Coronavirus Aid," *Nikkei Asian Review,* April 8, 2020, https://asia.nikkei.com/Spotlight/Coronavirus/US-counters-China-s-mask-diplomacy-with-225m-coronavirus-aid.
the White House said: Judd Deere 45 Archived (@JuddPDeere45), "Today, @realDonald Trump Spoke with President Xi Jinping of China. President Trump Expressed Confidence in China's Strength and Resilience in Confronting the Challenge of the 2019 Novel Coronavirus Outbreak.," Twitter, February 7, 2020, https://twitter.com/JuddPDeere45/status/1225627973635715072.

266 *tweeted on March 12:* Lijian Zhao (@zlj517), "CDC was caught on the spot. When did patient zero begin in US? How many people are infected? What are the names of the hospitals? It might be US army who brought the epidemic to Wuhan. Be transparent! Make public your data! US owe us an explanation!," Twitter, March 12, 2020, 7:37 a.m., https://twitter.com/zlj517/status/1238111898828066823.

267 *a new study:* Ben Hu et al., "Discovery of a Rich Gene Pool of Bat SARS-Related Coronaviruses Provides New Insights into the Origin of SARS Coronavirus," *PLoS Pathogens* 13, no. 11 (November 30, 2017): e1006698, https://doi.org/10.1371/journal.ppat.1006698.

269 *issued a moratorium:* Sara Reardon, "US Suspends Risky Disease Research," *Nature News* 514, no. 7523 (October 23, 2014): 411, https://doi.org/10.1038/514411a.
an article in Nature: Declan Butler, "Engineered Bat Virus Stirs Debate over Risky Research," *Nature News,* November 12, 2015, https://doi.org/10.1038/nature.2015.18787.

271 *released a statement:* Peng Zhou et al., "A Pneumonia Outbreak Associated with a New Coronavirus of Probable Bat Origin," *Nature* 579, no. 7798 (March 2020): 270–73, https://doi.org/10.1038/s41586-020-2012-7.
Shi claimed: Jonathan Latham and Allison Wilson, "A Proposed Origin for SARS-CoV-2 and the COVID-19 Pandemic," Independent Science News, July 15, 2020, https://www.independentsciencenews.org/commentaries/a-proposed-origin-for-sars-cov-2-and-the-covid-19-pandemic/.

According to one researcher: Xiaolu Tang et al., "On the Origin and Continuing Evolution of SARS-CoV-2," *National Science Review* 7, no. 6 (June 1, 2020): 1012–23, https://doi.org/10.1093/nsr/nwaa036.

may be overestimated: Yue Li et al., "The Divergence Between SARS-CoV-2 and RaTG13 Might Be Overestimated Due to the Extensive RNA Modification," *Future Virology* 15, no. 6 (April 24, 2020): 341–47, https://doi.org/10.2217/fvl-2020-0066.

such as a pangolin: Li et al., "Divergence."

there's no evidence: Ping Liu et al., "Are Pangolins the Intermediate Host of the 2019 Novel Coronavirus (SARS-CoV-2)?," *PLoS Pathogens* 16, no. 5 (May 14, 2020): e1008421, https://doi.org/10.1371/journal.ppat.1008421.

272 *In an interview:* Jane Qiu, "How China's 'Bat Woman' Hunted Down Viruses from SARS to the New Coronavirus," *Scientific American*, June 1, 2020, https://www.scientificamerican.com/article/how-chinas-bat-woman-hunted-down-viruses-from-sars-to-the-new-coronavirus1/.

published a paper: Xing-Yi Ge et al., "Coexistence of Multiple Coronaviruses in Several Bat Colonies in an Abandoned Mineshaft," *Virologica Sinica* 31, no. 1 (February 1, 2016): 31–40, https://doi.org/10.1007/s12250-016-3713-9.

274 *was immediately tarred:* Alexandra Stevenson, "Senator Tom Cotton Repeats Fringe Theory of Coronavirus Origins," *New York Times*, February 17, 2020, https://www.nytimes.com/2020/02/17/business/media/coronavirus-tom-cotton-china.html.

275 Washington Post *column:* Josh Rogin, "State Department Cables Warned of Safety Issues at Wuhan Lab Studying Bat Coronaviruses," *Washington Post*, April 14, 2020, https://www.washingtonpost.com/opinions/2020/04/14/state-department-cables-warned-safety-issues-wuhan-lab-studying-bat-coronaviruses/.

276 *"no scientific evidence":* "Fauci: No Scientific Evidence the Coronavirus Was Made in a Chinese Lab," *National Geographic*, May 4, 2020, https://www.nationalgeographic.com/science/2020/05/anthony-fauci-no-scientific-evidence-the-coronavirus-was-made-in-a-chinese-lab-cvd/.

Chinese CDC officials declared: James T. Areddy, "China Rules Out Animal Market and Lab as Coronavirus Origin," *Wall Street Journal*, May 26, 2020, https://www.wsj.com/articles/china-rules-out-animal-market-and-lab-as-coronavirus-origin-11590517508.

277 *little-noticed study:* Shi-Hui Sun et al., "A Mouse Model of SARS-CoV-2 Infection and Pathogenesis," *Cell Host and Microbe* 28, no. 1 (July 2020): 124–133.e4, https://doi.org/10.1016/j.chom.2020.05.020.

279 *released its own study:* Qiu, "How China's 'Bat Woman.'"

280 *tried to erase:* "Brief Introduction," Wuhan Institute of Virology, Chinese Academy of Sciences, accessed October 1, 2020, https://web.archive.org/web/20150823141414/http://english.whiov.cas.cn/About_Us/Brief_Introduction/.

published a paper: Xiaoxu Lin and Shizhong Chen, "Major Concerns on the Identification of Bat Coronavirus Strain RaTG13 and Quality of Related Nature Paper," Preprints, June 5, 2020, https://doi.org/10.20944/preprints202006.0044.v1.

283 *tried to patent it:* "Wuhan Institute of Virology (China) Sought to Patent Gilead's Remdesivir," TrialSite News, March 16, 2020, https://www.trialsitenews.com/wuhan-institute-of-virology-china-sought-to-patent-gileads-remdesivir/.

284 *wrote on March 4:* Emily de La Bruyère and Nathan Picarsic, *Viral Moment: China's Post-COVID Planning*, Coronavirus Series (Horizon Advisory, March 2020), https://www.horizonadvisory.org/news/coronavirus-series-report-launch-viral-moment-chinas-post-covid-planning.

286 *focused on a statement:* "Statement by NCSC Director William Evanina: Election Threat Update for the American Public," Office of the Director of National Intelligence, August 20, 2020, https://www.dni.gov/index.php/newsroom/press-releases/item/2139-statement-by-ncsc-director-william-evanina-election-threat-update-for-the-american-public.

287 *Nikki Haley declared:* Jennifer Medina, "Full Transcript: Nikki Haley's R.N.C. Speech," *New York Times,* August 25, 2020, https://www.nytimes.com/2020/08/25/us/politics/nikki-haley-rnc-speech.html.

said Democrats: Josh Rogin, "The Republican National Convention Highlights Political Abuse of the China Challenge," *Washington Post,* August 25, 2020, https://www.washingtonpost.com/opinions/2020/08/25/republican-national-convention-highlights-political-abuse-china-challenge/.

EPILOGUE

289 *reportedly was under:* Brian Spegele et al., "Fundraising at Company Tied to Steve Bannon and Guo Wengui Faces Probe," *Wall Street Journal,* August 19, 2020, https://www.wsj.com/articles/fundraising-at-company-tied-to-steve-bannon-and-guo-wengui-faces-probe-11597857467.

290 *"the hard drive from hell":* Steve Bannon's War Room — COAR, "WarRoom: Global Election Night Special 2020," YouTube video, 8:35:10, streamed live on November 3, 2020, https://www.youtube.com/watch?v=ZVWvZFWBE9Y&t=3080s.

291 *issued a statement:* "Statement by NCSC Director William Evanina: Election Threat Update for the American Public," Director of National Intelligence, August 7, 2020, https://www.dni.gov/index.php/newsroom/press-releases/item/2139-statement-by-ncsc-director-william-evanina-election-threat-update-for-the-american-public.

armies of social media accounts: Didi Kirsten Tatlow, "Exclusive: 600 U.S. Groups Linked to Chinese Communist Party Influence Effort with Ambition beyond Election," *Newsweek,* October 26, 2020, https://www.newsweek.com/2020/11/13/exclusive-600-us-groups-linked-chinese-communist-party-influence-effort-ambition-beyond-1541624.html.

292 *legions of his followers:* Nick Aspinwall, "Steve Bannon Ally Guo Wengui Is Targeting Chinese Dissidents," *Foreign Policy,* October 28, 2020, https://foreignpolicy.com/2020/10/28/guo-wengui-sending-mobs-after-chinese-dissidents-bannon-ccp/.

295 *spent over twenty-five hours:* Michael Crowley, "'Strategic Empathy': How Biden's Informal Diplomacy Shaped Foreign Relations," *New York Times,* July 5, 2020, https://www.nytimes.com/2020/07/05/us/politics/joe-biden-foreign-policy.html.

296 *"if he loses":* Ashley Parker et al., "How Trump's Erratic Behavior and Failure on Coronavirus Doomed His Reelection," *Washington Post,* November 7, 2020, https://www.washingtonpost.com/elections/interactive/2020/trump-pandemic-coronavirus-election/.

298 *Xi was crushing Ma:* Enda Curran, Sofia Horta e Costa, and Lulu Yilun Chen, "Derailing of Jack Ma's Ant IPO Shows Xi Jinping's in Charge," Bloomberg, November 4, 2020, https://www.bloomberg.com/news/articles/2020-11-04/derailing-of-jack-ma-s-mega-ant-ipo-shows-xi-jinping-s-in-charge.

299 *"It is in a spirit":* "Remarks by Deputy National Security Advisor Matt Pottinger to London-Based Policy Exchange," The White House, October 23, 2020, https://www.whitehouse.gov/briefings-statements/remarks-deputy-national-security-advisor-matt-pottinger-london-based-policy-exchange/.

300 *"The smart phones we use":* "Remarks by Deputy National Security Advisor Matt Pottinger to London-Based Policy Exchange," The White House, October 23, 2020.

301 *The official communiqué:* "Communiqué of the Fifth Plenary Session of the 19th Central Committee of the Communist Party of China — Current Affairs — People's Daily Online" [in Chinese], Chinese Communist Party, October 29, 2020, http://politics.people.com.cn/n1/2020/1029/c1001-31911511.html.

303 *"America's strategic position is weaker":* Reuters, "Biden Adviser Says Unrealistic to 'Fully Decouple' from China," *US News,* September 22, 2020, https://money.usnews.com/investing/news/articles/2020-09-22/biden-adviser-says-unrealistic-to-fully-decouple-from-china.

304 *China's careful statement:* Ben Westcott and Steven Jiang, "China Offers Belated Congratulations to US President-Elect Joe Biden," CNN, November 13, 2020, https://www.cnn.com/2020/11/13/asia/biden-china-trump-election-intl-hnk/index.html.

305 *in a long piece:* Alexandra Stevenson et al., "A Chinese Tycoon Sought Power and Influence. Washington Responded," *New York Times,* December 12, 2018, https://www.nytimes.com/2018/12/12/business/cefc-biden-china-washington-ye-jianming.html.

a 2019 New Yorker *profile:* Adam Entous, "Will Hunter Biden Jeopardize His Father's Campaign?," *New Yorker,* July 1, 2019, https://www.newyorker.com/magazine/2019/07/08/will-hunter-biden-jeopardize-his-fathers-campaign.

were both partners: Andrew Duehren and James T. Areddy, "Hunter Biden's Ex-Business Partner Alleges Father Knew About Venture," *Wall Street Journal,* October 23, 2020, https://www.wsj.com/articles/hunter-bidens-ex-business-partner-alleges-father-knew-about-venture-11603421247.

Index